Charles Carleton Coffin

Drum-beat of the nation: the first period of the war of the rebellion

From its outbreak to the close of 1862

Charles Carleton Coffin

Drum-beat of the nation: the first period of the war of the rebellion
From its outbreak to the close of 1862

ISBN/EAN: 9783337118549

Printed in Europe, USA, Canada, Australia, Japan

Cover: Foto ©ninafisch / pixelio.de

More available books at **www.hansebooks.com**

SERGEANT HART NAILING THE COLORS TO THE FLAGSTAFF OF FORT SUMTER.

DRUM-BEAT OF THE NATION

THE FIRST PERIOD OF

THE WAR OF THE REBELLION

FROM

ITS OUTBREAK TO THE CLOSE OF 1862

BY

CHARLES CARLETON COFFIN

AUTHOR OF "THE BOYS OF '76" "THE STORY OF LIBERTY" "OLD TIMES IN THE
COLONIES" "BUILDING THE NATION" &c.

Illustrated

NEW YORK

HARPER & BROTHERS, FRANKLIN SQUARE

1888

Dedicated

TO THE

SONS AND DAUGHTERS OF THOSE WHO FOLLOWED THE DRUM-BEAT

THAT THE NATION MIGHT LIVE

INTRODUCTION.

NEARLY a third of a century has rolled away since the outbreak of the war between the northern and southern sections of the United States, known in history as the War of the Rebellion. Since then a generation has come upon the active stage of life. One-fourth of the inhabitants of the United States at the present time have no personal knowledge of the war, and to fully one-half it is but a dim and fading memory. The conflict was one of the mightiest of all time, waged between people having a common ancestry, speaking the same language, living three-fourths of a century under the same flag, attaining an exalted position among the nations, and looking forward to a great and unexampled destiny.

In 1860 thirty-three States composed the United States of America. Of these, fifteen permitted the holding of slaves. The slave-holders living in the States which produced cotton brought about the secession of their respective States from the Union, seized forts, arsenals, cannon, ships, and other property belonging to the United States. South Carolina was the first to withdraw, followed by Mississippi, Florida, Alabama, Georgia, Louisiana, and Texas, which united to form a Confederacy of States, electing Jefferson Davis President. North Carolina, Tennessee, Arkansas, and Virginia soon after withdrew from the Union and joined the Confederacy. The slave-holders put forth as a justification of their action the claim that some of the original and reserved rights of the slave-holding States were not protected under the Constitution. Of the seceding States, Virginia, North Carolina, South Carolina, and Georgia took part in the formation of the Constitution. Alabama and Mississippi were originally a part of Georgia, and claimed that any original right that belonged to Georgia inhered to them upon their admission. Florida, Louisiana, and Arkansas had been created from territory purchased from Spain and France after the formation of the Constitution, and could put forth no such plea; neither could Tennessee, which had been created from territory owned by the United States. Texas had been annexed. These five States last named had accepted the Constitution without any expressed reservation. They severally joined in the war against the United States.

As the years go by, it is seen that the upholding of the "rights" of the States as against those of the United States was not the real and primal object which the leaders of the Rebellion had in view, but that their true and genuine purpose was to arrest the progress of free labor, the development of free institutions, and the growing power of the people; that it was an attempt to overthrow the democratic government founded by the people and establish instead an aristocratic government of the few over the many; that it was, in reality, a conflict between two civilizations—one the development of free, and the other of slave labor.

The conflict was marked by three distinct periods. The first includes the conspiracy to bring about the disruption of the Union, withdrawal of the cotton-producing States, formation of the Confederacy, seizure of property belonging to the United States, bombardment of Fort Sumter, gathering of great armies; the period of enthusiasm, expectation, egotism, braggadocio, and ignorance in both sections; of mortification throughout the North and exultation in the South over the issue of the first great battle, followed in the North by the sober second thought, the rise of true patriotism, voluntary enlistment in the armies, the resolute determination that, cost what it might of life or treasure, the Government of the people should not perish; the enrolment of Missouri, Kentucky, Maryland, Delaware, which held slaves, also a large portion of the people in West Virginia and East Tennessee, on the side of the Union; the success of the army and navy in the West, on the Mississippi and the Atlantic coast; skilled labor putting forth its energy to arm, equip, feed, and clothe the million of men in arms — this, with defeat and disaster, incapacity and mismanagement, the ebbing of the cause of the Union to low-water mark at the close of 1862; the gradual awakening of the people of the North to the comprehension that slavery, instead of being an element of weakness, was a source of strength to the Confederacy; that slaves were constructing fortifications and tilling the soil while the white men were fighting the battles, and that to preserve the Union slavery must be exterminated; followed by the immortal Act of Emancipation by President Lincoln.

The second period includes the year 1863 — the victories of Gettysburg, Vicksburg, Lookout Mountain, Missionary Ridge, and other battles; opening of the Mississippi; the turning of the tide; the results of the Proclamation of Emancipation; the enrolment of slaves as soldiers of the Republic.

The third period includes the months from the appointment of Ulysses S. Grant commander-in-chief of the armies of the Union to the final breaking up of the Confederacy and the re-establishment of the authority of the United States.

"The Drum-beat of the Nation" treats of the first period of the conflict between free and slave labor. In writing it I have endeavored to present briefly and impartially the cause, scope, progress, and meaning of the war by grouping the leading events. I have endeavored to lay aside prejudice, to see the questions at issue as the people of the seceding States saw them, duly recognizing their sincerity of conviction and adherence to the idea that the authority of the State was higher than that of the Nation. I have endeavored to do full justice to the endurance of hardship and bravery of the soldiers of the Confederacy in battle, and to recognize the great ability of the officers who commanded them.

In the month of May, 1861, I began my labors as correspondent of the *Boston Journal.* It was my privilege to witness many of the great battles, to have personal acquaintance with nearly all the generals commanding the armies of the Union, and with those prominent in legislative and executive affairs. Since the war I have had personal acquaintance with many of the generals who commanded in the Confederate armies.

History is valuable only as it is truthful. It is comparatively easy for an historian to comprehend the general plan and design of a campaign, but there is no task surrounded with greater difficulties than that of ascertaining the sequence of events in a great battle. The commander-in-chief of a large army sees but little of what takes place upon a battle-field. Commanders of corps, divisions, brigades, and regiments can have but partial knowledge of the various movements. The story of the private is his individual experience. A correspondent having the freedom of the army, if faithful to his trust, has exceptional opportunities for observation. Official reports, in the very nature of things, can present but one side of a battle. Human nature makes the most of success, and is ever ready to give a reason for defeat. The victor glorifies the part performed by his army; the vanquished ever finds extenuating circumstances for his defeat. Official reports and narratives written by officers in command are not always the truth of history. From my note-books of the battle-field, from official reports, later narratives, from a great mass of material, I have endeavored to arrive at the probable facts.

The statistical record during the years 1861 and 1862 gives seven hundred and twenty engagements between the opposing forces, most of them between small parties, and of little account in a history. Only those events which have been fruitful of result, or given direction to campaigns, have been considered. The chief object of this volume will be attained if those who have come upon the stage since the close of the war, by a perusal of its pages, are enabled to comprehend the meaning of the great historic drama—what this Government of the people has cost and what it is worth, what their fathers accomplished for the continuance of the nation, the wiping out of slavery, and the welfare of the human race through all coming time.

CHARLES CARLETON COFFIN.

BOSTON, *September*, 1887.

CONTENTS.

ILLUSTRATIONS.

DRUM-BEAT OF THE NATION.

CHAPTER I.

CAUSES WHICH BROUGHT ABOUT THE WAR.

THE war between the northern and southern sections of the United States, which began in April, 1861, and lasted till April, 1865, was a conflict of ideas and institutions. The moral and political causes which brought it about are so many that I think of them as I think of the rivulets springing from far-off mountain ranges, which united become a mighty river, broadening and deepening as it flows to the sea. The fountain-heads are far away.

In those days when Rome was mistress of the world, the Angles or Saxons of Germany lived in villages which were called *tuns*. Each man had the right of voting in tun meeting, which was held at the *moot*, or meeting-place. The meeting was a parliament in which the majority ruled. Each tun was independent and sovereign, but ever ready to unite with other tuns against a common enemy. From the tuns along the shores of the Baltic Sea a band of Angles sailed across the German Ocean and landed in Britain, gaining a foothold on the banks of the Thames. They carried to Britain individual freedom, the organizing faculty, and obedience to the will of the majority. They conquered the country, making it Angle-land, or England.

We come down to an October day, 1066, when William of Normandy and his followers won the battle of Hastings on the white cliffs of Dover, conquering the Saxons, or Angles, dividing the land, giving the estates to the soldiers, with titles of honor to those who had been brave in the battle. Out of the victory came the barons, lords, earls, and dukes; the titled nobility of England on the one hand, and on the other the subjugated Saxons and Britains, who became the common people of England.

1

In all ages men have worshipped power, and have assumed that the conferring of a title made men noble; that the descendants of those thus honored, by some inexplicable process, were more worthy than the common herd of men. The nobility could look disdainfully down upon the multitude, regarding them as of inferior make, with the taint of low condition in their blood.

From London, in 1606, sailed three vessels which bore the first permanent English settlers to America. Of the one hundred and five on board the ships, four were carpenters, twelve laborers, four gold-refiners, while forty-eight regarded themselves as gentlemen, far superior to the joiners and carpenters. So it came about that class distinction, sense of superiority, and antagonism to labor were transplanted from English soil to the banks of the James, in Virginia. These features of society were made more prominent when the merchants who established the colony sent over indentured servants to work in the tobacco fields who could have no social rights, and they became a permanent force affecting the community, when a Dutch ship-master, in 1619, sailed up the James with sixteen slaves stolen from Africa, which were purchased by the planters. In those years no one thought it wrong to steal or hold negroes or Indians in slavery. Sir John Hawkins, who engaged in the traffic, thought himself a special servant of God elected to bring blessings to the negroes, who would be better off as slaves in a Christian land than remain barbarians in Africa. Besides, it was very profitable. Little did that Dutch ship-master, or any one else, comprehend what would be the outcome of that cargo of slaves—that the little rivulet would become a river—the mightiest of all the forces to bring about the greatest civil war of all the ages.

There came a time when there was trouble between King Charles and Parliament, resulting in civil war in Great Britain. Most of the noblemen sided with the King. They called themselves Cavaliers. To be a Cavalier was to be brave, to have exalted ideas of honor, and be quick to resent insult. To be spoken of as a true Cavalier was regarded as the highest praise. The King was defeated in battle and executed. Many of the men who had sided with him made Virginia their home, bought large tracts of land, owned slaves, and dispensed lavish hospitality. It was natural for them to regard themselves as superior to those who were obliged to labor for their bread. They believed in class distinction, gave direction to society, and left their impress upon the State. One of the emigrants was Sir John Washington, who had followed King Charles in all his misfortunes; but when the King lost his head, when the outlook for the future, as Sir John saw it, was only dark and gloomy, he sold his old home in England, bade farewell to all that was dear, crossed the Atlantic, and made himself a home in Virginia.

Following another rivulet, we are led back to that day when, by order of Henry VIII., King of England, a Bible was placed in every church throughout the realm. From reading it people began to think for themselves, and to obtain exalted ideas of the worth and dignity of man; that men have natural rights which cannot be justly taken away by king or bishop, or any one else.

Many of the parish ministers of England preached to the people to reform their lives, to stop their brutal sports—the fighting of cocks and dogs and worrying of bulls. Lords, ladies, king and queen, as well as the common people, delighted to see bull-dogs tear each other to pieces. Men who reformed their lives and became zealous for a purer religion were derisively called Puritans by the rollicking Cavaliers, who found little pleasure in attending church or listening to a psalm or sermon.

The movement for purer morals began with the common people, some of whom met in their own houses for worship instead of attending church. Such independence could not be tolerated by King James and the bishops of the Church of England, and out of their persecutions came the flight of the men and women of the little hamlets of Scrooby and Austerfield to Holland, where they lived ten years, and then, fearing that their children would forget that they were Englishmen, determined to leave Holland, cross the Atlantic, and establish themselves in the wilderness of America. On the 16th of September, 1620, they bade farewell to all friends, sailing from Plymouth, England. They were one hundred and one persons. They were casting loose from all old things. They loved law and order. No one had given them authority to elect a governor, but nevertheless they chose one of their number—John Carver. In the cabin of the *Mayflower*, riding at anchor in the waters of Cape Cod, they signed their names to a compact organizing themselves as a body politic, agreeing to obey all the laws which they might make, and the governors whom they might choose. The world never before had seen such a paper or government. It was a constitution formed by a Christian people—the beginning of the government of the people.

The men of the *Mayflower* called themselves Pilgrims. They were poor; they were laborers. Labor was not only a necessity, but they regarded it as a duty—a blessing. Idleness, in their estimation, led to vice; industry to virtue.

In that company of one hundred and one persons there were no inherited privileges, no class distinctions conferred by birth or positions in society. A democratic State crossed the Atlantic to establish itself upon the barren shores of Massachusetts, on a soil and in a clime where growth was possible only through unremitting industry. On Sunday they assembled in their moot, or meeting-house, for worship, listening to the preaching of Elder Brewster, their bishop, elected by themselves. They elected their governor in the same building, where they discussed all questions affecting the welfare of the community, each man having the right to be heard and to hold up his hand in voting. The Saxon tun became the New England town-meeting. Each citizen cultivated his own land, and there were no large estates.

That their children might not grow up in ignorance, comprehending that ignorance is weakness and knowledge is power, they established free schools. With schools came the printing-press and the establishment of newspapers.

In contrast, from the settlement of Virginia to the beginning of the war in 1861, in no Southern State was there a complete system of common schools. "I thank God," wrote Governor Berkeley, of Virginia, in 1671, "that there are no free schools nor printing in Virginia, and I hope we shall not have them these hundred years."

During the reign of Queen Anne a corporation was formed in England under the title of the Royal African Company, organized for carrying on the slave-trade. It was composed of dukes, lords, nobles, and merchants. Queen Anne reserved one-quarter of the stock for herself. She instructed the Royal governors of the American colonies to give all possible encouragement to the trade, and it is estimated that several hundred thousand slaves were transported to America by the company. So many were brought that the colonists began to be alarmed, and Pennsylvania, in 1712, passed a law restricting the importation. Virginia, in 1726, imposed a tax on the slaves brought from Africa. In 1760 South Carolina enacted a law against the trade. All of these laws were disallowed by the English government. But there was no commercial enterprise which brought in such rich returns. Those engaged in it purchased molasses in the West Indies, shipped it to New England or to Old England, distilled it into rum which was sent to Africa, where it was exchanged for slaves captured in the wars between the negro tribes, which were transported to the West Indies and the American colonies. In 1772 the Virginia assembly sent an address to George III., pleading with him not to thwart their efforts to put a stop to the trade. "The interest of the country manifestly requires the total expulsion of the slaves," read the address. Thomas Jefferson and Henry Lee, of Virginia, were earnest in their efforts not only to put a stop to the importation of slaves, but to inaugurate measures for the final abolition of slavery. The obstinate King, influenced by those who were reaping a rich harvest, would not listen to the appeal of the Virginians, and thus it came about that slavery was forced upon the people. The legislature of Massachusetts, in 1771, and again in 1774, appealed to the crown to put a stop to the slave-trade without avail. It was British greed which planted slavery in America.

With the coming of the Revolution slavery ceased in the New England States, and Virginia, in 1778, prohibited the further introduction of slaves. Societies were organized in the Southern States to bring about its gradual abolition, and people looked forward to the time when it would become extinct. When the Constitution of the United States was adopted in 1787, and the Union established, each State surrendered some rights before exercised, that the good of all might be secured. It was agreed that Representatives to Congress should be apportioned according to population. The South demanded that three slaves should be regarded as equal to two white men. The slaves were citizens, but not voters. The North assented. It was the thistle seed of all future trouble. It was agreed that the African slave-trade might be continued till 1808, when it should cease altogether. This agreement was regarded as a compromise between the diverse interests of the States. Each State claimed the right to manage its own institutions in its own way, and to make its own laws in regard to slaves. Slavery was an institution belonging to the several States, and not to the nation. Under the Constitution the States were no longer a Federation but a Union, a Government of the people, with a Constitution which was to be the supreme law of the land. In 1787 an ordinance was passed for the government of the north-west territory, the great region of country now covered by the States of Ohio, Indiana, Illinois, Michigan, and Wisconsin, which prohibited slavery, but which declared that slaves escaping into the territory should be given up. This last provision was a seed which was to bring about a great crop of thistles sixty years later.

In the Southern States agriculture was the only occupation—carried on almost wholly by the slaves, except in the mountain region, where slavery could not be made profitable, and where it degraded white labor. There was a class which lived solely upon the labor of the slaves. In the North there was a great diversity of occupations—agricultural, commercial, industrial, and mechanical. All men were regarded as laborers. The result was, as the years rolled on, a springing up of bustling towns and thriving cities in the North, while in the South there was only the shire

town of the county or the house of the planter with negro huts around it.
New Orleans was the only city of magnitude in the South.

Though the people of the entire country, when the Constitution was
adopted, looked forward to the time when slavery would be gradually extinguished, the progress of events wholly unforeseen changed the aspect
of affairs.

When we study the history of the human race, the development of nations and their character, we see that climate—heat and cold, currents in
the sea and air, rivers and mountains—as well as the fertility and produc-
tions of the soil, have had much to do with the moulding of nations. With
the earth turning on its axis from west to east, there is ever a current
flowing westward along the equator in the Atlantic and Pacific oceans.
That in the Atlantic strikes against the coast of Brazil, and sends a large
portion of its flood, together with the mighty volume of water coming
down the Amazon and Orinoco, northward into the Caribbean Sea and
the Gulf of Mexico, and having no outflow except between Florida and
Cuba, there must of necessity be a great rush of water at that point, which
is the beginning of the Gulf Stream. The warm currents of air rising
above the waters, laden with moisture drifting landward, give to the
southern tier of States the climate which surpasses all others for the cultivation of cotton. Up to the close of the Revolutionary War, people in
temperate climes wore clothing manufactured almost wholly from wool
or flax, but it was discovered that the fibres of the cotton-plant could be
used for the manufacture of clothing. The first cotton used in England
was grown in India, but some seeds were brought to South Carolina,
where the plants grew luxuriantly. Its cultivation began immediately
after the close of the Revolutionary War. In 1784 eight bags of cotton
were shipped to England, and in 1788, the year after the adoption of
the Constitution, two hundred and eighty-two bags were shipped, and
more called for. James Hargreaves, in England, had invented a spinning-
machine, by which one person could do the work of several hands, thus
cheapening the price of cloth and giving great impetus to the manufacturing industries, and increasing the demand for cotton. It was slow work
to pick the cotton seeds from the fibres, but this difficulty was overcome
by Eli Whitney, of Massachusetts, who invented the machine called the
cotton-gin.

We have seen that from the first settlement of the country there were
two distinct and diverse civilizations—two forms of society—one based on
free, and the other on slave, labor. The demand of the world for cotton,
the invention of the spinning-frame and of the cotton-gin, brought about

HENRY CLAY.

a state of affairs entirely different from what had been anticipated by those who expected the gradual dying out of slavery. These inventions had a tendency to perpetuate the two distinct forms of society. Manufacturing began in New England at the close of the last century, increased the demand for cotton, and in turn there was a call for more slaves in the cotton-growing States. The cessation of the African slave-trade in 1808, together with the demand for slaves, made it profitable for the slave-

holders of Virginia, Kentucky, Tennessee, and Missouri to raise slaves for
the southern market. Thus it came about that the commercial and industrial pursuits of the Northern and Middle States were intimately re-
lated to the one great industry of the South. Slavery, instead of dying
out, became a great source of wealth and political power. From its nature it must be aggressive upon free labor, and must have new States and
territories to maintain its political position.

There are few things so slow of growth as an idea. Down to 1798
the people did not comprehend that the United States were a nation.
The course of the French government towards the United States awakened resentment throughout the country. During that year Mr. Nichols,
of Kentucky, offered a series of resolutions setting forth the rights of
the States as superior to those of the nation. The insolence and arro-
gance of the Governor of Algiers in 1800 brought on the war with that
country, which awakened in some slight degree an enthusiasm for the
Stars and Stripes. Up to that time there had been no background of
history, of sacrifice and devotion, except that of the Revolution.

The question was arising as to who owned the ocean. Great Britain
claimed to be mistress of the seas. The merchants of England wanted to
do all the carrying of the world, and they looked with jealous eyes across
the Atlantic to the United States, whose merchant-ships were spreading
their white wings on every sea. England and France were at war. Bonaparte was sweeping Europe with his armies, while England with her
navy was asserting her power upon the ocean. England not only destroyed the war-ships but the merchant-vessels of France. The United
States was England's only competitor for the carrying trade of the world.
France and England both began to seize American ships, and England
began to seize American sailors for her navy. The United States was
powerless to protect American merchant-vessels. Members of Congress
thought that if all trade between the United States and foreign countries
were stopped, the necessities of England and France would compel them
to come to terms, and a law was passed laying an embargo, or prohibition,
on trade. The result was far different from what they expected it would
be, for in a very short time the vessels were rotting at the wharves, ship-
masters and sailors, ship-carpenters, calkers, and sail-makers, were roam-
ing the streets of the seaport towns with nothing to do. In the country,
on the other hand, the spinning-wheels and looms were never so busy—
women and girls at work from morning till night. Instead of depending
upon England for cloth, they were manufacturing it. The people in the
seaports were suffering, while those in the country were prospering under

the law. The natural result was a divided opinion as to the benefits of the Constitution and the Union. England and France, the while, went on seizing American vessels. England had taken nine hundred and seventeen, and France five hundred and fifty-eight, valued at more than seventy million dollars. England had also forced nearly twelve thousand Ameri-

JOHN C. CALHOUN.

can sailors into her navy. The people of the United States became very angry, but were divided in opinion, some desiring to go to war with both England and France, others with England only. On June 19, 1812, Congress, in secret session, passed a bill declaring war with England. The United States had twenty vessels in the navy, the largest carrying forty-four guns, while Great Britain had one thousand and sixty vessels, many

1—2

of them carrying seventy-four guns. On the 19th of August, 1812, the frigate *Constitution* fell in with the British ship *Guerriere*, and in a few minutes compelled her surrender, so badly damaged that she soon went to the bottom of the sea. From the adoption of the Constitution to that hour no event had aroused such enthusiasm for the flag of the country. The successes of the American navy, and the victories along the Canadian frontier and at New Orleans, made the United States a nation. Although the war was unpopular in the Northern States, though a convention was held at Hartford, Connecticut, in opposition to the war, the people comprehended as never before that in unity only could there be power and peace for the nation.

The war was very popular in Kentucky, where Henry Clay, orator and statesman, used his great influence to arouse the people of that State. He was born at Ashland, in Virginia, about twenty miles north of Richmond, and like many other Virginians made Kentucky his home. Nearly every man in that State was a hunter, and with his rifle could bring down a squirrel from the tallest tree. The hunters volunteered in great numbers to serve under General Harrison in the North-west, and under General Jackson at New Orleans. For many years after the war, ballads were sung throughout the country extolling their deeds and awakening a loyal sentiment for the flag. There can be no doubt that the part taken by the people of Kentucky in the war of 1812 created a deep and abiding love in that State for the Union.

A very different sentiment existed in the cotton-growing States, which took no part in the war, contributing few if any soldiers to the army. No loyal sentiment for the Union was awakened in those States. The people of South Carolina had always disliked the form of government. The great planters were aristocratic while the government was democratic. The aristocrats had little in common with the mass of people. Just after the war with Great Britain, Commodore Charles Stewart, commanding the frigate *Constitution*, had this conversation with John C. Calhoun, member of Congress from South Carolina :

"You of the South," said Mr. Stewart, "are the aristocratic portion of the Union. You are aristocratic in your habits, modes of living, and action, and yet you assume all the professions of democracy."

"I admit," said Mr. Calhoun, "that we are essentially aristocratic, but we yield much to democracy. It is our sectional policy. It is through our affiliation with the democratic party in the Middle and Western States that we hold our power. When we cease thus to control the nation, we shall dissolve the Union."

ANDREW JACKSON.

Mr. Calhoun believed with Jefferson that the sovereignty of the State was superior to that of the nation; the Union was only an agreement between the States, and not a system of government. He was sincere in his opinions, a man of keen, incisive intellect, who wielded great influence. Through his teachings, far beyond those of any other man, the doctrine that the rights of the States were superior to those of the nation was accepted by the people of the South, and that it was their right and privilege to secede from the Union whenever, in their judgment, there was sufficient cause.

In 1818 a decision was made by the Supreme Court of the United States which was far-reaching in its results. The decision is known as the Dartmouth College case. The college is in New Hampshire. It began as a school for Indians before the Revolutionary War. The Earl of Dartmouth and other benevolent men contributed to its support, and it became a college, receiving a charter from the State. There arose a disagreement among the trustees as to its management. The legislature changed its charter, making it a university, and electing a portion of the trustees. The highest court in the State decided that the legislature had the right to change the charter, whereupon the old trustees appealed to the Supreme Court of the United States, and employed Daniel Webster, who argued the case for the State against the college. When he was but eight years old, having had a few cents given him, he purchased a pocket-handkerchief with the Constitution printed on it, and studied it until he knew it by heart. He claimed that the charter originally given was a contract between the State and the men who had given their money to the college, and that to change the charter was a violation of the contract. The Supreme Court of the United States so decided, reversing the decision of the State court. It was an exaltation of the Constitution of the United States over the several States. It was felt in every legislative hall and in all courts. Not the cannon-balls of the frigate *Constitution*, crashing through the sides of the *Guerriere*, not from the musketry flaming over the breastworks at New Orleans, came the grand idea of Nationality, but from the plain, intelligent argument of Daniel Webster on the obligation of contract, which seemingly had nothing to do with the Constitution and the Union. The decision is one of the landmarks of American history.

In 1824 Congress passed a Tariff Bill which gave great offence to the planters of South Carolina. Under the lead of Mr. Calhoun the legislature of that State passed a law nullifying the law of Congress. No immediate effort was made by the State to put its law in force, but it was an offensive declaration that the State was superior to the nation.

In 1830 Senator Hayne, of South Carolina, advocated the doctrine of nullification in the Senate of the United States. Daniel Webster replied, setting forth the meaning and power of the Constitution. The newspapers printed his speech, which was read by the people far and wide. School-boys declaimed its closing words, "Liberty and Union, now and forever, one and inseparable." It was a speech which, above all others, educated the people as to the meaning of the Constitution. The Governor of South Carolina issued his proclamation for the enforcement of the State law relative to the collection of revenue from vessels entering Charleston harbor. Andrew Jackson, who commanded the hunters of Kentucky and Tennessee at New Orleans, was President. He was smoking his pipe before

DANIEL WEBSTER.

the open fire in the White House when the proclamation reached him. He leaped from his chair, dashed the pipe into the fire, lifted his right hand as if taking an oath, and said, " The Union must and shall be preserved, by the Eternal !" He ordered a fleet of war-vessels to Charleston to enforce the laws, and South Carolina was compelled to submit. The words of President Jackson electrified the country.

During these years a large number of poor white people were leaving the slave States and moving into Ohio, Indiana, and Illinois. They could not stay where they were degraded by contact with slave labor.

One of the emigrants from Kentucky was Thomas Lincoln, a descendant of Samuel Lincoln, who left Norwich, England, in 1638, when troubles were arising between King Charles and Parliament. He was one of the great company of liberty-loving men who preferred to seek a home in the wilderness of America rather than submit to the usurpations of the King. He settled in Hingham, Massachusetts. His descendant, Thomas Lincoln, disliked slavery. He was poor, and decided to cross the Ohio and make his home in Indiana. When his son Abraham was seven years old he loaded a little raft with his property—his carpenter's tools and a cask of whiskey—and floated down the Ohio to Perry County, in Indiana, where friends were living, and where he built a log-cabin for his future home. We shall see this boy Abraham many times during the unfolding of the events of the war.

The provision in the Constitution which recognized slaves as property entitled to representation was becoming a great political power. In 1820 Maine and Missouri were admitted to the Union, but there was an angry discussion in Congress, with threats of a dissolution of the Union unless Missouri, which had been largely settled by people from Kentucky, was made a slave State. It was the first conflict between slavery and freedom under the Constitution, and slavery won. The State was admitted, with no restriction against holding slaves, but it was agreed that in all other territory north of the southern boundary of that State slavery should be forever prohibited.

The slave-holders, to maintain their political power, brought about the annexation of Texas, which resulted in war with Mexico and the acquisition of a vast area of country. The slave-holders expected that it would be settled by a slave-holding population, but their plans were overturned in a way which no one could have foreseen—the discovery of gold in California. Thousands of hard-working men made their way to the Pacific coast in 1849 who voted that California should be a free State.

The spirit of the age in all civilized lands was changing. In 1775 England was forcing slavery upon America; in 1830 England was liberating all the slaves in the West Indies, and was declaring to the world that wherever her flag floated there was freedom for every man. Agitation had begun in the Northern States for the abolition of slavery in the territories over which Congress had jurisdiction, and in the District of Columbia. Slaves were sold at auction like pigs and cattle, within a stone's-throw of the Capitol, where floated the Stars and Stripes. Slave-gangs, handcuffed and chained, wives and husbands, parents and children, separated forever, with weary steps and weeping eyes, were taken from the slave prison through the streets of Washington, on their way to the southern market. The people of the Northern States said that it was wicked, a shame and disgrace; that slavery was an institution of the States, and not of the nation. They petitioned Congress to abolish it in the District of Columbia. The presentation of the petitions gave great offence to the slave-holders. California was south of the line of the Missouri Compromise agreed upon in 1830. The slave-holders would not consent to its admission as a free State, except on the condition that slaves who had run away and escaped into the free States should be returned to their masters. The Fugitive Slave Law, passed in 1850, made it a crime to aid a slave in escaping, or to refuse to aid in recapturing one who had escaped.

Everywhere, except in the Southern States, people were beginning to comprehend that liberty is the birthright of every man; that what God has given him cannot be taken away. They were beginning to see that what in itself is wrong can never be made right by act of Congress or Legislature. The law was hateful because it was repugnant to their sense of right. What the world looked upon as right in other days, had come to be regarded as all wrong in 1830. "We will not be slave-catchers," said the people of the Northern States, and they passed laws which made it very difficult for a slave-holder to recapture those who had escaped. "If the Constitution will not protect our property, we will dissolve the Union," said the slave-holders. The great mass of the people in the Northern States had no thought of interfering with slavery in the States, but they were determined that it should not be recognized in any way as a national institution. The Abolitionists demanded that the Union should be dissolved, and denounced the Constitution as "a covenant with Death and a league with Hell." There were riots and mobs, which increased the bitterness between the North and South. In 1854 the law of 1820, which prohibited slavery north of the southern boundary of Missouri, was repealed. The object was the extension of slavery into Kansas and Nebraska. The slave-holders of Missouri hastened into Kansas. The people of the free States organized emigration societies to assist in making it a free State. There was much fighting, which intensified the growing bitterness. A majority of the settlers were opposed to slavery, and Kansas became a free State.

Times had changed. No one in the South now expected that slavery would die; on the contrary, every effort was made to extend it over the whole country. It was regarded as a blessing, a beneficent institution. A class of men had risen in the South who regarded themselves as born to govern.

"The right to govern resides in a very small minority; the duty to obey is inherent in the great mass of mankind. The real civilization of a country is in its aristocracy." So wrote Mr. De Bow, of New Orleans. "To make an aristocrat," he said, "in the future we must sacrifice a thousand paupers. We would, by all means, make aristocracy permanent by the laws of entail and primogeniture."

That was the plan of the great slave-holders—to set up a government in which a poor man should always be poor and low down in the world, with no opportunity to better himself; the rich to have everything their own way; the plantation descending from father to son, the oldest son having the best chance.

Said Mr. De Bow, "We must teach that slavery is necessary in all societies, as well to protect as to govern the weak, poor, and ignorant. . . . It is the duty of society to protect all its members, and it can only do so by subjecting each to that degree of government constraint, or slavery, which will best advance the good of the whole. . . . To protect the weak, we must first enslave them. . . . Slavery is necessary as an educational institution, and is worth ten times more than all the common schools of the North." The state of society which this class desired to bring about was slavery for the colored people, degradation for the poor white men, wealth, power, landed estates, offices, titles, and nobility for themselves.

The writings of some of this class will read strangely a century hence. Rev. Mr. Thornwell, of Columbia, South Carolina, was a learned and able writer, a doctor of divinity, respected and reverenced through the South. In a sermon preached in 1860, he said, "We confidently anticipate the time when the nations which now revile us would gladly exchange places with us. In its last analysis slavery is nothing but an organization of labor. . . . Society is divided between princes and beggars. . . . The only way by which labor can be organized as a permanent arrangement is by converting the laborer into capital; that is, by giving the employer a right in the capital employed; in other words, by slavery. . . . Strange as it may seem to those not familiar with the system, slavery is a school of virtue."

Rev. Mr. Palmer, a Presbyterian preacher in New Orleans, a native of South Carolina, maintained that slavery was a divinely ordained institution, and that the social condition of the South was much better than that of the North. He deplored the condition of the people of the Northern

States. "The so-called free States," he said, "are working out a social problem under conditions peculiar to themselves. These conditions are sufficiently hard, and their success is too uncertain to excite in us the least jealousy."

The preachers, writers, politicians, leaders of thought, those who wanted to belong to the aristocracy, were for the extension and perpetuation of slavery.

A convention of slave-holders was held at Nashville, Tennessee, in 1857, which appointed a committee to report upon affairs at the next meeting, which was held at Montgomery, Alabama, in May, 1858. Thus read the report: "Two antagonistic forms of society have met for contest on this continent. The one assumes that all men are equal; that equality is right. On that theory it is levelling its members to the horizontal plane of democracy. The other assumes that all men are not equal; that equality is not right; and standing on that theory, is taking to itself the rounded form of social aristocracy. The former is the view of the North, the latter of the South."

The committee advocated the reopening of the slave-trade with Africa. They said, "It will give us political power; it will give us population; it will draw foreign enterprise to its embrace, foreign capital to its support; it will drive the North from every field of competition. If the South were to stand out for itself, crowns would bow before her, kingdoms and empires would break a lance to win the smile of her approval, and it will be her option to become the bride of the world rather than remain, as now, the miserable mistress of the North."

In June, 1857, a fast sailing-vessel, the *Wanderer*, owned by Mr. Lamar, of South Carolina, sailed to Africa, obtained a cargo of slaves, landed them at Brunswick, Georgia, whence they were taken into the interior and sold. In former years Congress had passed a law which made the slave-trade piracy, and this cargo was brought as a deliberate violation of the law and to reopen the trade. Mr. Lamar notified the Secretary of the Treasury, Mr. Howell Cobb, of Georgia, who was a slave-holder, that he intended to violate the law. Nothing was done to prevent him.

Said the leading magazine of the South, *De Bow's Review*, "An exasperated South will blow the Union to shivers if hordes of Northern immigrants continue to seize upon and monopolize the whole of that territory which the South mainly acquired. The revival of the African slave-trade, the reduction in the price of negroes, and the increase of their numbers, will enable us successfully to contend in the settlement of the new territories with the vast immigration of the North. Nothing else can."

2

The slave-holders knew that the time was at hand when they could no longer control the government; that they must lose the political power which they had long enjoyed.   They believed that the North was prosperous because of its connection with the South.   They were ignorant of the laws which govern the economic world, and had little comprehension of the rising spirit of the age.   They were blind to the great movements

JOHN BROWN.

which have characterized the century—the rise of the people everywhere to a larger liberty and nobler civilization ; they knew almost nothing of the power of a free people and their institutions.   The record will ever stand in history that they deliberately determined to destroy the Union and establish a government based on slavery and class distinction.

In the development of the historic drama, an actor, unheralded, appeared upon the scene—John Brown, who had taken a conspicuous part in making Kansas a free State, who had seen one of his sons ruthlessly murdered by ruffians set on by the slave-holders. In October, 1859, with seventeen men he seized the United States arsenal, where the waters of the Potomac break through the Blue Mountains at Harper's Ferry, Virginia. He believed that the slaves of Virginia would flock to him, that he could arm them with muskets from the arsenal, and that he could in a short time bring about the abolition of slavery.

It was a plan devoid of reason. There was no chance of success. He was captured by a company of United States marines commanded by Robert E. Lee, whom we shall frequently see in this story of the war. He was hung at Charleston as a criminal, Henry A. Wise, governor of Virginia, signing his death-warrant. The world thought John Brown a lunatic, but Wendell Phillips, Boston's greatest orator, looking down into his grave, said, "He has abolished slavery;" and James Russell Lowell, poet, said,

> "Truth forever on the scaffold,
> Wrong forever on the throne,
> But that scaffold sways the future,
> And behind the dim unknown
> Standeth God within the shadow,
> Keeping watch above his own."

John Brown went to his death as a criminal, but a million men, a few months later, sung his apotheosis in the march, by the bivouac fire, in the uproar of battle. I heard it rising like a dirge upon the evening air along the green banks of the Potomac. I heard it like the voice of many waters when the accompaniment was the diapason of the cannonade; but noblest, grandest, most impressive, was the mighty chorus which I heard ascending to heaven in the streets of Charleston, South Carolina, on a calm, still night, when a brigade of colored troops marched past old St. Michael's church, where the moon was throwing the shadow of the church-spire across the grave of Calhoun, the great apostle of the rights of the State as superior to that of the nation—a brigade of men, slaves once, sold on the auction-block within a stone's-throw of that church-yard—freemen evermore, citizens of the Republic, soldiers of the mighty army, with the protecting folds of the Stars and Stripes above them, redeemed and elevated to citizenship by Abraham Lincoln. This the song:

> "John Brown's body lies a-mouldering in the grave;
> His soul is marching on."

The people of the South regarded the attempt of Brown to liberate the slaves as indicative of the future action of the people of the North. It aroused indignation and intensified the bitterness. Those who were

planning for the secession of the slave States improved the opportunity to increase the antagonism. The time had come to carry out their plans. It was not the people of the South that started the movement, but the great planters and politicians.

HARPER'S FERRY.

South Carolina took the lead. On the 30th of November, 1859, the legislature of that State passed a resolution favoring the formation of a Southern Confederacy. Charles G. Memminger was sent to Virginia to present the resolution to the legislature of that State. He said that "the

Constitution of the United States should be amended so that slavery might be carried everywhere. The South has the right to demand the repeal of all laws hurtful to slavery."

A newspaper was established in Charleston to advocate the reopening of the African slave-trade.

The people of Virginia were not quite ready to accept that doctrine. South Carolina wanted the law repealed which prohibited the importation of slaves from Africa, while Virginia did not; for she was raising negroes for the Southern market, every year sending from ten to twelve thousand, worth ten million dollars.

Mr. Memminger, and others of South Carolina, formed an association to bring about the dissolution of the Union. It was called the "1860 Association," which sent out one hundred and sixty thousand pamphlets advocating secession. The legislature of South Carolina called a convention to provide for arming the militia of the State. The United States flag was taken down from the State House in Columbia. "Never again shall it float in the free air of South Carolina," said the great planters.

One of the leading secessionists was Robert Barnwell Rhett. His true name was Smith, which he did not like, and so changed it. His parents were poor, but he became wealthy and lived in a stately mansion, owned a large plantation and many slaves. His summer residence was at Beaufort, overlooking the beautiful bay of Port Royal, his winter home was in Charleston. In a speech delivered in the hall of the Institute of South Carolina, he said, "The Northern people are swollen with pride and insolence, and steeped in ignorance, selfishness, and fanaticism. They never will understand their dependence on the South until the Union is dissolved, and they are left naked to their own resources. Then, and not till then, will they realize what a blessing the Almighty conferred upon them when he placed them in connection with the South; and they will curse in bitterness and repentance the dark day on which they compelled us to dissolve it. Upon its dissolution their whole system of commerce and manufactures will be paralyzed and overthrown. Their banks will suspend payments, their stocks will fall in price, and confusion and distrust will walk the streets of their great cities; mobs will break into their palaces, and society will resolve itself into its original chaos."

Mr. Rhett and his fellow-secessionists did not see that the conflict which they were about to inaugurate would be a struggle between two systems of labor. Nearly seven million emigrants had crossed the Atlantic to become free citizens of the United States. They were hard-working men and women. They had been oppressed in their native lands.

They hated slavery and class distinction.   All of their instincts were for liberty.   They knew that slavery degraded labor, and cast their votes against its extension into the territories of the West.

The men in the South who hated the democratic form of government on which the Union had been established, who thought to establish a confederacy on aristocracy and class distinction, little comprehended the magnitude of their undertaking.   Slavery, from its nature, must be aggressive. The slave-holders saw that they must dissolve the Union, or, in time, slavery would die.   Jefferson Davis and other Southern writers would have the world believe that they brought about the dissolution of the Union for the preservation of the rights of the States, but the verdict of history will be that it was to establish a government based on slavery.

CHAPTER II.

THE CONSPIRACY.

WE come to 1860, the last year of the presidency of James Buchanan. The prediction made by John C. Calhoun in 1812 had come to pass. The Democratic party had been purposely divided by the great slave-holders, who made demands for the extension of slavery which the members of the party in the North would not listen to. The slave-holders nominated John C. Breckinridge, of Kentucky, while the Northern men nominated Stephen A. Douglas, of Illinois. The Whig party nominated John Bell, of Tennessee. A new party, the Republican, had risen, pledged to resist the aggressions of slavery. Its candidate was that boy whom we saw in the first chapter, floating down the Ohio on a raft, whose father was moving from a slave to a free State. Abraham Lincoln had attended school only a few weeks in a log-cabin, where the only window was a hole in the side of the building, covered with a skin dressed very thin, or a sheet of paper greased with lard. He had very few books—the Bible, "Robinson Crusoe," the "Pilgrim's Progress," a history of the United States, and a life of Washington. For want of other books he read the Dictionary, carefully studying the words to comprehend their meaning. He used to sit before the wide fireplace in the evenings with a wooden shovel before him, and work out problems in arithmetic upon it with a bit of charcoal. He frequently walked several miles to the house of David Turnham to read the laws of Indiana. In 1830, at the age of twenty-one, he moved with his father to Illinois. It was bitter cold, and the snow was deep on those December days when they made their way across the wind-swept prairies to their future home, on the north fork of Sangamon River. With John Hanks and John Johnston he went down the river to Springfield to build a flat-boat, working for fifty cents a day. When the boat was completed, they loaded it with country produce and started for New Orleans, where he saw slaves whipped and sold. His heart sickened at the sight. Returning to Illinois, he went to work splitting rails—four hundred of them for a pair of butternut-colored jean trousers, which Nancy Hanks made for him, walking seven miles each day to and from his work.

In 1841 he helped John Hanks build a flat-boat, and again went to New Orleans pulling an oar, seeing more of the hateful features of slavery. The water was low in the river when he returned on a steamboat, so that he was a long time in getting home. There was a gang of slaves on board, handcuffed and chained to prevent their escape, the sight of which made a deep impression upon him. Once more at home, he became clerk in a store, and kept his accounts with such exactness, and was so fair in trading, that people called him "honest Abe." All respected him and had such confidence in him that they elected him to represent them in the legislature, where he came in contact with public men and learned about government. At one time he thought of becoming a blacksmith, but concluded to survey land instead, and draw deeds. He finally went to Springfield, studied law, and was admitted to the bar. He was so exact in all his dealings, so able in argument, so clear-sighted upon questions of law, that the people liked him and elected him to Congress. Being a native of Kentucky, he had a great admiration for Henry Clay— Kentucky's great statesman and orator—and was a firm believer in the principles of the Whig party. The northern section of that party was opposed to the aggression of slavery. Most of those who supported the Whig party, together with many of the Democratic party, organized the new Republican party. Mr. Lincoln had been selected by the Republican party in Illinois as their candidate for Senator, but Stephen A. Douglas was elected instead. At the convention of the Republican party held in Chicago in 1860, Mr. Lincoln was selected as their candidate for the presidency.

It was on Saturday evening, after the adjournment of the convention, that I first saw Mr. Lincoln in his own home in Springfield, accompanying the committee of the convention who apprised him of his nomination. He received the committee in the parlor, standing before the open fireplace, wearing a black frock-coat. He listened to the address of Mr. Ashman, president of the convention, and replied briefly. There was no study of inflection or cadence for effect, but there was a sincerity of expression which won instant confidence from all present. With the utterance of the last syllable his manner instantly changed. A smile illuminated his face. Addressing Hon. William D. Kelley, of Pennsylvania, he said, "You are a tall man, judge. What is your height?" "Six feet three," was the reply. "I beat you. I am six feet four without my high-heeled boots." "Pennsylvania bows to Illinois," said Mr. Kelley, "and I am glad that we

ABRAHAM LINCOLN.

have found a candidate for the presidency whom we can look up to, for we have been informed that there were only little giants in Illinois." It was an allusion by Mr. Kelley to Stephen A. Douglas, who was called the "little giant" by his admirers.

The nomination of Mr. Lincoln was received with ridicule by the Southern newspapers, the editors of which delighted to call him an ape, a baboon, an ignoramus, an abolitionist; and the party which had nominated him was stigmatized as the Black Republican party. The editors

LINCOLN'S HOME.

informed their readers that the Republican party was in favor not only of abolishing slavery by act of Congress, but also was in favor of promiscuous marriage between white people and negroes, thus increasing the bitterness of the South towards the North.

Many Northern men had settled in the South, some as merchants, others as mechanics, who ran locomotives, who built and repaired machinery. Slavery did not produce skilled mechanics, nor did it educate the people. Nearly all the school-teachers in the Southern States were from the North. There were few common schools. The secessionists of Charleston, South Carolina, found fault with the school board of that city for employing teachers educated in the North. This was the excuse of the board: "We have looked through the South, searching through the colleges and academies in vain. The teacher's profession, unhappily, seems but little appreciated in the South." Only the sons and daughters of rich men in the South obtained an education. A very large proportion of the poor white people were unable to read or write. It was the legitimate outcome of the institution of slavery.

People from the Northern States, even those who had lived in the South many years, were regarded with suspicion and closely watched. Vigilance committees were formed to look after Northern men. A period of espionage began. William H. Crawford, living at Fort Worth, Texas, was suspected of being opposed to slavery, and was hung by a mob set on by the vigilance committee. They brought his body to his grief-stricken wife, then organized a meeting, and chose a committee to hunt up all suspicious persons in the county. More than two hundred persons were compelled to leave that region—some were whipped, others tarred and feathered. In several of the Southern States laws were passed which compelled all free negroes to leave the State or be sold into slavery. The steamboats on the Mississippi were thronged with negroes thus driven out. More than two hundred thousand free men were made liable to be sold by these inhuman laws. Slavery could not tolerate freedom in any form. There must be no free negroes to make the slaves discontented. Free speech must not be permitted. White men must not discuss the question of slavery. They must remain silent or leave the country. The vigilance committees opened mail-bags and assumed the right to read private letters. The spirit of slavery was inhuman, robbing men, hanging them or driving them from their homes. Thus said the *Richmond Whig:*

"A large amount of violence has been developed since the secession movement began, more than in the whole previous history of the State. There has been an intolerance of spirit never before known. It is on the increase, and bodes no good to law and order."

During the summer and fall of 1860 John B. Floyd, of Virginia, Secretary of War, was doing what he could to prepare the Southern States for war. He sent one hundred and thirty-five thousand muskets from Northern to Southern arsenals. "We are much obliged," said the *Mobile Advertiser*, "to Secretary Floyd for the foresight he has displayed in disarming the North and equipping the South in this emergency."

The United States army numbered only twelve thousand men. Most of the troops were in Texas, California, and Oregon, so far away that when the plans of the conspirators were ripe, they could carry them out without molestation.

The Secretary of the Navy, though from Connecticut, allowed himself to be used by the secessionists. There were ninety vessels in the navy, carrying two thousand four hundred and ninety-five guns. He sent five vessels to the East Indies, three to Brazil, seven to the Pacific coast, three to the Mediterranean, seven to the coast of Africa. Twenty-five were dismantled and unfit for service. Of the entire navy, the steamer *Brooklyn*, twenty-five guns, and the store-ship *Relief* were the only ones fit for service on the Atlantic coast.

The dissolution of the Union was brought about by a few men. We can count them on our fingers. The leaders were: Francis W. Pickens, William H. Gist, James H. Hammond, Robert Barnwell Rhett, Charles G. Memminger, Lawrence M. Keitt, James L. Orr, of South Carolina; Jefferson Davis, Jacob Thompson, of Mississippi; John B. Floyd, James M. Mason, Robert M. T. Hunter, John Tyler, Henry A. Wise, John Seddon, of Virginia; Robert Toombs, Howell Cobb, of Georgia; William L. Yancy, of Alabama; Judah P. Benjamin, John Slidell, of Louisiana; Louis Wigfall, of Texas; Stephen R. Mallory, of Florida. They announced their intention of dissolving the Union in case Mr. Lincoln should be elected President.

"If Abraham Lincoln is elected," said Henry A. Wise, "I will not stay in the Union one hour. Rather than submit to Republican rule, I would fight to the last drop of blood to resist its fanatical oppression. Our minds are made up. The South will not wait till the 4th of March, but we will be well under arms before then."

"South Carolina will shatter this accursed Union. She will throw her arms around the pillars of the Constitution, and involve all the States in a common ruin," said Lawrence M. Keitt, with confused and florid rhetoric.

There was great rejoicing in Charleston on the evening of election-day, November 6, 1860, when it was known that Mr. Lincoln was chosen. A few days later the legislature of South Carolina called a convention to act upon the question of seceding from the Union. Notices of the formation of military companies appeared in the newspapers. The drum-beat was heard in every village. The *Charleston Mercury* flung out a transparency from its windows with this inscription: "One voice and a million of strong arms to uphold the honor of South Carolina."

The Stars and Stripes became a hateful banner. Orators made inflammatory speeches against the Union, and at the same time set forth the glorious future that awaited the Palmetto State. She was to be the leader in a revolution which would bring about the establishment of a new nation, which would be so powerful that the Northern States would sue for peace, and Great Britain, from necessity, would bow meekly down before the new empire of the Western world.

On December 17th the convention assembled in Columbia, but adjourned to Charleston. Its sessions were held in secret, in the hall of the South Carolina Institute. On December 20th, at a quarter before one o'clock, it was voted that the union between the United States and South Carolina be dissolved. "The Union is dissolved!" was the cry which rang through the streets. Men tossed their hats into the air, women waved their handkerchiefs. All business stopped. Ladies appeared upon the streets wearing secession bonnets made of cotton cloth, ornamented with rosettes of red, white, and blue, and leaves of the palmetto. A procession was formed which marched to St. Michael's church-yard, where, around the grave of Calhoun, a solemn oath was sworn to give life, fortune, and honor to secure the independence of the State.

Evening comes. The ordinance of secession has been engrossed and is ready for signing. Two palmetto-trees have been placed on the platform in the hall. Mr. Alexander, an artist, has painted a banner representing the arch of the Confederacy, built on the ruins of the Union, South Carolina the key-stone. Cotton bales beneath a palmetto-tree, a rattlesnake darting its angry tongue, its emblems of power and vengeance.

The members of the convention signed their names, then the bells rang, cannon thundered, and an excited crowd surged through the streets hurrahing over what had been done.

Commissioners were sent to the other Southern States, urging them to secede. The legislature of Georgia was in session. Robert Toombs was at home from Washington and addressed the legislature. "Withdraw your sons," he said, "from the army and navy and every department of the Government. Buy arms and throw the bloody spear into the den of the assassins and incendiaries, and let God defend the right. Twenty years of preparation would not make up for the advantage your enemies would gain if the rising sun on March 5th should find you in the Union. Strike while there is yet time."

Alexander H. Stephens made a speech in opposition to Toombs. "I tell you frankly," he said, "that the election of a man constitutionally chosen President is not sufficient cause for any State to separate from the Union." A month later he became vice-president of the Confederacy.

Mississippi was the first State to follow South Carolina; then Florida, Alabama, Georgia, Louisiana, and Texas, the last on February 1, 1861.

Lieutenant-colonel Gardner, of Massachusetts, was commander of the forts guarding the harbor at Charleston. Castle Pinckney was an old-fashioned, circular, brick fort on Folly Island, about one mile east of the city. Fort Moultrie was on Sullivan's Island, still farther to the east, on the site

BUILT FROM THE RUINS.

of the old fort built of palmetto logs during the Revolution, which the British fleet bombarded, and where, when the flag-staff had been shot away, Sergeant William Jasper leaped from the rampart down upon the beach, picked up the flag, and planted it once more upon the parapet. Besides these there was Fort Sumter, built up from a reef in the harbor. There were twenty-two cannon in Castle Pinckney, besides two mortars and two small guns. In Moultrie there were forty-five heavy cannon and seven light pieces; in Sumter there were seventy-eight cannon. The last-named fort was pentagonal in form, built of brick made solid by cement, and rose sixty-five feet above the water. The engineers who planned it intended that the armament should be one hundred and thirty-five cannon, which should be placed in three tiers, two in casemates to be fired through embrasures, and the third on the top of the fort. Only seventy-eight of the guns, however, had been placed in position. Within the fort were wooden barracks for the privates and officers. The fort was about midway, Sullivan's Island on the north and Morris Island on the south, a little more than half a mile from each. The main ship-channel was between Sumter and Moultrie. The fort was two and one-third miles from Castle Pinckney and three and one-third miles from Charleston.

Lieutenant-colonel Gardner saw that the secessionists were getting ready to seize the forts and called for reinforcements. The members of Congress from South Carolina called upon the Secretary of War, Mr. Floyd, and asked for his removal. The request was granted, and Major Robert Anderson, of Kentucky, was appointed to succeed him.

The secessionists did not know how true a man he was, or what blood coursed through his veins. His father was from Virginia, a lieutenant-colonel during the Revolution, was wounded at Trenton, taken prisoner by the British at Charleston, and was aide to Lafayette at Yorktown. Major Anderson was born in Kentucky, whose sons had poured out their blood for the Union in the war of 1812, whose voice had ever been for the Union. Major Anderson was a religious man. He believed in God and loved the Bible. Nothing was so dear to him as the flag he had sworn to support. His headquarters were in Fort Moultrie, on Sullivan's Island. He, too, saw what the secessionists intended to do, and sent this message to General Scott: "Fort Sumter and Castle Pinckney must be garrisoned immediately, if the Government is to keep command of the harbor."

"Your communications in the future will be addressed to the Secretary of War," wrote John B. Floyd to Major Anderson.

Why did not Floyd remove him? Because he had something else to think of. A matter was coming to light which he would like to keep in the dark. Some bonds belonging to the Indian Trust Fund of the Interior Department were not in the safe where they ought to be. A relative of Floyd, Godard Bailey, had charge of the bonds; Floyd had made a contract with the firm of Russell & Co. to transport supplies for the army from St. Louis to Utah, and had paid them more than two million dollars in excess of work done, making the payments by drafts. The bankers in New York would not advance money on the drafts, whereupon Bailey took the bonds from the safe and gave them to Russell & Co., taking the drafts in exchange. It was in effect a robbery. The interest on the bonds would be due January 1st, and if not paid the theft would be made public. There was no money in the Treasury, which, under the administration of Buchanan, had become bankrupt. The Secretary of the Interior, Jacob

MAJOR ROBERT ANDERSON.

Thompson, of Mississippi, was in Raleigh, North Carolina, using his influence to bring about a secession of that State. He received a letter from Bailey informing him of the condition of affairs, which caused him to hasten to Washington, and it was his arrival, and the reflection that in two or three days the transaction would be known, that gave Floyd something else to think of.

There were still a few men in Charleston who were true to the old flag. James L. Pettigrew was regarded as the ablest lawyer in South Carolina.

3

On Sunday when the minister, where he attended church, omitted from the service the usual prayer for the President of the United States, Mr. Pettigrew rose in his seat and repeated very distinctly, "Most humbly and heartily we beseech Thee with Thy favor to behold and bless Thy servant, the President of the United States." He placed his prayer-book in the rack, motioned to Mrs. Pettigrew, who placed her arm within his, and together they left the church; nor did he ever enter it again until his lifeless body was carried there for burial.

There was still another loyal man in Charleston—Tom Hogan, born in Ireland, but who had made America his home. He was in an auction-room, where, among other goods, the Stars and Stripes was displayed, not in honor, but in derision. The auctioneer did not offer it for sale, but threw it upon the ground, saying he would not ask a bid for that worthless rag. "I'll give ten dollars for it!" shouted Tom Hogan, handing over his money, picking up the flag and carrying it away, the astonished secession-ists not daring to molest him. Through all the years of the war he kept it concealed in his house, and when Charleston was once more under the Stars and Stripes, Tom Hogan's flag waved above the headquarters of the general in command.

Christmas evening came. Major Anderson was at a dinner-party in Charleston, where he heard something which set him to thinking as to what he ought to do. No reinforcements had been sent him, and from what he heard he concluded that none were to be sent. He knew that the military companies of Charleston were intending to seize the forts under the direction of Governor Pickens. All night long he thought of his duty and obligation to the flag, and resolved to abandon Moultrie and transfer the troops to Sumter. His entire force consisted of two weak companies of artillery and some hired men employed by the engineer department about the forts, in all about one hundred, of which fifty-one were officers and soldiers. The day after Christmas was a very active day in Moultrie, where nearly all of the soldiers were stationed, and where Major Anderson had his headquarters. Only the officers were informed as to what Major Anderson intended to do. The secessionists had spies around him, and at night they had a boat patrolling the harbor. They attempted to keep close watch of every movement. Supper was ready, but the soldiers did not sit down to their mess; taking their supper with them, they stepped into the boats and made their way to Sumter. Morning dawned; the sun was rising. The soldiers stand around the flag-staff. Major Anderson kneels, holding the halyards, while Rev. Matthew Harris, the chaplain, offers prayer, and then the flag rises to the top-mast to float serenely in the morning air.

The people of Charleston, looking out from the balconies of their houses along the grand promenade, behold with astonishment a column of smoke rising above Moultrie, where the gun-carriages are slowly burning, having been set on fire by the departing garrison, while above Sumter floats the detested flag. All their plans have suddenly been overturned. Sumter cannot now be seized; the garrison must be starved out or the fort captured. They do not want to starve the garrison, but to win glory by capturing the fort. The telegraph flashes the startling news to Washington. Secretary Floyd hastens to the White House to see President Buchanan, demanding that Major Anderson be ordered back to Moultrie. The President refused to comply with the request, which greatly enraged the secessionists.

In Charleston there was a beating of drums, a mustering of the militia, who took possession of the arsenal, Castle Pinckney, and Fort Moultrie. There was great excitement throughout the State. The governor ordered out the Darlington Guards and the Columbia Artillery, which took possession of Morris Island, to begin the erection of batteries and the mounting of cannon for the bombardment of Sumter. The soldiers in their bright uniforms did not do the shovelling; that was done by slaves sent by the planters in their fiery zeal. Rev. Mr. Prentis, preacher of the Gospel, owner of many slaves, sent sixteen of them. It was the beginning of the struggle between the two systems of labor, two forms of society, two diverse civilizations. Had Major Anderson seen fit to open fire upon that gang of slaves and the militia drilling on the sandy beach, he would quickly have put an end to the shovelling. He had not gone to Sumter, however, for any hostile purpose; it was not his duty to begin hostilities. He had acted solely in self-defence, according to instructions from Washington. Day by day he saw the fortification rising upon Morris Island, and heavy cannon placed in position to open fire, but it was his duty to wait. The secessionists, and not the Government, must bear the responsibility of beginning a war.

The 1st of January came, and the coupons of the Indian Trust Fund were due. The money in the Treasury had been squandered. The people throughout the country were astounded at the news that the bonds of the Trust Fund had been stolen by trusted officials. Secretary Floyd had done what he could to destroy the government of the United States and build a Confederacy upon its ruins; he could stay no longer in office. He sent his resignation to the President, and fled to Virginia like a thief escaping justice. The court indicted him, and warrants were issued to the sheriff for his arrest. We shall see him once more for a moment as major-general in the Confederate army, then he will disappear, to be remembered only as a traitor and thief. Howell Cobb, Secretary of the Treasury, had already resigned. Their places were filled with loyal men.

President Buchanan made a great mistake in not dismissing Jacob Thompson, of Mississippi, Secretary of the Interior. At a meeting of the cabinet it was decided to send four companies of troops to reinforce Major Anderson. Thompson acted the part of a traitor by telegraphing to the Governor of South Carolina what had been done. The Government could not send a despatch to Major Anderson, as the secessionists would know all about it. The steamer *Star of the West*, with the troops on board, reached Charleston harbor, but was turned back by the batteries on Morris Island, which opened fire. Very boastful was the *Charleston Mercury* the next morning. "We would not," it said, "exchange or recall that blow for millions. It has wiped out half a century of scorn and outrage. The haughty echo of her cannon has, ere this, reverberated from Maine to Texas. The decree has gone forth. Upon each acre of the peaceful soil of the South armed men will spring up as the sound breaks upon their ears. By the God of our fathers, the soil of South Carolina shall be free!"

In one of the committee-rooms of the Capitol at Washington, on the night of January 5th, there was a secret meeting of the Senators from Florida, Georgia, Alabama, Mississippi, Louisiana, and Texas. The watchman who strolled through the corridors of the Capitol knew nothing of what was going on in the room; the public knew nothing of what was said by the men who had thus met to overthrow the Government; but during the night messages were flying along the wires urging the secession of the States which they represented, and the seizure of all the forts along the Southern coast, with all the arsenals.

Governor Brown, of Georgia, ordered the military companies of Savannah to take possession of Fort Pulaski. A military company from New Orleans went up the Mississippi to Baton Rouge, and occupied the arsenal there. In all the ports the secessionists were seizing the revenue-cutters belonging to the Government.

John Adams Dix, of New York, was appointed Secretary of the Treasury. He sent Mr. Jones to New Orleans with an order to Captain Breshwood, commanding the revenue-cutter at that port, to sail to New York. The captain was a secessionist and proposed to turn the vessel over to the Confederates, whereupon Secretary Dix sent this despatch: "*If any man attempts to haul down the American flag, shoot him on the spot!*"

What a glorious and heart-thrilling despatch it was! There had been apathy throughout the country over the state of affairs. People had stood appalled over the treachery at Washington and through the South. A sentiment so loyal, and uttered so fearlessly, awakened a lofty enthusiasm for the old flag which had never been lowered in dishonor.

Every fort in the South was seized, except Fort Pickens, on Santa Rosa Island, in the harbor of Pensacola, which was held by Lieutenant Slemmer and the troops under him.

General Twiggs was in command of twenty-five hundred troops at San Antonio, Texas. He entered into conspiracy with Ben McCulloch, who

GENERAL JOHN A. DIX.

called himself a Texan Ranger, who gathered one thousand men and rode into San Antonio at two o'clock on the morning of February 10th, yelling, firing their guns, and taking possession of the town. General Twiggs professed to be surprised, and surrendered the troops, all the stores, cannon, and supplies, worth one million two hundred thousand dollars. Twiggs was from Georgia. When the news of his treachery reached Washington, President Buchanan ordered his name to be stricken from the rolls of the

Treasury Department
Jan. 29, 1861

Tell Lieut. Caldwell to arrest
Capt. Breshwood, assume command
of the Cutter and obey the order I gave
through You. If Capt. Breshwood
after arrest undertakes to interfere
with the command of the Cutter, tell
Lieut. Caldwell to consider him
as a mutineer & treat him accordingly. If any one attempts to haul
down the American flag shoot
him on the spot. —

John A. Dix
Secretary of the Treasury.

FAC-SIMILE OF GENERAL JOHN A. DIX'S DESPATCH.

army as a traitor. The people of New Orleans gave him an ovation, but his name has gone down to history covered with infamy. From the time of Judas men have despised a traitor.

Florida seceded January 12th. It had been purchased from Spain by the money of all the States, and the forts at the entrance of Pensacola Bay had been built by the United States. The State of Florida had no claim to them. Men sent by the governor demanded the surrender of the forts.

There were three — Fort McRea and Fort Barrancas on the mainland at the entrance to the harbor, and Fort Pickens on Santa Rosa Island, guarding the eastern side. Young Lieutenant Slemmer, in command, knew that he would be powerless against the troops which would soon appear, but he was loyal to the flag which he had sworn to support. He was quick to act. He drove spikes into the vent-holes of the cannon in the forts on the main-land, jumped into a boat with his men, rowed across the bay, threw himself into Fort Pickens, and determined to keep the Stars

MAP OF PENSACOLA.

and Stripes flying above that fortress of stone. He held it until the middle of April, when reinforcements arrived. It was the one place on the Atlantic shore south of the Chesapeake where the flag of the Union, through all the years of the war, waved in grandeur and glory.

February 15th was a great day in Montgomery, Alabama. A crowd surged through the streets. Delegates from the seceding States were there, sitting in convention, organizing a Confederacy, and electing Jefferson Davis president and Alexander H. Stephens vice-president. Mr. Davis was at his home in Mississippi. There was great enthusiasm at all the railroad stations on his route to Montgomery. He made twenty-five speeches, one from the balcony of the Exchange Hotel in Montgomery. It was ten o'clock in the evening; cannon were thundering, bonfires blazing, the crowd hurrahing. On each side of the newly elected president of the new Confederacy stood a negro, holding a tallow candle, that the people might see the great man of the hour.

"England will not allow," said Mr. Davis, "our great staple—cotton—

to be dammed up within our present limits. She will aid us. If war must come, it must be on Northern, not on Southern, soil. A glorious future is before us. The grass will grow in Northern cities where the pavements have been worn off by the tread of commerce. We will carry war where it is easy to advance, where food for the sword and torch await our armies in the densely populated cities."

He had some reason for uttering such language, for there were people in high positions in the Northern States who had assured the slave-holders that they were in sympathy with them.

JEFFERSON DAVIS.

"If there is any fighting, it will be within our own borders and in our own streets," wrote ex-President Franklin Pierce, of New Hampshire, to Jefferson Davis. Fernando Wood, mayor of New York, proposed that there should be a separation of the States, and that New York City should be independent of them all.

"If force is used it will be inaugurated at home," said the politicians belonging to the Democratic party, in convention at Albany.

"If the cotton States can do better out of the Union than in it, we insist on letting them go in peace," wrote Horace Greeley, editor of the *New York Tribune*, one of the leaders of the party which elected Mr. Lincoln. It was a natural conclusion which the secessionists arrived at, that the people of the North were so divided in sentiment that they would not go to war, or if they did, it would be an easy matter for the Southern States to establish their independence. The merchants of New York, Boston, and Philadelphia became alarmed at the prospect of losing their trade, and were ready to give their friends in the South long credits, hoping thereby to induce the Southern States to remain in the Union. The merchants of Charleston, Savannah, and New Orleans accepted the offers, and purchased large stocks of goods, giving notes which never were paid.

Let us keep in mind, as we go on with this story of the war, that it was a conflict between two systems of labor. The South had few manufactories of any kind. On the 18th of February Raphael Semmes, who had resigned his commission in the United States navy, called upon Jefferson Davis at Montgomery, and received authority to visit the Northern States and obtain skilled mechanics, to be employed in making machinery for the manufacture of arms, ammunition, and percussion-caps. "So exclusively," writes Mr. Semmes, "had the manufacture of these articles been confined to the North, that we had not even enough percussion-caps to fight a battle." In the month of March Mr. Semmes was inspecting the manufactories in Connecticut and Massachusetts and New York. He says that he found people everywhere not only willing, but eager to trade with him. He purchased large quantities of percussion-caps and sent them by express to Montgomery, and made contracts for machinery to manufacture rifled cannon. Mr. Semmes bears this testimony: "The people did not think it possible that the South was in earnest."

Jefferson Davis and the cotton-planters thought that England must have cotton to supply the manufactures of that country, to keep millions of people from becoming paupers; that if the Northern States attempted to blockade the Southern seaports, England would send her ships to break the blockade; that the spinners and weavers of Lowell, Manchester, Fall River, and all the cotton manufacturing towns of New England, not having any more cotton, would become mobs, parading the streets and crying for bread. The Southern newspapers informed their readers that the North would soon be starved into submission. "The Northern people," said the *Charleston Courier*, in December, 1860, "have a long, dark winter of cold and hunger impending over their heads. Before it is over

they will have millions of operatives without work and without bread.
When cold and hunger do their work, this deluded rabble will ask alms at
the door of the rich with pikes and firebrands in their hands."

On February 11th Abraham Lincoln left his home in Springfield,
Illinois, for Washington. He was the chosen representative of free labor.

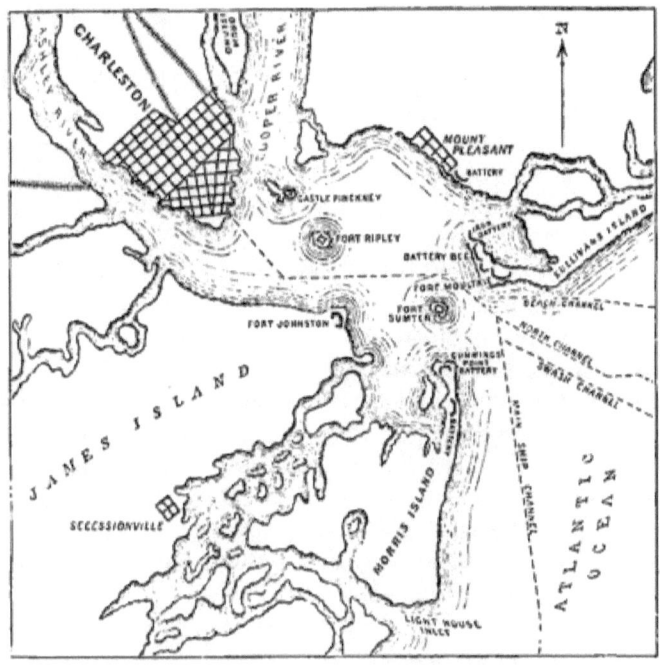

MAP OF CHARLESTON HARBOR.

Crowds greeted him at every station. This was what he said at Indianap-
olis: "When the people rise in mass in behalf of the Union and the lib-
erties of their country, truly may it be said that the gates of hell cannot
prevail against them."

On March 4th he became President.

"I have no intention of interfering with slavery in the States where it
exists," he said; and he went on to say that the Union is perpetual; that
acts of violence against the authority of the United States are insurrection-
ary, and that the Union would defend itself and hold its property; that
beyond that there would be no invasion, no using of force against the people, no bloodshed, unless forced upon the national authority.

"In your hands," he said to the people of the South, "and not mine, is the momentous issue of civil war. The Government will not assail you; you can have no conflict without being yourselves the aggressors."

An attempt was made to conciliate the seceding States by holding a "Peace Congress," but the States that had seceded had no desire to be conciliated.

What should be done about Fort Sumter? That was the one great question.

"I have but one month's provisions," wrote Major Anderson. If provisions were not sent, he would be compelled to evacuate.

Jefferson Davis sent commissioners to Washington to negotiate for the surrender of the fort, but instead of surrendering it, President Lincoln and a majority of his cabinet decided that provisions should be sent to the garrison.

"You will not be permitted to purchase provisions in Charleston," said the authorities of South Carolina to Major Anderson, stopping the commissary who had purchased vegetables in the market. The garrison had nothing left but salt pork and one barrel of flour.

A fleet sailed from New York with supplies.

"My batteries are ready. I await instructions," was the message of General Beauregard, commanding the troops on Morris Island, to Jefferson Davis. For three months the slaves had been at work with shovels, throwing up intrenchments. For three months the Palmetto Guard, the Columbia Artillery, and other companies—five thousand troops in all—had been placing cannon and mortars in position.

A floating iron-clad battery had been constructed, which was towed by a steam-tug into a chosen position and anchored where it would rain its shot and shell upon the weakest wall of the fort. Major Anderson had seen it all, but yet he did not attempt to prevent it, for President Lincoln had determined that if there was to be war the Southern States should fire the first gun.

"Demand the immediate surrender of Fort Sumter," was Jefferson Davis's order to Beauregard, and on the afternoon of April 11th two officers went out to the fort from Morris Island with the demand.

"I cannot surrender the fort. I shall await the first shot, and if you do not batter me to pieces, I shall be starved out in three days."

South Carolina and the Confederate government cannot wait.

Every morning through the winter the people of Charleston had seen the Stars and Stripes go up the flag-staff of Sumter, and its crimson folds and fadeless stars float serenely in the breeze through the day; at nightfall they had seen the flash and heard the thunder of the sunset salute to the hated banner. The colonels, majors, captains, lieutenants, the soldiers in the batteries, longed to humiliate the emblem of national authority. The governor of the State, Francis W. Pickens, Jefferson Davis, all who had labored with hot and fiery zeal to overthrow the Union, with blood at fever heat, were eager for war. The flag of the United States must be trailed in the dust. The "mud-sills," as Senator Hammond, of South Carolina, had called the working-men of the Northern States, must understand that the Cavaliers of the South were their masters.

"It is a gross mistake," wrote George Fitzhugh, of Virginia, "to suppose that Abolition is the cause of dissolution between the North and the South. The Cavaliers, Jacobites, and Huguenots of the South naturally hate, contemn, and despise the Puritans who settled the North. The former are master races; the latter a slave race, the descendants of the Saxon serfs."

Virginia had not seceded. The convention to consider the question was in session, composed largely of men who did not wish to secede.

"I will tell you what will put Virginia in the Southern Confederacy in less than an hour," said Roger A. Pryor, a red-hot secessionist of Virginia, to the people of Charleston; "sprinkle blood in their faces."

From the beginning the secessionists were bold and aggressive. Not by appeals to reason, not by fair argument, but by denunciation of the Northern people, by constant talking of "State Rights," they brought about the secession of the several States. The leaders in the conspiracy saw that a blow must be struck. Having gone so far, they must go farther, and they deliberately resolved to bring on the war.

At 3.20 on the morning of April 12th a boat glides over the calm waters to Fort Sumter, bearing a messenger with a note from General Beauregard to Major Anderson: "I shall open fire on Fort Sumter in one hour." The people of Charleston knew that the message was to be sent, and many have sat up through the night to see the ushering in of the new era in the history of the Palmetto State.

Half-past four. The hour has come. They see the flash of a cannon and hear its thunder rolling up the bay. An old man with long white hair flowing upon his shoulders—Edmund Ruffin, of Virginia—whose beautiful home stands on the bank of the James, who has given heart and soul to the cause of Secession, claims to have fired it. Little does he comprehend what will come of it; that before the cannon of the Nation have ceased their thundering, great armies bearing the Stars and Stripes will pitch their tents upon his wide-spreading acres; that the soldiers of the

GENERAL BEAUREGARD.

Union will eat the fruits of his orchards; that his home will disappear in the devastating flames; that his slaves will be freemen, citizens of the Republic; that his own weak and trembling hands will twist a rope for his own neck; that the time will come when his body will be swaying lifeless in the air—that he will commit suicide through mortification over the failure of his hopes and expectations.

From the sand-hills on Morris Island, from the floating battery, from Moultrie, came flashes in quick succession. White powder clouds floated in the morning air, and the deep thunder rolled across the hitherto peaceful waters of the bay. Six o'clock. As yet there is no answering from Sumter. Major Anderson and his men are eating their breakfast of fried salt pork. Seven o'clock. At last the cannon of Sumter open their lips. Their waiting is symbolic of the patience, endurance, and long-suffering of a great people. Through the day the bombardment goes on, the forts and batteries raining a concentrated fire upon the beleaguered garrison. Major Anderson's heart is momentarily gladdened by the appearance of the fleet which has been sent to his relief, but the batteries on Morris Island command the channel, and the vessels cannot approach the fort. At sunset the fort ceases its thunder, but through the night the Confederate batteries, at regular intervals, send their shells across the water.

Morning dawns, and once more the batteries are in lively action. Again the fort replies, but more slowly than before, for no more cloth can be had for cartridges. The soldiers tear up their blankets, and when those are gone, strip off their shirts and hand them over to the gunners.

From the roofs and steeples of Charleston, from the balconies along the promenade, the people look exultingly upon the scene. The Confederate soldiers in Moultrie send red hot cannon-balls crashing into the wooden barracks, setting them on fire. In vain the efforts of the Union soldiers to extinguish the flames, and fearing that the heat will explode one of the magazines, they throw most of the powder into the sea. The flag-staff is shot away, but Peter Hart, who was once a sergeant under Major Anderson, but who is now working at his trade as a carpenter for the Government, and Mr. Davy, run up the stone steps to the parapet, where shells are exploding and solid shot ploughing across the masonry, and fix the flag once more in its place.

Major Anderson has so little powder that he can only fire once in ten minutes. He has eaten his last meal; there is not a biscuit left, no flour, nor rice, nothing but salt pork, but he has no thought of surrendering the fort; he will stay till the last moment. He will be compelled to evacuate on Monday morning, when he can no longer give his starving soldiers food.

A boat glides over the water from Morris Island, bearing General Wigfall, of Texas, who climbs into one of the embrasures and informs Major Anderson that he has come from General Beauregard. He is a self-appointed messenger, unauthorized, but through his action the cannonade ceases. It is finally agreed that the fort shall be surrendered, that Major Anderson and all his men shall have the privilege of saluting the flag, taking it with them, and that they shall be placed on board the Government vessels outside the harbor.

Never before has Charleston been so intoxicated with joy amounting to delirium as on that Saturday night, April 13, 1861. Crowds surge the streets, hurrahing and shouting. Houses are illuminated, bells ring. In the stately mansions ladies fill wineglasses, and the young men drink to the health of General Beauregard, Jefferson Davis, Governor Pickens, the honor of South Carolina, and to the ladies. Never before such a night of revel in Charleston.

"Thank God!" said Governor Pickens, standing on the balcony of the Charleston Hotel, addressing the multitude—"thank God! the day has come; the war is open, and we will conquer or perish. We have defeated their twenty millions, and we have humbled the proud flag of the Stars and Stripes that never before was lowered to any nation on earth; we have lowered it in humility before the Palmetto and Confederate flags, and have compelled them to raise the white flag and ask for honorable surrender. The Stars and Stripes have triumphed for seventy years, but on this 13th of April it has been humbled by the little State of South Carolina. And I pronounce here, before the civilized world, that your independence is baptized in blood; your independence is won upon a glorious battle-field, and you are free now and forever, in defiance of the world in arms."

Little did Governor Pickens think what changes four years would bring; that grass would be growing on those time-worn pavements; that the air would be voiceless to all sounds of business, every house desolate, every home rent by cannon-balls, or shattered by exploding shells; that all would be ruin and desolation. Governor Pickens had a great plantation. Slaves did his bidding. Ere four years they would be free men, soldiers in the army of the Republic, enjoying the rights of citizenship, and all the fond dreams which had come to him of a confederacy built on slavery would fade away before the mighty power of a free people, and the old flag would once more be floating over the shapeless ruins of Sumter.

CHAPTER III.

THE UPRISING OF THE PEOPLE.

SINCE the founding of the nation, men had never looked into one another's faces as on Saturday evening, April 13, 1861. Never had there been such sinking of hearts and hopes as at the sunset hour of that day of gloom. People wept as they weep when looking down into the coffin of a departed friend. The flag that never before had been dishonored, the brightest banner that ever waved on earth, the emblem of the world's best hope—insulted! Bitter the thought. Never before such a Sunday in this Western Hemisphere or in the history of the human race—on which thirty millions of people pondered the all-absorbing question whether the Union and the Government of the people was to live or die. Monday morning—the answer is on their lips. It is to live. Abraham Lincoln has written it with his own hand.

"I, Abraham Lincoln, President of the United States, in virtue of the power in me vested by the Constitution and the laws, have thought fit to call forth, and hereby do call forth, the militia of the several States of the Union, to the aggregate number of seventy-five thousand, in order to suppress this combination against the laws, and to cause the laws to be duly executed."

The telegraph flashes it east to Bangor, westward to San Francisco, to every city and town. A great hour has come—the beginning of a new era in the history of our country. Men read it with quivering lips and moistened eyes. For months and years, while the slave-holders have been directing the affairs of Government, lower and still lower has burned the patriotic fire, but now it flames from the Atlantic to the Pacific shore. In every fibre of their being the people feel that the nation shall live. Their fortunes, their lives—all the strength that God has given them shall be devoted to the preservation of the Union.

A week ago the people of the Northern States were divided into political parties; now there is only one party. On Sunday afternoon, while the ink is still wet on the paper upon which President Lincoln has written his proclamation, Stephen A. Douglas walks with quickened steps to the White House. He has been Mr. Lincoln's political antagonist. They were candidates for Senator from Illinois. Through that senatorial contest they stood face to face, waging political warfare. Mr. Douglas won. They were candidates for the presidency, and Mr. Douglas lost; but now that the Union is in peril, he forgets the past. He knows nothing but the duty of the hour. They clasp hands. "We must wage relentless war," are the words of Mr. Douglas. "Every man must be for the United States or against it; there can be no neutrals—only patriots and traitors."

One State was ready to respond to the call of the President—Massachusetts, which had thirteen thousand citizen soldiers. Massachusetts had been foremost in the Revolutionary War. Her citizens had ever been ardent lovers of liberty. Most of the leading antislavery men were of that State. During the year 1860, the governor, Nathaniel P. Banks, looking into the future and apprehending the possible coming of war, had taken measures to bring the militia to a high degree of efficiency. There had been a mustering of all the troops of the State on the historic field of Concord. His successor, John A. Andrew, also looked into the future and saw the necessity of having the troops ready to respond at any moment to any call which might be made upon them. Benjamin F. Butler, citizen of Lowell, who had earnestly supported Breckinridge for the presidency, had visited Washington in December to attend a meeting of his political party. To his astonishment, in conversation with a gentleman from Mississippi, he learned that the South intended to secede from the Union. "You men of the North will not fight," said the Mississippian. "Yes, they will fight," responded Butler. "Who will fight?" "I will." "Oh! there will be plenty of men in the South to take care of such as you." "When we march to the defence of the Union we will hang on the trees all the men left behind who undertake to break up the Union," responded Butler. Returning to Boston, he informed Governor Andrew of the intentions of the secessionists.

There was still another citizen of Massachusetts who fully comprehended the designs of the secessionists—Henry Wilson, Senator, like Abraham Lincoln, a man of the people, who was very poor in early life, but who, by patriotic devotion, hard study, and perseverance, had won the confidence of the people. He had been one of the foremost to resist the aggressions of slavery, was bold and energetic, and who, whenever he wished to know just what to do, made the trip from Washington to Massachusetts to learn the opinions of the people. He was an adroit politician, and took measures to find out all he could about the plans of the secessionists, and

4

had kept the governor of the State informed as to their intentions. During the month of January, Governor Andrew ordered the colonels of regiments to ascertain who of their commands would be ready to respond upon the instant to any call. During the month of February two thousand overcoats were made and other equipments provided.

"If you have troops ready, forward them at once to Washington," is the message which comes to him. Out of the State House men hasten with orders. Twenty companies are wanted. The soldiers are scattered far and wide, in more than twenty towns, driving teams upon their farms,

THE PIG.

making shoes, pushing the plane; some are clerks in counting-rooms, or laborers in mills where spindles are whirling and shuttles flying.

Down by the sea-side, where the waves of the Atlantic break upon the granite ledges of Marblehead, are men with sunburnt, weather-beaten faces, who have braved the storms of the sea. All are sons of toil, representatives of labor. They are men who earn their daily bread. Little dream they of the place they are to occupy in history. It is four o'clock in the afternoon when a messenger rides up to the house of Captain Knott V. Martin. The captain has killed a pig and is ready to dress it, when the messenger hands him a slip of paper. With knife in hand he reads it:

"You are ordered to appear with your company on Boston Common at the earliest possible moment." He throws down the knife to put on his uniform.

"What will you do with the pig?" asks Mrs. Martin.

"—— the pig!"

Not an instant does he wait; the members of his company must be summoned, his knapsack packed.

Major Watson, of Lowell, is a lawyer. He has important cases in court, with interests of clients at stake, but he turns the key of his office door. Months will pass before he again will enter it. The spiders can spin their webs in peace across the windows through the coming summer. The dust will be thick upon his briefs before he will again ponder points in law. General Benjamin F. Butler leaves his multitudinous law business to take command of the troops hastening to the rendezvous.

Morning dawns, and in every village there is a beating of drums and gathering of citizens to see the soldiers take their departure. The day is dark and dreary—the wind east, the storm-clouds flying in from the sea, but the streets are filled with people. There is a steady tramping of feet upon the pavement, a swinging of hats and loud hurrahs as the companies arrive, marching to Faneuil Hall, the building where the nation in its infancy was cradled.

The Sixth Regiment is the first to leave. A great crowd assembles to witness its departure and rend the air with their cheers. The next morning the troops are in New York, marching down Broadway beneath a sea of banners. Hundreds of thousands of people cheer them. They breakfast at the Astor House. Mr. Colman, the proprietor, will receive no pay for what they eat. At Philadelphia they sit down to a sumptuous entertainment provided by the citizens. In their loyalty they cannot do enough for the men who, at a moment's notice, have left everything to save Washington from the hands of the Confederates.

April 19th. It is the anniversary of Lexington and Concord. Eighty-six years have rolled away since Major Buttrick marshalled his fifty men in the meadows of Concord, with Rev. Mr. Emerson, minister, in the ranks, his gun upon his shoulder, and now three of Major Buttrick's descendants are whirling towards Washington in response to their country's call.

They are in Maryland, a slave State, which the secessionists hope to secure to the Confederacy. They have stirred up the ruffians of the city to prevent the passage of Northern troops to Washington.

"I fear that you will have trouble in Baltimore," are the words of General Davis to Colonel Jones, commanding the regiment.

"Load your guns," is the order of the colonel to his men as he passes through the cars distributing twenty cartridges to each man. The cars whirl into the northern depot; horses are hitched on, and one by one they are drawn through the streets. Six companies go through to the southern depot before the ruffians can muster their forces; but a mob quickly gathers, digs up the pavement, and hurls the stones into the cars. They tear up the rails. The four companies left behind must fight their way. The officers are cool and determined. They see that there must be a single commander, and elect Captain Follansbee. Clubs and stones are hurled upon them. The ruffians bring boxes, barrels, and carts to form a barricade, but the troops toss them aside. They are two hundred and twenty against five thousand.

"We'll dig your graves!"

"Down with the Yankee cowards!"

"Hurrah for Jeff Davis!"

One by one the soldiers drop. Luther Ladd, Sumner H. Needham, Charles A. Taylor, and Addison O. Whitney are killed—the first to give their lives that the nation may live. The ranks close and the troops move on. The mob divides before the advancing columns as the air divides before an arrow shot from the bow. Besides the four killed, thirty-six are wounded. Of the ruffians, no one will ever know how many went down. The regiment reaches the cars and the train moves on to Washington.

While the cars are carrying the Massachusetts troops to the Capitol of the nation, the people throughout the country are holding mass-meetings, and passing resolutions to sustain the Government. In every village drums begin to beat. From flag-staff and steeple wave the Stars and Stripes. Presidents of banks in Boston hasten to Governor Andrew, offering loans. In New York a great meeting is held in Madison Square. Some of the newspapers of that city have favored the secessionists, but now, under the pressure of the demands of the people, they fling out the Stars and Stripes and give their allegiance to Abraham Lincoln. The feeling becomes intense when they learn what is going on in Baltimore.

By the order of the mayor of that city, the bridges on the railroad to Philadelphia and Harrisburg were burned, so that no more troops could reach Washington. The secessionists rejoiced in the anticipation that in a few days the Confederate flag would be waving over the Capitol, and that Jefferson Davis would be occupying the White House.

"I will prophesy," said L. P. Walker, Confederate Secretary of War at Montgomery, "that the flag of the Confederacy will float over the dome of

THE MASSACHUSETTS SIXTH ATTACKED WHEN MARCHING THROUGH BALTIMORE.

the Capitol in Washington before the first of May. Let them try Southern chivalry, and it may float eventually over Faneuil Hall in Boston."

Great events were taking place in Richmond. The State Convention was in session. A majority of its members, when elected, were opposed to secession, as were a majority of the people of the State. Nor is there much doubt that the majority of the people throughout the South, with the exception of South Carolina, were at heart opposed to seceding from the Union. But the slave-holders were aggressive, determined to trample down all opposition. The men who had brought about the secession of the cotton-growing States knew that it was necessary for them to secure Virginia. The leaders of the movement in that State, before the firing on Sumter, called on Governor Letcher, who at heart was a secessionist, but who had sworn to support the Constitution of the United States. He had a peculiar feeling of honor, and regard for his oath of office. Among those who called upon him were John Seddon, of Richmond, and Mr. Lacey, who owned a large estate and many slaves on the Rappahannock. They presented a plan for seizing Fortress Monroe and the navy yard at Norfolk, which would give the Confederacy command of Chesapeake Bay, the war-ships at Norfolk, the immense amount of supplies in the ship-yards, and nearly three thousand heavy guns. They included in the plan the seizure of the arsenal at Harper's Ferry, where there were fifteen thousand muskets and the machinery for the manufacture of arms. Mr. Lacey offered his check for ten thousand dollars to carry out the enterprise. Governor Letcher informed them that he was in favor of the secession of the State, but until the Convention voted to secede, he would not permit the carrying out of their proposed plan. "Wait till the Convention secedes, and I will be with you; but if you attempt it before action by the Convention, I will hang you." And yet he laid plans to act with great promptness the moment the State seceded.

In order to influence the Convention, the conspirators made a great demonstration in Richmond — holding a mass-meeting, employing brassbands, making speeches, inciting the passions of the people, ridiculing Abraham Lincoln, dwelling upon the aggressions of the North, glorifying the rights of Virginia. They organized a grand procession, and made a display of fireworks in the evening. The ladies of Richmond, who ardently favored secession, did what they could to help it on by standing on the balconies of their homes waving flags and wearing rosettes of red, white, and blue. The demonstration had its intended effect. In secret session the vote was passed April 17th, with the condition that the question should be submitted to the people for ratification. The secessionists knew that before the day for taking the vote arrived, regiments from the other Southern States would be tramping through the State, and that voting would be a farce. When the day of election came, the voters of Winchester found a regiment of Louisiana troops guarding the polls. When the vote of the Convention was announced, the people of Richmond were wild with excitement. Cannon thundered, ladies waved their handkerchiefs from window, door-way, and balcony, and a drunken rabble surged the streets, hurrahing for Jefferson Davis and the Confederacy. "Virginia walks out of the Union like a queen," said the *Richmond Examiner*.

In Montgomery, Jefferson Davis and the members of the Confederate congress are packing their trunks for removal to Richmond. They will make that city the capital of the Confederacy till they can take Washington. That it would soon be theirs they do not doubt. This is what the *Richmond Examiner* said : " From the mountain-tops and valleys to the shores of the sea there is one wild shout of fierce resolve to capture Washington City at all and every human hazard. That filthy cage of unclean birds must and will assuredly be purified by fire. . . . It is not to be endured that this flight of abolition harpies shall come down from the black North for their roosts in the heart of the South, to defile and brutalize the land. . . . Our people can take it—they will take it—and Scott, the arch-traitor, and Lincoln, the beast, combined cannot prevent it. The just indignation of an outraged and injured people will teach the Illinois ape to retrace his journey across the borders of the free-negro States still more rapidly than he came, and Scott, the traitor, will be given the opportunity at the same time to try the difference between Scott's tactics and the Shanghae drill for quick movements.

" Great cleansing and purification are needed and will be given to that festering sink of iniquity—that wallow of Lincoln and Scott—the desecrated city of Washington, and many, indeed, will be the carcasses of dogs and caitiffs that will blacken the air upon the gallows before the work is accomplished. So let it be."

On the very hour that the Virginia Convention was voting in secret session to secede, Jefferson Davis virtually was declaring war against the United States by issuing his proclamation, offering "letters of marque and reprisal" to armed ships to capture the unarmed ships belonging to Northern merchants. The South owned very few ships, while those of the North swarmed on every sea. He expected that privateers would soon be capturing the vessels of the North. Two days later, President Lincoln issued a proclamation, which announced the intention of the United States to blockade all the ports of the seceding States.

The succession and sweep of events was like the rush of a whirlwind. In the arsenal at Harper's Ferry were fifteen thousand muskets and the valuable machines for the manufacture of arms. There was no time to remove the muskets. "Three thousand troops are on their way to capture the arsenal," was the message which reached Lieutenant Jones, in command of the arsenal, on the evening of April 18th. The militia of Virginia intended to seize the muskets, make their way to Baltimore, arm the secessionists there, then march to Washington and hold the Capitol. It had all been planned in advance by Governor Letcher, and in anticipation of the secession of the State. Lieutenant Jones had expected such a movement. He received orders from Washington to destroy the building, and had piled wood around the stacks of arms and saturated the floors with oil. He had watchmen out on all the roads. One came with the information that the Virginians were close at hand. The soldiers, sixteen of them, ran with torches and shavings, and the flames were soon leaping from the windows and curling through the roof. Down the hill came the Virginians, while Lieutenant Jones and the soldiers crossed the river and made their way up the Maryland hills.

There were thousands of secessionists in Washington ready to rise and seize the city. On the day Abraham Lincoln was inaugurated, a majority of the inhabitants were secessionists at heart, or utterly indifferent to the great question of the hour. The Union men discovered their plot. General Scott had six companies of United States troops, two batteries, and a company of marines whom he could rely upon. The clerks in the departments were organized into military companies. None was accepted who would not swear to sustain the Government. Beneath the trees in front of the War Department they held up their hands and made oath to be truly loyal. Fearing that an attempt might be made to assassinate the President, three hundred citizens guarded the White House, cannon were planted to sweep Long Bridge and the bridge at Georgetown. The burning of the arsenal at Harper's Ferry upset the well-laid plan.

At Norfolk was the navy yard, with its great ship-houses and buildings filled with supplies for the navy; with more than two thousand cannon, a quarter of a million pounds of powder, and thousands of cart-loads of solid shot and shell, with vessels on the stocks and in the stream, among them the new frigate *Merrimac*, carrying forty guns—ten million dollars' worth of property. Captain McCauley was commander of the yard.

"Remove the *Merrimac* to Philadelphia at once," was the order that came from Washington. An engineer came to work the engines. It was

Saturday, April 12th ; the cannon were booming at Sumter. If Captain
McCauley was not himself a traitor, he was surrounded by traitors, who
persuaded him to disobey the orders. The fires had been kindled, but he
ordered them to be put out. He did not comprehend that he had reached a

supreme moment in life ; that then
and there he might write his name
large upon the scroll of fame—so
large that people would read it
with admiration through all coming time. In the stream, riding at
anchor, is the frigate *Cumberland*,
with twenty · four guns, with a
loyal crew on board. The military companies of Norfolk are drilling. He hears their drum - beat.
He knows that they are meditat-
ing the seizure of the navy yard.
How easy for him to say, "The
moment you attempt it I will
sweep the streets of Norfolk clean
with grape and canister, and level
it to the ground." Instead of

VORTRESS MONROE.

that, before Virginia secedes, he permits Governor Letcher to sink vessels
across the channel to prevent his taking away the *Merrimac*.

"I will not remove any of the vessels, nor will I fire a shot except in
defence," he says to the secessionists, and sets men to work cutting holes
in the bottom of the *Merrimac* and the other ships to sink them.

Captain Paulding, appointed to supersede McCauley, arrives with several hundred Massachusetts troops just in season to see the *Merrimac* settle beneath the waves.

"Save the navy yard if you can, but hold Fortress Monroe in any
event," are the orders of General Scott. He has not troops enough to
hold both. Confederate troops are hastening in. He sets the houses and
ships on fire—the *Pennsylvania*, *Delaware*, and *Columbus*, each carrying
seventy-four guns; the *Merrimac*, *Raritan*, and *Columbia*, frigates, and several smaller vessels. From ground to roof, from hull to top-mast, leap the
flames, illuminating all the surrounding country. The houses and ships
are destroyed, but the fire will not burn the cannon, the shot and shell, and
so at the outset the Confederates obtain enough cannon to arm all their
forts and batteries. So much lost to the nation, so much gained by them.

It was four o'clock in the afternoon, April 19th, when the New York Seventh Regiment marched down Broadway. Everywhere — from window, door-way, staff, steeple—waved the Stars and Stripes: flags of the costliest silk, flags of the homeliest bunting, flags of painted cotton cloth. Street, sidewalk, doors, windows, were crowded with people—a sea of human faces. Never before such cheers as swelled up from the lips of five hundred thousand people. From the armory to the ferry that bore them to the Jersey shore it was one prolonged hurrah. Men worth millions of

BURNING NORFOLK NAVY YARD.

dollars were in the ranks. No more the making of money; no more plans for mercantile transactions. Farewell to ease and comfort. Welcome the weary march, the bivouac, the battle. The nation shall live, perish everything else. Women become like men, strong of heart, and wave their farewells to those most dear without a tear upon their cheeks; strong men become like women, and weep through excess of joy and emotion.

Not only in New York, but in Philadelphia, Chicago, Cincinnati—in every city, town, hamlet of the North—the new tide of life rolls in.

Gen. Benjamin F. Butler, with the Massachusetts Eighth Regiment, reached the Susquehanna River at Havre de Grace. "The bridges are burned; you cannot reach Washington," was the word that came to him. The great ferry-boat, the steamer *Maryland*, was in the stream. "Seize it," was the order. In a very short time the regiment was on board, and the *Maryland* steaming down Chesapeake Bay for Annapolis.

The New York Seventh Regiment was steaming down Delaware Bay on the steamer *Boston*, and up the Chesapeake to the same point.

Great the consternation of the secessionists at Annapolis when the *Maryland* entered the harbor. The *Constitution*—"Old Ironsides," the ship that won so many victories in 1812 — was there without a crew. The secessionists were planning to take possession, but General Butler was too quick for them. The flag of the Confederacy never was to float above her deck.

The secessionists had torn up the railroad; but the men of the Eighth Massachusetts knew how to build railroads, and began to spike down the rails. They had taken the locomotive to pieces. "I helped make this locomotive; there is my mark," said a soldier, who laid aside his musket and went to work with a wrench and hammer to put it in order. "Are there any soldiers here who can run the engine?" asked the colonel. Nineteen stepped from the ranks in response. The slave-holders had left out of their calculations the greatest factor of all—labor. How little did they comprehend, when they began the war, that the laborers—the men who worked for their daily bread, the men who wore blue blouses and handled wrenches and hammers, who filed iron, who pushed the plane, who followed the plough—were the men who would reconstruct what slavery destroyed. There they were, at the outset, reconstructing the locomotive, the railroad, and in the end they would reconstruct the nation. Together the Massachusetts Eighth and the New York Seventh relaid the rails and made their way to Washington.

In Baltimore the secessionists had triumphed for a moment, but up in western Maryland, at Frederick and Hagerstown, the Union men were running up the Stars and Stripes. One evening, greatly to the astonishment of the secessionists, General Butler, at the head of his troops, marched into the city, planted the Stars and Stripes, arrested the police-commissioners who were plotting treason, seized all the muskets and pistols they had collected, and set men to work repairing the bridges which had been burned. The Union men rejoiced; the secessionists gnashed their teeth. The slave-holders were confident that the State would secede. James R. Randall wrote the song "My Maryland," which was set to an old German

THE NEW YORK SEVENTH REGIMENT MARCHING DOWN BROADWAY.

melody by Miss Carey, of Baltimore. She and her sister, Miss Hetty, were ardent secessionists. Their house was regarded by the Union men as the headquarters of secession. The ladies of Baltimore who sympathized with the South met there to make uniforms for Confederate soldiers. The song was first sung by Miss Carey in June, 1861. It was greatly applauded, and became very popular. It was sung everywhere throughout the South:

MARYLAND! MY MARYLAND!

"The despot's heel is on thy shore, "I hear the distant thunder hum,
 His torch is at thy temple door,   The old-time bugle, fife, and drum;
 Avenge the patriotic gore   She is not dead, nor deaf, nor dumb,
 That flecks the streets of Baltimore, Huzza! she spurns the Northern scum,
 And be the battle queen of yore, She breathes, she burns, she'll come—she'll come!
  Maryland! my Maryland!   Maryland! my Maryland!"

Vain the song! Ineffectual all the machinations of conspirators at Richmond and in Baltimore to bring about the secession of the State!

CHAPTER IV.

FIRST WEEKS OF THE WAR.

THE first week in June, 1861, I became a correspondent in the army. My first observations were at Baltimore. In Boston, New York, Philadelphia, and in all Northern cities patriotism was at flood-tide. Everywhere flags were waving; the drum-beat was heard in every village; troops were drilling, companies and regiments organizing. Ladies wore Union rosettes of red, white, and blue. The music of the hour was "Yankee Doodle" and "Hail Columbia." Baltimore presented a striking contrast to the other cities. It was dull and gloomy; only here and there were the Stars and Stripes to be seen. Business was at a standstill. It was a Southern city, but the secessionists, who in April had all but succeeded in taking the State out of the Union, finding that they had been foiled by the vigilance of the Government, were leaving Baltimore secretly, and making their way to Richmond to join the Confederate army. Ladies who sympathized with the South looked upon the Union soldiers as low, mean, vile, hateful creatures. They forgot their high breeding and ceased to be ladies when they daintily gathered up their skirts and spat at them upon the street. A regiment of Pennsylvania troops was drilling near Fort McHenry. A few days before they had been driving their teams afield or working in coal-mines, but now they were soldiers of the Republic. They knew very little of military affairs. They came, in their marching, upon a pool of water, and the colonel, not knowing the proper word of command to avoid it, shouted, "Gee round that hole!" They understood it. Out of such material the mighty armies of the Republic were organized.

Washington, on the other hand, was in a hubbub. Troops were pouring in, raw, undisciplined, yet of material such as the world had never seen—artisans, artists, farmers, mechanics, merchants, printers, painters, poets, bankers, men of letters, ministers of the Gospel; men from every calling and occupation were in the ranks, responding to the call of the President, and obeying the promptings of their own patriotic hearts. There was a rumble of baggage-wagons in the streets and a constant tramping of men. Soldiers were quartered in the Capitol, spreading their blankets in the corridors. General Scott, who had served his country faithfully in the war with England in 1812, and in Mexico, was popularly regarded as the Hercules of the time. He was a native of Virginia, but was true to the old flag. The newspapers in the South were calling him a traitor to Virginia. He was seventy-five years of age, and his powers were failing. He could walk only with difficulty, but day and night he gave his waning energies to his country in this its trying hour.

GENERAL SCOTT.

Could I have gone to Richmond, I should have seen equal activity in that city — regiments of men in gray parading the streets or hurrying northward to Manassas or Harper's Ferry. Throughout the South the blood of the secessionists, those who believed that the States were superior to the Nation, was at fever-heat. Those who still loved the old flag were

5

awed into silence. Mr. Semmes, who later in the war commanded the
Confederate ship *Alabama*, gives this picture of Mobile the week after
the firing on Sumter: "I found Mobile, like the rest of the Confederacy,
in a great state of excitement. It was boiling over with enthusiasm; the
young merchants had dropped their day-books and ledgers, and were forming and drilling companies by night and day, while the older ones were
discussing the question of the Confederate Treasury, to see how it could
be supported. The Battle House was thronged, 'and all went merry as
a marriage bell.'"

The cotton States had seceded under the hallucination that cotton was
"king." Jefferson Davis had pictured the glory of the future South, and
its power, based on slavery. The merchants of New Orleans had brought
themselves to believe that its commercial greatness would be far superior
to that of New York; but before the month of April had passed a great
change came over the city. This is the picture by Mr. Semmes: "I arrived in New Orleans on Monday, the 22d of April. A great change was
apparent. The levee was no longer a great mart of commerce, piled with
cotton-bales and with supplies going back to the planter, and densely packed
with steamers, and thronged with a busy multitude. The long lines of
shipping had been greatly thinned, and a general air of desolation hung
over the river front. It seemed as though a pestilence brooded over the
doomed city, and that its inhabitants had fled before the fell destroyer.
But this first simoom of the desert which had swept over the city, as a
foretaste of what was to come, had not discouraged its patriotic inhabitants.
The activity of commerce had ceased, but another activity had taken its
place. War now occupied the thoughts of the multitude, and the sound
of the drum and the tramp of armed men were heard in the streets. The
balconies were crowded with lovely women in gay attire to witness the
military processions, and the Confederate flag in miniature was pinned
on every bosom."

Mr. Jones, of Richmond, who kept a record of events during the war,
gives this picture of Richmond: "The ladies are postponing all engagements until their lovers have fought the Yankees. Their influence is great.
Day after day they go in crowds to the Fair-ground, where the First
South Carolina volunteers are encamped, showering upon them their smiles
and all the delicacies the city affords. They wine and cake them—and
they deserve it. They have just taken Fort Sumter, and have won historic
distinction. They are worth from one hundred thousand to half a million
dollars each, these rich young men, and are dressed in gray homespun."

On the 6th of May Arkansas seceded from the Union, and was followed

RICHMOND, FROM A SKETCH MADE IN 1861.

by North Carolina on the 21st and Tennessee on the 8th of June. In all the mountain region of West Virginia, North Carolina, and Tennessee there were but few slaves. The people of that section were hard-working men and women, who loved the old flag, and who could not see that they would be any better off in the Confederacy under Jefferson Davis than in the Union under Abraham Lincoln. In Kentucky there were eleven hundred and sixty thousand people, and of these two hundred and fifty thousand were slaves. There were strong ties to bind that State to the Union. Through all the years the people had lived in peace with their neighbors across the Ohio River, which with its many windings formed their northern boundary for nearly eight hundred miles. Young men from Ohio, Indiana, and Illinois had found their true-hearted wives south of the river. Many of the citizens of those States had been born in Kentucky, but had settled for life where there were no slaves to degrade their labor. There were frequent visits to the old homes to see brothers and cousins.

More than this, the little log-cabin in which Abraham Lincoln was born was still standing, and the people of the State — those who did not have any slaves — remembering how he struggled with poverty and hardships, how he had triumphed over adversity, how he had chopped wood, split rails, pulled at the oar on a Mississippi flat-boat, were not sorry that he was President. He had been constitutionally elected. They believed in fair play. Why should he not be President? Why should Kentucky join the Confederacy? Why should the hard-working farmers who held with their own hands the plough join a government under which labor was regarded as degrading?

The people of Kentucky had not forgotten the teachings of their great statesman, Henry Clay; they had just erected a beautiful monument of marble to commemorate his virtues and greatness. His voice had ever been for the Union. Men advanced in years who had listened to his eloquent words rehearsed them to their sons. Old soldiers who had fought for their country under General Harrison and General Scott in Canada, and who had stood with Jackson behind the breastwork of cotton-bales and hogsheads of sugar at New Orleans, who were receiving their pensions from Government, could not bear to think that the old flag had been insulted. They took pride in the thought that it had been defended at Sumter by a son of Kentucky, Major Anderson. The Rev. Doctor Breckinridge, father of Senator Breckinridge, who had been Vice-president under Buchanan, loved the Union. He wielded great influence among the Presbyterians of the State. Kentucky did not raise cotton. Very few of those who owned slaves had any thought of building up an em-

5*

pire based on slavery. On the contrary, many of them were willing to
see slavery abolished, if it could be done peacefully. Such were some of
the ties which bound the State to the Union.

The Governor of Kentucky, Mr. McGoffin, was a "States-rights" man,
and when President Lincoln called upon him for troops to put down the
rebellion, he replied that Kentucky would take no part in the war, little
comprehending that in a contest between two forms of society, the one
based on slave labor and the other on free labor, there could be no neutral
ground; that before many weeks the people of the State would range
themselves on one side or the other.

The planters of Missouri, who cultivated tobacco and hemp, and owned
slaves, had done what they could to make Kansas a slave State. Like
the planters of Virginia, they raised slaves for the Southern market.
Many of them were originally from Virginia, others from Kentucky.
But emigrants from Germany had been pouring into the State, especially
into St. Louis. They hated slavery; they crossed the ocean to become
American citizens; they could not understand the provincial pride of the
secessionists which made a State of more consequence than the Nation.
They were all for the Union, as were a majority of the American-born
citizens of Missouri. Claiborne F. Jackson became governor January 1,
1861, and did what he could to bring about the withdrawal of the State
from the Union. A convention was called, but not a single secession
delegate was elected. It was a bitter disappointment to the South. It
upset all the plans which had been laid by Jackson for arming the State
before turning it over to the Confederacy.

There were a few far-seeing men in St. Louis who loved the Union,
and who determined to thwart the secessionists. One of these level-headed
men was Francis P. Blair. In December he called the leading Union men
together for consultation. "The State authorities," he said, "are working
to bring about secession. There are sixty thousand muskets in the United
States arsenal which they intend to seize. We must form a military organization to prevent it." Seventy-three names were enrolled, and Blair
was chosen captain. It was the first military organization formed in the
country to maintain the Union. Other companies were soon organized.
They called themselves Home Guards.

The hot-blooded young Southerners began to organize themselves as
minute-men, under the lead of Basil W. Duke. Their special object was
to gain possession of the arms. The commander of the arsenal, who was
from North Carolina, had an understanding with Governor Jackson in
regard to turning it over to the State; but this plan was upset by the

arrival of another officer sent by General Scott to command the United
States troops, to take charge of the property of the United States at
St. Louis, Nathaniel P. Lyon, of Connecticut, bold, fearless, resolute. He
erected barricades around the building.

Under the laws the Governor had the right to order out the militia
for drill. He sent a messenger to Jefferson Davis for cannon and muskets. The secession militia under General Frost were in camp just out
of St. Louis. When Fort Sumter was fired upon, and President Lincoln

F. P. BLAIR.

called upon the governors for troops, Governor Jackson replied that Missouri would furnish no troops to coerce a sister State, whereupon Blair
telegraphed that Missouri would furnish her share, and the Home Guards
were mustered into the service of the United States.

Strange-looking boxes were landed on the levee in the darkness of
the night, May 8th, from a steamer just arrived from Memphis. A sharp-
eyed man was lounging along the levee, and as the boxes were tumbled
out he saw that they were heavy. "Marble," was the label. He saw

them loaded upon drays. He had the curiosity to follow them till they reached Camp Jackson.

It was a nice carriage which drove out to Camp Jackson on the morning of May 9th. It contained a gentleman and lady. The sentinels admitted it, and it was driven over the field leisurely where the soldiers were drilling. The lady admired their marching. She saw soldiers opening the boxes of marble. They had changed to cannon, shot, and shell. The lady drove to her lodgings, took off her bonnet and gown, and put on her hat and uniform—no longer a woman, but Captain Lyon of the United States army.

Two o'clock P. M. The Home Guards are marching through the streets. They are six regiments, with six pieces of artillery. Half the regiments march through one street, half through another, very rapidly, as if seeing how fast they can keep step to the drum-beat. They reach the open field and turn towards Camp Jackson. The cannon unlimber and the gunners stand by their pieces.

General Frost beholds it in amazement.

"Your command is regarded as hostile to the United States. I demand your surrender, with no other conditions than that all persons shall be humanely and kindly treated," are the words of Captain Lyon.

General Frost sees that he is in a trap, with no chance to escape, and therefore surrenders. Thus, again, all the plans of the slave-holders and secessionists are overturned in Missouri.

Ruffians in the street shook their fists at the Home Guards, threw paving-stones, drew their pistols and fired. The Guards returned the fire, and for a few moments there was a mêlée, in which several soldiers and citizens were killed and others wounded; but the Stars and Stripes were not to go down in St. Louis, and that great commercial centre was thus saved to the Union.

When you look at the map of Virginia you will notice that the Appalachian Mountains lie in successive ranges, like the waves of the sea. East of the mountains the country is a succession of plateaus and plains all the way to Chesapeake Bay. It was in this section that the Cavaliers of England, when that State was settled, laid out their broad plantations, built their spacious mansions, and cultivated their fields of tobacco. The people who lived in the mountains were hunters, lumbermen, and coal-miners. They had small farms. They traded with the inhabitants of Wheeling more than with the merchants at Richmond. What they had to sell found a better and more convenient market westward than eastward.

NIGHT MARCH INTO VIRGINIA. FROM A SKETCH MADE AT THE TIME.

In the section of the State east of the mountains there were nearly half a million slaves; in the country between the Blue Ridge and the Ohio River less than twenty thousand.

The people of West Virginia had no sympathy with secession. In June, delegates from forty counties met at Wheeling and repudiated what had been done at Richmond. They formed a State government, and elected F. H. Pierpont governor. So the State which had gloried in the name of the Dominion, before a month had passed after voting to secede lost one-half of her domain.

Confederate troops were gathering at Harper's Ferry and at Manassas Junction. There were several companies at Alexandria. Arlington House, the home of Robert E. Lee, who had been greatly trusted by General Scott, but who had resigned his commission to become a major-general under Jefferson Davis, was within cannon-shot of the White House. "Washington will be ours before many days," was the boast of the newspapers at Richmond. General Scott saw that Arlington and Alexandria must be occupied, or some morning cannon-shot would be crashing through the White House.

The moon was shining, the air calm and still, at two o'clock on the morning of May 24th, when the soldiers rolled up their blankets, fell silently into line, and moved towards the bridges crossing the Potomac. They were commanded by General McDowell. Three regiments marched through Georgetown, four across Long Bridge, while the regiment of Zouaves under Colonel Ellsworth went on board a steamer, which moved down the river to Alexandria, where the gunboat *Pawnee* was lying. The Zouaves landed, swept through the streets, the Confederates fleeing to Manassas. A Confederate flag was flying over a hotel kept by a Mr. Jackson. Colonel Ellsworth climbed the roof and pulled it down. He was descending the narrow stairs when he was shot dead by the land-lord, who in turn was shot by one of the Zouaves. The Northern people said that Jackson was an assassin, while the Southern people regarded him as a martyr to liberty.

Through the South there was great indignation because the troops of the Union had invaded the State of Virginia. "The minions of Abraham Lincoln must be driven from the sacred soil of the State," said the Richmond papers. Troops from other Southern States were tramping through the State controlling the voting on the day of election, but the newspapers published no protest.

"Brave Virginians," said the *Charleston Courier*, "and all true sons of the South, will cling to their true and honored flag with more zeal and devotion, and, if compelled to fall beneath it, will sell their lives dearly, striking especially at the leaders and officers of the insolent and invading hirelings and ruffians who seek to disgrace the chosen standard of a redeemed people."

"The corner-stone of the Confederacy is African slavery," said Alexander II. Stevens, Vice-president of the Confederacy. "Our negroes will do the shovelling while our brave cavaliers will do the fighting," said one of the Richmond newspapers. But before a battle had been fought the corner-stone began to crumble.

The slave-holders around Norfolk and Hampton, in Eastern Virginia, sent their slaves with shovels to throw up fortifications. Some of the

BENJAMIN F. BUTLER.

slaves, watching their opportunity when night came, crept through the woods, swam rivers, and made their way to Fortress Monroe. General Benjamin F. Butler was there with Massachusetts and New York troops. The slaves knew instinctively that the Union soldiers were their friends, that the slave-holders had begun the war to perpetuate slavery. The colored people had never studied logic, did not know the meaning of the word, did not know a letter of the alphabet, but they comprehended the meaning of this gathering of armies—that it was a war between slavery and freedom.

One slave named Luke made his way to Fortress Monroe, and became a servant to Captain Tyler.

Luke's owner, Colonel Mallory, came to get him. "If you will take the oath of allegiance to the United States I will give him up," said General Butler. The negroes in the camp heard of it, and were much excited. Luke, with tears upon his cheeks, came to Captain Tyler. "I don't think that you will be sent back, for General Butler has not any authority to send you." A moment ago the negroes were weeping and moaning, but now they were wild with joy. The news spread. General Butler heard of it, and ordered Captain Tyler to appear before him.

"I understand, sir," said the general, "that you have been telling the negroes that they can't be sent back to their masters. Now, sir. I want to know by what authority you have told them so?"

"By the authority of common-sense."

"What do you mean by that, sir?"

"The case is this: Luke's former master sent him to work on the Confederate fortifications: that act made Luke contraband of war, and liable to be confiscated to the United States in case he should ever be found within our lines, either by his own act or by the advance of our troops. While thus employed he escaped to our lines; that extinguished his master's right. Luke instantly acquired what he never had had before—freedom. His master cannot demand him, for he held him only as property, and employed that property in acts of war against the United States. The United States cannot hold him as a chattel, because, as a government, we do not recognize slavery as a national institution. Luke, as property, is contraband of war, and confiscated to the United States. He is free; nor can he ever again legally be a slave."

"Slaves are contraband of war," was the proclamation made by General Butler, and sent out from Fortress Monroe.

Never had the men who laid their plans to build the Confederacy and perpetuate slavery dreamed that the institution, before a battle had been fought, would begin to settle from its foundations. They began to see that military law was far different from civil law. Colonel Mallory and all the other planters went sadly back to their homes. Thousands of dollars' worth of property had walked away, nor was there any law by which they could recover it.

A few days before Virginia seceded, Lieutenant-colonel John Bankhead Magruder, of the United States Artillery, called upon President Lincoln and said, "Mr. President, every one else may desert you, but I never will." Two days later he was in Richmond, offering his services to Jefferson Davis. He was sent to Yorktown to command the Confederate troops gathering at that point. He impressed slaves to work on the fortifications. One of them escaped to Fortress Monroe.

"Massa Magruder is building forts," said the slave, George Scott. Major Theodore Winthrop, private secretary and aide to General Butler, went with him up the road towards Big Bethel, creeping through the woods, getting so near that Major Winthrop obtained a good view of the fortifications. General Butler resolved to make an attack, and Major Winthrop drew a plan for the movement and made this note: "GEORGE SCOTT IS TO HAVE A SHOOTING-IRON."

Military law, the week before, had assumed superiority to statute law by making slaves contraband of war, and now this clear-headed young man, who, before the war began, was writing delightful literary articles, saw what none of the statesmen had discovered, that the same law which made slaves contraband of war for working on rebel fortifications would in like manner give them the right to bear arms. The people of the North, however, were reluctant to accept that conclusion. Not till many thousands of brave men had laid down their lives would they consent to the enrolling of the freed men as soldiers of the Republic.

General Pierce commanded the expedition to Bethel, composed of two columns, one marching from Hampton, under Colonel Duryea, the other from Newport News, under Colonel Bendix. It was a night march, and "Boston" was the watchword. The soldiers were to wear a piece of white cotton cloth on the left arm. Unfortunately, the officer who was to attend to that service forgot to inform Colonel Bendix, and his men fired into the other column, killing two and wounding ten. General Pierce captured thirty prisoners at Little Bethel, but the alarm was given, and Magruder had ample time to make preparations.

It was ten in the morning when the Union troops reached Big Bethel. The men had marched all night, had had no breakfast, and were weary; the sun was hot; the Confederates were in a strong position behind breastworks mounting several guns. Unwisely the attack was ordered. Lieutenant Greble, commanding the two pieces of artillery, the only cannon, opened fire. The Zouaves advanced through the woods on the right of the road, the other regiments through a cornfield and orchard. The Union troops were six regiments; the Confederate not quite so many, but were behind breastworks, with cannon, which made them much the strongest. Lieutenant Greble aimed his cannon with accuracy, and silenced several of the enemy's guns, but fell mortally wounded. The battle went on till the ammunition of the Union troops was spent and they retreated, having lost

GENERAL BUTLER DECLARING THE NEGRO "CONTRABAND OF WAR."

forty men killed and wounded. Among the killed were Lieutenant Greble and Major Winthrop, beloved and lamented. The Richmond newspapers magnified the affair into a great victory.

From Staunton, the first week in June, General Garnett, with several Confederate regiments and six cannon, marched north-west over the mountains to Beverly, in West Virginia, to hold that region. He reached Beverly, where there are two turnpikes, one running nearly north, through a pass in Laurel Mountain, the other north-west, through a pass in Rich Mountain. He sent Colonel Pegram up the turnpike which runs over Rich Mountain with six cannon. Pegram crossed the summit, went almost down to Roaring Creek, threw up breastworks, felled trees, planted his cannon, and pitched his tents. General Garnett went up the other turnpike to Laurel Mountain. "These are the two gate-ways to the north-western country," he said.

MAP OF BETHEL.

Troops from Ohio had crossed the Ohio River at Wheeling to protect the Baltimore and Ohio Railroad. They were commanded by General McClellan, who was a lieutenant in the war with Mexico. When war broke out between France and England and Russia, he was sent by Jefferson Davis, then Secretary of War, to the Crimea to make observations. He had been appointed major-general by the Governor of Ohio, and was protecting the railroad east of Wheeling.

General McClellan detached General Morris with five regiments to make a feint of attacking the Confederates on Laurel Mountain, and moved with the rest of his force from the town of Buckhannon to Roaring Creek against Pegram, who was in a strong position. One of the Union brigades was commanded by General W. S. Rosecrans, who proposed to make a flank movement, climb the mountain, gain the rear of the rebels, while McClellan made a show of attacking in front. The plan was satisfactory, and was accepted.

At daylight on the morning of June 11th General Rosecrans starts. He has four regiments—nineteen hundred men. Storm-clouds are rolling along the mountain sides, the rain is pouring, the bushes are dripping, the clothes of the soldiers are soaked with rain; but all through the forenoon

6

they pick their way up the steep ascent south of the turnpike.   A farmer guides them.   Walking by his side is Colonel Lander, who, before the war began, piloted a body of troops through the passes of the Rocky Mountains to Oregon.   The farmer's knees shake from fear; he can go no farther, and Colonel Lander pushes on, picking out a route for the soldiers.

They gain the top of the ridge, rest a few moments, and then turn north, marching along the crest of the mountain towards the turnpike.

GENERAL McCLELLAN.

Colonel Pegram, fearing a movement upon his rear, has sent three hundred men and two cannon back to the house of Mr. Hart.   The Confederate soldiers are behind breastworks.

It is three o'clock before General Rosecrans reaches Mr. Hart's farm. The soldiers are wet and weary, but advance to the attack.   The Confederate cannon open fire. The Union troops pour in their volleys, and the Confederates throw down their guns and flee, panic-stricken, into the woods, leaving their cannon and all their supplies.

Great was the commotion in Colonel Pegram's camp at Roaring Creek. The soldiers left everything and rushed up the mountain-side, stealing along the summit northward, hoping to make their way to Laurel Mountain. But they never reached General Garnett, who, hearing of the disaster, and finding his retreat cut off by General McClellan, who crossed Rich Mountain and took possession of the turnpike at Beverly, fled north along a mountain road. The road was narrow and rough. His teamsters had hard work to get along. He had thirty-five hundred soldiers, but they lost all heart, and began to drop out of the ranks.

General Morris was following, and overtook Garnett at Carrick's Ford. There was a booming of cannon and rattling of musketry for a few moments, but the disheartened Confederates soon fled to the next ford, where they rallied once more, and where General Garnett was killed. With his fall all fled in terror, throwing away their guns.

General Rosecrans planned and executed the movement by which the two gate-ways had been opened, which annihilated the Confederates and secured Western Virginia to the Union. General McClellan, however, was commander-in-chief, and received the honor. He sent a despatch which electrified the country: "Garnett and forces routed, his army demolished,

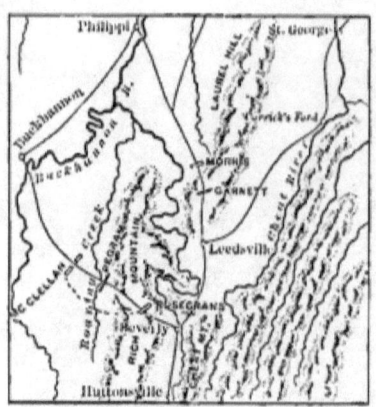

MAP OF RICH MOUNTAIN.

Garnett killed. We have annihilated the enemy in Western Virginia, have lost thirteen killed and not more than forty wounded. We have, in all, killed at least two hundred of the enemy, and their prisoners will amount to at least one thousand. Have taken seven guns in all. The troops defeated are the crack regiments of Eastern Virginia, aided by Georgians, Tennesseeans, Carolinians. Our success is complete, and secession is killed in this country."

Like the bulletins which Napoleon was accustomed to issue, and which electrified the people of France, so this despatch awakened the enthusiasm of the people, who looked upon McClellan as a great commander. The routing of Garnett and Pegram secured West Virginia permanently to the Union, and made McClellan commander-in-chief of the armies of the United States.

Passing once more to the West, we see Governor Jackson of Missouri doing what he can to help on the Confederate cause. Captain Lyon has been appointed general by President Lincoln. Jackson sends a message proposing that the State remain neutral. A conference is held in the Planter's House, St. Louis.

"Rather," said Lyon, "than concede to the State of Missouri the right to demand that Government shall not enlist troops within her limits, or bring troops into the State whenever it please, or move its troops at its own will, I would see every man, woman, and child in the State dead and buried. This means war."

Governor Jackson hastened to Jefferson City, issued a proclamation calling the people to arms, burned the bridges on the railroad leading to St. Louis and across the Osage River, and fled southward. General

GENERAL LYON.

Lyon was quick to act. He started up the Missouri River on steamboats, came upon a party of Jackson's troops at Booneville, quickly routing them. It was a blow which secured Missouri to the Union. Thousands who had hesitated gave their allegiance to the Government, and enlisted to put down the rebellion.

The newspapers of the South at this period of the war ridiculed the Northern troops. Said the *Mobile Advertiser*:

"The Northern soldiers prefer enlisting to starvation; scurvy fellows from the back slums of cities. But these are not soldiers, least of all to meet the hot-blooded, thorough-bred, impetuous men of the South; trencher soldiers, who enlisted to war upon rations, not upon men. They are such as marched through Baltimore, squalid, wretched, ragged, half-naked, as the newspapers of that city report them; fellows who do not know the breech of a musket from its muzzle; white slaves, peddling

wretches, small-change knaves, and vagrants, the offscouring of the popu-
lous cities. These are the levied forces which Lincoln arrays as candidates for the honor of being slaughtered by gentlemen such as Mobile
sends to battle. Let them come South, and we will put our negroes to
the dirty work of killing them. But they will not come South; not a
wretch of them will live on this side of the border longer than it will
take us to reach the ground to drive them off."

There was also foolish boasting in the newspapers of the North; the
people were confident that the war would not last more than a month
or two. The Secretary of State, William H. Seward, expressed the opinion that it would be over in three months. It was believed that the
Union men in the Southern States would rise against the secessionists.
On the other hand, the Confederates believed that those in the North
opposed to the war would rise against the Government. The farthest-
sighted, whether living North or South, had little conception of what
the conflict was to be, how vast its proportions, how tremendous in
results.

CHAPTER V.

THE FIRST GREAT BATTLE.

THE mustering of armies began. Mountains, rivers, railroads — the physical geography of a country — were to determine military campaigns. The great Appalachian chain of mountains covers a wide section of country; it was plain that the great movements of armies must be either east or west of this region. In the east two Union armies were gathering: one at Chambersburg, in Pennsylvania, the other at Alexandria, in Virginia, commanded respectively by Generals Patterson and McDowell. General McDowell issued an order to the troops to respect private property. Officers were to keep a strict account of all land taken for camps, to estimate all damage in the destruction of fences or buildings, or trees cut down, and to obtain the names of the owners that they might be reimbursed. Very few men at the beginning had any comprehension of what destruction would come to the South.

Two Confederate armies were gathering in Virginia: one at Manassas, under General Beauregard, the other at Harper's Ferry, under General Joseph E. Johnston. On June 6th Beauregard issued this address to the people of Loudon, Fairfax, and Prince William counties:

"A reckless and unprincipled tyrant has invaded your soil. Abraham Lincoln, regardless of all moral, legal, and constitutional restraints, has thrown his abolition hosts among you, who are murdering and imprisoning your citizens, confiscating and destroying your property, and committing other acts of violence and outrage too shocking and revolting to humanity to be enumerated.

"All rules of civilized warfare are abandoned, and they proclaim by their acts, if not on their banners, that their war-cry is 'Beauty and Booty.' All that is dear to man — your honor, and that of your wives and daughters, your fortunes and your lives, are involved in this momentous conflict."

It is not to be supposed that General Beauregard sincerely believed what he had written. He had been in the service of the United States more than twenty years. When South Carolina seceded he was in command of the military school at West Point, mingling with the refined, intelligent people of New York. He knew that they were not what he represented them to be, and that the address was a slander. It was the spirit of slavery and the madness of the hour that prompted him.

General Johnston was stationed at Harper's Ferry, because it was supposed to be an important position. Jefferson Davis said that it was a natural fortress, and that it commanded the Shenandoah Valley. The military men at Washington made the same mistake. It commanded nothing.

The Union army gathering at Chambersburg, Pennsylvania, was designed to confront that under Johnston. General Patterson had served in Mexico. He was sixty-nine years old, indecisive, easily influenced. He advanced to Williamsport, on the Potomac, above Harper's Ferry, whereupon Johnston spiked the heavy cannon which he had brought up from Norfolk Navy-yard and placed in position, and retreated to Winchester, more than twenty miles. General Patterson could not comprehend it, neither could his brigade commander, General Cadwallader, nor his adjutant-general, Fitz-John Porter.

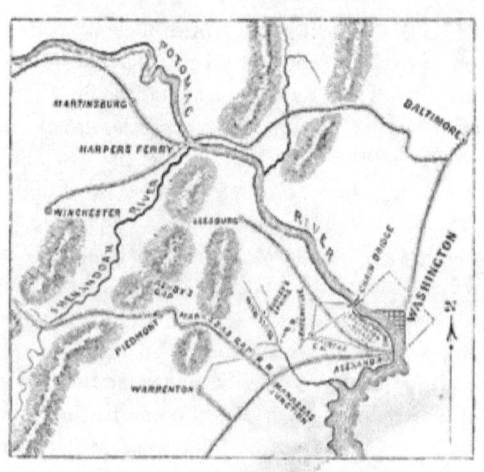

MAP OF BULL RUN

"I believe it is designed for a decoy; there may be a deep-laid plot to deceive us," wrote Patterson. "The whole affair is a riddle," said Cadwallader. But it was not a decoy; it was plain common-sense on the part of Johnston, who saw that the position had no particular military value; that Patterson could march past him, gain his rear, and cut off his retreat. In studying the war, we are to consider that the generals in command at the beginning knew very little about war except what they learned from books, and that some of them never had commanded even a company. A large number were made generals because they had been prominent in political affairs.

General Scott, commander-in-chief of the Union armies, planned a campaign. The people demanded that the armies should move. "On to Richmond!" was the cry. The rebellion must be crushed. At Alexandria and Arlington were between thirty and forty thousand troops, under General McDowell, confronted by the Confederate army under Beauregard, supposed to number twenty-five thousand. McDowell was to advance against Beauregard, and Patterson, at the same moment, was to move upon Johnston at Winchester. General Scott was apprehensive that Johnston would make a quick movement, join Beauregard, and outnumber McDowell, and he very emphatically informed Patterson that he must not permit any such movement. He assured McDowell that if Johnston attempted

GENERAL McDOWELL.

it he would have Patterson at his heels. Patterson had twenty-two thousand men, Johnston about twelve thousand.

From the beginning the Confederates artfully and successfully deceived the Union generals as to their numbers. The timid Patterson accepted as truth all the stories told by men who came from Winchester pretending to be Union men, but who were spies. "Johnston has forty-two thousand men and fifty cannon," said one. General Scott and the War Department knew better; but there was very little reliable information as to what was going on in Richmond or in the Confederate lines, while Jefferson Davis had accurate accounts of matters at Washington. When the war began it was a Southern city, and a large number of the people sympathized with the South. They were in the Departments, in position to know all the secret movements. There was an organized mail-route between Washington and Richmond. Every evening a man left the city on horseback, riding eastward to Port Tobacco. The country around is very poor. One hundred and fifty years ago there were tobacco plantations, with gangs of slaves cultivating the ground. Now the once waving fields are overgrown with pines, and Port Tobacco is a sleepy place. The people of that region were in sympathy with the South.

On the bluff overlooking the Potomac stood the house of Mr. Watson, who had a son in General Lee's army. Across the Potomac, in Virginia, stood the house of Mr. Grimes. These gentlemen owned boats, and used to ferry people across the river in the night who carried percussion-caps, quinine, and other things purchased in Baltimore, to Richmond, making a great deal of money. There were Union gunboats in the river and soldiers on land; but Mr. Watson had a daughter whose sympathies were with the Southern army, and who kept a sharp lookout for the gunboats and soldiers. When neither was near she hung out a shawl from her chamber window as a signal to Mr. Grimes that the coast was clear, and when night came, light skiffs darted out from the creek along the shore and glided across the river. Mr. Jones, who lived near Mr. Watson, was the Confederate mail-agent; his post-office was a hollow tree at the foot of the bluff. When night came he made his way with letters and newspapers through the thick pines to the bank of the river, leaving the packages in the hollow tree, and taking those that he found there. He knew where the Union sentinels were, and how to avoid them. Every day when the New York newspapers arrived at Annapolis, a Confederate agent made up a package, which before night was in the hands of Mr. Jones, and which the next night would be in Richmond, Mr. Grimes sending a messenger across the country with the bag.

We come to July 15th. The time of the soldiers called out for three months has nearly expired; the movement to Manassas must be made at once, or not at all. General Patterson is at Martinsburg, and marches to Bunker Hill, within nine miles of Winchester. He has no definite plan.

On the morning of the 16th the cavalry makes a reconnoissance, and finds the Confederates in line of battle behind stone walls north of Winchester. There are three things which Patterson can do, either of which

will be effective: attack Johnston, make a feint of attacking, or take a
position which will prevent him from joining Beauregard. He does
neither, but retreats to Charlestown, leaving Johnston free to move in
any direction. There is no doubt that Patterson, up to the evening of
the 16th, intended to attack, but that Fitz-John Porter, his adjutant-
general, for some reason was opposed, and did what he could to persuade him to move to Charlestown. So, on the morning of the 17th,
we see the army especially instructed to prevent a junction of the two
Confederate armies deliberately moving away.

GENERAL J. E. JOHNSTON.

General Beauregard knew that McDowell was getting ready to march
towards Manassas, and sent Colonel Chestnut, who had been a clerk in the
War Department, to Washington to obtain information. He crossed the
Potomac below Alexandria in the night, reached the city in the early
morning of the 16th, and ate breakfast at the house of a friend. His
friend's wife wrote these words on a scrap of paper: "Orders issued to
McDowell to march to Manassas to-day." She had a confidential friend
in the War Department who secretly sympathized with the South. Colonel Chestnut jumped into a buggy, was driven by a friend down the north
bank of the Potomac to a spot where a boat was drawn up beneath the

bushes, and was ferried across the river. Before nightfall Beauregard was reading the information.

The army under McDowell is in five divisions, commanded by Generals Tyler, Hunter, Heintzelman, Miles, and Runyon. The troops for active service number about twenty-eight thousand, with forty-nine cannon.

At noon, July 16th, the division under Tyler takes up the line of march. There has been much talk about masked batteries. The orders for the movement contain the following cautions: "The three following things will not be pardonable in any commander: to come upon a battery or breastwork without a knowledge of its position; to be surprised; to fall back."

The march is very slow. The troops stop when they please, to pick blackberries or rest themselves, but the bands strike up now and then, and the column moves on in glee, never doubting that in a few days the army will be in Richmond, and the rebellion ended. On the 17th it is nine o'clock before the troops are on the march, and the movement is slower than ever, for fear of masked batteries. General Tyler comes upon a body of Confederates at Germantown with two cannon who make a rapid retreat. The newspaper correspondents, in their eagerness for news, enter Germantown in advance of the troops. So rapid the retreat of the Confederates that the sick in the hospital are left behind, together with a large amount of flour, several barrels of sugar, with frying-pans and kettles. Just beyond Germantown a baggage wagon has broken down, and the driver has cut the harnesses from the horses and is scampering towards Centreville, all of which puts the troops in the best of spirits.

At nine on the morning of the 18th the army is in motion once more, the correspondents in advance, climbing over the abandoned breastworks at Centreville, and learning all the news before the troops arrive.

At noon Richardson's brigade turns south to reconnoitre the ground towards Bull Run in the vicinity of Blackburn's Ford. The skirmishers discover a Confederate battery with troops. It is Longstreet's brigade. General Tyler orders up Ayres's battery, places two cannon in position, and a shell goes screaming across Bull Run, strikes a house, exploding inside, tearing away the chimney, and spoiling General Beauregard's dinner cooking over the fire. The next moment a shell comes from the woods down by Bull Run which explodes above the Union cavalry, setting the horses to dancing and wounding two men. General Tyler makes a mistake in sending Ayres with his two guns down the slope, followed by Richardson's brigade. Suddenly there comes a volley from beneath the green foliage along the winding stream, and the air is thick with leaden rain. A white cloud rises above the trees, and a wild yell, not a cheer, not a hurrah, but more like the war-whoop of the painted warrior of the Western plains, is heard above the din of battle. It was Longstreet's brigade delivering its first volley, and sending out its first battle-cry, often repeated during succeeding months. Richardson's men hurrah in turn. The firing is quick and sharp. Longstreet's men are thrown into confusion, and he sends to General Early for assistance. General Tyler is beneath the

peach-trees near a small house overlooking the field; he walks nervously, and finally orders the troops to withdraw. Between sixty and seventy men have been killed or wounded. The loss on the Confederate side has been about the same. Tyler had exceeded his orders, and nothing had been gained. The Confederates regarded it as a great victory, while the Union troops looked at it in the light of a repulse. It had disarranged General McDowell's plans.

Returning now to the Shenandoah Valley, we see General Johnston at this moment reading this despatch from Richmond: "General Beauregard attacked; go to his assistance." The way is clear, for

GENERAL LONGSTREET.

Patterson marched towards Charlestown at daybreak, and is eighteen miles away. A few moments later the soldiers of Jackson's brigade are on their way towards Ashby's Gap, in the mountain wall bounding the eastern horizon. Seventeen miles will take them to Piedmont on the Manassas Railroad. Major Whiting gallops in advance, to have engines and cars in waiting. At eight o'clock the next morning the troops are in the cars, whirling towards Manassas.

Bull Run is a branch of the Occoquon River, rising in the Bull Run Mountains, running south-east through a beautiful reach of fields, pasture, and woodland. As we go up stream from the Occoquon we come to McLean's Ford. Another mile brings us to Blackburn's. Two miles farther and we are at a stone bridge on the turnpike leading a little south of west from Centreville to Warrenton. There are several places above the bridge where the stream may be forded. Two miles more brings us to Mr. Sud-

THE BATTLE OF BULL RUN.

ley's mill, with its great water-wheel. A road crosses the stream by the mill leading south to Manassas. Leaving the run and going down the road, we pass a little church in a grove of oaks. A mile and a half brings us to the house of Mr. Matthews, on the east side of the road, with woods extending eastward towards the stone bridge. There is a beautiful field west of the house. Looking across the field, we see the house of Mr. Dogan. Going on, we descend a gentle slope, and come to a pretty little brook trickling over a rocky bed eastward towards Bull Run. It is Young's Branch, and empties into Bull Run below the bridge. The turnpike is built alongside. We pass a stone house at the junction of the roads, and then ascend a hill. There is a grove of young pines and cedars on the right hand. East of the road is Mr. Henry's house; across the field, still farther east, is the house of Mr. Robinson. We see a lone tree in the field a few rods south of Mr. Henry's, and a short distance beyond a rail fence, with a thicket of pines.

In making this itinerary we have traversed the ground on which the first great battle of the war was fought.

On the afternoon of the 18th General Beauregard had his troops along Bull Run, facing east. He had nearly twenty-two thousand men, with twenty-nine cannon. His brigades were stationed as follows: farthest down stream, at Union Mills, were Ewell's and Holmes's; at McLean's Ford, Jones's and Early's; at Blackburn's Ford, Longstreet's. Next came Bonham's, Cocke's, and Evans's, holding the line covering all the fords and the turnpike bridge. On Friday and Saturday, while McDowell's troops are resting at Centreville, Johnston's troops are being transported over the railroad. Jackson's brigade is the first to arrive, and is placed near Longstreet's brigade. Bee's and Bartow's brigades are in reserve between McLean's and Blackburn's fords. Johnston brings nearly nine thousand men and twenty-two cannon. General Holmes, who has been south of the Occoquon, comes with his brigade and six guns. The consolidated Confederate force numbers thirty-two thousand and seventy-two men and fifty-seven cannon.

McDowell's engineers are riding along Bull Run, seeking a place where the troops can cross. They discover Poplar Ford, one mile above the bridge, but learn that there is a much better crossing at Mr. Sudley's mill. McDowell intended to attack the Confederate right flank, but the intrenchments are so strong that he must make a new plan, and he decides to leave Richardson's brigade to make a demonstration at Blackburn's Ford, to send General Tyler with the remainder of his division down the turnpike, to make a show of attacking, to march with Hunter's and

Heintzelman's divisions through the fields and woods in the night to
Sudley's Ford, march down the road leading towards Manassas, and strike
the Confederate left flank and rear.
At the right time Tyler is to change
his demonstration to a real attack, cross
the stream, and join Hunter and Heintzelman.

POSITION AT 3 A.M.

It is Saturday night. Going over
to the house of Mr. McLean, we see
Beauregard and Johnston in consultation. Johnston is the senior officer,
but as Beauregard is familiar with the
ground, defers to his judgment. Beauregard proposes that they cross Bull
Run and attack McDowell's rear at
Centreville. Johnston accepts the plan, and the order is written for the
movement on Sunday morning.

It is two o'clock in the morning when the troops of Tyler's division
fold their blankets and move down the turnpike towards the stone bridge.
A mistake has been made at the outset. Hunter and Heintzelman ought
to have been the first to move; they have a long distance to march.
Tyler's men block the way. The flanking column ought to be at the
ford at sunrise, but it is nine o'clock, and the sun high in the heavens,
before the head of the column reaches the old mill. The march has been
tediously slow. When the soldiers reach the ford they stop to fill their
canteens and munch their meat and bread, but finally cross the stream and
move down the road.

Half-past five. Confederate officers are carrying the orders to the several brigade commanders to attack McDowell, when the stillness of the
peaceful morn is broken by a single cannon on the turnpike east of the
bridge. It is Ayres's battery beginning the battle. His second shot passes
through the tent of Captain Alexander, a signal-officer to Beauregard. A
moment later the guns with Richardson's brigade open their brazen lips.
General Tyler sends a company of skirmishers towards the bridge. There
is a rattle of musketry, a booming of cannon, but nothing more. Tyler
made a mistake on Thursday in attacking with too much vigor; now he
is over-cautious, and Beauregard and Johnston soon discover that it is a
feint.

Just before the troops reached Sudley's mill Mr. Cunningham, who
lives near the mill, discovered them, ran to his stable, mounted his horse,

crossed the stream, dashed down the Manassas Road, and informed the
pickets of Evans's brigade that the Yankees were coming to turn their
flank. Evans, without waiting for orders, changes front and marches
north towards the house of Mr. Matthews.

General Burnside, commanding the leading brigade of Union troops
in Hunter's division, throws out the Second Rhode Island Regiment as
skirmishers. They move nervously through the woods and fields. Suddenly there bursts upon them a rattling fire from Evans's men. Two
cannon open upon them. For half an hour the contest goes on in this
fashion. Hunter makes the mistake of attacking slowly when it should
be with vigor, and with a force strong enough to sweep Evans in an instant from the field. Wheet's battalion of Confederates comes upon the
run to help Evans, but receives a volley which is very destructive. And
now the brigades of Bee and Bartow, six regiments of Johnston's troops,
hasten across the turnpike, with Imboden's battery of four pieces, the
horses upon the gallop.

Just as these Confederate regiments are coming into position General
Hunter is wounded by a piece of shell, and is carried to the rear, and
General Andrew Porter assumes command. In a few moments the four
Union regiments of Burnside's brigade are engaged, together with Reynolds's battery, which the Confederates attempt to capture, but are stopped
by Sykes's battalion of regulars, which General Porter brings into line.
Griffin's Union battery comes upon the gallop and wheels into position,
and opens fire. Burnside's officers are falling; Colonel Slocum is mortally
wounded, Colonel Marston receives a bullet in his shoulder, Major Balch
falls, with one leg crushed by a cannon-ball. General Porter has sent
Sykes east of the road, but the other regiments and Griffin's battery are
west of it, the line extending towards Dogan's house. Ricketts's Union
battery, near Dogan's, joins in the conflict.

The fire of the Union troops is so destructive that General Bee orders
the Confederates to fall back. They go faster and farther than he intended, down the slope, across Young's Branch, up the hill to Mr. Henry's
house, where Imboden's battery is stationed. The battle has opened favorably for the Union troops. There comes a lull. It is past eleven, and
the advance regiments of Heintzelman are just coming upon the field,
swinging out towards Dogan's house. If their bayonets had flashed in the
sunlight an hour earlier, far different, in all probability, would have been
the result.

Looking eastward, we see Sherman's and Keyes's brigades of Tyler's
division marching up the east bank of Bull Run to Poplar Ford, crossing

7

the stream, turning south, and advancing towards the turnpike. They
could not cross by the bridge, because it was covered by a Confederate
battery; besides, the report was current that it was mined, and would be
blown up the moment the Union troops attempted to cross.

At ten o'clock General Beauregard is at Mitchell's Ford, waiting
to hear the opening of the battle at Centreville, towards which General
Ewell is slowly advancing. He hears instead a cannon in the direction
of the north-west. "There is a cloud of dust towards Sudley's Ford,"
is the report of the signal-officer. The cannonade increases, and there
are volleys of musketry. The conviction comes to Beauregard that

ROBINSON'S HOUSE.

McDowell is turning his left flank. "March towards the sound of battle," is the order to all the brigade commanders, and Johnston and Beauregard both ride as fast as their horses will carry them towards the
Henry house, Beauregard taking command of the troops east of the
house, Johnston west of it. They come out of the woods south of the
house, and see the troops of Bee, Bartow, and Evans retreating in disorder
up the hill. The lines are broken, the fugitives are streaming down the
road towards Manassas. The officers are trying to stop them. A few
turn about, but the greater number keep on. "Every segment of line,"
says General Beauregard, "we succeeded in forming, was again dissolved
while another was being formed. More than two thousand men were

shouting, each some suggestion to his neighbor, their voices mingling with the noise of the shells exploding amid the trees overhead, and all word of command was drowned in the confusion and uproar."

General Jackson's brigade has arrived, and stands by the fence in the thicket of pines south of Mr. Henry's. Jackson has drilled his men, and has been strict in discipline. If some of the men feel like running, they do not go. General Bee sees them, and thus calls out to his wavering men,

STONEWALL JACKSON.

"See Jackson standing like a stone wall!" Possibly it does not have much effect upon the Alabama and Mississippi regiments under him, but he has made "Stonewall Jackson" evermore a historic name.

The Confederate line at this moment, with the exception of Jackson's brigade, is in great confusion. Towards Manassas stream the fugitives, crying that all is lost. "The disorder," says Beauregard, "seemed irretrievable; but the thought came to me that if their colors were planted out to the front the men might rally round them. I gave the order, which was executed. The soldiers advanced, and the line was formed."

It was a position much higher than the ground on which McDowell was forming for an advance, and the Confederate artillery could send a plunging fire upon the Union troops.

It is two o'clock Sunday afternoon. The Union troops began their march at midnight, have come twelve miles, have only nibbled a little hard bread and bit of meat, and are weary and thirsty. A scorching sun has beaten upon them. The lines are growing thin. There is little discipline. Soldiers leave to get water, and do not return. I stand upon the roof of a house overlooking the field and see the brigades of Sherman, Franklin, Wilcox, and Porter advancing towards the houses of Mr. Robinson and Henry; Burnside is resting on the ground from which the Confederates have been driven; Howard's brigade is moving towards the turnpike by Dogan's house; Keyes's brigade is near the stone bridge. There are parts of fourteen Union regiments advancing to assail the Confederate line.

At this moment nearly every Confederate brigade is hastening towards the spot, where the uproar is going on, with a quicker cannonade and livelier volleys of musketry. There are twenty-two Confederate cannon pouring a heavy fire upon the advancing men in blue, and twelve regiments delivering their volleys, only three of which, with six cannon, belong to the army under Beauregard; the others belong to the army from the Shenandoah, under Johnston.

CONFEDERATE POSITION 5 P.M.

The batteries of Griffin and Ricketts are on the plateau east of Dogan's. They have been nobly served, and the Confederates have all been driven across Young's Branch southward. General McDowell at this moment commits another error: he orders the batteries to go across the stream in advance of the infantry. Ricketts does not like the order, but he is a soldier in the regular army, and believes in obeying commands. The battery moves down the road, crosses the stream, ascends the hill towards the Henry house, and opens fire at close range. The Confederate sharp-shooters behind the picket-fence and under the peach-trees begin to pick off his horses, but he rains canister upon them and riddles the house with shells. Mrs. Henry, old and feeble, is killed, and the sharp-shooters are compelled to retreat. Griffin comes, with his horses upon the gallop, across the stream, and takes position to the left of Ricketts. Major Barry, chief of artillery, has brought him the order to take this position. He, too, has objected, not having any infantry supports.

"The Zouaves will support you," says Barry.

"Why not let them go in advance until I get into position? then they can fall back."

"It is McDowell's order for you to go."

"That settles it; but mark my words, the Zouaves will not support me."

A ball has lodged in one of the guns and it cannot be used. The other five open, and with Ricketts's deliver a destructive fire.

From my position I can see a dust-cloud in the west rising above the tree-tops. A little later a regiment comes out of the woods south of the turnpike and west of the road leading to Manassas. The men are in gray, as are several of the Union regiments. They climb over a rail-fence. The colonel walks along the ranks as if saying something to them. Griffin sees them, believes them to be Confederates, and wheels his guns to mow them down with canister. The cannon are loaded, and the gunners stand ready to send the double-shotted charges into the line.

We have arrived at a turning-point in the history of our country.

"Don't fire!" It is Major Barry, commanding the artillery, who shouts it.

"They are rebels," Griffin replies.

"No, they are your supports."

The Fourteenth New York Regiment has gone up into the woods, to the right of Griffin's battery, and Major Barry makes a mistake in supposing that the men in gray, which have just come out of the wood, are those who a few moments ago entered it.

"Sure as the world, they are rebels!" Griffin shouts again.

"I know that they are your supports."

Griffin wheels his guns in the other direction towards the Henry house, and opens fire once more. The officer addressing the men in gray has finished his speech, and now faces them to the left, marches a few rods, faces them to the right, as deliberately as if at drill in camp, advances steadily towards Griffin, then comes to a halt. The men bring their guns to a level, and take aim. There is a flash, a white cloud, a roll of musketry. The air is filled with leaden hail. Men and horses go down. Hardly one of the gunners that is not killed, wounded, or taken prisoner. The horses plunge madly down the ravine. The Zouaves in rear of Griffin behold the spectacle in amazement, then break, and stream over the field

towards Dogan's house, a few only remaining to fire parting shots. In
vain the efforts of the officers to rally them.

The men in gray that have given this deliberate volley are the troops
of General E. Kirby Smith, the last of Johnston's army. They left the
cars at the point where the railroad crosses the Warrenton turnpike, and
have come upon the run down the pike and through the fields, guided by
the sound of the cannon and the white cloud rising above the tree-tops.
Without orders from Beauregard, Johnston, or any one, Smith has poured
in his volley, changing the tide of affairs.

Five minutes ago, and the fortunes of the hour were setting against the
Confederates. Five minutes ago, and Griffin and Ricketts, if they had
done what they were about to do, would have cut Smith's brigade to pieces.
One round from those eleven guns, double-shotted, would have made great
gaps in those ranks, and have sent the living a routed rabble to the rear.

For a short time the contest goes on. The Thirty-third Virginia advances to seize the cannon, but are driven by the First Michigan of Wilcox's brigade. General Howard's brigade is advancing at the moment up
the slope towards the Henry house. It delivers its volleys, holds its
ground a while, but at last begins to melt away. Going over to the left
near the Robinson house, we see Sherman's brigade, which has come across
Bull Run, crossing Young's Branch, marching up the hill, pouring in a
deliberate fire. At this moment the Confederate troops, animated by the
destruction wrought by Smith's brigade of two thousand five hundred,
redouble their energy. Men who a moment ago were faint-hearted, who
were just ready to give way, take on fresh courage. Stragglers return,
new troops arrive. On the other hand, the Union army has lost its aggressive energy. Under the disaster it begins to melt away. The troops
fall back down the hill to the turnpike. There is no reserve behind which
they can be rallied, and the tide drifts back over the ground wrested from
the Confederates in the forenoon.

There are days when the air is calm, no breath rippling the placid
waters—so calm that the aspen leaf ceases to be tremulous; but suddenly,
we know not whence, there comes a gentle breeze, which catches up the
finest dust, whirling it in widening circles, gathering straws and sticks and
broken twigs, whirling faster, in larger circles, with louder noise and wild
commotion, sweeping over field and plain, hill and dale, levelling fences
and houses, twisting trees like withes, becoming the uncontrolled devastating tornado.

Such a whirlwind arises. Just where it begun it is not possible to say,
but somewhere on the field men started to run. Why they ran it would

not be easy to say, for the Confederates were not in pursuit. A body of Confederate cavalry a little later rode towards the Union hospital; another company dashed across Bull Run near the bridge; and though the exploits of the Virginia Black Horse Cavalry, of which every horseman regarded himself as a "cavalier," were the themes of the hour, but there was no grand charge.

The panic was far greater among the teamsters and the crowd of sight-seers that had gone out from Washington to see the battle than among the troops. The turnpike was crowded with army wagons. The team-sters stopped, not to inquire as to what had happened, but cut their horses loose, mounting one, handing the others over to the frightened Zouaves, and all dashing towards Centreville. Members of Congress had come from Washington in carriages, and the frightened drivers lashed their horses to a run. I was drinking at a spring near the stone bridge, a few rods south of the turnpike, when the whirlwind came sweeping across the stream. I had just left General Schenck's brigade. Captain Carlisle, commanding a battery, had taken the bits from the mouths of his horses and was feed-ing them when the Confederate Black Horse battalion came through the woods. Ayres's guns opened upon the cavalry, sending canister into their ranks, and scattering the force in an instant. Having done this, Ayres came tearing along the turnpike towards Cub Run, gaining the eastern bank, wheeling into position, and standing ready to hurl destruction upon the Confederates. Not so fortunate Carlisle, who was compelled to leave four of his guns because the bridge across Cub Run broke down. It would not be an accurate statement were I to say that all the troops were panic-stricken; far otherwise. Many of the regiments left the field in good order, returning to Centreville by the route of the morning. There was disorder at Centreville through the incompetency of Colonel Miles, who after the battle was accused before a court-martial of being intoxicated. The only guns lost on the field were those of Griffin and Ricketts, the others were lost through the breaking down of the bridge at Cub Run.

General McDowell rallied the troops at Centreville, and thought of making a stand at that point, but decided to fall back to Washington; and so through the night the army which had marched to Centreville with confident expectation of victory, which had been all but secured, made its weary way back to Alexandria and Arlington, leaving twenty-five of its cannon and nearly fifteen hundred men, killed and wounded, upon the plateau of Bull Run. The Confederate loss in men was greater; but Beauregard and Johnston had secured the prestige of victory almost at the moment of defeat.

CHAPTER VI.

THE CLOSE OF 1861.

"EVERY one believes," wrote one of the clerks at Richmond in his diary, "that our banners will wave in the streets of Washington in a few days, and the Union army will be expelled from Maryland; that peace will be consummated on the banks of the Schuylkill." The people of the South were wild over the victory of Bull Run. Many thousands who had hesitated to join the Confederate army now hastened to enroll themselves. It was the universal belief that Jefferson Davis would soon be in the White House, and the flag of the Confederacy waving above the Capitol.

The people of the North had not dreamed of defeat, and the disappointment was very bitter; but as the lightning clears the murky air on a sultry summer day, so the defeat cleared the vision, and they comprehended that the war was to be a conflict vast in its proportions, and to be waged to the bitter end.

Cost what it might, the rebellion must be crushed, was the resolve of every loyal heart.

"Three hundred thousand men are called for to suppress the rebellion," was the message which flashed over the wires from Washington. People left their occupations—the farmer his plough, the mechanic his hammer, the joiner his plane, the salesman his yardstick, scholars their books. Men worth a million dollars enlisted as privates, ready to give life and fortune to their country. In every village drums were beating, soldiers marching.

They must be fed and clothed; they must have guns, cartridge-boxes, knapsacks, tents, and wagons. For the closing of the Southern seaports ships must be built. Never before was there such a commotion in the Northern States. Labor, which the slave-holder had despised, suddenly became a giant, and was getting ready to put forth its strength.

General Scott was too far advanced in life, and too feeble, to be commander-in-chief of the army; but there must be a commander, and General McClellan, who had won the battle of Rich Mountain, in West Virginia, was selected. That battle was a small affair, but it had compelled the Confederates to abandon that section of country, and General McClellan was already regarded as a great commander. He was called to Washington, and commissioned by President Lincoln.

"General McClellan would like to meet the correspondents in Washington. Please be at Willard's Hotel this evening at eight o'clock."

Such was the invitation which the newspaper correspondents received on the morning of August 1, 1861. They assembled at the hotel, stepped into omnibuses, were taken to General McClellan's headquarters, and introduced to him.

"I have one request to make—that you will be careful not to write anything from which the enemy will learn what is going on," he said.

His words were few, but pleasant. The next day all the country was reading about the interview; how General McClellan looked and acted. One correspondent said that he resembled Napoleon Bonaparte, and the people began to speak of him as "Little Napoleon," and to have great expectations of victory with such an officer as commander-in-chief.

It takes much money to carry on a great war—to pay the soldiers and officers, and buy horses, tents, wagons, muskets, swords, cannon, boots, clothing, oats, corn, hay; to build ships and steamboats.

"Which will win, the North or the South?" was the question a banker in London asked of Baron Rothschild, who had a great deal of money, and who never lent it without getting good security and interest.

"The North."

"Why?"

"Because it has the longest purse."

It is industry that keeps the purse full. Baron Rothschild knew that the Southern people had no manufactories; that they had invented no labor-saving machines; that their property was in land and slaves. He knew that they had only cotton and tobacco to sell; that with all the seaports blockaded they would have no market; that the slaves might run away or be set free, and that in a short time they would be of little value.

He knew that the people of the North had set mill-wheels to whirling, and were employing the energy of nature to do the work of human hands; that their property was in small farms, houses, mills, machinery; that labor was free; that it could tax itself; that it could borrow money, promising to pay in the future. This far-seeing man comprehended that the Southern people would see their property disappear; that they would exhaust the country of supplies; that they would create a debt which they never would be able to pay; and that after a while the Confederacy, reared on slave labor, would go down with a crash.

This story of the war would be very incomplete were I to leave out the position and influence of England in the struggle. Very soon after the surrender of Fort Sumter, and before Mr. Charles Francis Adams, who had been appointed Minister to England, reached London, the British Government recognized the Confederates as belligerents—or as a people exercising war powers—which the people of the United States regarded as a very unfriendly act. But the great manufacturers of England who wanted cotton, the merchants who wanted to sell goods, saw that if the Southern ports were blockaded all trade with the Southern States would cease. They were greatly offended, also, because Congress, in order to get money to carry on the war, put a high tax on all goods manufactured in other countries and brought to the United States for sale. So it came about that the manufacturers, merchants, and traders of Great Britain sympathized with the Southern people. They subscribed money to buy cannon, muskets, powder, and shells, which they gave to the Confederates. They built fast-sailing ships, and loaded them with all kinds of goods to run the blockade, sailing from Liverpool for the Bahama Islands, which lie only two hundred miles east of the coast of Florida, thence for Charleston, running past the blockading-vessels at night, supplying the Confederates with arms, ammunition, and supplies, and carrying cotton back to England.

Most of the nobles, dukes, lords, and barons hoped the government which the people of the United States had established would be destroyed. Their sympathy was with the people of the South. Most of the newspapers in England praised the Southern people as gentlemen fighting for the freedom of their country against the Northern people, whom they called low-born, selfish Yankees.

"The North," said the London *Times*, when it received the news of the battle of Bull Run, "has lost all—even military honor. We have been cheated out of our sympathies. We don't like to laugh. Seventy-five thousand American patriots have fled twenty miles in an agony of fear, though there was nobody pursuing them. The United States of America have ceased to be. The Union has burst asunder by explosive forces generated within itself, and now the two republics stand like cliffs which of old were the same rock, but which can never be united."

The men who owned cotton mills wanted the South to triumph; not so the men and women who tended the spinning frames and looms in Lincolnshire. They had little cotton to spin and little food to eat, but when times were hardest, when their cheeks were thin and pale for want of food, when their children were asking for bread, they came together and held prayer-meetings, asking Almighty God to give victory to the people of the Northern States. They knew that it was a struggle between free and slave labor; that the people of the North were fighting a battle for the oppressed of every land.

> "For mankind are one in spirit, and an instinct bears along
> Round the earth's electric circle the flash of right or wrong."

Turning once more to the distant West, we see General Lyon in south-western Missouri, at Springfield, with about five thousand men, most of whom are soon to return to their homes, the term of enlistment being nearly expired. They are, many of them, without shoes; their uniforms are in tatters. General Lyon has called for reinforcements, but the Government has calls from every quarter. It is the 8th of August, and on the 14th the time of the three months' men will expire. There is a Confederate army at Wilson's Creek, ten miles beyond Springfield, towards the south-west, under General McCulloch and General Price. General Lyon estimated them at twenty thousand; General Price's adjutant-general, Sneed, says that there were eleven thousand. It is probable that the Confederates outnumbered the Union soldiers nearly three to one. Another Confederate army, under General Hardee, numbering nine thousand, farther east, was advancing to get between General Lyon and St. Louis, thus cutting off his retreat.

We must not forget that the people of Missouri are taking sides as in no other State. The great majority are for the Union. Shall General Lyon abandon this section of the State? Shall he turn back from the people who are looking to the old flag for protection? The Confederates have a large force of cavalry, and if he attempts to retreat, the cavalry will gain the advance, McCulloch will follow in swift pursuit, and his little force will be ground to powder. He believes it will be far better to advance and strike a powerful blow before retreating.

The sun has gone down, the stars are shining. The day has been hot and sultry, but the night is cool and refreshing. The soldiers eat their supper, the battery horses munch their corn. At nine o'clock the bugles sound, and the artillerymen jump upon their seats. The drums tap lightly, and the soldiers fall into line. The columns wheel into the road—one, under Colonel Sigel, with six guns, taking a road which leads south; the other, under General Lyon, leading south-west. Colonel Sigel is to attack the right flank and rear of the Confederates, while General Lyon is to hurl his troops upon their front. A small force is left to guard the camp.

General Lyon had in his column the First Missouri, First Iowa, First and Second Kansas regiments, two companies of the Second Missouri Riflemen, eight companies of United States Regulars, ten cannon, two companies of cavalry—about three thousand five hundred.

Colonel Sigel had the Third and Fifth Missouri regiments, six cannon, and two companies of cavalry—about one thousand one hundred. Colonel Sigel was to make the attack, and when General Lyon heard the sound of his cannon he was to attack in front.

Wilson's Creek is a small stream winding amid wooded swells of land, with here and there a field or pasture.

The morning was dawning. Some of the Confederate soldiers were asleep, others rekindling their fires and putting their frying-pans upon the coals, cutting slices of ham for their breakfast, when they heard a rattling of musketry a mile away. A picket came running in. "The Yankees are coming!" he shouted.

The drums beat the long roll, the bugles sounded; frying-pans were tossed aside; soldiers ran hither and thither. The regiments formed in hot haste, for General Lyon was driving in the pickets. Captain Totten's battery was sending its shells into camp from the north, and Sigel's guns were opening from the east.

We see General Lyon's line moving down the road, the battalion of regulars, under Captain Plummer, in advance. Major Osterhaus commands the skirmishers on the right. Captain Totten wheels his six cannon into position, and the shells go hissing into the Confederate camp. Lieutenant-colonel Andrews, with the First Missouri, supports him. The First Kansas comes up on the left. Up the ridge they drive the Confederates.

Leaving General Lyon's troops for a moment, let us go through the woods south-east to the other road, on which Sigel is moving. His two companies of cavalry are in advance. In the dim gray of the morning the cavalrymen see Confederate soldiers coming down the road from their camp with pails and kettles, on their way to the creek for water. The cavalrymen ride into the fields, circle around them, and the Confederates suddenly discover that they are prisoners.

The troops press on. They can see the white tents of the Confederates on the slope of a hill. The smoke is curling up from the camp-fires. Sigel whirls four cannon into position and opens fire. There is a sudden commotion. Some of the Confederates flee, panic-stricken, through the fields. Far better for Sigel—far better for the fortunes of the day, if, instead of firing, he had pressed on with his troops; then he could have captured many prisoners. The Third and Fifth regiments crossed the creek and took possession of the camp. He had fallen upon the Commissary Department of the Confederate army. Around the camp were quarters of beef hanging on stakes and poles. There was a corral of cattle, another of horses.

The Confederate troops had fled, but they were rallying on another hill. Sigel brought up his cannon and once more opened fire. He could hear the uproar on the other road growing louder and coming nearer. Lyon was advancing. Looking across the hills towards the north-west he could see the battle-cloud rising above the tree-tops. General Lyon is driving all before him, was the thought that came to him.

"Lyon's men are coming up the road towards us," said Sigel's skirmishers.

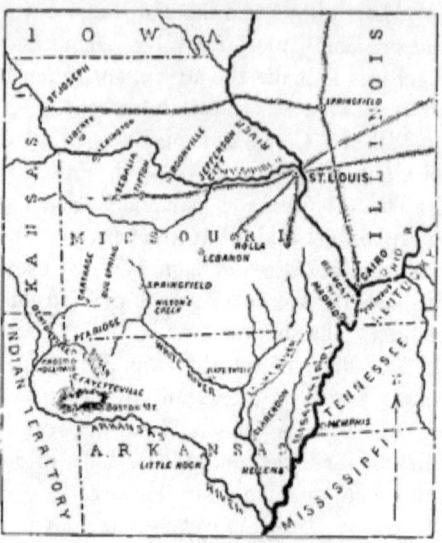

CAMPAIGN IN MISSOURI.

Lieutenant-colonel Albert, commanding the Third Missouri Regiment, and Colonel Salomen, commanding the Fifth, saw a brigade of troops coming through the fields. Above them floated the Stars and Stripes. The color-bearer was waving it as a signal to them not to fire.

"They are Lyon's troops. Don't fire!" said the officer. The men stand at ease. The advancing line halts. Suddenly muskets flame, and shells from a battery crash through the woods.

"They are Lyon's troops firing on us!" The cry runs along the line. Up, almost to the muzzles of Sigel's cannon, rush the Confederates, shooting horses, capturing five of the guns, killing and wounding nearly three hundred men. Back through the fields flee Sigel's troops—their part in the battle ended.

Passing over now to the Confederate camp, we see General McCulloch marshalling his forces. It is half-past five when the rattle of musketry breaks on the skirmish line.

In front of the position where General Lyon is advancing are the troops commanded by Generals Slack, Clark, McBride, Parsons, and Rains.

They file towards the left. Captain Woodruff, with his six cannon, comes into position and replies to Totten's guns. Colonel Herbert, with his Louisiana regiment, and Colonel McIntosh's Arkansas regiment join them, marching up to a rail-fence enclosing a cornfield, coming against the Union regulars under Captain Plummer and the troops from Kansas.

Forward and backward, through the scrubby oaks, surge the lines of battle, the Confederates greatly outnumbering the Union troops.

General McCulloch hears the thundering of Sigel's guns upon his rear. Leaving General Sterling Price in command of the troops in front of Lyon, he marches east with Churchill's and Greer's regiments of Missourians, two companies of Louisiana troops, and Reid's battery.

General McCulloch, in his report of the battle, makes no mention of the way in which he deceived Sigel by marching with the Stars and Stripes, but nevertheless, according to Sigel's account, under its protecting folds he advanced close up to the unsuspecting troops before opening fire;—at a volley putting Sigel to rout and enabling McCulloch to wheel about and march back to confront Lyon, who is driving all before him. The hill on which the contest has raged is thickly strewn with the dead and dying. The battle is going against the Confederates on the left. McCulloch throws in Carroll's, Greer's, McIntosh's, and the Louisiana regiments. These are not enough. General Pearce's brigade, the last reserve, is called upon. Reid's battery comes to take part.

Once more let us go back to the Union lines. From a hill overlooking the field where the Confederates are standing, amid the sheltering corn-rows, Captain Dubois's and Captain Totten's pieces are still thundering. The Missourians in Lyon's regiments look across the space between the two lines and see old acquaintances in the Confederate ranks. The Confederates recognize them in turn.

There are no hatreds like those engendered by civil war. Old-time friends become implacable enemies, ready to fight to the bitter end.

Some of General Lyon's regiments' have fired away all their ammunition. A soldier of a Missouri regiment has fired the last bullet that will fit his gun, but has some of large size. He sits down beneath a tree and begins to whittle them.

"What are you doing?" asks an officer.

"Whittling the bullets to fit my gun."

"Don't stop to do that. Look into the cartridge-boxes of the men who have been killed; you will find some that will fit your gun."

In a few moments he is loading and firing once more.

Colonel Gordon Granger is on General Lyon's staff. There is a gap between two regiments, and as he looks over to the Confederate line he discovers a regiment preparing to rush in. He brings three companies into the intervening space. "Lie down in the grass. Don't show yourselves. Wait till I give the word," are his orders. The men lie low. Up the slope march the Confederates. There is a blaze and rattle, and many of the Confederates reel to the earth. Back over the field flee the living.

General Lyon has been wounded in one leg, a bullet has struck his head. Blood-stains are on his face. He has put his last battalion into the line. His horse has been killed, and he has mounted a second. Altogether, he has but a handful of troops. Sigel is routed; McCulloch is bringing up every Confederate soldier, outnumbering him three to one.

"I fear the day is lost," General Lyon says; but he rides along the line, swinging his hat and encouraging the men. They rally round him, and follow him into the thick of the fight. A bullet pierces his breast, and he falls from his horse dead. The army has lost its great-hearted leader. Only those around him know of it. Though dead, his bravery has so stirred the soldiers that for another half-hour the fight goes on.

It is half-past eleven. For five hours the battle has raged. All night long the Union men were on the march. They have had no breakfast; they are hungry, thirsty, faint, weary. Notwithstanding all this, once more they charge the advancing Confederates and drive them, but cannot hold the field. There is but one thing to do—retreat.

One-third of those engaged have been killed, or are wounded. The battle is lost, but they have struck a blow which, in its moral effect, will make it a victory. Out of it will come a taking of sides by the people of Missouri—thousands of men wavering before the battle, after it will decide to stand by the Union.

The troops which marched from Springfield under General Lyon numbered not quite four thousand; of these more than fourteen hundred were killed, wounded, and missing. The Confederate loss was proportionally great, and the blow so damaging that McCulloch and Price made no attempt to follow the retreating troops, which made their way to Rolla, a distance of one hundred and twenty-five miles.

Leaving now the West, let us look at events on the Atlantic coast.

Very soon after the first battle of Bull Run, when the Confederates saw—as did the people of the North—that the war was to be a trial of strength and endurance, they began to build forts along the coast.

A gang of slaves was building Fort Hatteras, which stands on a point of land nearly surrounded by water, on the North Carolina coast. The white waves of the Atlantic break along the narrow strip of sandy beach, which is washed on the other side by the waters of Pamlico Sound. The Confederates are building a bomb-proof large enough to afford shelter for five hundred men. The bank of sand is twenty-five feet in thickness; it is turfed over, and there are ten heavy cannon mounted — two of them thirty-two-pounders.

. On Tuesday, August 27, 1861, the Confederate soldiers in the fort, looking seaward, saw a Union fleet coming down from the north — the frigate *Minnesota*, with the flags of Commodore Stringham and General Butler flying in the breeze; the frigate *Wabash*, the sloop-of-war *Pawnee*, and three war-steamers — the *Monticello*, *Harriet Lane*, and *Quaker City*. There were also two steamers with nine hundred troops on board, commanded by General Butler.

The *Cumberland*, a sailing-frigate, came from Fortress Monroe with her white sails spread to the winds. The *Wabash* took her in tow, and the whole fleet steamed in towards the forts.

It was nearly ten o'clock before the vessels were ready, and then the sides were all aflame sending a storm of shells into the forts. While the cannon were thundering, two hundred soldiers jumped into boats and rowed towards the shore. The white surf was breaking on the sands, but they dashed through it, and running up the beach formed in line. Colonel Weber, of New York, was in command. The Confederate cannon in the fort returned the fire of the ships, but the shots were badly aimed, and did no harm. For four hours the bombardment went on, and was so terrific that the Confederates pulled down their flags. The *Monticello* steamed in, when suddenly the guns of Hatteras opened upon the ship, and solid shot crashed through her sides, while shells exploded around her. Fortunately, however, the captain got out of range and saved his ship from destruction. It was an act of perfidy.

The Confederates finally abandoned Fort Clark, and two or three of the skirmishers, under Captain Weigel, ran in and hoisted the Stars and Stripes. The Confederates in Hatteras, thinking Fort Clark was full of Union soldiers, opened upon it with all their guns, wasting their ammunition and hurting no one.

At sunrise the next morning the Confederate steamer *Winslow* opened fire upon the troops on shore; but during the night Colonel Weber had placed two howitzers and a rifled six-pounder in position behind an embankment, and the *Winslow* was obliged to keep at proper distance. It was a grand sight when the *Susquehanna*, *Wabash*, *Minnesota*, *Harriet*

Lane, Pawnee, and *Cumberland,* one after another, opened their broadsides upon Hatteras. Commodore Barron was the Confederate commander in the fort. Once more the Confederate flag came down, but Commodore Stringham paid no heed to it; he was not to be deceived a second time, and the shells kept pouring in till a white flag went up. Then the sailors gave a hurrah and let the cannon cool. More than seven hundred prisoners were captured, with one thousand muskets and thirty-one heavy cannon. Nearly fifty of the Confederates had been killed or wounded, while not a Union soldier or sailor had been injured.

No longer could English vessels enter and depart through Hatteras Inlet; and several which arrived during the next few days, unconscious of danger, were captured, to the great chagrin of the captains and crews.

The loss of the forts and their occupation by the Union troops was an unexpected blow to the Confederates, for now a Union fleet could gain entrance to Pamlico and Albemarle sounds, and a Union army could secure a foothold in North Carolina.

Taking events in their chronological order, and returning once more to Missouri, we find General Sterling Price issuing a proclamation glorifying the battle of Wilson's Creek as a great victory for the Confederates, and calling upon the young men of Missouri to join his army, which soon numbered twenty thousand. He advanced to Lexington, on the Missouri River, where there were three Missouri volunteer regiments and two of Home Guards, numbering twenty-eight hundred, under Colonel Mulligan, who threw up intrenchments, upon which were mounted six cannon and two howitzers; but the howitzers were useless for want of ammunition. He had only forty rounds for his men. On September 11th the Confederate artillery opened fire, but Price decided to begin a siege instead of making an attack. Reinforcements

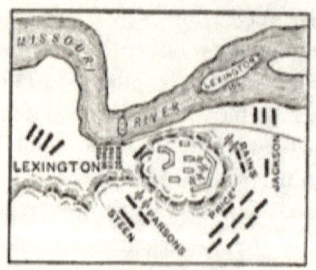

DEFENCE OF LEXINGTON.

swelled his force to twenty-five thousand. He captured a steamboat ascending the river with supplies for Mulligan. The Union troops could get no water, and their food was running short. The Confederate batteries kept up a constant fire; the shells exploded among the horses of the Union cavalry, strewing the ground with their mangled bodies. The rebels charged upon the hospital, but were driven by the Montgomery Guards of Chicago, who in turn were driven. For three days Mulligan held out against Price's whole army, till his ammunition was exhausted, and the

8

tongues of his men hung out of their mouths for want of water, bravely waiting for reinforcements which would never reach him. A shower came, and the soldiers spread their blankets to catch the falling drops, and then wrung them into their kettles. The Home Guards became disheartened at last, and Major Becker, without authority, raised the white flag, but Mulligan tore it down. The rebels opened fire once more, and the Home Guards retreated. Mulligan was twice wounded, nearly two hundred of his men killed or wounded, and he was forced to surrender. But this success of General Price could not swerve the great majority of the people of that State from their allegiance to the Stars and Stripes.

We are to remember that the border line was fifteen hundred miles long; that the Government was obliged to send troops in every direction. It must help the loyal men of Missouri—must hold St. Louis, the great commercial centre west of the Mississippi, with its iron-founderies, its great fleet of steamboats. If the Confederates were to get possession of the State, or hold any part of it, the cause of the Union would suffer. General Fremont was appointed commander of the Department; his head-quarters were at St. Louis. He gathered a large number of troops for a movement towards the south-west, which would compel General Price to retire from the Missouri River.

It was seen by the Government at Washington and by the Confederate Government at Richmond that the Mississippi, the Ohio, Tennessee, Cumberland, and Arkansas rivers would be great lines of communication as well as the railroads in the mighty struggle. Railroads could be torn up, but the rivers would be always running. Cannon might be planted upon the banks to stop the passing of steamboats, but the rivers would always be there.

In West Virginia General Cox, with several regiments, was making his way up the Kanawha Valley, to give protection to the Union people. General Floyd, who, while Secretary of War, had violated his oath of office and done what he could to destroy the Union, was at Carnifex Ferry, on the Gauley River, a branch of the Kanawha. General Robert E. Lee, with a body of Confederates, was at Cheat Mountain, confronted by General Rosecrans. We see Rosecrans leaving General Reynolds with a portion of his force to hold the ground against Lee, then marching with the rest from Clarksburg southward. He climbs mountains and moves through narrow defiles. At noon, September 9th, he is on the summit of Gauley Mountain. After a march of more than one hundred miles he comes suddenly upon Floyd near Summerville, who has strong intrenchments and twelve cannon. Rosecrans advances; there is a skirmish, which almost

BATTLE OF BALL'S BLUFF.—DEATH OF COLONEL BAKER.

becomes a battle, waged with such vigor that Floyd steals away in the night, crossing the river on a log bridge, leaving all his tents, a large amount of supplies, and does not stop till he reaches Sewall's Mountain, thirty miles away.

It was the 21st of October, a sweet, calm, and restful day, with the glory of autumn on all the hills. I was in Washington. There were whispers in the air of something going on near Edwards Ferry, on the Potomac, above Washington. I hastened to General McClellan's headquarters to ascertain what it might be. The headquarters were in a large brick building; there were aides and clerks in the numerous apartments, but they had no information to give to a correspondent. There was an air of mystery, a reticence which usually stimulates a correspondent to get at the bottom of things. While waiting to obtain an interview with General McClellan, President Lincoln entered the room. I had seen him in his Springfield home, and he gave me a cordial greeting. An aide passed into the room occupied by General McClellan, and announced the presence of the President. I could hear the click of the telegraph within. Several minutes passed, and then the lieutenant invited the President to enter the inner room. While waiting, the President rested his head upon his hand, and seemed lost in thought; there were lines of trouble in his sunken checks. He soon came out, with his head bowed. His hands were clasped upon his heart; he walked with a shuffling, tottering gait, reeling as if beneath a staggering blow. He did not fall, but passed down the street, carrying not only the burden of the nation, but a load of private grief, which, with the swiftness of the lightning's flash, had been hurled upon him.

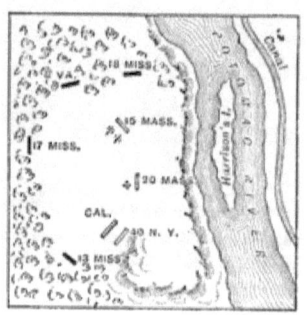

MAP OF BALL'S BLUFF.

"We have met with a disaster up the river: fifteen hundred men have been lost and Colonel Baker is killed," said General Marcy, in response to my inquiry. It was at Ball's Bluff, where the Fifteenth and Twentieth Massachusetts, the Tammany Regiment of New York, and the California Regiment, also recruited in New York, commanded by Colonel Baker, had been sent across the Potomac to make a demonstration towards Leesburg. The crossing was made on a canalboat and two smaller boats. Colonel Baker was confronted by a force much larger than his own. He fell, and the troops were forced back to the river. There was a rush for the boats. Many plunged into the

8*

swirling waters, to be swept away, a few to gain the other shore, some to be shot by the exultant Confederates, firing with deliberate and deadly aim upon the helpless and unresisting victims. It was a needless movement which was ordered by General McClellan, and not well managed. The disaster aroused the indignation of the people and awakened criticism. Colonel Baker was President Lincoln's intimate friend; he had lived in Springfield, practised at the same bar, ridden in the same circuit, and they were animated by the same lofty ideas. Colonel Baker served in the Mexican war, made California his home in 1852, and had been elected Senator. On the floor of the Senate-chamber his voice had been eloquent for the Union. When the war began he raised his regiment in New York, equipped it largely at his own expense, naming it the "California" Regiment. He had fallen in its first battle, and the telegraph had flashed the news of the terrible disaster to the President.

On September 4th, General Ulysses S. Grant, who had been appointed to command the Department of South-eastern Missouri, reached Cairo, at the junction of the Ohio and Mississippi rivers. When the war began he was a clerk in a leather store at Galena, Illinois. He had been educated at West Point, and had seen service in Mexico. He drilled the volunteers of the first company raised in the town, went with them to Springfield, where Governor Yates asked him to assist in the Adjutant-general's office. He mustered in the soldiers as they arrived, went with the regiments ordered to St. Louis, and was there on that morning when General Lyon marched out and captured the camp of the secessionists. The Governor appointed him colonel of the Twenty-first Illinois Regiment. He had been commissioned a brigadier-general, and had arrived in Cairo.

The Confederates had invaded Kentucky, violating the neutrality which the State attempted to assume. Bishop Leonidas Polk had left the ministry of the Episcopal Church, and had been appointed a major-general by Jefferson Davis. With several thousand men he took possession of Columbus, twenty miles below Cairo. The next morning after General Grant reached Cairo a Union scout came to him and said that the Confederates were getting ready to start from Columbus to seize Paducah, at the mouth of the Tennessee River. General Fremont, at St. Louis, General Grant's superior commander, was informed by Grant that he intended to send several regiments up the river that night and get ahead of the rebels. No instructions came to the contrary.

At daylight on the morning of the 6th the people of Paducah were astonished to see a fleet of steamboats crowded with Union soldiers moored at the landing. Most of the people were secessionists, and were greatly disturbed; they had expected to welcome General Jeff Thompson and an army of Confederates instead. The quick action of General Grant had upset all their expectations. The seizure of that town was an act of incalculable benefit to the Union.

We come to the first week in November. General Fremont was moving with an army towards south-western Missouri. Word reached General Grant that a large portion of the Confederates at Columbus were getting

HOUSE IN WHICH GENERAL GRANT WAS BORN.

ready to leave on steamboats, go down the Mississippi and up White River, in Arkansas, and join the force under General Price, and thus enable him to overwhelm Fremont. General Grant was to execute a movement which would keep the rebels from carrying out the plan. He directed General C. F. Smith, who was at Paducah, to march towards Columbus, but to halt before reaching that place. General Grant himself gathered up the troops at Cairo, about three thousand, and went down the river, accompanied by

two gunboats. A portion of the rebels were on the high bluffs of Columbus, where they had mounted heavy guns; but there was also an encampment on the low ground on the Missouri side, at Belmont. General Grant
landed a few men on the Kentucky side to make a demonstration towards
Columbus, as if he were intending to join General Smith, who was coming
from Paducah. He had no intention of fighting a battle, but made the
movement to keep the rebels from leaving. His soldiers were eager to
do something, and he determined to land at Belmont and break up the
Confederate camp at that point.

The Confederates at Columbus were at their wits' ends as to his intentions, but at daylight he drew in the men on the Kentucky side, crossed
the river, and landed the troops. He had two companies of cavalry, six
cannon, and five regiments. It is eight o'clock
when the troops advance. A mile and a half
brings them to the rebel pickets, which are
quickly driven in. The troops charge upon
the camp and capture it. They swing their
hats, then stack their arms and break ranks
to seize the plunder. Some of the officers, in
their enthusiasm, mount a stump and deliver
speeches glorifying the Union. While this
is going on, steamboats are ferrying several
thousand Confederates across the river from
Columbus. General Grant, finding it impossible to restore discipline, orders the camp to
be set on fire. The Confederates who have

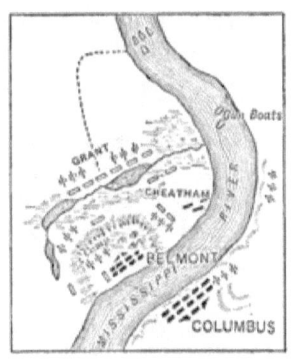

MAP OF BATTLE OF BELMONT.

fled to the bank of the river, finding that they are not pursued, and that
reinforcements are landing, reform, advance along the bank, flanking the
Union troops. "We are surrounded!" is the cry. Some of the officers
who have been making speeches suddenly become faint-hearted, and are
all but ready to surrender. "We have cut our way in, and we can cut our
way out," is the quiet remark of General Grant. The lines are formed,
the skirmishers advance, the Confederates are again driven, and the troops
reach the boats. General Grant rides alone out towards the enemy to
reconnoitre. He reaches a corn-field quite near the Confederates, looks at
them a moment, turns his horse, walks him a short distance before breaking into a gallop. General Polk and one of his staff see him. "You may
let your soldiers try their marksmanship on that Yankee, if you like," said
General Polk, but no one fired. The two gunboats were sending their
shells upon the Confederates. The troops were on board the steamers,

BATTLE OF BELMONT.

The Confederate batteries are seen on the bluff and at its base. The steamboats are drawn up against the western shore.

and the boats ready to move away, when General Grant came riding in from the corn-field. All supposed him to be on board. The captain of one of the steamers sees him, runs out the plank, and the noble horse which he is riding slides down the steep bank and walks the plank to the deck, with the rider in the saddle. General Grant goes upon the upper deck, and sits on a sofa a moment in the captain's room. He rises, and an instant later a bullet passes where he has been sitting.

It has been a sharp battle; the Union loss is nearly five hundred, the Confederate, six hundred and forty-two. The newspapers of the North spoke of the battle as a defeat because General Grant went back to Cairo, but the object which he had in view was fully accomplished. The enemy did not send any troops to join General Price, nor were any sent to capture General Oglesby, who was fifty miles south-west of Cairo. The battle, instead of being a defeat, must therefore be regarded as a victory for the Union.

On this same day another engagement was taking place at Port Royal, on the coast of South Carolina, which in its results was of great value. On the morning of October 29th a fleet of gunboats, with the frigate *Wabash*, all under the command of Admiral Dupont, together with a great number of steamers carrying an army of twelve thousand men, commanded by General T. W. Sherman, sailed out from Fortress Monroe. None of the captains knew whither they were bound, but each had a letter which was to be opened after sailing. No one in the fleet, except Admiral Dupont and General Sherman, was supposed to know the destination of the expedition; but there were so many traitors in Washington that on the next morning Mr. Benjamin, Confederate Secretary of War in Richmond, telegraphed to Governor Pickens, of South Carolina, that it was bound for Port Royal.

Port Royal is a deep and capacious harbor. The Government saw that the navy must have a harbor where the vessels blockading Charleston, Savannah, and all the other ports, could obtain coal and make repairs. The Confederates had erected two forts to defend it — Fort Walker, on Hilton Head, and Fort Beauregard, on the opposite northern shore. There were fifty-two guns in both works. General Drayton, with several hundred men, held Fort Walker, and Colonel Donavant Fort Beauregard. The Confederates had a small fleet of steamers, under Commodore Tatnall, but they were not of much account.

It is half-past nine in the morning when the signal for attack flutters out from the mast-head of the *Wabash*. There are thirteen vessels in the fleet; they are to sail in a circle, delivering their fire first on one fort

and then on the other. The *Wabash* leads, followed by the *Susquehanna*
and the gunboats. The forts are the first to open fire, but with little effect, for the vessels are moving and the guns are not well aimed. When
half a mile away the sides of the vessels begin to flame, pouring solid shot
and shells into Fort Walker. Round and round, in an ellipse, the vessels
move in majestic order, the shells exploding in the forts, tossing up clouds
of sand and dismounting the guns. Three times the fleet rounds the circles, coming nearer Fort Walker, and sending such a storm into it that the
garrison flees in consternation through the woods. The gunboats steam up

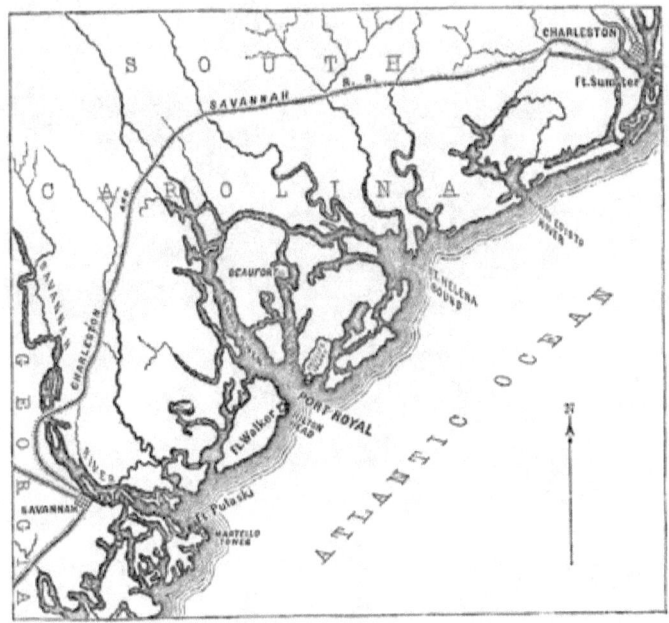

SOUTH CAROLINA COAST.

the bay to Beaufort, the beautiful town which has been the pride of the
wealthy planters and the citizens of Charleston, who have made it their
sea-side home, and who have been foremost to bring about secession, little
thinking how soon retribution would overtake them. They have thought
that the war would be far away on Northern soil. Through the morning
they have heard the thunder of the cannonade rolling up the river. Couriers have been stationed to bring the news of the expected discomfit-
ure of the fleet. There is sudden silence, a few moments of suspense,
and then a horseman rides into town with the news that the forts are

GENERAL GRANT ON HIS HORSE GOING ON BOARD THE STEAMER.

abandoned and the gunboats are on their way up the bay. Never before was there such consternation in Beaufort. There is running to and fro, wringing of hands, quick loading of wagons, shoutings to the slaves to go to the main-land; but instantly the negroes disappear in the woods or hide in their cabins. The planters and their families flee, leaving all behind. When the gunboats reach the town the negroes are having a saturnalia, making themselves at home in the stately mansions, drinking the costly wines, plundering and destroying property. The troops land and take possession of the town and restore order.

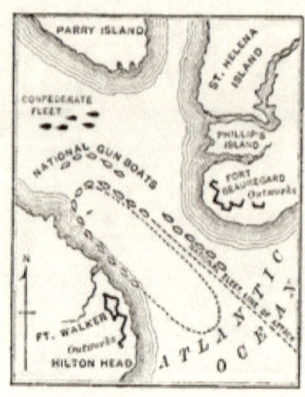

CAPTURE OF THE PORT ROYAL FORTS.

The year closes with the border states — Kentucky, Missouri, East Tennessee, West Virginia, and Maryland — loyal to the Union, all the other Southern States joining the Confederacy. Midsummer opened with disaster to the Union at Bull Run, but autumn closes with victory for the old flag at Port Royal.

CHAPTER VII.

THE BEGINNING OF 1862.

THE year 1862 opened with the Union armies, east and west, doing nothing. The Army of the Potomac in and around Washington numbered one hundred and thirty thousand men. Throughout the autumn there had been grand reviews, attended by the President and Cabinet, members of Congress, and great crowds of people. There had been much pomp and parade, and promise as to what the army would do; but 1861 closed with nothing accomplished, and no plan of a campaign on the part of General McClellan. New troops were constantly arriving, and by midwinter the army around Washington numbered nearly two hundred thousand. The inaction of General McClellan was producing discontent throughout the country. Everything he had asked for had been granted, but as nothing had been accomplished, the people were beginning to lose confidence in him. The "peace party," which was opposed to the war, applauded his inaction, and the natural result was that those who were earnest for its prosecution began to think that his heart was not in it. He had issued an order that no damage should be done to the property of the Confederates; slaves were not to be molested. When the Hutchinson family—three brothers and a sister, who had given many concerts throughout the country—visited the camps and sang songs to cheer the soldiers, they were ordered to leave because some of their songs were anti-slavery in sentiment. From the beginning of the war the Potomac River had been closed to navigation by Confederate batteries along its southern bank. General McClellan made no attempt to reopen the river. Every night the correspondents sent the despatch, "All quiet along the Potomac," until it became a byword.

Seeing no indications of any movement by the Army of the Potomac, I left Washington for Kentucky, where General Buell was in command.

Tennessee had joined the Confederacy; Kentucky had not. The Governor of Kentucky was hoping that the State would take no part in the war. Jefferson Davis planned otherwise. Several thousand Confederate troops, under Major-general Polk, had entered the State and planted cannon on the bluffs of Columbus. The Confederates hoped that the act would make the State decide to join the Confederacy, but instead it made the people more determined than ever to stand by the Union.

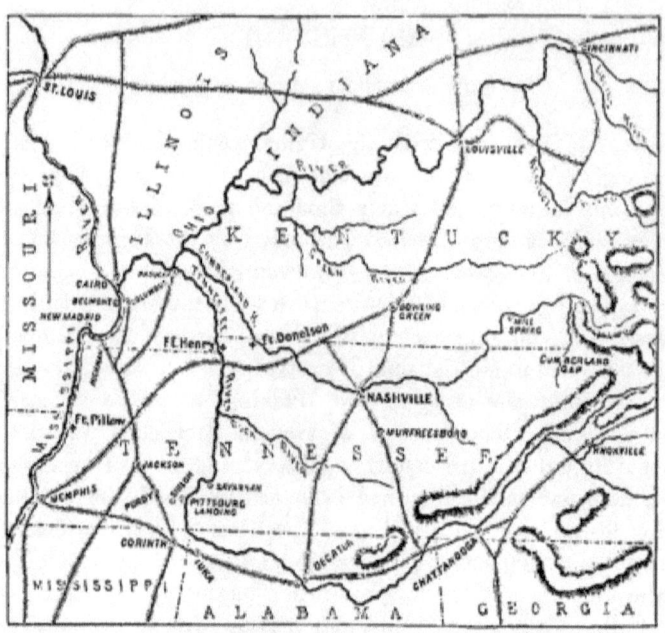

THE CAMPAIGN IN TENNESSEE.

Jefferson Davis appointed Albert Sydney Johnston, born in Kentucky, to command the Confederate troops in the West. Before he arrived, General Lovell laid out Fort Henry and Fort Donelson, on the Tennessee and Cumberland rivers. They were only twelve miles apart, close to the boundary of the two States. Five hundred slaves were set to work.

General Johnston, on the afternoon of his arrival at Nashville, sent General Buckner to take possession of Bowling Green with five thousand men, and ordered General Zollicoffer, with several thousand men, to advance from Knoxville, in Tennessee, through Cumberland Gap, and take position east of Bowling Green. Still farther east, General Humphrey Marshall, with three thousand troops, entered the State from Virginia and descended the valley of the Big Sandy River, which runs north to the

9

Ohio.   General Marshall thought that he could bring all eastern Kentucky under the Confederate Government.

James A. Garfield was at Columbus, Ohio, a young colonel, who was born in a log-cabin with a bark roof, a stone fireplace, and mud chimney.

GENERAL JAMES A. GARFIELD.

His parents were poor; they had a frying-pan, a bake-pan, and some wooden plates, and a few other things in the kitchen—the one room in the cabin. He began life by driving mules to tow a canal-boat. He chopped wood, helped a farmer make potash, and by hard work made his way through college. He had taught school, and had been president of a college in Ohio. He was colonel of the Forty-second Ohio Regiment, at Columbus. He received a despatch from General Buell, who was at Louisville, to send his regiment to Prestonburg, on the Big Sandy River, while he was to hasten to Louisville.

"If you were in command of the sub-department of eastern Kentucky, what would you do? Let me know to-morrow morning," said General Buell.

Through the night Colonel Garfield studied the map of Kentucky, the Big Sandy, the valleys, the gaps in the mountain-ranges leading to Virginia and Tennessee. He went over the census tables to see where he could find forage and supplies for troops, laid his plan before General Buell, and was appointed to command a brigade. He was directed to "drive the enemy back or cut him off." He had his own and the Fortieth Ohio and the remnant of the Fourteenth Kentucky—a half-organized regiment, poorly supplied with arms and clothing. He had no cannon. Rain was falling, but the soldiers marched through deep mud up the valley of the Big Sandy. They had no tents; at night they bivouacked in the woods, kindling great fires.

A steep and wooded hill, with rocky ledges at the summit and a creek winding through a narrow valley at its base, was the position selected by Marshall. With his four cannon he could sweep the valley. The valley was so narrow, and the hills so steep and high, that the Union troops could not turn his flank; they must attack in front.

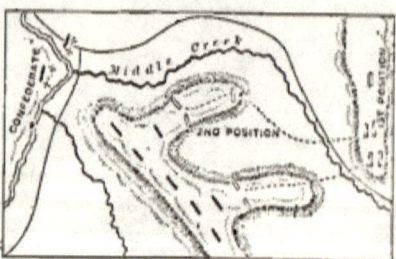

MAP OF MIDDLE CREEK.

On the evening of January 9, 1862, the Union troops found themselves face to face with the Confederates. A few shots were fired; but the cold gray winter night was setting in, and the soldiers of both armies lay down to sleep in the mud and rain, which changed to sleet, and beat pitilessly upon Union and Confederate alike. No fires were kindled. Garfield was in the valley, the Confederates on the hill, with every advantage of position, outnumbering him two to one, with four cannon, while he had not a single piece of artillery. In the morning the Union troops advanced.

General Marshall was getting ready to charge, but suddenly changed his mind, for down the valley he beheld twelve hundred Union troops coming as fast as they could run. They had been marching all day, and had come twenty miles through the mud since daylight. They had heard the thunder of the Confederate cannon rolling down the valley, and had hastened to take part in the fight.

General Marshall fears that he is to be flanked, and gives the order to retreat. The frightened Confederate soldiers throw away their guns and flee through the woods.

Night is closing in. Suddenly a bright light illumines the sky: General Marshall has set fire to his stores and supplies, and is fleeing through the mountain-passes towards Virginia. There has been little fighting, but that little has brought about a great result; it has secured all eastern Kentucky to the Union. It is the first break in the Confederate line of defence west of the Alleghanies.

Let us go up now to the head-waters of that beautiful stream, the Cumberland River. From its mountain springs it gurgles over a rocky bed westward to the town of Waitsboro. Just below that town the water is deep enough for small steamboats, which can come all the way from the Ohio, past Nashville, to that point.

A little farther down, on the south side of the Cumberland, is a grist and saw mill, also springs which gush from the hill-side. The place is known as Mill Springs.

General Zollicoffer was there with nine thousand troops. He had been a member of Congress from Tennessee, but had given heart and soul to the Confederate cause. He knew little about military affairs, and General George B. Crittenden was sent to take command. General Crittenden was a Kentuckian; his brother was a general in the Union army, and his father, who had been a Senator in Congress, was giving the strength of his declining years to maintain the Union.

Before General Crittenden arrived, General Zollicoffer, eager to advance, by using two steamboats and some flat-boats crossed the Cumberland and threw up intrenchments at Beech Grove, on the north bank of the river.

There was a brigade of Union troops at Somerset, under General Schoepf, twenty miles from Beech Grove, and another brigade at Columbia, thirty miles north-west, under General George H. Thomas, both moving towards Mill Springs.

While the Union troops are making their toilsome march along the miry roads, let us see how things look at Beech Grove. General Crittenden finds nine thousand men, but so many are sick that only six thousand are fit for duty. They have little to eat. The country around is poor;

the mire is so deep that the wagons which bring provisions and supplies cannot move. Many of the soldiers are armed with shot-guns; they are destitute of overcoats; their shoes are wearing out. Why have they left their homes to become soldiers? Because they have been led to believe that they owe allegiance to the State in which they were born rather than to the nation, and because they have dreamed of winning glory on the field of battle. There is no glory in remaining in camp. General Zollicoffer does not wish to wait for the Union troops to attack; he would rather march out and attack them. General Crittenden opposes the plan; but the colonels, the captains, the men—all are eager to advance. A council of officers decided in favor of the plan. General Thomas is only nine miles away. They will make a night march, attack him at daylight, rout him, then move on to Somerset and rout the troops under Schoepf. By one vigorous stroke they will sweep the Union troops back to the Ohio River.

The night is cold and dreary, the rain falling; but the Confederate soldiers hail with joy the news that they are to move out and attack General Thomas. They will eat breakfast in his camp upon rations supplied by the United States.

The war has become more than a conflict between two sections of the country. In Kentucky it is a war between old neighbors and friends—a civil war. Union soldiers from Tennessee are to fire into the faces of Confederate Tennessee soldiers. Though Kentucky has not joined the Confederacy, hot-blooded young men have left their homes to enlist in the Confederate service.

General Thomas, commanding the Union troops, was born in Virginia. He was in the battle of Buena Vista, in Mexico. He is clear-headed and self-possessed. His soldiers love him, for he is kind-hearted, brave, and looks after their comfort and welfare. He always has his eyes open. To guard against surprise, he stations his cavalry pickets out on all the roads leading to his camp, and behind them infantry pickets.

He reached Logan's Cross-roads on the night of January 17th. The troops pitched their tents on Mr. Logan's farm, and the cavalry pickets went two miles out on all the roads, with infantry behind them.

We see the Confederate cavalry mounting their horses at midnight at Beech Grove. Zollicoffer's brigade moves first—two cavalry battalions, one Mississippi and three Tennessee regiments, and Rutledge's battery, four guns. General Carroll follows with two Tennessee regiments, two cannon of McClung's battery, then the Sixteenth Alabama and two cavalry battalions.

The dim light of the winter morning is dawning (January 19th) when the foremost cavalryman comes upon the Union pickets.

"Halt! Who goes there?"

The answer is a Confederate pistol-shot.

A Union cavalryman goes down the road as fast as he can ride to Colonel Manson's tent. In an instant the drum is beating the long-roll.

General Thomas has four thousand men: the Tenth Indiana, Colonel Kise, and Fourth Kentucky, Colonel Frye, from Colonel Manson's brigade; the First and Second Tennessee and Twelfth Kentucky, from General Carter's brigade; the Ninth Ohio and Second Minnesota, from Colonel McCook's brigade. The three batteries are commanded by Captains Kenny, Randall, and Wetmore. He has only one battalion of cavalry. Besides these he has a battalion of engineers from Michigan and one company of the Thirty-eighth Ohio Regiment, who are ordered to guard the camp. Out from their tents leap the soldiers of the Tenth Indiana and Fourth Kentucky, and form in line across the road.

Ten minutes, and both regiments are ready and waiting the word of command. The Tenth Indiana is on the west side of the road in the woods, the Fourth Kentucky on the east side, both facing south. The men in blue, as they stand there with their muskets loaded and capped, see the skirmishers falling back, and in the dim and misty light the flashes of the muskets. And now they catch a glimpse of an advancing line of Confederates, who halt, raise their guns, and fire. It is a regiment from Mississippi. Behind the Mississippians come the Nineteenth Tennessee upon a run through a field. The battle furiously begins; volley after volley rolls from the opposing lines. The Fourth Kentucky is in rear of the Tenth Indiana.

"Where shall I go into position?" Colonel Frye asks.

"Go out and take position in those woods," Colonel Manson replies.

The Fourth Kentucky passes through a field, enters a piece of woods, and comes out into Mr. Logan's field. The men leap over a rail-fence and form once more. Suddenly from the other side of the field there comes a volley.

"Back to the other side of the fence!" Colonel Frye gives the order.

"Ha! ha! they are retreating!" the Confederates shout; they think that the Union troops are panic-stricken. Across the fields they rush, but suddenly five hundred muskets flame in their faces, and Kenny's Battery sends shell after shell through the advancing line, which comes to a stand-still.

The air is misty and the smoke so thick that the men in blue and the men in gray can see only the quick flashes of one another's guns.

Colonel McCook comes with his brigade. The Second Minnesota

swings up behind the Fourth Kentucky, and the Ninth Ohio takes the place of the Tenth Indiana. The Mississippians are in front of the Minnesota regiment. Colonel Frye rides down by the rail-fence. He sees in the dim light an officer on a white horse, wearing a rubber blanket concealing his uniform. Colonel Frye does not know him, but rides up so near that they might shake hands.

"We must not shoot our own men," says the officer.

"Of course not."

"Those are our men."

The officer points, but Colonel Frye cannot see any soldiers in that direction, and rides a few steps away. He turns his horse to look once more. Suddenly an officer by the side of the man on the white horse fires a pistol at Colonel Frye, missing him, but wounding his horse.

What! A Confederate! The man on the white horse not a Union officer! Colonel Frye raises his pistol, fires, and General Zollicoffer falls from his saddle dead. How strange Zollicoffer's mistake! for Colonel Frye has no cloak or blanket concealing his uniform.

For a half hour the struggle goes on east of the road. Stepping over, now, west of the road we see the Ninth Ohio fixing bayonets. They have fired away nearly all their ammunition, and they will finish the battle by a charge. The line closes—shoulder touching shoulder. They break into a run. The Confederate Tennesseeans give way. A panic seizes the whole Confederate line; officers and soldiers alike think only of saving themselves.

What a pitiful scene it was! More than four hundred Confederates killed and wounded, the living throwing away their guns and everything that hindered them. Back to Beech Grove, across the Cumberland River, they fled, most of them crossing on the steamboats, but some attempting to swim were swept away by the swirling ice-cold stream.

They had nothing to eat; all had been lost. Hungry, weary, faint, footsore, freezing, the regiments melted wholly away. It was a terrible blow; Kentucky was hopelessly lost to the Confederacy. The Union men in eastern Tennessee, hearing the news, took heart.

Never, never would they yield, but stand forever for the flag of the Union!

On January 9th I reached Cairo, with credentials from the Secretary of War to the general in command. I entered the headquarters—a mean room in an old building, up a flight of rickety stairs. "Come in," was the response to my knock. Entering, I found a gentleman with a close-cut beard, wearing a blue blouse, without sign of any rank, sitting on an empty nail-cask at a pine table, smoking a pipe, with a pile of papers before him. He had the appearance of being a clerk.

"Is General Grant in?" I asked.

"Yes, sir," was the reply.

"Will you be kind enough to give him this letter?"

Instead of carrying it to an adjoining room, the gentleman opened it, ran his eye over the page, greeted me cordially, and said, "I am happy to see you. Please take a nail-cask. Colonel Webster will give you a pass." It was my first interview with General Grant.

In the ship-yards at Cincinnati and St. Louis there had been a clattering of axes: carpenters hewing oaken timbers, building vessels — broad, flat-bottomed, with sloping sides, flat roofs—to be clad with iron plates. Never before had floated on the waters of the Ohio and Mississippi such strange craft.

A GUNBOAT OF THE MISSISSIPPI.

"They look like mud-turtles," said the soldiers when the gunboats *Essex, Carondelet, Cincinnati, St. Louis,* and *Benton* steamed up to the levee at Cairo.

But these queer-looking gunboats, with cannon peeping from their port-holes, were destined to play an important part in the war. Let us keep in mind that the war was a revolt against free labor. The working-men of the great States of the West, the iron-workers and the ship-carpenters, had wielded hammers and axes, and here were the vessels which they had constructed, with which they proposed to open once more to commerce the Cumberland, Tennessee, and Mississippi rivers.

The Cumberland and Tennessee run side by side northward from the northern boundary of the State of Tennessee. They are only twelve miles apart. Just south of the State line stood Fort Henry, on the east bank of the Tennessee, while Fort Donelson stood on the west bank of the Cumberland. There was no bluff at Fort Henry, and the mud fortification thrown up by slaves under the direction of Major Gilmer was on a low bank, screened by a thicket of willows. There were sixteen cannon —one of which threw a ball ten inches in diameter, one sixty-pounder, twelve thirty-two-pounders, and two twelve-pounders. They were so arranged that they could all be pointed down the river to knock the gunboats to pieces, or inland to throw shells upon troops advancing to attack it from the rear. Outside of the fort were rifle-pits and breastworks. The tall trees were cut down to form an abatis.

Inside the intrenchments were nearly four thousand men, under General Tilghman. At Columbus, on the Mississippi, were twenty-two thousand Confederates, under General Leonidas Polk. At Fort Donelson was General Buckner, with nearly twenty thousand troops. At Bowling Green, in Kentucky, on the south bank of the Big Barren River, in a very strong position, was General Johnston, with twelve thousand troops.

Opposite the Confederates, at Bowling Green, in central Kentucky, was a Union army, under General Buell. At Cairo was another army, under General Grant. General Garfield, by his victory in eastern Kentucky, and General Thomas, by the victory at Mill Springs, had broken the Confederate lines of defence. Where, now, would it be easiest for the Union troops to break through?

On January 28th Commodore A. H. Foote, commanding the gunboats at Cairo, sent this despatch to General Halleck at St. Louis: "General Grant and myself are of the opinion that Fort Henry can be carried with four gunboats and the troops."

"From Fort Henry," wrote General Grant, "it will be easy to operate either on the Cumberland, twelve miles distant, on Memphis, or Columbus."

If Fort Henry were taken, it would be easy to land an army on the east bank, march across and attack Fort Donelson in the rear; or the army could land on the west bank and attack Columbus in the rear.

"I strike where the enemy least expects me, and I move to turn his positions," were the military rules adopted by Napoleon.

If Fort Henry could be taken, it would turn the Confederate position.

There was so much to be done that a month passed before the gunboats were ready. But up the Ohio, on February 2d, they moved, followed by a fleet of steamboats, with ten regiments of soldiers crowding the cabins and the decks. The gunboats turned up the Tennessee. The melting snow on the far-off mountains was sending down a flood, which was overflowing all the lowlands. At daylight the next morning the steamboats ran their prows against the bank and tied them up to the trees. The troops went on shore. Scouts called at a farm-house.

"You never will take Fort Henry," said a woman.

ADMIRAL FOOTE.

"Oh yes, we shall; the gunboats will knock it to pieces."

"They will be blown sky-high before they get near the fort."

"How so?"

"The river is full of torpedoes."

The scouts reported the information to Admiral Foote, and the sailors, jumping into the boats, went out with grappling-irons, and in a short time fished up six torpedoes.

General Grant and Commodore Foote agreed that the gunboats should commence the attack at twelve o'clock.

"I shall take the fort in about an hour," said the commodore. "I shall commence firing when I reach the head of Panther Island, and it will take me about an hour to reach the fort, for I shall steam up slowly. I am afraid, general, that the roads are so bad the troops will not get around in season to capture the enemy. I shall take the fort before you get into position."

The boats reach the head of the island, and the fort is in full view. It is thirty-four minutes past twelve o'clock. There is a flash and a creamy cloud of smoke at the bow of the *Cincinnati*. An eight-inch shell screams through the air. The gunners watch its course; their practised eyes follow its almost viewless flight. The fort accepts the challenge, and instantly twelve guns open upon the advancing boats. The shot and shell plough furrows in the stream, and throw columns of water high in air.

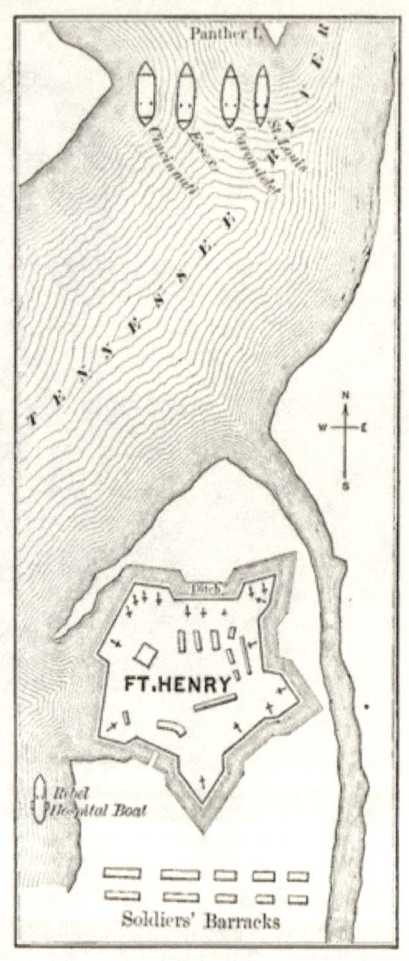

FORT HENRY.

The gunboats move on slowly and steadily; their fire is regular and deliberate. Every shot goes into the fort. The Confederate gunners are blinded and smothered by clouds of sand; the gun-carriages are crushed, splintered, and over-turned; men are cut to pieces. Something unseen tears them like a thunder-bolt. The fort is full of explosives. The heavy rifled gun bursts, crushing and killing those who serve it; the flag-staff is splintered and torn as by lightning.

Yet the fort replies. The gunners have the range of the boats, and nearly every shot strikes the iron plating. They are like the strokes of sledge-hammers, indenting the sheets, starting the fastenings, breaking the tough bolts. The *Cincinnati* receives thirty-one shots, the *Essex* fifteen. the *St. Louis* seven, and the *Carondelet* six.

Though struck so often, they move on. The distance lessens. Another gun is knocked from its carriage in the fort; another—another. There are signs that the contest is about over. But a shot strikes the *Essex* between the iron plates; it tears through the oaken timbers and into one of the steam-boilers. There is a great puff of steam; it pours from the port-holes, and the boat is enveloped in a cloud. She drops out of the line of battle. Her engines stop, and she floats with the stream. Twenty-eight of her crew are scalded, among them her brave commander, Captain Porter.

The Confederates take courage. They spring to their guns, and fire rapidly but wildly, hoping and expecting to disable the rest of the fleet. But Commodore Foote does not falter; he keeps straight on as if nothing had happened. A shell from the *Cincinnati* dismounts a gun, killing or wounding every gunner. The boats are so near that every shot is sure to do its work. The fire of the boats increases, while the fire of the fort diminishes. Coolness, determination, energy, perseverance, and power win the day. The Confederate flag comes down, and a white flag goes up. Cheers ring through the fleet. A boat puts out from the *St. Louis*. An officer jumps ashore, climbs the torn embankment, stands upon the parapet, and raises the Stars and Stripes.

Thus, in an hour and twelve minutes, the fort which the Confederates confidently expected would prevent the gunboats from ascending the river was forced to surrender, and there was unobstructed water communication to the very heart of the Confederacy. The line of defence was again broken.

There was but little loss of life in this engagement—twenty to thirty killed and wounded on each side.

Up the river steamed the gunboats, capturing the nearly completed Confederate gunboat *Eastport*. During the preceding months the Confederates have partly altered an old river steamboat into a gunboat. They had built it up with thick timber, and partly plated it with iron; but suddenly they cut the steam-pipes, chopped holes in the bottom, and fled to the woods. On the Union side during these months the men of the ironmills, the carpenters of St. Louis and Cincinnati, had constructed the gunboats, and there they were, making their way up the Tennessee to the border of Alabama.

Although Governor Harris, of Tennessee, and his fellow-confederates

THE GUNBOATS AT FORT HENRY.

have voted the State out of the Union; although the great mass of the people in western Tennessee are for the Confederacy, there are those who swing their hats and give a cheer, with the tears rolling down their cheeks, when they behold once more the dear old flag floating from the flag-staffs of the gunboats.

With consternation General Albert Sidney Johnston, at Bowling Green, read the message that came to him announcing the surrender of Fort Henry. Through the months his troops had been digging trenches, throwing up breastworks in front of the Union army under General Buell, but now it was lost labor. He must make a quick retreat, or General Grant with a great army would be in his rear. Johnston had twelve thousand men; Buell a much larger force, and was getting ready to advance.

There was a sudden commotion, a packing up of baggage, loading it into the cars and in wagons—barrels of flour, beef, pork, tents, cannon, ammunition. They set fire to buildings containing thousands of bushels of corn. In the engine-house of the railroad were six engines laid up for repairs. They piled wood around them and set it on fire and hastened away. The work of destruction of material forces had begun in the Confederacy.

On the morning of February 14th, General Mitchell's division of Union troops marched into Bowling Green. Mitchell looked at the locomotives.

"It will not take long to repair them," he said.

It was the difference between the North and the South. A few days later and the engines were running. Labor was winning its victories.

It is twelve miles from Fort Henry to Fort Donelson. There are two roads, which wind through the forest, with here and there a farm-house. The soil is not very fertile, and the farmers do not raise much corn; but the oak-trees in the fall of the year are full of acorns, and the farmers keep large herds of pigs, which roam the woods, feeding upon the nuts.

Out from Fort Henry marched the troops under General Grant—McClernand's and Smith's divisions—leaving General Lew. Wallace's division to hold that fort. The baggage-wagons had not arrived from Cairo, and the soldiers carried three days' rations of bread and meat in their haversacks. They bivouacked at night beside a brook, and kindled great fires, shooting the pigs and roasting them by the glowing coals. They sang songs, shouted, danced, told stories till the drums beat the tattoo; then they scraped the dead leaves into heaps for a bed, wrapped themselves in their blankets, and lay down to sleep.

While the Union army is working its way towards the Cumberland River, let us go in advance and look at Fort Donelson.

We see the town of Dover located where the river runs north-west, and then bends north. The ground rises fifty feet above the water; the stores and dwellings are on the hill-side.

Low down we see a bank of fresh earth, and higher up a second line of works, and seventeen cannon peeping from the embrasures—most of them thirty-two pounders—all pointing down the river. Those in the upper work are so high that they will pour a plunging fire upon the gun-boats when they steam up the river, while Admiral Foote will find that if he approaches near the fort he will not be able to elevate the muzzles of his cannon sufficiently high to do any damage.

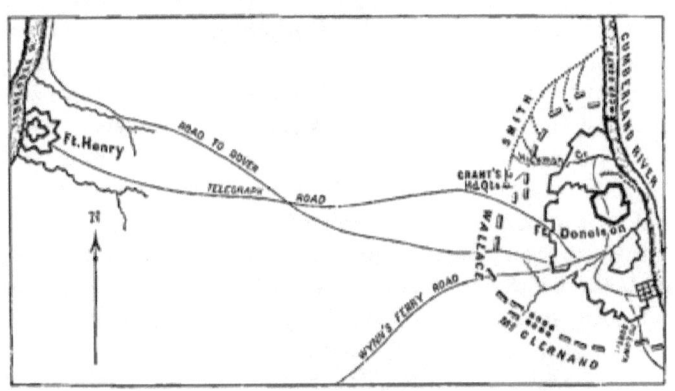

FORTS HENRY AND DONELSON.

From the south-west corner of the fort a line of breastworks runs south along the crest of a ridge. Following it a mile, we come to a deep ravine, with a creek flowing through it; crossing the creek, we follow the line, now bending east another mile to Lick Creek, which flows north to the river, and which is too deep to be forded.

The fortifications consist of three distinct parts—the water batteries and fort, the line of breastworks, and beyond them a line of rifle-pits and abatis.

The rifle-pits are built of logs. There is a space between the upper log and the one beneath it, behind which the Confederate riflemen can lie and pick off the Union troops. The country beyond is broken into ridges and hills covered with forests.

At midnight on the day of the loss of Fort Henry the Confederate troops from that fort, under Colonel Heiman, reach Fort Donelson. Troops arrive from Nashville, sent by General Johnston. General Gideon J. Pillow arrives on the 9th. He had served in the Mexican War. It was said that in that war he ignorantly constructed a fortification with the ditch on the wrong side of the embankment; but he had an exalted opinion of his abilities, was jealous of his superior officers, besides being ever ready to find fault with their plans. He once attempted to supersede General Scott. Another Confederate general arrived on the 11th, Simon B. Buckner, who several years before the outbreak of the war had had a falling out with Pillow, and their personal relations were not cordial. General Johnston was very unfortunate in his selection of officers for the defence of this important point. The major-general in command was John B. Floyd, the man who, as Secretary of War under President Buchanan, had done what he could to furnish the Southern States with arms, who had been indicted by the Grand Jury at Washington as a thief for the embezzlement of the funds of the United States—this man, with no military experience, by virtue of the date of his commission was senior officer. It is quite certain that General Buckner, the junior general officer, was much better fitted to command. General Floyd arrived on the 13th and assumed command, which was not relished by Pillow.

There were twenty-eight regiments of Confederate infantry, besides two battalions, one regiment of cavalry, six batteries of light artillery, and seventeen heavy guns. General Buckner, with six regiments and two batteries, was assigned to hold the ground north-west of the town; the rest of the army—six brigades—the remainder of the line, under General Pillow. General Bushrod R. Johnston was selected by General Floyd as chief of staff, and a great deal of the energy of the defence of Donelson was due to him and General Buckner rather than to Floyd or Pillow. The first brigade in line was Heiman's, holding the right; then Davidson's, Drake's, Wharton's, McCausland's, and Baldwin's, with twenty-four cannon. During the winter four hundred log-cabins had been built, so that the Confederates were much better sheltered than the Union troops, who had no tents, but who must bivouac on the frozen ground.

The Union army left Fort Henry on the 11th of February. On the 12th the videttes come in sight of the Confederate pickets outside the breastworks. General McClernand's division swings south towards Lick Creek, while General Smith takes position north-west of the fort. General Grant makes his headquarters at the house of Mrs. Crisp, a log-cabin with a chimney outside. He has twenty-five regiments and seven batteries: in all, forty - two guns. McClernand's division has three brigades — Oglesby's, W. H. L. Wallace's, and Morrison's—all the troops from Illinois, with the exception of a company of United States cavalry. General Smith's division consists of McArthur's, Lauman's, Cook's, and Morgan L. Smith's

10

brigades.   One of the regiments in Lauman's brigade is commanded by Colonel Berge.   The men are sharp-shooters; their rifles have telescopes attached.   They have fired at targets till they have become expert in aim.

The morning of the 13th dawns.   The sharp-shooters have filled their cartridge-boxes, and are in advance of the rest of the army, working their way towards the Confederate lines.   They crouch behind logs or lie upon the ground, screened from sight by the gnarled roots of the trees.   Before the sun is up there is a rattling fire between the sharp-shooters and the Confederate pickets.   A little later the Confederate cannon throw shells at random towards the Union lines.   Some of the Union batteries make their way through the thick woods, and come into position and aim at the puffs of smoke which rise above the trees.

General Grant sees that he has not troops enough to cover the entire line, and sends a courier to Fort Henry for General Lew. Wallace's division.   Other regiments are on the way, coming up the river, which are turned over to Wallace upon his arrival, who organizes them into brigades, commanded by Colonel Cruft and Colonel Thayer.   He comes into position between Smith and McClernand, directly west of Fort Donelson, forming the centre of the army.   The arrival of these troops enables McClernand to move farther east towards the river, and close the road which leads south from Dover, thus cutting off all chance of escape on the part of the Confederates in that direction.

While this is going on, the gunboat *Carondelet* comes up the river and opens fire upon the batteries with her long-range guns.

One cannot understand just what General Floyd intended to do.   Probably he had no definite plan.   Had he been a commander of ability he would have fallen suddenly, with an overwhelming force, upon McClernand before the arrival of General Wallace, when there was a wide gap between the right and left wings of Grant's army, but he waited instead till ten additional Union regiments had arrived.   He waited to be attacked instead of attacking, and lost his best opportunity of winning a victory.

The morning sun was bright and clear, the air balmy as April, but before night the wind changed, clouds drifted across the sky, the wind increased to a gale, and a furious snow-storm swept over the contending armies.   Many of the Union soldiers had thrown off their overcoats and left them behind in the march, and now paid the penalty by shivering through the night.

General Grant does not wish to bring on an engagement.   He has closed all the roads leading from Fort Donelson.   The Confederates can receive no supplies except by the river.   He hopes, with the aid of the

ATTACK OF THE GUNBOATS ON FORT DONELSON.

The view is south-west. The attack of General Smith was from the ground behind the house on the right.

gunboats under Commodore Foote, to capture the entire force without much fighting. The fleet arrives on the morning of the 14th. While Commodore Foote is getting ready to open fire upon the fort, General McClernand is taking matters into his own hands. General Grant has directed him to do nothing that will bring on an engagement, but McClernand is a lawyer, a nervous, restless, brave, impulsive man, and was a member of Congress before the war. He has not yet comprehended that strict obedience to the command of his superior officer, except in extreme cases, is one of the most important rules. A Confederate battery on a hill in front of Morrison's brigade is sending its shells upon his line. There are three Confederate batteries, which have a wide sweep, and are very annoying to McClernand. His own batteries reply. When the Confederates stop firing, McClernand, thinking that they are silenced, resolves to order Morrison to advance and capture them. He does not take into account the five regiments of infantry under Heiman crouching behind the breastworks near by.

There are three regiments in Morrison's Union brigade. They move through the woods and come to the foot of the slope in front of the Confederate works. Instantly the Confederate cannon open upon them. The Forty-ninth Illinois, Morrison's own regiment, comes into a clearing, and moves more rapidly than the other regiments. The men begin to fall, but they open fire upon the cannoneers. Captain Maney, commanding one of the Confederate batteries, is wounded; also his first and second lieutenants. The Union troops thinking that with a rush the battery will be theirs, give a cheer and run up the hill. Suddenly the breastworks flame. The Confederates, resting their muskets on the logs in front of them, fire a volley. Men firing down hill, especially in the excitement of battle, almost always aim too high. Men fall from the Union ranks, but for fifteen minutes they stand on the slope of the hill loading and firing— not only the Forty-ninth Illinois, but the Seventeenth and Forty-eighth. They fall back at last, but at the foot of the hill halt, reform their lines, advance once more, again fall back, and a third time go up almost to the breastworks to retreat again, leaving many of their number upon the dead leaves, close up to the works. It is a horrible sight which they behold when they see the leaves set on fire by the burning wadding of the Confederate cannon, and the flames sweeping over the wounded, whom they cannot help. More than three hundred men—just how many we do not know—have fallen in this assault made against the orders of General Grant.

Not till three o'clock in the afternoon were the gunboats ready to attack. During the two days of waiting, the *Carondelet* has thrown one hundred and thirty-nine shot into the fort, dismounting three of the guns. All the cannon in the fort have replied, and sent hundreds of solid shot in return, but only two have done any damage. One has gone through the side of the boat, and killed or wounded a dozen men. Several men have been killed in the fort.

The plan of Commodore Foote is to attack the batteries on the bank of the river, silence them, then run past the town, and cut off all commu-

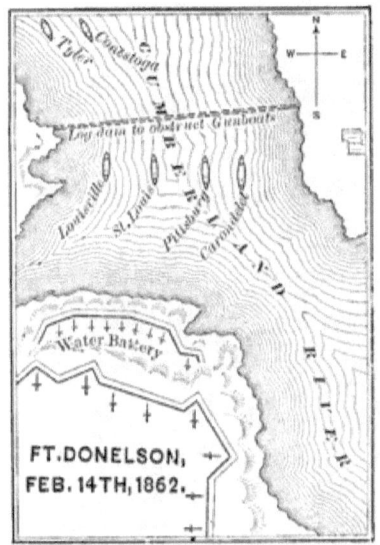

FT. DONELSON,
FEB. 14TH, 1862.

nication between the army and Nashville, which will soon compel Floyd to surrender. The fleet comes into position. The boats are to steam slowly and fire deliberately. It probably would have been better to have gone ahead with the utmost speed and run past, without attempting to silence the batteries. If attempted, it might possibly have been accomplished.

When within one mile of the fort the *St. Louis* opens fire, quickly followed by the *Pittsburg*, *Louisville*, and *Carondelet*. The *Conestoga* and *Taylor*, wooden vessels, are in rear, firing at long range. The battle opens earnestly. There is the deafening roar of the guns, the crash of solid shot, the bursting of shells, whirring of the ragged pieces, ripping up of the iron plating, and loosening of bolts. The boats move steadily on. The mile lessens to half a mile; the smoke-stacks are riddled, and the fire under the boilers, for want of proper draught, begins to grow dull, reducing the speed. But on they move till within one-quarter of a mile, when a shot strikes the pilot-house of the *Carondelet*, killing the pilot. A solid shot cuts the rudder-chains of the *Carondelet*, and she became unmanageable. The thirty-two-pound balls go through the oaken sides of the boats as you can throw pease through wet paper. A shot splintered the helm of the *Pittsburg*, and that boat also became unmanageable. A third shot crashed through the pilot-house of the *St. Louis*, killing the pilot instantly. Commodore Foote was standing by his side, and was sprinkled with the blood of the brave man. The shot broke the wheel and knocked down a timber, which wounded the commodore in the foot. He sprang

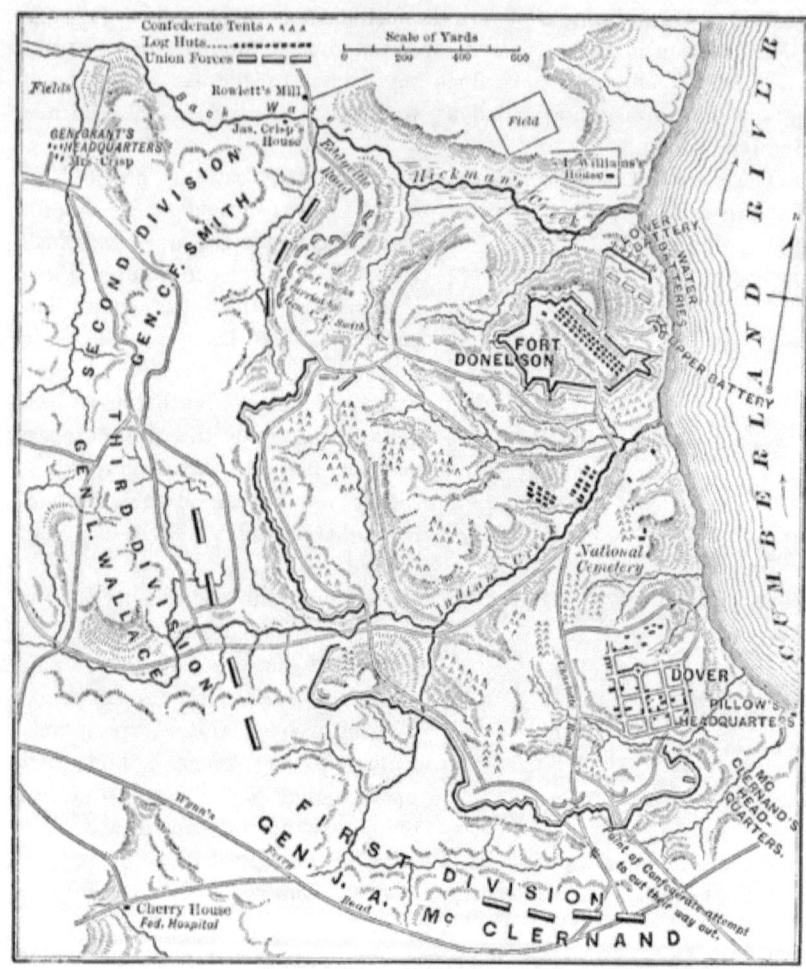

MAP OF FORT DONELSON, AS INVESTED BY GENERAL GRANT; BASED ON THE OFFICIAL
MAP OF GENERAL J. B. McPHERSON.

to the deck, limped to another steering apparatus, and endeavored with
his own hands to keep the vessel's head to the stream; but the other
apparatus also had been shot away. Sixty-one shots had struck the *St.
Louis*; some had passed through from stem to stern. The *Louisville*
had received thirty-five; twenty-six had crashed into and through the
Carondelet. One of her guns had burst, killing and wounding six of the
crew. The *Pittsburg* had been struck twenty-one times. All but the

Louisville, of the iron-plated boats, were unmanageable. At the very last moment—when the difficulties had been almost overcome—the commodore was obliged to hoist the signal for retiring. Ten minutes more, five hundred feet farther, and the Confederate trenches would have been swept from right to left their entire length. When the boats began to drift down the stream the Confederates were running from their guns, to escape the fearful storm of grape and canister which they thought would soon sweep over them. Fifty-four were killed and wounded on the gunboats in this attack.

General Floyd called a council of war, which met that Friday evening.

"I am satisfied," he said, "that Grant will bring up all his reinforcements, and will be able to prevent our getting supplies. I propose to attack him at daylight to-morrow morning. One-half of the army under General Pillow will attack McClernand's division, while General Buckner with the other wing will attack General Smith."

General Floyd hoped by this movement to throw the Union troops into confusion. At any rate, by driving McClernand, the Confederate army would be able to get away before Grant's reinforcements arrived. All preparations were made. The soldiers received extra rations, their cartridge-boxes were filled, and the regiments placed in position. All night long the marching and countermarching went on.

Saturday morning, out from the trenches moves Baldwin's brigade, Pillow's division in advance, and Drake's and Simonton's brigades following. The soldiers pick their way slowly through the woods. The skirmishers deploy, and come sooner than they expected upon the Union pickets in front of General Oglesby's brigade. The drummers of that brigade were beating the reveille when there came the sharp crack of rifles. The Union soldiers sprang to their feet.

General Pillow's troops marched south-west on the Ferry Road, as it was called, half a mile, then turned to the north-west. The Twenty-sixth Mississippi began the attack; but instead of catching Oglesby's men asleep, they found them wide awake and in line.

"The enemy is in front of me in force," was the message sent by Colonel Baldwin to Pillow, who moved forward the Eighth Kentucky and Twentieth Mississippi, making a fierce attack on Oglesby. The conflict was in the woods. There were no tall trees, but underbrush and scrubby oaks. There was a field with a rail-fence around it. There were ravines and knolls. In some places the bushes were so thick that you could see but a few feet. On such ground the battle raged—at first a rattling fire, then the thunder of the batteries, then a deep and heavy roll from thousands of muskets at once. Oglesby holds his ground till his men are out of ammunition. McArthur with his brigade does the same. But Pillow has the most men, and finally drives them. He falls upon W. H. L. Wallace's brigade, on the left of Oglesby, who has six Illinois regiments, with McAllister's two twenty-four-pound howitzers, and Taylor's, Schwartz's, and Dresser's batteries.

The falling back of McArthur and Oglesby exposes Wallace's right flank, and he falls back to a new position, making in part a change of front along a low ridge. The Confederates rush forward, but are swept back. They attempt to take McAllister's guns, but are driven. Farther round, facing north, move Pillow's troops.

"I must have reinforcements," is the word from McClernand to Wallace, who sends Cruft's brigade.

Just at this moment Buckner's division comes out of the intrenchments, passing in front of the rifle-pits at the foot of the hill to attack W. H. L. Wallace's left. Two guns of Taylor's Battery which have been firing towards the south wheel round towards the north-east and pour canister upon the Confederates. Three-fourths of Floyd's troops are falling upon McClernand's one division. They seize several of Schwartz's and McAllister's guns. Wallace sees that he must retreat, but his troops fall back steadily, loading and firing.

At eleven o'clock General Pillow has folded the Union line so far back that the road is open for the withdrawal of the Confederates. Why does not Floyd improve the opportunity? Because General Pillow is a weak, vain, egotistical man. He has led the movement, and wishes to reap all the glory. He thinks that he has defeated General Grant and routed his army. Ignoring Floyd, he sends this despatch to Nashville to General Johnston: "On the honor of a soldier, the day is ours." He regarded himself as a great general, and looked down upon Floyd, his superior in command, as only a political general, ignorant of the art of war. Without consulting Floyd, he ordered Buckner to march out and attack the Union troops. Buckner obeyed the order, and moved towards the position occupied by General Lew. Wallace, who at the moment was talking with Colonel Rawlins, of General Grant's staff. An officer came riding down the road as fast as his horse could run. "Save yourselves! All is lost!" he shouted. But Wallace, instead of saving himself, put his troops in motion up the road to confront Buckner. He meets W. H. L. Wallace riding coolly to the rear with what troops he has left.

"Are they pursuing?"

"Yes."

" How far behind ?"

" You will have just about time to form your line right here."

The men of Thayer's brigade come into line upon the run.   Up the road leap the horses of Wood's Battery, the men jumping from their limbers and wheeling the guns into position.   A moment later the battle opens with great fury.   The struggle is in the woods.   A cloud of smoke rises above the trees.   The hazel-bushes are whipped into shreds by the bullets.   The Confederates can make no impression upon this line of men who have thus thrown themselves across their path.   W. H. L. Wallace and Oglesby are reforming in the rear.   An hour passes, and then there comes a lull.

General Grant the while has been on the gunboat *St. Louis*, in consultation with Commodore Foote.   He has heard no cannonade ; no uproar of musketry has fallen upon his ears, nor intelligence of the attack reached him.   He is on his way to his headquarters at Mrs. Crisp's house, a log-cabin, when he meets Captain Hillyer of his staff, very white in the face over what has happened.   He is five miles from the scene of conflict.   The mud is deep; he rides through it as best he can, to find the men in groups, the regiments disorganized, their cartridge-boxes empty.   There is an abundant supply of ammunition, but the officers have not thought of refilling the empty boxes.

> "There is a tide in the affairs of men
> Which, taken at its flood, leads on to fortune."

A great hour has come to the man, who a few months ago was selling leather in Galena, so obscure a citizen that very few of his townsmen even knew that such a man as Ulysses S. Grant existed.   He turns to his chief of staff, Colonel Webster, and says, "Some of our men are pretty badly demoralized, but the enemy must be more so, for he has attempted to force his way out, but has fallen back ; the one who attacks now will be victorious, and the enemy will have to be in a hurry if he gets ahead of me."

On that instant decision hangs all the future—of Donelson, Vicksburg, Chattanooga, and Appomattox.   Intuition, with clear reasoning, leads him to correct conclusions.   The Confederates have come out in force ; their lines inside the fort must be thin somewhere, and now is the time to break them.

" Fill your cartridge-boxes ; quick—and get into line ; they are trying to escape ; they must not be allowed to do so !" he shouts, and the officers of his staff ride along the lines repeating it.   As an organist touching the keys of the mighty instrument brings the myriad pipes responsive to his touch, so this man, whom the world has not yet heard of, brings the thousands of human wills upon the instant responsive to his own. A moment ago they were despondent, but now their cheers ring out upon the wintry air. They fill their boxes, take their places in line, and stand ready to obey commands. Five minutes ago, confusion; now, discipline and order.

In a moment the plan of attack is decided upon. General Smith's division, which has not been engaged, will attack with all its energy. Smith had advanced his skirmishers in the morning. He is an old soldier; of all Grant's troops his are the best disciplined. Colonel Cook's brigade is directed to make a feint of attacking the fort. Major Cavender brings his heavy guns into position and opens a furious cannonade, under cover of which Colonel Lauman's brigade is to advance upon the rifle-pits on the outer ridge. If he can get possession of these, Cavender can plant his guns there and rake the inner trenches.

The Confederates, Colonel Hanson's brigade—the Second Kentucky, Twentieth Mississippi, and Thirtieth Tennessee—are in the rifle-pits. There are six pieces of artillery and another brigade behind the inner intrenchments, all ready to pour their fire upon the advancing columns. Colonel Hanson's men lie secure behind the breastworks, their rifles thrust between the logs. It is fifteen or twenty rods to the bottom of the slope, and there you find the fallen trees, with their branches interlocked, and sharp stakes driven into the ground. Beyond is the meadow where Lauman forms his brigade.

General Smith leads the Union troops—Lauman's men—to the meadow, while Colonel Cook moves upon the left and begins the attack. The soldiers hear far down on the right Wallace's division driving the enemy from the hill.

It is almost sunset. The rays of light fall upon the backs of Lauman's men and into the faces of the Confederates. The advancing brigade is in solid column of regiments, the Second Iowa in front; then the Twenty-fifth Indiana, the Seventh and Fourteenth Iowa—four firm and unwavering lines, which throw their shadows forward as they advance. Birge's sharp-shooters are flung out on each flank.

The brigade halts upon the meadow. General Smith rides along the line and informs the troops that they are to take the rifle-pits with the bayonet alone. He sits firmly on his horse, and his long gray hair, falling almost to his shoulders, waves in the evening breeze. The Confederate cannon cut them through with solid shot; shells burst above and around them; men drop from the ranks, or are whirled into the air; there are sudden gaps, but not a man flinches. They look not to the rear, but towards

the front. There are the fallen trees, the hill, the line of a thousand muskets, the cannon thundering from the height beyond. There is no whis-
pering in those solid ranks, no loud talking; nothing but the "Steady!
steady!" of the officers.

They move across the meadow. A line of flame runs along the Confederate works. Men drop from the advancing ranks to lie forever still
beneath the forest-trees. With all the energy of life centred in one effort
the living pass on, charging up the hill into the white smoke, driving the
Confederates. The woods resound with their lusty cheers as they take
possession of the works.

Going down to Lew. Wallace's line, we see the Eighth Missouri and
Eleventh Indiana regiments, under Morgan L. Smith, ready to advance.
He lights a cigar and gives the order to move on. A bullet strikes the
cigar from his lips. A soldier gives him another. "Thank you." He
does not forget to be courteous, though the air is thick with bullets. The
two regiments, followed by others, rush up the hill, reach the road over
which the Confederates intended to retreat, closing it once more.

There was a council of Confederate officers at General Floyd's headquarters. Nearly all the brigade commanders were present. They were
downhearted. General Floyd and General Pillow blamed General Buckner for not advancing earlier.

"I advanced as soon as I could, and my troops fought as bravely as
others," said Buckner.

"Well, here we are, and it is useless to renew the attack with any hope
of success. The men are exhausted," said Floyd.

"We can cut our way out," said Major Brown, commanding the Twentieth Mississippi.

"Some of us might escape, but the attempt would be attended with
great slaughter," said Floyd.

"We have got to surrender, for aught I see," said an officer.

"I will not surrender the command; neither will I be taken prisoner,"
said Floyd.

"I don't intend to be taken prisoner," added Pillow.

There were three small steamboats in the river. Floyd marched his
Virginia regiments on board. Pillow accompanied him. The boats swung
into the stream and moved up the river. So they fled, leaving Buckner
to surrender to General Grant.

At daybreak a white flag waved above the breastworks, and an officer
came out with a letter for General Grant, asking for an armistice till noon.

"No terms other than unconditional and immediate surrender can be accepted. I propose to move immediately upon your works," was the answer. General Buckner has no alternative, and accepts the terms.

I had passed the night on a steamboat with the fleet. Leaping ashore, I climbed over the embankment of the water-batteries, where the cannon, dismounted by the shot from the gunboats, were lying — one with its muzzle knocked off, others half buried in the yellow earth. The regiments of General Smith's division were marching into the fort, their banners waving in the bright sun, the bands playing. Down by the river and in the town were the Confederate regiments, their arms stacked, their knapsacks thrown upon the ground. They were woe-begone, weary, and hungry. They were kindling fires, using the picket-fences of the gardens. They felt that they had fought bravely, but that the battle had been lost through the incapacity of Floyd and Pillow. They said that Floyd was not only a thief but an imbecile.

Passing through the shivering ranks, receiving courteous treatment from the soldiers, I entered the old hotel, with a wide veranda covering its front, and found General Buckner eating his scant breakfast of poor bacon, corn-bread, and coffee. General Grant arrived about noon. I was present at the formal surrender of the troops. The interview between Grant and Buckner was in the cabin of the steamboat *Uncle Sam.*

In the cabin lay Colonel John A. Logan upon a cot. He had been wounded, and his wife was by his side ministering to his needs. On the day of the battle the Confederate force, so far as can be ascertained, exceeded twenty thousand. More than fourteen thousand soldiers were surrendered. The Union troops numbered about twenty-seven thousand.

Let us go up to Nashville on this Sunday morning. At noon on Saturday General Pillow had sent his despatch: "On the honor of a soldier, the day is ours."

There is great rejoicing. The newspapers have put out bulletins, and the crowds in the streets are reading them:

"Enemy retreating! Glorious result! Our boys following and pressing their rear! A complete victory!"

A horseman comes tearing through the street, shouting "Fort Donelson has surrendered, and the Yankees are coming!"

Never before such an excitement in Nashville as at that moment. People began to pack up their goods, loading them on wagons.

Before noon the steamboats arrived with Floyd and Pillow. Johnston's troops soon came from Bowling Green, passing through the city towards Murfreesboro. The people had supposed that Johnston would defend the city, but when they saw the troops moving away they became frantic.

When the army was across the Cumberland, the beautiful wire suspension-bridge which had cost more than two hundred thousand dollars was destroyed. The Confederates had more than a million dollars' worth of supplies in the city which they could not remove. The people rushed into the storehouses, helped themselves to flour, sugar, meat, clothing, shoes, and whiskey.

In an hour they passed from wild enthusiasm to despair. There was one Union man in Nashville who had stood resolutely for the old flag—Stephen Driver—who before the war was a sea-captain, sailing from Salem, in Massachusetts, to foreign lands. Once, when in a foreign port, he rendered important service to the place, and the people presented him with a beautiful flag. A priest pronounced a blessing upon it as it rose to the mast-head of his ship, and he made a solemn promise to ever defend it, with his life if need be. He had made Nashville his home. He opposed secession. When the war began he was obliged to secrete the flag. He sewed it into a quilt, and every night slept beneath it. He named it "Old Glory." Many times the Confederate soldiers searched his house to find it. "I shall yet raise it above the State-house!" he said to them. They threatened him with death, and he bade them do their worst. His hour of triumph came when the troops under Buell entered Nashville. He told the soldiers the story of "Old Glory," brought it out, went with them to the roof of the State-house, and flung it to the breeze, with the men in blue swinging their caps and shouting their hurrahs.

CHAPTER VIII.

THE SPRING OF 1862.

THE theatre of the war was wide, and the drama one of many scenes. The first one in the month of March, 1862, was in the far West, on the line between Missouri and Arkansas.

There were at the breaking out of the war 50,000 Indians in New Mexico, 30,000 in Texas, 20,000 in Kansas and Nebraska : in all there were more than 400,000 who received supplies from the Government.

Very soon after the war began, Albert Pike, who was born in Boston, Massachusetts, who lived in Arkansas, and who was known to the world as a poet, was sent by Jefferson Davis to make a treaty with the Indians of the South-west. He told the Indians that they had been wronged by the United States ; that the Confederacy was thenceforth to be the government of the country; and that they would be well cared for.

He induced the chiefs to call the Indians together, and a great council was held August 21, 1861. Four thousand braves were there. John Ross was the principal chief of the Cherokees, and signed a treaty to act with the Confederate Government. The Creeks joined them. They were supplied with arms, and in a short time several thousand warriors were enrolled as soldiers in the Confederate army.

Sterling Price and Benjamin McCulloch were commanders of the Confederate troops, but they could not act in harmony, and General Earl Van Dorn was placed in command of the Department west of the Mississippi. He was born in Missouri, was educated at West Point, fought in the war with Mexico, and had deserted the flag of his country. When the war began he gathered a band of Texans and captured the troops of the United States Army in that State.

Jefferson Davis appointed him to command the Department, hoping that he would induce the young men of Missouri to enlist in the army. There was great rejoicing in the Confederate army when he arrived. Forty cannon fired a salute. He made an address.

"Soldiers," he said, "behold your leader. He comes to show you the way to glory and immortal renown. He comes to hurl back the minions of the despots at Washington, whose ignorance, licentiousness, and brutality are equalled by their own craven natures. They come to free your slaves, lay waste your plantations, burn your villages, and abuse your loving wives and beautiful daughters."

He issued a proclamation, which was distributed by messengers through all the towns of Arkansas and northern Louisiana. Confederate sympathizers in Missouri distributed it in that State.

"We have voted to be free," it read; "we must now fight to be free, or present to the world the humiliating spectacle of a nation of braggarts more contemptible than the tyrants who seek to enslave us. The flag of our country is waving on the southern border of Missouri, planted there by my hands under authority of our chief magistrate. It represents all that is dear to us in life. Shall it wave there in melancholy loneliness as a fall leaf in our primeval forests, or shall its beautiful field and bright stars flaunt in the breeze over the bright fields of Arkansas, Texas, and of Louisiana, as they are marshalling to do battle with Missouri for victory, for honor, and for independence?

"Awake, young men of Arkansas, and arm! Beautiful maidens of Louisiana, smile not upon the craven youth who may linger by your hearths when the rude blast of war is sounding in your ears! Texas chivalry, to arms! Hardship and hunger, disease and death are preferable to slavish subjugation; and a nation with a bright page in history and a glorious epitaph is better than a vassalled land, with honor lost and a people sunk in infamy!"

To fire the hearts of the people of Arkansas and arouse his troops to action, he forged a telegraphic despatch that there had been a great battle on the Mississippi, in which three Union gunboats were destroyed and twenty thousand Union troops were killed, wounded, or taken prisoners.

General Pike, who had been commissioned brigadier-general by Jefferson Davis, was placed in command of the Indians.

The whole force, under Van Dorn, moved towards Pea Ridge to crush the only Union army south-west of St. Louis, under General Curtis, who had advanced to the boundary line of Arkansas. He had eleven thousand troops: the brigades of Osterhaus and Asboth, under General Sigel, the brigades of Davis and Carr, with thirty-eight cannon and howitzers.

General Van Dorn's army had been hastily gathered. The Arkansas, Louisiana, and Texas troops numbered eleven thousand, and were commanded by General McCulloch; the Missouri troops were under General Price, and numbered eight thousand. General Pike had two white regiments besides the Indians, numbering four thousand, making the Confederate army above twenty thousand.

General Van Dorn was in the Boston Mountains, on the border of the Indian country, fifty miles from Pea Ridge, and he determined to make a rapid march, get in rear of General Curtis, and strike a sudden blow, cutting off his retreat.

It was a windy morning, March 5, 1862, when the Confederate troops broke camp, packed up their iron kettles and tin dishes, and marched north along the road to Pea Ridge. They had no long line of baggage-wagons, and marched rapidly, though the snow was whirling in their faces. The movement was so rapid that Van Dorn confidently expected to make it a surprise.

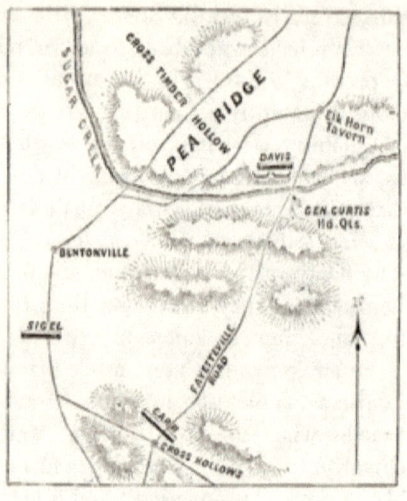

PEA RIDGE.

"The Union troops are widely scattered," said the Confederate scouts.

It was true. Sigel was south of Bentonville, several miles from the Third and Fourth divisions under Curtis. Some of the regiments were out after forage, which would make the work all the easier for the Confederates.

Startling news reached General Curtis at two o'clock on the afternoon of March 5th. Men came riding into camp with the information that the Confederates were advancing. He is quick to act. He must concentrate his troops. Cavalrymen ride across the country with orders to the officers who are out after forage and to Sigel. He resolves to fight a battle, although the Confederates outnumber him two to one. He selects his ground on Pea Ridge.

The road from Springfield to Fayetteville runs south-west. Leaving Elk Horn Tavern, where the landlord has a pair of antlers for a sign, and going south, we come to Sugar Creek and the hamlet of Mottsville, near which the Third and Fourth divisions of the Union army are in camp. Bentonville is ten miles west, near which Sigel is stationed. Ten miles brings us to Cross Hollows—a place where three hollows or ravines cross

11

one another. The ravines are narrow—seventy-five feet wide—the banks steep, and the position one of great strength. Just south of Cross Hollows General Van Dorn pitches his tent. Keeping these points in mind, we shall see just how the Confederates moved to surprise General Curtis.

General Curtis had formed his line facing south, expecting that Van Dorn would advance from Cross Hollows; but that was not Van Dorn's plan. He sends a small force up the road towards General Curtis, but the main army turns west towards Bentonville to strike Sigel.

Messengers have brought orders to Sigel to retreat to Pea Ridge. He has two hundred wagons, which he sends in advance. The Confederate cavalry ride rapidly round him and gain his rear, but he fights his way through them, losing twenty-eight killed and fifty prisoners, and joins General Curtis, who has discovered what Van Dorn is intending to do, and who quickly changes his front, forming his line facing north-east instead of south-west.

MAP OF PEA RIDGE.

General Curtis sends General Carr's division up the road on the morning of March 7th to Elk Horn Tavern. The troops of this division are to hold the right of the line. They are to be in the thick of the fight, which is to rage around the tavern, and which is to give a name to the battle—the Confederates calling it the battle of Elk Horn.

Next in line is General Davis's division, and beyond him the troops under Sigel.

General Price, with the Missourians, has led the advance of the Confederates. They have made a long march, have reached the road north-east of Elk Horn Tavern, and confront General Carr. Next in line, towards Cross-timber Hollows, are the Arkansas troops, under General

McCulloch, while the Texans, Louisianians, and Indians are in front of Sigel.

It was half-past ten in the morning when Colonel Osterhaus, with the Third Iowa Cavalry, a detachment of the First Missouri Cavalry, the Twenty-second Indiana, and Davidson's battery advanced to reconnoitre the Confederate position. The cavalry drove in the enemy's pickets, who retreated to the woods; but suddenly the woods were thick with Confederates, who rushed upon the Union battery and captured two guns. At the same moment there was a ripple of musketry in the woods north of the tavern. Price was advancing, and the Union pickets were falling back.

The battle was raging so fiercely on the left that General Curtis sent General Davis to assist Osterhaus. The woods were alive with Indians, under General Pike and the celebrated chief, John Ross. The Texans and Louisiana troops charged with fury. In the fight General McCulloch was killed and General McIntosh wounded.

General Davis saw that the Confederate left flank was exposed, and sent the Eighteenth Indiana to attack it. The regiment fell upon the Indians, driving them, and strewing the field with killed and wounded, rushing upon the cannon, capturing them, wheeling them into position, and turning them upon the fleeing Confederates. The battle on the left centre was over.

General Carr placed Dodge's brigade east of the road, and Colonel Vandever's brigade west of it. Captain Jones's battery was the first to open fire. Colonel Vandever was at Huntsville, forty miles away, when General Curtis's orders reached him. The brigade had marched the distance, stopping three times only, making a rest at each halt of fifteen minutes. The troops had arrived the night before, but they were rested, and ready for the battle.

We see the brigade advancing half a mile north of the tavern, and Captain Hayden's battery from Dubuque, Iowa, coming into position and opening fire. Sterling Price determines to strike with all his force. He presses on, drives the Union troops towards the tavern, making a sudden rush, and capturing one of the cannon.

General Carr was outnumbered two to one. "I must have reinforcements," is his message to Curtis.

"I send you my body-guard; you must hold them," was the response, and Major Bowen's battalion of cavalry went down the road with a howitzer. They were all the troops that could be spared at the moment.

"I cannot hold on much longer," was the second message from Carr.

"You shall have help," was the reply, and a battery came up from the left with a battalion of infantry.

A few minutes later Curtis himself, with Asboth's division, came over the ridge to Carr's aid. Through the afternoon Price had pressed on, Carr disputing every inch of ground. He had been driven a mile; a bullet had pierced his arm, one-fourth of his men had been killed or wounded, but his line had not been broken.

Asboth's batteries wheeled into position south of the tavern. The Second Missouri and Third Iowa Infantry had fired away all their ammunition, but they charged and drove the Confederates.

Night came, with the Confederates defeated on the left, but well satisfied with what they had accomplished on the right. They had captured one cannon, had possession of the road to Springfield, cutting off Curtis's retreat. Van Dorn made his headquarters at the tavern and prepared for the morrow.

It is not a very bright outlook for General Curtis when the sun goes down. His line of retreat is cut off, his supplies nearly exhausted. His mules and horses have had little to eat for forty-eight hours. He is hemmed in. He must be ready to fight in the morning, and must win the victory. He does not sit down and wring his hands in despair, for he is confident that he will win. He knows the ground, and reforms his line, with Davis's division on the right, where the fighting is to be most severe, and places Carr in the centre, with Sigel on the left. His line is shorter than it has been. He knows that Van Dorn will advance from the tavern with all his force.

Eight o'clock, and the Confederates have not advanced. General Curtis resolves to begin the battle. The cannon open, and Sigel brings his infantry forward, attacking the right flank of the Confederates.

It would be a long account were I to narrate all the details: how Pattison's brigade and the First Indiana battery fought in the fields south of the tavern and east of the road; how the Confederate batteries opened upon them, compelling them to fall back; how White's brigade and Davidson's battery made the line a sheet of flame; how the Twenty-fifth Illinois took position behind a fence on the left, and the Twelfth Missouri, with twelve guns, on the ridge in their rear, the men lying down, and the cannon sending shells into the Confederate lines, silencing Van Dorn's batteries, discouraging his troops; the Indians fleeing, the Arkansas and Louisiana troops losing heart, the Confederate fire growing fainter, the troops fleeing at last—some towards Cross-timber Hollows, the Missourians, under Price, running along the road towards Springfield, then fleeing west, scattering in every direction so suddenly that General Curtis is at a loss which way to turn in pursuit.

Eight miles away, Van Dorn gathered a portion of his scattered troops, and sent a request to General Curtis to bury the dead and care for the wounded.

It was not a pleasant scene that General Albert Pike beheld — the bodies of the Union dead hacked to pieces by the Indians, the wounded scalped and tomahawked. General Curtis charged Van Dorn with having permitted the horrible work to go on, and the Confederate general did not deny the charge.

BATTLE OF PEA RIDGE.

The victory was won, but at a cost of more than thirteen hundred Union soldiers killed and wounded. How many Van Dorn lost will never be known; but as the Confederates attacked, while General Curtis stood on the defensive, there was probably a greater Confederate loss.

On Saturday and Sunday, March 8 and 9, 1862, near Fortress Monroe, was enacted the most dramatic event of the war—an engagement between two naval vessels the like of which never before had been witnessed. We have already seen that when Virginia seceded it became necessary to destroy the navy yard at Norfolk, that the frigate *Merrimac* was scuttled, set on fire, and that it sunk before the hull was very much injured.

The Confederates had raised the *Merrimac*, and men were at work night and day rebuilding it, making the sides sloping, like the roof of a house, and plating it with iron nearly four inches thick. The engines and boilers had not been injured. Spies which went to Norfolk from Fortress Monroe told the Union officers of what was going on, and said that before long the *Merrimac* would be a match for all the Union war-ships. It would have four eleven-inch guns on each side, and an Armstrong rifled one-hundred-pound cannon at the bow and one at the stern—ten guns in all.

There was one man in the country who had been thinking about naval vessels, and the best way to construct them: John Ericsson, who was born in Sweden in 1803. As soon as he was old enough to use a jack-knife he began to whittle. He made water-wheels and a little saw-mill, which he set to running in the brook by the roadside. He used a piece of watch-spring for a saw, cutting the teeth with a file which he borrowed from a blacksmith. For the crank of the water-wheel he used part of a tin spoon. He learned to draw on birch-bark, and made a pair of wooden compasses, using needles for the points. He picked out the fine hair from the fur on his mother's cloak and made soft and delicate brushes to use in coloring his drawings. This John Ericsson was soon known as an ingenious boy. He made his way to England. From England he came to the United States. In 1854 the idea came to him of building a war-ship on a new plan, to be plated with iron, and with an iron revolving dome, or turret, in which he would have two powerful cannon. Such a ship would be invulnerable, and would be more than a match for all the great wooden vessels afloat.

In October, 1861, he went to Washington to see if the Government would employ him to build such a vessel.

"It will be top-heavy and tip over, and go to the bottom with all its crew," said the admiral who examined his drawings.

That stirred the blood of John Ericsson, who explained his plans so well that Admiral Paulding said, "I have learned more about the stability of a vessel from what you have said than I ever knew before."

A contract was made with him to have one of his vessels ready in just one hundred days. The Navy Department was in trouble over the news which spies brought from Norfolk.

One hundred days! How quickly they go by when a great work is on hand! But in the Novelty Iron Works, in Brooklyn, forges were flaming and steam-hammers pounding. The vessel was one hundred and twenty-four feet long; the frame of oak, twenty-seven inches thick, and out-

JOHN ERICSSON.

side of it were five iron plates, each an inch thick; the deck was flat, like a raft, covered with iron; the turret was twenty feet in diameter inside, formed of iron—eight plates, each an inch thick. In front of the turret was the pilot-house. In the turret were two eleven-inch guns. The vessel had no masts or sails, but was to move wholly by two steam-engines. The keel was laid October 22d, and on January 30, 1862, the strange craft, unlike any vessel ever seen, glided into the water.

What name should she bear? Captain Ericsson believed that the vessel would bring about a new order of things in naval architecture; that it would astonish and admonish all the naval officers of the world. It would be a "monitor," to give instruction and advice; and so he named it the *Monitor*.

In Hampton Roads, blockading Norfolk and James River, lay a fleet of twenty war-ships, carrying two hundred and ninety-one guns. The frigate *Congress* had fifty guns; *St. Lawrence*, fifty; *Minnesota*, forty-eight; *Roanoke*, forty; *Cumberland*, twenty-four. The other vessels were small. The *Congress* and *Cumberland* were old sailing frigates; the *Minnesota* and *Roanoke* steamers, but the engines of the latter were out of order.

Saturday, March 8, 1862. It was washing-day on board the fleet, and the sailors of the *Congress* and *Cumberland*, near Newport News, washed their shirts in the morning and hung them in the rigging to dry.

It was eleven o'clock when they saw three vessels coming down from Norfolk — the *Virginia* and two small steamers, the *Teaser* and *York-town* — carrying rifled guns.

Captain Frank Buchanan, born in Maryland, commanded the *Merrimac*, which the Confederates had renamed *Virginia*. He was educated by the United States Government, and had served under the Stars and Stripes thirty-five years. He had grown gray in the service of his country, but had joined the Confederacy. Maryland had not seceded. He could have no excuse such as Robert E. Lee, Joseph E. Johnston, and most of the Confederate officers could put forth—that the State to which they owed allegiance had seceded. Maryland was loyal to the Union, and Captain Buchanan was fighting not only against the nation, but against the State that gave him birth.

It is low tide. Captain Buchanan has selected the hour when the sailing-vessels will not be able to get a spring on their cables and swing their broadsides towards the *Merrimac*.

Lieutenant Morris commands the *Cumberland*, Lieutenant Smith the *Congress*. The drums beat, the sailors spring to their guns, kicking off their shoes, throwing aside their jackets, and tying their handkerchiefs around their heads.

A tug-boat, the *Zouave*, with one gun, runs alongside the *Congress* to take her in tow, just as it used to tow canal-boats loaded with grain in the harbor of New York; but the tug is weak, her machinery breaks down, and the frigate runs aground.

Captain Buchanan sees that she is helpless; he will not stop for her now, but will make for the *Cumberland*. The one-hundred-pounder Armstrong gun at the bow sends a shot which kills and wounds ten men on the *Cumberland;* a second shot kills and wounds twelve more. The *Teaser* and *Yorktown* pour in their fire. The guns of the *Cumberland* flame, but the ten-inch solid shot glance like pease from the sloping sides of the *Merrimac.*

Upon the *Cumberland* steams the *Merrimac*, her great iron beak running into the frigate's bows. The oaken timbers are crushed into splinters. A shell tears through the sides of the frigate as you could throw a bullet through a sheet of paper, killing four of the men already wounded. The *Cumberland* is beginning to settle.

HAMPTON ROADS.

"To the pumps!" shouts Lieutenant Morris, and some of the sailors work the pumps, while the others fire the guns or lift the wounded to the upper deck.

Through the sides come the solid shot and shells, tearing great gaps, knocking knees, timbers, braces into kindlings, killing and wounding the men, making terrible havoc. Down, down, lower in the water, sinks the *Cumberland*, with her cannon still flaming, the sailors shouting to keep up the fight. The vessel keels over till the upper deck is like the roof of a house.

"Do you surrender?" shouts Buchanan.

"No, sir," is the answer of Morris.

> "'Strike your flag!' the rebel cries,
> In his arrogant old plantation strain.
> 'Never!' our gallant Morris replies;
> 'It is better to sink than to yield!'
> And the whole air pealed
> With the cheers of our men."

The last gun on the upper deck is level with the water. Matthew Tenney pulls the lanyard, and a shot is hurled into a port-hole of the *Merrimac*, dismounting a gun. At that instant the *Cumberland* goes down, sucking him into the whirlpool. The cannon on the upper side break from their fastenings and crash amid the drowning crew, of whom one hundred and seventeen are killed or drowned.

The water is sixty feet deep, but the top-mast is above the surface, with the flag still flying.

"Next morn, as the sun rose over the bay,
    Still floated our flag at the main-mast head.
Lord, how beautiful was Thy day!
        Every waft of the air
        Was a whisper of prayer
Or a dirge for the dead.

"Ho! brave hearts, that went down in the seas,
    Ye are at peace in the troubled stream.
Ho! brave land, with hearts like these,
        Thy flag that is rent in twain
        Shall be one again,
And without a seam."

That last shell of the *Cumberland* struck into the muzzle of the Armstrong gun at the bow of the *Merrimac*, exploding it and killing seven men and wounding Captain Buchanan.

The *Merrimac* steers for the *Congress*, aground and helpless, takes position four hundred feet astern of the frigate, and fires a shell, which kills seventeen men. The frigate has only two guns which she can use. In a few minutes one is dismounted and the other knocked to pieces. The *Merrimac* comes nearer, fires hot shot, which set the *Congress* on fire and make awful havoc, killing and wounding nearly one-half of the men. It is murder; the crew can make no resistance.

Commander Smith is killed, and the officer next in command hauls down the flag. The flames burst forth and burn a while; the sailors leap overboard, some to escape, some to drown; then comes the explosion, and the noble frigate disappears forever.

The *Merrimac* makes for the *Minnesota*, but draws too much water to get at her. The *Yorktown* and *Teaser* run near, and with their rifled guns kill and wound several men on board; but the *Minnesota* keeps them at bay.

Night sets in, and the *Merrimac*, like a great spider coming out of its den, having made a good meal for the day, steams back to Norfolk. On Sunday morning it will make a breakfast of the *Minnesota*, *Roanoke*, *St. Lawrence*, and all the rest.

Captain Buchanan has killed and wounded more than three hundred of his old associates. He has won a great victory for the Confederacy, but will the world regard it as an honorable record?

What rejoicing in Norfolk, in Richmond, Charleston, Savannah, and throughout the South, as the news flashed over the wires! In a few days the *Merrimac* would be at Baltimore, New York, and Boston, carrying havoc and consternation. There was nothing afloat that could destroy her. The cannon in the forts guarding the harbor of New York would be only pop-guns; the eleven-inch solid shot would glide harmlessly from her sides. In imagination, Jefferson Davis and the people of Richmond saw France and England and all the world recognizing the Confederacy, and the great powers of Europe reconstructing their navies.

It is early dawn Sunday morning when the spider, with an appetite sharpened by its luncheon of yesterday, eager to make a full meal, steams down to Hampton Roads. Captain Catesby Jones has succeeded Captain Buchanan as commander.

Captain Jones sees something moving through the water. It is a very strange craft; never before has he seen anything like it. There is a flat surface, even with the water, a short piece of funnel, a round turret, a small cupola, and the Stars and Stripes flying from a staff—nothing more. It is coming fearlessly, insolently towards the *Merrimac*.

It is the *Monitor*, which reached Fortress Monroe at nine o'clock Saturday night, John L. Worden commander. Samuel Howard has volunteered to act as pilot.

"Steer straight towards her," is the order of Captain Worden.

The *Teaser* and *Yorktown*, which have come down to take a share in the feast, turn back. They do not like the looks of that "cheese-box on a raft," as one sailor calls her, steering fearlessly up to the *Merrimac*, which opens fire, but whose shot glance harmlessly from the revolving turret.

Nearer glides the *Monitor*, like a weasel approaching its prey. The turret ceases to turn for a moment, the thick iron slides covering the two port-holes swing, the two guns flame, and the eleven-inch solid shot, each weighing one hundred and sixty-eight pounds, rip up the iron plates of the *Merrimac*. The slides fall back over the port-holes, the turret turns once more, the gunners ram in the cartridges, lift the solid shot, and again the guns of the *Monitor* belch their flames. The vessels are side by side, so near that the clouds of smoke from each become one cloud, for the moment hiding them from the people standing on the shore at Sewell's Point and Newport News. Two shot strike the turret, but do no harm, while those of the *Monitor* are splitting the iron plates of the *Merrimac* and shattering the timbers.

The *Merrimac* is heavy and unwieldy, the *Monitor* light and agile. The leviathan puts on steam to run down the puny craft.

"Hard-a-port the helm!" shouts Captain Worden, and the *Monitor* swings round in such a way that the blow does no harm.

A shell explodes against the pilot-house, blinding Captain Worden, and Lieutenant Green takes command. The *Monitor* has used up all the solid shot which had been hoisted into the turret, and steams away to get ready for another attack.

The *Merrimac*, no longer attempting to make a meal of the *Minnesota*, steams towards Norfolk with her men at the pumps, for the water is pouring in through the seams and rents made by the shot of the *Monitor*. Tugs take her in tow; but only with constant pumping and bailing can she be kept afloat. Her sides are broken, the massive timbers crushed; great pieces of iron have been torn away.

The recognition of the Confederacy by England, France, and the governments of Europe is not so near as it appeared to be. The *Merrimac* will not bombard New York or set Boston on fire. The day of wooden ships has gone by forever, and the iron age has come.

All the world talked about this battle of the iron ships. The one was likened to Goliath, the other to David with his sling.

The hopes and jubilant expectations of the people of the South began to fade away; for in the Northern workshops forges were blazing and steam-hammers pounding, building other monitors; while in the South there were no iron-mills, nor were there any workmen to construct an iron-clad navy. Labor and invention were winning victories on the sea as well as on the land.

It was seen that Hatteras Inlet could be used to good advantage; that a fleet of gunboats, accompanied by troops on light-draft vessels, might use it as a door-way to reach the eastern portion of North Carolina.

The Secretary of War and President Lincoln thought favorably of the plan, and very soon there were lively times at Fortress Monroe: the arrival of a great fleet of steamers and war-ships, and the gathering of fifteen thousand men under General Burnside. Most of the troops were from New England.

General H. A. Wise had been Governor of Virginia before the war. It was he who signed the warrant for the execution of John Brown. He had been a member of Congress for many years, and had wielded great influence. Being a general in the Confederate service, he was sent to defend the North Carolina coast. The Confederate Secretary of War,

Mr. Benjamin, and Jefferson Davis had no great love for General Wise, because he was very independent, and was in the habit of criticising their administration of affairs. General Wise called for ten thousand men to defend Roanoke Island. Mr. Benjamin told him that he must get the

MAP OF THE NORTH CAROLINA COAST.

men of North Carolina to enlist; but recruits did not come. General Wise bitterly complained that he could get no supplies from the Secretary of War, who was accused of allowing his personal feelings to influence his action.

By employing gangs of slaves, General Wise soon had a line of fortifications on Roanoke Island, with twenty-two heavy cannon. He had eight small steamers, each carrying one or two guns.

On Sunday, January 11th, a fleet of nearly one hundred steamers and sailing-vessels took their departure from Fortress Monroe. None of the captains, none of the officers of the army of fifteen thousand, except the commander, General Burnside, knew their destination till the captains opened their sealed instructions, and found that they were to make for Hatteras Inlet. On Monday a storm came on, and six of the vessels were wrecked and three men drowned. Not till the first week in February was the fleet in Pamlico Sound.

Not till February 7th was Commodore Goldsborough ready to bombard the Confederate forts. At ten o'clock the sailors on the gunboats saw a line of signal flags flying at the mast-head of the *Southfield*, the flag-ship of the fleet. This is what they read:

"On this day our country expects every man to do his duty."

The *Stars and Stripes* led the way, and the other vessels followed.

Down from the northern end of the Sound steamed the Confederate fleet, under Commodore Lynch. It was past eleven o'clock when the *Stars and Stripes* sent a shot from its one-hundred-pounder rifled gun spinning towards Fort Bartow. It was the signal for battle. Commodore Lynch's largest vessel, the *Curlew*, was quickly riddled by solid shot that crashed through her sides. The water was pouring in, and the captain ran her ashore.

A continuous storm of shells rained upon the fort, tossing up clouds of sand, ploughing through the embankment, dismounting cannon, cutting down the flag-staff, setting the barracks on fire. Through the afternoon the bombardment went on, the fire of the forts growing fainter, the Confederate fleet moving away beyond the reach of the long-range rifles.

Behind the gunboats came the transports, with the Union troops on board. By the side of General Burnside stood a colored boy, Tom. He was only twenty years old. He had been a slave of John M. Daniel, of Roanoke. He longed for liberty. He knew that there was a Union fleet and Union soldiers at Hatteras Inlet, and one morning when his master called him, Tom did not answer. He had crept away in the darkness, and managed to get across the water and into the Union lines. He knew all about Roanoke Island, the forts, the piles and sunken vessels in the sound, and the number of Confederate troops on the island. He knew where there was a landing-place—Ashby's Harbor—a little inlet on the west side of the island, half-way up to Fort Bartow; the troops could land there, and save wading through the marshes. He pointed out the place, and was of great service.

General Burnside had three brigades: one commanded by General J. G. Foster, who was in Fort Sumter when the South Carolinians began the war, one commanded by General Parke, and one by General Reno. In

GENERAL BURNSIDE.

the woods by Ashby's Harbor were some Confederate troops, with their cannon; but the shells of the gunboats soon sent them upon the run up the narrow road towards their breastworks.

Night sets in. Rain is falling, but the soldiers leap into their boats, reach the marsh, wade knee-deep in mud, and before midnight ten thousand men are on shore.

BOMBARDMENT OF ROANOKE ISLAND.

There are two thousand five hundred Confederate troops on the island, commanded by Colonel Shaw. Three hundred of them are behind a breastwork built across the road a mile from Ashby's Harbor. Up the road march the soldiers of Foster's brigade, the Twenty-fifth Massachusetts in advance, followed by the Twenty-third Massachusetts. They come upon the Confederate skirmishers, who fire a volley and then flee to the breastworks. The Confederate cannon open. The howitzers reply, and the musketry begins. The Twenty-seventh Massachusetts and the Tenth Connecticut arrive, and the fight rages more fiercely.

General Reno's brigade pressed on to take part in the conflict, the Twenty-first Massachusetts, Fifty-first New York, Fifty-first Pennsylvania, and Ninth New Jersey pushing out through the swamp on the left, wading waist-deep in water, forming on Foster's right towards Roanoke Sound.

General Parke's brigade relieves General Foster's. The soldiers gave little heed to the volley that burst upon them. A few dropped, but the line went on — over the embankment. With a hurrah they seized the cannon and poured a volley upon the panic-stricken Confederates fleeing up the road, casting aside guns, knapsacks, and cartridge-boxes.

The battle was over. The Union troops soon overtook the Confederates, who gave themselves up as prisoners. All were captured, with forty heavy cannon.

Among the Confederate wounded was Captain Wise, son of the general. When the war began he was editor of a paper in Richmond, and captain of the "Richmond Blues." He had written hard things about "Lincoln's hirelings," as he called the Union troops, had shown his devotion to the Confederacy by fighting bravely to the last. He was mortally wounded, and died soon after the battle; his body was tenderly cared for by General Burnside.

How strangely things come round! It was but a little while before the breaking out of the war that General Wise, then Governor of Virginia, sat unmoved while a beautiful girl kneeled before him pleading for the life of her father. It was the daughter of Cook, one of John Brown's soldiers. Tears rolled down her cheeks, but no moisture gathered in his eyes as he listened to her prayer.

HENRY A. WISE.

"Your father has forfeited his life to the law, and the law must have its course," he said; took up his pen, dipped it in the ink, signed the death-warrant of Cook and John Brown. Then he took out his cigar-case and turned to one of his officers: "Do you smoke, colonel? these are good Havanas."

But now a flag of truce comes from General Wise, begging for the body of his son, and General Burnside courteously complies with the request.

In Portsmouth the bells are tolling, and a mournful procession winding through the streets. The gray-haired man looks down upon the face of his son, takes the cold hand in his; tears roll down his cheeks.

"He has died for me! he has died for me!" he cries, in bitter anguish.

His son has fallen, and he feels that disaster has come to the Confederacy through the incompetency of the Secretary of War and the personal pique of Jefferson Davis. He dictates a protest to the Confederate Congress, censuring the Secretary and President.

There was a commotion in Richmond when the people beheld, one morning, in the street near Jefferson Davis's house, a black coffin, with a

12

rope and a noose at one end coiled upon it. The police never could discover who placed it there, but it made a great sensation; and General Wise's protest to Congress caused the appointment of a committee to investigate affairs and see who was to blame for the disasters that had come to the Confederacy in North Carolina and in the West.

"If blame attaches to any one, it ought to fall on the Secretary of War and General Huger," read the report.

General Huger might have sent ten thousand men from Portsmouth through the Dismal Swamp Canal to Roanoke Island, but did not. So unpopular was Mr. Benjamin that he had to resign his position as Secretary of War; but Jefferson Davis appointed him Secretary of State, which had the effect of weakening the confidence of the people in the Confederate Government.

MAP OF ROANOKE ISLAND.

General Burnside did not wish to retain the prisoners he had captured, and so released them upon the condition and oath that they never again would serve against the United States.

South of Cape Lookout is the harbor and town of Beaufort, with a railroad running west. The River Neuse comes down from the centre of North Carolina, and empties into Pamlico Sound. The entrance to the harbor of Beaufort was commanded by Fort Macon, which the Governor of the State had seized before the war began. Steamers from England were finding shelter under its guns, running the blockade, bringing supplies for the South, and carrying back cotton. It was determined to put a stop to all this. Having captured Hatteras Inlet and Roanoke Island, it would be an easy matter to approach the fort on the side where the walls were weakest. Before attempting it, Newbern, on the railroad and river, where a Confederate army was gathering, must be captured.

That we may see how important a place Beaufort was to the blockade-

JUDAH P. BENJAMIN.

runners, and what they were doing for the Confederacy, let us go over to Southampton, in England, where the Confederate war-steamer *Nashville* is lying, February 1, 1862. Near her is the United States war-ship *Tuscarora*, which has been sent across the Atlantic to watch the *Nashville* and follow her the moment she sails. When three miles from land the *Tuscarora* is to open fire upon her. The British war-ships *Dauntless* and *Warrior* are there to prevent the *Tuscarora* from sailing till twenty-four hours after the *Nashville* departs.   On February 3d the *Nashville*, which was a fast sailer, left Southampton; twenty-four hours later the *Tuscarora* was allowed to depart, but of course could not overtake her.

While Burnside was getting ready to move into Pamlico Sound, the *Nashville* reached Bermuda.   The British Government had issued an order that no American war-ship should take coal in that port, but the *Nashville* was allowed to fill her bunkers, and on the 28th of February she slipped past the blockaders and entered Beaufort with a cargo valued at more than three million dollars.   She stayed two weeks, taking on a load of cotton, and then slipped out past the blockaders at night, while the cannon, arms, and ammunition which she brought were being whirled through Newbern to Raleigh, and thence to Richmond.

The River Trent comes from the south-west and joins the Neuse at Newbern.   The Neuse comes from the north-west, and is very broad below the town.   General Branch was in command of the Confederate troops.   He built seven forts on the banks of the Neuse, and carried from that stream a line of breastworks to the Trent.   The fortifications were two miles from the town, crossing the railroad and the highway.   The slaves threw up the redoubts, and there were heavy cannon in position to open upon the gunboats.

In Fort Thompson, where his line began, there were thirteen heavy guns; in Fort Dixie, four; in Fort Brown, eight; in Fort Ellis, eight; in Fort Low, eight; in Union Point Battery, two—in all, forty-three heavy cannon.   To prevent the gunboats from getting up to the town, old hulks were sunk in the river, and spars, with great iron spikes driven into them, to pierce the hulls of the gunboats.   Torpedoes were also planted in the river.   With such defences and obstructions, and ten thousand troops, General Branch expected to defend the place, and keep the Union army and fleet at bay.

Colonel Estvan, of England, who was in the Confederate service, was sent by the Confederate Secretary of War to examine the defences.   The Confederate officers had a jolly dinner-party.

"As soon as the champagne went round," Colonel Estvan says, "every man present was eager to make a speech.   General Branch proposed a toast in honor of the Confederacy, after a speech of half an hour.   The colonel of the Second North Carolina Cavalry responded.   He dilated on the matchless gallantry of his troops, their prowess being such as to throw the deeds of the Greeks and Romans into the shade.   The whole corps was ready to die to the last man.   Let us make Newbern a second Sebastopol, before the walls of which the enemy must perish."

"Hurrah! We'll make it a Sebastopol!" shouted the company, filling their glasses.

"With ten thousand troops such as I have," said Colonel Speil, "I would have taken Sebastopol in fourteen days, and not left one stone upon another."

General Branch had seven regiments of infantry—the Seventh, Sixteenth, Nineteenth, Twenty-fifth, Thirty-fifth, Thirty-sixth, and Thirty-seventh North Carolina—and two regiments of cavalry, with thirty-six pieces of field artillery, and all the heavy guns in the forts.

LANDING AT NEWBERN.

On the morning of March 12, 1862, the steamers, with the Union troops on board, ran as near as they could to the shore, eighteen miles from Newbern. The troops landed, and marched through a forest of pines in a drenching rain. At daylight they ate a bit of cold beef and bread, then took their places in line. General Foster's brigade move on the right of the road, the Twenty-fifth Massachusetts leading and taking position near the Neuse River. Then came the Twenty-fourth Massachusetts, the left of the regiment reaching to the road. West of the road stood the Twenty-seventh and Twenty-third Massachusetts.

Along this part of the line, on both sides of the road, were placed some boat-howitzers, manned by marines, and a twelve-pounder steel cannon,

12*

under Captain Bennett, of the gunboat *Cossack*, who had twenty sailors. in their blue jackets, to man the cannon. Captain Drayton, of the gunboat *Highlander*, had a battery farther to the left. General Parke's brigade occupied the centre, while General Reno's troops filed from the road. crossed the railroad, and came into line to attack the Confederates' right wing.

The Twenty-seventh Massachusetts was the first to open fire. There was no rattling fire from skirmishers, but first the howitzers, then the roar of the Confederate heavy artillery, and then the volley of the Twenty-seventh Massachusetts, with a roll of musketry from a half-dozen Confederate regiments.

In a few moments all of General Foster's troops were engaged except the Twenty-fifth Massachusetts, which was brought from the extreme right back to the road. A fog hung over the marshes, and the smoke of the battle drifted down upon Reno's troops, making the air so murky that they could see but a few rods.

"There is a battery," said one of the skirmishers, peering through the mist and smoke. He could see the Confederates getting two thirty-two-pounder guns into position.

There was a deep cut for the railroad through a sand-hill, and the cannon were planted to sweep the approach near Mr. Wood's house and brick-yard. There was an engine on the track and a train of cars, from which the Confederate soldiers were taking ammunition.

A company of the Twenty-first Massachusetts moved rapidly forward. raised their guns, and fired. There was consternation in the Confederate lines. The engineer on the locomotive quickly reversed the engine and backed the cars towards Newbern. The soldiers who were taking the ammunition from the cars ran behind Mr. Wood's house to a ravine in rear of the brick-yard.

"Plant your colors on that building," said General Reno to Sergeant Bates, of the Twenty-first Massachusetts, who ran forward, sprang upon the low roof of a house, and waved the colors amid a storm of bullets. The regiments rushed forward.

The first man to fall was Frazer Augustus Stearns, son of the President of Amherst College, Adjutant of the Twenty-first Massachusetts. He was only twenty-one years old, but was very brave and of noble character.

"Charge!" he shouted; but the next moment he fell. General Reno thought a great deal of him, and the tears rolled down his cheeks when he heard that he was killed.

It was a brave defence which the North Carolina troops made, but the battle was going against them. Their ammunition was failing. The gunboats were steaming up the Neuse and sending shells into Fort Thompson.

In front of the Union howitzers the Confederates had a large cannon, drawn by four mules. A lieutenant of the navy was out in front watching the shot. He came running back swinging his cap.

"Now's your time. One of the mules is down. Come on! come on!" he shouted.

In battle men do strange things. The lieutenant had nothing to do with the Twenty-fifth Massachusetts; the soldiers were not under him, but with a hurrah they went forward. The Twenty-fourth caught the

ENCAMPMENT OF THE ARMY.

enthusiasm, and together they rushed on. The Confederates threw away their guns and cartridge-boxes, and fled towards Newbern.

"Who ordered that charge?" asked General Burnside.

"I do not know; and it makes no difference, now that it is done," said General Foster.

Colonel Estvan had reached the town from Richmond just before the battle closed. He says: "As I approached Newbern the roar of cannon became more and more distinct. Suddenly a number of horsemen galloped past me in full flight, and among them I could discern the gallant colonel with whom I had dined. He gave me a hurried nod and passed on. Newbern I found looking bad enough. General Branch had secured a railway-carriage for himself. Troops without their officers were passing me in confusion, throwing away their arms. They all told wonderful stories of the feats performed by their respective regiments. According to their accounts, they had all fought like so many devils, but the force of the enemy not being less than one hundred thousand, they had no chance. The fact is, General Branch had run away, and all discipline was at an end."

The Confederates set the long bridge across the Trent on fire. In the town all was confusion, the people fleeing panic-stricken from their houses. The Confederates set the town on fire, and a great black cloud rose heavenward from the burning buildings.

One of the Union steamers came up, ferried the troops across the river into the town, and the soldiers laid aside their guns to put out the flames. Out of twelve hundred people not one hundred white people remained. The colored people did not flee, but welcomed the troops as their best friends.

The victory was complete, but nearly six hundred Union troops had been killed and wounded in the conflict.

General Parke's brigade embarked on the steamers and sailed back to Slocum's Creek, landed, marched to Moorehead City and Beaufort. There were no troops to oppose them, but the Confederate flag was flying on Fort Macon. Colonel White, a nephew of Jefferson Davis, was commander of the fort. General Parke sent a summons to him to surrender. It was a resolute reply which came back — "He would not yield till he had eaten his last biscuit." There were five hundred Confederates in the fort, and Colonel White was confident that he could hold it.

The gunboats came, mortars were landed, and in a few days General Parke had eight of them and three thirty-pounder rifled cannon in position to bombard the fort. Colonel White knew that something was going on behind the sand-hills, and he found out what it was when, at six o'clock on the morning of April 25th, the shells began to fall into the fort. Four of the gunboats also opened fire, which was so hot and heavy that at four o'clock in the afternoon Colonel White ran up a white flag; and when the firing ceased Captain Guion came out and said that they would surrender. So the five hundred men who would fight till they had eaten their last biscuit gave themselves up.

By their capture all the harbors north of Wilmington were closed to the blockade-runners, and the blockading vessels of the North Atlantic could have a harbor of refuge when the storms came on. A severe blow had been struck against the Confederacy.

There are so many islands in the Mississippi River that the pilots of the steamboats have numbered them from Cairo to New Orleans. Island No. 10 was about sixty miles below Cairo. It is washed away now, but in 1862 it was three-quarters of a mile long and a quarter of a mile wide, located in a bend of the river opposite the boundary between Tennessee and Kentucky.

The river runs south, then west, then north-west, and at New Madrid turns south again. The banks are low. Behind New Madrid there are swamps and bayous. On the Tennessee side there are swamps and a large lake.

When Fort Donelson surrendered, General Polk, who was at Columbus, saw that he must evacuate the place, for the Union troops could march across the country and attack him in the rear. He thought, however, that he could fortify Island No. 10, and hold it against the gunboats, and shipped the heavy guns to the island. He erected batteries on the Tennessee shore, and built two forts at New Madrid, behind the town, to prevent the Union troops from coming down the Missouri side. The Confederate troops on the island would be under the necessity of receiving their supplies from steamboats, as there was no road through the swamp on the Tennessee side.

The officer sent to take command of the troops was General Mackall, who, upon his arrival, issued a pompous address. He said: "Soldiers, we are strangers. Let me tell you who I am. I am the general selected by Beauregard and Bragg for this command when they knew that it was in peril. Soldiers, the Mississippi Valley is intrusted to your discipline and to your patience. Exhibit the coolness and vigilance you have hitherto, and hold it."

Besides the cannon in the batteries, he had six steamboats armed with cannon. There were between nine and ten thousand men. The swamps were so wide, and the water in them so deep on the Tennessee side, that General Mackall had no fear of being attacked from that direction. He stationed most of his soldiers at New Madrid.

On February 22, 1862, General Pope, with several thousand men, landed at Commerce, opposite Cairo, in Missouri. The river was rising, rain falling, the mud deep. Very slow and toilsome was the march towards New Madrid. The troops could only make five miles a day.

When General Pope reached New Madrid he found fourteen heavy

guns in one fort and seven in the other—twenty-one in all—placed to
sweep all the surrounding country, with a line of breastworks connecting
the forts, and the trees cut down and made into abatis.

"The forts are impregnable," writes an officer to the *Memphis Appeal*. "All are hopeful and ready. We will make this an American Thermopylæ."

Below New Madrid ten miles, on the Missouri side, is a place called Point Pleasant. General Pope quietly sent Colonel Plummer, with three regiments and a battery of rifled cannon, through the woods to take possession of it. The soldiers went to work with their shovels, and in a short time threw up strong embankments. The cannon were placed in position, and when a Confederate steamboat came along they opened fire upon the astonished captain and crew. The roar of the cannon rolled along the river. Commodore Hollins, commanding the Confederate gunboats, heard it, and hastened down, opened fire, but Plummer's artillerymen compelled him to withdraw, and the unpleasant conviction came to General Mackall that the river below was being blockaded; but he determined to hold the place. He had a large amount of supplies, and would defend it to the last.

It is energy that wins. At sunset on March 11th four rifled thirty-pounder siege-guns reached General Pope. The Confederates looking out from the forts saw nothing unusual going on in General Pope's camp. They could see the Union soldiers sitting round their camp-fires—nothing more; but when the twilight faded, Colonel Morgan's brigade marched out with picks and spades. General Stanley's division followed. They marched up within eight hundred yards of the forts and began their work, Colonel Bissell telling them where to dig. All through the night the men worked in silence, for only a quarter of a mile distant the Confederate sentinels were pacing their beats.

When morning dawned there were breastworks eighteen feet thick and five feet high, and a curtain nine hundred feet long, nine feet thick, and three feet high connecting them.

In thirty-four hours from the time the guns arrived at Cairo from Pittsburg they had been taken across the Mississippi, loaded on railroad cars, taken to Sykestown, twenty miles, dragged through the mud twenty miles, and placed in position. This work was done so quietly that the Confederate pickets heard nothing. They thought it a rifle-pit in the dim light, and opened fire, but were astonished when a shell from a thirty-two-pounder cannon exploded above them.

It was a foggy morning; the air was still, and the deep thunder rolled far away. It woke up the slumbering Confederates. The fog lifted, and

BOMBARDMENT OF ISLAND NO. 10.

all the guns of the fleet and boats began to play. All through the day
the uproar went on.   Just at night General Paine's division advanced
towards the lower fort, but a thunder-storm and hurricane came on, and
the troops waited till it should pass.

Through the following night the rain pelted them.   Morning dawned,
but no enemy was to be seen.   A citizen of the town came towards them

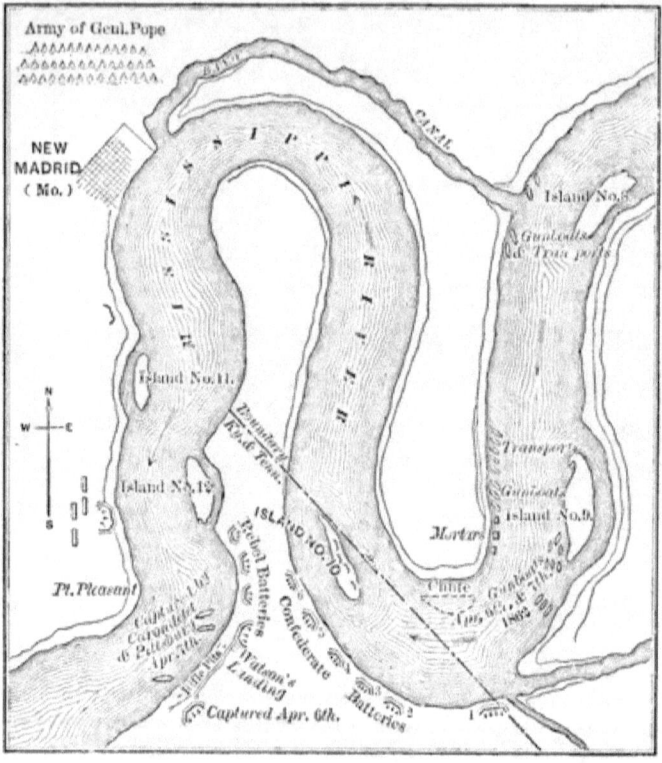

MAP OF ISLAND NO. 10.

with a white flag, informing them that during the night General Mackall,
who was going to make New Madrid a Thermopylæ, had marched his
troops upon the steamboats and taken them to the Tennessee shore,
spiking the guns.

The soldiers rushed into the deserted works.   Before night the spikes
were removed from the guns, and the heavy cannon placed upon the bank
of the river.

The gunboats which were so badly injured at Fort Donelson had been repaired, and on that morning were steaming down the river from Cairo to bombard Island No. 10.

I was on the gunboat *Benton* with Commodore Foote. We came to anchor above the island. A man on the Missouri shore was making a signal. It was a messenger from General Pope with this despatch: "I have possession of New Madrid. The river is closed; no escape for the enemy by water."

Commodore Foote had seven gunboats and ten thirteen-inch mortars on boats built like rafts, with thick timbers laid crosswise and bolted together.

To fire a mortar accurately requires a good knowledge of mathematics —the relations of curves to straight lines; for the shell is fired into the air at an angle of thirty or forty degrees, and the gunner must calculate the distance from the mortar to the object he wishes to destroy. He must calculate the time it will take for the shell to pass to its highest elevation; it must burst at the right moment. Captain Maynadier had command of the mortar-boats. I went with him out through a cornfield, across a point of land, to a farm-house. We climbed upon its roof, and had a clear view of the Confederate fortifications. It was an easy matter for us, by using a compass and by sighting the mortar-boats in one direction and the batteries on Island No. 10, to calculate how far away they were, and at what angle the shells ought to be fired. It was very interesting to sit there and see the flash of the mortar and the great cloud of smoke, and then to watch the shell sailing high above us, making a beautiful parabolic curve, bursting above the enemy, sending its fragments in every direction. It was all very interesting till we heard something coming towards us, and a solid shot tore through the house beneath us. The Confederates had discovered us, and the shot and shells came so thick and fast that it was far more interesting to be somewhere else.

The Southern people were confident that the island could not be taken. The *Memphis Argus* said: "For the enemy to get possession of Memphis and the Mississippi Valley would require an army of greater strength than Secretary Stanton can concentrate. The gunboats in which they have so much confidence have found their weakness. They cannot stand our guns of heavy calibre. Foote, the commander of the Federal fleet, served his time under Commander Hollins, and should he attempt to descend the river Hollins will teach him a lesson."

It is a beautiful morning. The gunboats are ready. They float slowly with the current till they are within easy cannon-shot, and anchor with their bows down stream, so that they can use their heavy rifled guns.

THE "CARONDELET" PASSING THE BATTERIES.

The mortars open fire, ten of them sending shells into the air. The gunboats open their bow-ports and run out the cannon. You have seen battle-pictures by great painters, but no painter can portray the grandeur of the scene—the gunboats and mortars enveloped in flame and smoke: the unfolding clouds slowly floating away; handfuls of white cloud suddenly bursting out high in air, or great columns of water thrown up from the eddying stream. A round shot skips along the water and pierces the embankment; another crashes through a tree, cutting it down in a twinkling. The air is filled with sulphurous clouds, broken timbers, branches of trees. There are deep explosions, a lifting of cart-loads of earth into the air. There are answering shots. A thirty-pound ball strikes the upper deck of the *Benton*, tears up the iron plates, breaks the stout timbers, crushing them to kindlings, falls upon the lower deck, bounds once more against the timbers above, and drops into Commodore Foote's writing-desk.

In the thick of the bombardment a gun on the *St. Louis* bursts, killing two men and wounding thirteen.

The gunboats stop their firing at sunset, but all night long the mortars hurl their shells upon the island.

"If I had a steamboat, and if you could send down a gunboat, I would cross the river from New Madrid and take them in the rear."

Such was the message which General Pope sent to Commodore Foote.

A bright thought came to Carlton Ela, one of the soldiers of Company F, Tenth Iowa, as he paced his beat on the picket-line. He saw the bayou—that it was once the bed of the Mississippi; that if the drift-wood and other obstructions were cleared out, steamboats could be brought below the batteries. It so impressed him that he mentioned it to General Hamilton, who commanded the division.

The water was overflowing the banks of the river, filling all the bayous. He saw that if a canal were cut through a ridge of land for a short distance, and if the trees were cut from a bayou, a steamboat might leave the river above the gunboats and be taken across to New Madrid. Commodore Foote found that Island No. 10 was so strongly fortified that he could not take it. He could only carry on the fight with his bow-guns and mortars, and the mortars were not doing much damage.

Engineers examined the bayous to see if the canal could be cut, and reported that they could accomplish it. Soldiers went to work once more with shovels. There were great trees that must be sawed off four feet under water. They rigged a sawing-machine on a flat-boat, with an engine to drive it. So well did it work that more than one thousand trees were

13

cut down and removed. Some of the trees were sawn by hand, the men standing up to their necks in the water.

For nineteen days the work went on, General Mackall having no suspicion of what was being done. Every day the mortar-boats tossed shells upon the island, to make the Confederates think that the bombardment had not been given up.

"I think that we can capture the upper battery," said Commodore Foote.

It was on the Tennessee shore. Night came, April 1st. Black clouds are rising in the west. The wind blows a gale, swaying the tall trees. There are vivid lightning flashes. While the storm is wildest, five boats filled with men silently push out from the shore and drift with the current. The oars have been muffled; no word is spoken. In the boats are one hundred resolute men; each knows just what he is to do.

Onward they sweep, the rowers bending to their oars, gliding now as swiftly as a race-horse. Colonel Roberts of the army is commander. Two Confederate sentinels are standing in the battery, keeping watch amid the storm. Suddenly they behold by the lightning flash a fleet of boats sweeping up to the shore. Their guns flash. A few rods away a regiment is sleeping.

"Lay in, quick!" shouts Colonel Roberts.

A stroke, and the prows of the boats run upon the shore. Up the bank leap the soldiers, running to the cannon with files of hardened steel, which they drive into the vents. A moment's work, and every cannon in the battery is spiked. There is a commotion in the Confederate camp— officers shouting, soldiers, waking in fright, leaping to their feet. Colonel Roberts examines each gun.

"All aboard! Push off!" he shouts. He is the last to leap in. A few strokes, and they are beyond musket-shot. Six guns have been rendered useless.

All is ready—the canal complete, the water flowing through, and four boats making their way towards New Madrid.

It is midnight, April 3d, a dark and stormy night. The *Carondelet* is ready to run past Island No. 10. She has a barge loaded with bales of hay alongside. The engineer has screwed down the valves of the boilers, and the pent-up steam is struggling to escape.

"Cast off!" Captain Walke, commanding the *Carondelet*, issues the order, and the gunboat floats out into the stream.

Although the night is stormy, the Confederate sentinels are on the watch, and give the alarm. The soot in the chimney of the *Carondelet* takes fire, and a lurid flame spouts high in air, leaving a long trail of sparks behind. There are sudden flashes from the batteries on the island, but swiftly the *Carondelet* sweeps past them. If she reaches New Madrid in safety Captain Walke is to fire three signal-guns.

I stand upon the bank in the darkness, waiting to hear them. The up-roar at the island dies away. A minute seems an hour. At last they come—three peals of thunder rolling up the valley. The soldiers spring to their feet and swing their caps.

"Three cheers for Commodore Foote!"

"Three more for Captain Walke!"

"Three for the crew!"

The *Carondelet* has not been struck.

Night comes again, and the *Pittsburg* runs the gantlet. Four steam-boats are through the canal.

Down the river steamed the two gunboats, pouring their broadsides upon a Confederate battery, and putting the soldiers to flight. In the darkness of the night General Pope moves his troops across the river to the Tennessee shore. They are in rear of Island No. 10.

The Confederate troops flee from the tents, throwing away their guns, knapsacks, clothing, plunging into the swamp.

In the early morning the troops under General Pope push on, coming suddenly upon the fugitives, capturing General Mackall, nearly seven thousand prisoners, and one hundred and twenty-three cannon, seven thousand muskets, an immense amount of ammunition and camp equipage.

The victory was almost bloodless. During the bombardment of the island and of the forts at New Madrid few had been killed or wounded.

By this victory, and by the victory gained in the battle of Pea Ridge, near south-western Missouri, the last of the Confederate troops were swept from that State. The love for the old flag, the determination to stand by, the Union, became, as in Kentucky, a deep and abiding force, making it one of the truly loyal States of the Union.

CHAPTER IX.

THE BATTLE OF SHILOH.

THERE was consternation in Richmond over affairs in the West. Immediately after the battle of Mill Springs General Beauregard had hastened to Tennessee, to aid General Albert Sidney Johnston. The people gathered at the railroad stations to see the man who was regarded as the hero of Sumter and Manassas. At Nashville he was presented to the Legislature, and received a hearty welcome. On the 4th of February, the day before the attack on Fort Henry by Commodore Foote, he reached Bowling Green, in Kentucky, and had a conference with Johnston. He was at Nashville when the astounding news came that Fort Donelson had surrendered. He saw that a new army must

MAP OF THE SHILOH CAMPAIGN.

be created, the Confederate forces concentrated; that the army under General Grant, with the gunboats, could make its way up the Tennessee River to northern Alabama, and that Corinth, the junction of the railroad running from Columbus, in Kentucky, to Mobile and New Orleans, with the road running east from Memphis to Chattanooga, was the best place for the gathering of the new army. While General Johnston did what he could to recruit the disheartened troops at Murfreesboro, Beauregard began the concentration of troops at Corinth. Regiments came from General Lovell, in command at New Orleans. General Bragg came with his brigade from Mobile. Steamers were sent up the Arkansas River to bring down the troops under Van Dorn. Governor Harris, of Tennessee, ordered out the troops of that State, and aroused the enthusiasm of the people to such a pitch that in a few days the new army, including the troops from Bowling Green, which had been taken to Corinth in the cars, numbered between forty and fifty thousand. Beauregard asked the people to contribute their plantation bells, to be recast into cannon. The women in their enthusiasm gave their brass fire-dogs and candlesticks. It is not probable that the recast bells sent out their tones from the brazen lips of the cannon on the field of Shiloh, but the readiness of the people in responding shows that they were very much in earnest.

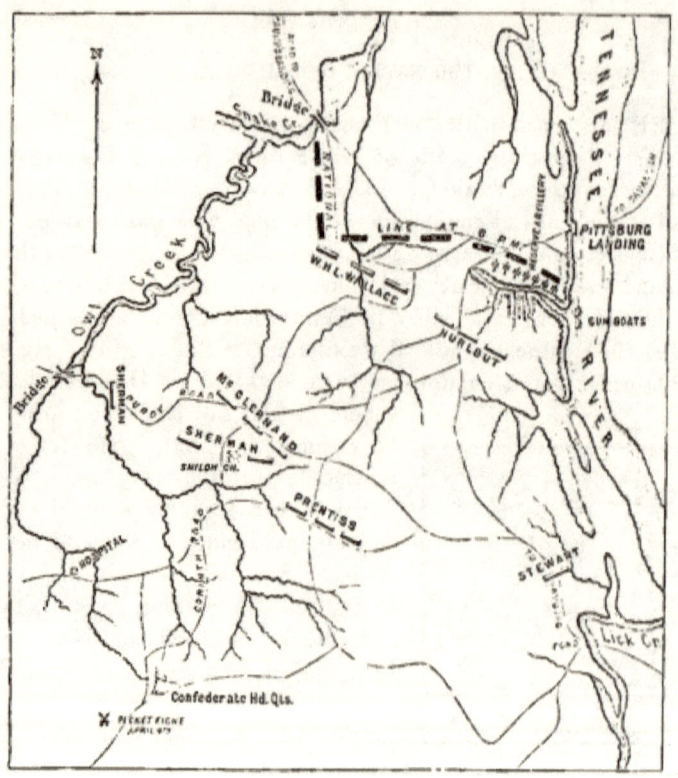

THE BATTLE OF SHILOH.

Up to the taking of Donelson, General McClellan had been commander of all the Union armies, but President Lincoln appointed General Henry W. Halleck to command the troops west of the Alleghanies. General Halleck was educated at West Point. When the war began he was a lawyer in San Francisco. Soldiers delight to call their commanders by pet names. The Army of the Potomac called General McClellan "Little Mac." Later in the war they called General Thomas " Papa," because he

was careful to see that they were fed and clothed.   They called General
Halleck "Old Brains."   He directed the army which had captured Donelson to go up the Tennessee River to Savannah, and ordered General Buell
to march from Nashville to the same point.   The steamboat *Golden Gate*,
with the Fortieth Regiment of Illinois, was the first to reach Savannah,
and was followed by a great fleet of steamboats loaded with troops.   Ten
miles above Savannah, on the west bank of the Tennessee, was a log-house,
with a clearing and a road winding up the bank.   Down by the river the

ALBERT SIDNEY JOHNSTON.

willow-trees bend their branches into the stream, but as we go up the bank
we come to tall oaks and gum-trees, and an undergrowth of chincopins
and hazels.   Going out a little more than two miles, we come to a log
meeting-house.   A spring bubbles up near by, where the people who
attend church eat their luncheon and drink the clear running water.
They call it Shiloh church.   People who think highly of General Albert
Sidney Johnston as a commander say that he picked out in advance this
little log building as the spot where a great battle would be fought.   So

historians have said that Wellington picked out the field of Waterloo as a place where he intended to defeat Napoleon. It is probable that there is not much truth in either of the stories. It takes two parties to bring on a battle, and a general cannot very well decide just where it shall be fought. When the Confederates began to concentrate at Corinth, it was plain that the Union army would be likely to move in that direction. General Johnston was for selecting a place farther South, along the Hatchie River, but Beauregard began to assemble the troops at Corinth, which is twenty miles from the Shiloh meeting-house. He sent a battery down to Pittsburg Landing, which opened fire on one of the gunboats. In turn the gunboat sent its shells crashing through the willows and oaks, compelling the Confederates to fall back into the woods. It was the firing of that Confederate field-piece which attracted the attention of General Sherman to the spot as a suitable one for the Union army to occupy. He had been up to Eastport, and had tried to reach the railroad at Iuka, but the river was overflowing its banks, and he had to abandon the attempt. He went ashore at Pittsburg Landing and examined the ground. He saw that Snake Creek came in from the west just below the landing, and Lick Creek just above it. Five miles below was Crump's Landing. The ground was a broken plateau, mostly covered with trees, with clearings here and there. He pitched his tents around the church. The other divisions of the army arrived and went into camp between the church and the river.

General Buell was marching slowly from Nashville towards Pittsburg Landing. The Confederates had burned the bridge over Duck Creek, and the stream was swollen by the rains. He set about rebuilding the bridge. The river was falling. General Nelson, commanding one of the divisions of the army, was impatient to get on, and directed the soldiers to put their cartridge-boxes on their bayonets, hold them above their heads, and ford the river. His troops crossed, and thus were in the advance. We shall see what came of it. The troops under Buell numbered thirty-seven thousand, while those already at Pittsburg Landing numbered about thirty-eight thousand. United, the army would number seventy-five thousand. General Halleck was coming from St. Louis to take command.

General Johnston, at Corinth, knew that the army under Buell was on its way, and his scouts informed him that it would reach Pittsburg Landing by the 6th of April. What should he do? He had between forty and fifty thousand men; he expected General Van Dorn with twenty thousand more. Should he wait at Corinth and let the united Union armies attack him, or should he march at once from Corinth to Shiloh and attack Grant before Buell's arrival? With his superior force, by surprising Grant he might completely crush him; for he was between two creeks, with a deep river behind him, and no means of escape. It was the unanimous opinion of the Confederate generals that Grant should be attacked. Johnston hoped to be ready to move on April 1st, but was not. It was ten o'clock on the evening of the 2d when a messenger from General Cheatham, who was north of Corinth, came to Beauregard with the information that the Union army was divided, that one division was north of Snake Creek. "Now is the time to strike," said Beauregard. Johnston hesitated; said that the army was not ready. His adjutant, General Jordan, was earnest for the movement, and finally persuaded him to issue the order. The troops were to take three days' cooked rations in their haversacks, and three days' uncooked in wagons.

Drums were beating the next morning at Corinth. The Third Corps, under General Hardee, filed out from its camp and took the lead. General Hardee was from South Carolina; he had been educated at West Point. The Second Corps followed, under General Braxton Bragg, born in North Carolina and educated at West Point. He was in the battle of Buena Vista, in Mexico, and commanded a battery which did excellent service. When the war began, in 1861, he was a planter in Louisiana, raising cotton and sugar-cane. He was brave and energetic, but had such a temper that his officers did not always find it easy to get on with him. The First Corps, under General Polk, came next, followed by the reserves, under General Breckinridge. There had been heavy rains, and the roads were deep with mire. It was Thursday morning. Johnston expected to be ready to strike the blow on Saturday morning, but it rained on Friday, and when the sun went down at night the army was not in position to fall upon the unsuspecting Union troops.

One division of the Union army, commanded by Lew. Wallace, is north of Snake Creek, to protect the provisions at Crump's Landing; one brigade down by the river, one two miles out, and the third one mile beyond, towards the town of Purdy. General Wallace has constructed a bridge across Snake Creek, north of Shiloh church. Starting at Pittsburg Landing, we can turn to the right, cross the creek, on the road leading to Crump's, or we can go on towards the church and turn north, and cross the new bridge, and so reach the position occupied by Wallace's second brigade. It is between nine and ten miles by either road. Two brigades of General Sherman's division are around the church. General McClernand's is in Sherman's rear about half a mile; General Prentiss's is three-quarters of a mile south-east of Sherman; General Hurlbut's and General W. H. L.

GENERAL W. T. SHERMAN.

Wallace's divisions are towards the landing.   Stuart's brigade, of Sherman's division, is east of Prentiss, guarding the ford over Lick Creek. Sherman, Prentiss, and Stuart form the front line.   It is just about three miles from where Stuart stood to Owl Creek.   This is the only place where the Confederates can strike their contemplated blow, for the water is high in the Tennessee, and has flowed back into the creeks, so that the attack, if made, must be directly in front, and not by any flank movement. To be successful, the attack must be a surprise.

General Grant knew that a large Confederate army had gathered at
Corinth, but he did not expect that Johnston and Beauregard were about
to fall upon him.   The success at Donelson had made the Union army
over-confident; officers and soldiers alike had unbounded faith in themselves.   Precautions which were taken later in the war—the throwing up
of breastworks—were not thought of at Pittsburg Landing.   The army

SHILOH CHURCH.

was getting ready to move to Corinth, and was not expecting to be attacked by the Confederates. The divisions were not stationed with any
reference to a battle line. There was no forethought of battle. The
headquarters of General Grant was at Savannah. The immunity from
attack on either flank had somewhat to do with the feeling of security
which pervaded the army, from the generals to the men in the ranks.
General Grant had very little cavalry, and his information in regard to
the Confederates had to be obtained mostly through spies and infantry
scouts. His picket lines were not as far out as they might have been.
On Thursday and Friday General Buckland went out with a brigade five
miles to the farm of Mr. Michey, when suddenly the Confederate cavalry
swooped down upon his videttes and captured a lieutenant and seven men.
Buckland did not like that, and pushed out two miles farther, where he
found himself confronted by cavalry and artillery. He did not know that

he had encountered Cleburne's brigade, of Hardee's corps, advancing from Corinth. In the skirmish Major Crockett of Buckland's command was killed, but ten Confederates were captured. On Saturday morning Captain Mason, of the Seventy-seventh Ohio, saw squirrels and rabbits coming through the woods from the south-west, as if suddenly startled from their haunts. He had a suspicion that something was going on beyond the picket line, and reported to General Sherman, who sent out several companies to strengthen the pickets.

LEW. WALLACE.

General Lew. Wallace had two scouts whom he relied upon for information. One of them was Mr. Carpenter, who obtained his information from the negroes on the farms in the vicinity, who were, in turn, in communication with the negroes in the Confederate army—the servants who waited upon the Confederate officers, and who were doing work in the camp. He instructed them to keep their ears and eyes wide open to hear all that was said by the Confederate officers at dinner, or in consultation over maps, and to make a note of what was going on. The Confederate officers little knew that the slaves, brushing their clothes, blacking their boots, or waiting upon them at the mess table, were listening intently to their conversation, and that a few hours later it would be reported to a Union officer. Mr. Carpenter did not accept all that the negroes reported, but by comparing the different accounts was able to arrive at the probable truth. General Wallace's other scout was a very shrewd man, who was in the pay not only of General Wallace but of General Johnston. General Wallace accepted his reports as truthful because they were corroborated by the accounts brought by the negroes. At two o'clock on Saturday afternoon the scout Carpenter came in through the picket line and reported to General Wallace that the whole Confederate army was advancing. Two hours later the other scout came in with the same information, which was sent to General Grant. In many of the first accounts of the battle of Shiloh it is represented that the army under General Grant was taken completely by surprise, but it is now known that the division commanders understood that the Confederates were not far away. General Grant knew that a large body of the enemy was in front of him. He was most apprehensive for the safety of Crump's Landing, where nearly all of his supplies were stored. He feared that a rapid dash might be made upon Lew. Wallace, and the supplies destroyed before the main body of the army could be brought to Wallace's assistance. He expected that some sort of a movement would be made by the Confederates. He remained at Savannah to meet Buell, whom he was hourly expecting. While General Grant was riding towards the front on Friday he was severely injured by his horse falling, and for two or three days was unable to walk except with crutches. On Saturday, April 5th, General Nelson's division of Buell's army, which had forded Duck Creek, arrived at Savannah. General Grant ordered him to move up the east bank of the river to a position where he could be ferried over to Crump's Landing or to Pittsburg, as he might be needed. General Buell arrived at Savannah on the same evening, but did not inform General Grant, who did not learn of his arrival until after the battle had begun on Sunday morning. All through Saturday there was skirmishing between the Union and the Confederate pickets. Although the signs were multiplying that the Confederates were advancing, there was no preparation for a great battle on the part of General Grant or his division commanders, but at the same time there was a growing apprehension that something might happen.

General Prentiss sends Colonel Moore on Saturday with three companies of the Twenty-first Missouri to reconnoitre. They march obliquely past General Sherman's position towards the west three miles. They see nothing of the enemy. If they had marched south-west two miles they would have come plump upon General Hardee's line.

Through Saturday General Lew. Wallace's men, north of Snake Creek, are under arms, for the pickets out on the Purdy road discover a large force of Confederates. Wallace does not know that it is General Cheatham moving south to get into position. General Sherman knows that the Confederates are in front of him, but he does not expect to be attacked. He writes a note Saturday evening to General Grant: " Probably nothing will occur to-day more than picket firing. The enemy is saucy, but got the worst of it yesterday, and will not press our pickets."

General Grant sent this to General Halleck by telegraph Saturday afternoon: " I have scarcely the faintest idea of an attack (general one) being made upon us, but will be prepared should such a thing take place."

Walking now beyond the Union pickets, let us see the Confederate troops. They have no tents. It has been a weary march. They lie down upon the cold, damp ground, knowing that at daylight they are to strike a blow which they believe will drive the Union troops into the river.

The front line is composed of Hardee's corps, with Gladdin's brigade on the right. The artillery is in front, with the infantry behind. Bragg's corps is next in line. Eight hundred yards in rear of Bragg's is General Polk. Behind all is Breckinridge with the reserve. In each line there are from ten to twelve thousand men.

No loud talking is allowed, no drums beat the tattoo, no bugle sounds out its blast.

It is ten o'clock Saturday evening. The night is clear. In rear of the lines one dim fire burns. Around it stand the Confederate generals, who have come to receive their last orders. Beauregard is talking. He is restless, nervous, throws aside his cloak, walks here and there because he cannot keep still. General Breckinridge is lying upon the ground, wrapped in his blanket, pale and thoughtful. A few months ago he was Vice-president of the United States. In July he was expelled from the United States Senate, has turned his back upon the Nation and upon his State to join the Confederacy. To-morrow he will be in the thick of the fight. Polk, no longer a preacher, but a major-general, sits upon a camp-stool, leaning forward, his elbows upon his knees. He is silent and motionless. General Bragg is wide awake. He speaks with energy as to how the attack should be conducted. General Albert Sidney Johnston, command-

er-in-chief, stands apart from the rest.   He is tall, his shoulders are broad,
his hair tinged with gray.   His face is pale; the wrinkles are coming in
his cheeks.   He has felt deep chagrin over his forced evacuation of Bowling Green and the disaster at Donelson and Nashville.   To-morrow he
will retrieve all.

"Hammer them, gentlemen — hammer them," he says.   He has but
one plan — to hurl his troops upon Prentiss's and Sherman's divisions,
drive them back upon McClernand, Hurlbut, and W. H. L. Wallace, and
sweep all into the river, or compel their surrender before Buell arrives.

It is not Johnston but Beauregard who says, "Gentlemen, we sleep
in the enemy's camp to-morrow night."   All are confident of success, for
spies have been through the Union lines, and have reported the exact situation of the Union troops.

General Beauregard is second in command, but he is regarded as a hero
and a great general by the Confederate soldiers.

"If you were to ride in front of my lines," says General Hardee, "and
show yourself to the men, it will greatly encourage them."

"The men must not cheer me, for we are so near that the enemy will
hear them," Beauregard replies.

Officers ride in advance and inform the men that Beauregard is coming, but that they must not cheer.   He rides along the entire line.   The
men behold him with admiration.

It is fourteen minutes past five Sunday morning.   General Johnston is
eating his breakfast.   Suddenly there is a rattling fire of muskets.   It is
not the Confederate troops advancing, but three companies of Union troops
of the Twenty-fifth Missouri, under Colonel Moore, sent out by General
Prentiss on a reconnaissance.   They started at half-past three, and have
come upon Hardee's pickets—the Third Mississippi—under Major Hardcastle.   So the battle was not begun by the advance of the Confederates,
but by General Prentiss's troops, only that the Union troops did not dream
that they were opening one of the most terrible conflicts of the war.

For an hour the firing goes on between the three companies and the
Confederates.   Major Hardcastle says, "We fought the enemy an hour
or more without gaining an inch.   At about 6.30 A.M. I saw a brigade
formed in my rear and I fell back."

I write these facts because some writers have said that the Union army
was completely surprised, which is not true.   The soldiers were not asleep
in their tents, but eating their breakfasts, when the three companies of the
Twenty-fifth Missouri encountered the Confederate pickets.

General Buckland, of Sherman's division, is awake early, for he is to go out on a reconnaissance. He is eating breakfast when the rattle of musketry falls upon his ear.

"Beat the long-roll," he shouts to the drummer, and in a moment his brigade is in line. He leaps into his saddle, gallops to General Sherman's headquarters, and informs him that the Confederates are advancing in force.

In a few moments all of Sherman's brigades are in line. He has three batteries—Waterhouse's, Taylor's, and Behr's. Sherman rides to the front and sees the Confederate troops advancing upon his left east of the church.

"Support my left," is his word to McClernand.

"The enemy is upon you in force," is his message to Prentiss. No need of sending that, for Prentiss has discovered it.

"Support Prentiss," is the word to Hurlbut, in rear of Prentiss.

While Sherman is at the front, along the edge of a ravine, by the Fifty-third Ohio, General Albert Sidney Johnston is on the other side of the ravine, putting Thomas's Confederate brigade in position, and Thomas's skirmishers kill Sherman's orderly. Johnston places Wood's brigade, and then brings Cleburne's brigade up in front of Buckland.

The Fifty-third Ohio pours two volleys into Wood's brigade, which holds it in check; but the colonel commanding the Fifty-third loses his self-control and orders the regiment to fall back. It is a sad mistake. At eight o'clock, all along the line in front of Sherman and Prentiss the cannon are thundering.

On the Confederate side, General Anderson's brigade, with Hodgson's battery of the Washington Artillery, comes up from Johnston's second line, to fill a gap between Hindman and Cleburne, but Taylor's battery and the Fifty-seventh and Seventy-fifth Ohio confront Anderson.

Cleburne, who holds the extreme left of Hardee's line south-west of the church, comes with six regiments and two batteries to attack Buckland, who has posted his men along the edge of a ravine. The ravine is boggy, and when Cleburne attempts to cross it his troops sink into the mire and suffer great loss. The Sixth Mississippi comes into the battle with four hundred and twenty-five men, but in a short time three hundred are killed or wounded. Cleburne loses one-third of his men.

General Johnston, with twelve Confederate regiments of Bragg's corps and two batteries, fell upon Prentiss's flanks. Prentiss's men were fighting their first battle; they held their ground a while, but broke at last and fled from their camp. The Confederates ran to the tents to secure plunder, seizing knapsacks, blankets, and finishing the breakfasts which they had captured. They danced and sang. They had captured three hundred prisoners, and thought the victory won.

Sherman tried to hold his position by the church. The battle was raging fearfully along his lines east of the church. His horse was shot, and he mounted another; that was killed, and he took a third. His clothes were riddled with bullets. He encouraged his men, but the giving way of Prentiss had exposed his left flank, and he must fall back. He held his ground till ten o'clock, and then retreated, leaving his camp in the hands of the Confederates. Other Confederates were forming a line half a mile in his rear towards Pittsburg Landing.

The drivers and gunners of Behr's battery became frightened, and rode off with the caissons, leaving five cannon to fall into the hands of the Confederates.

General Grant was eating breakfast at Savannah when the thunder of the cannonade reached him. He wrote a note to General Buell and went on board a steamboat, which moved rapidly up the river to Crump's Landing. General Wallace was there on a steamboat. Before Grant's arrival, Wallace, hearing the cannonade, and comprehending its meaning, had sent orders to his brigade commanders, to the one farthest out to fall back to the position of the second, to send all its camp equipage to Crump's Landing. It was half-past eight when General Grant's boat came alongside the steamer which General Wallace was using as his headquarters. "Be ready," said General Grant. "I am ready," was the reply. General Grant, not stopping, went on to Pittsburg Landing, arriving there a little past nine o'clock.

In a battle there comes a time when the assailing party begins to lose its aggressive force. That hour has come to the Confederate army. The soldiers have made a wearisome march from Corinth. They slept little on Saturday night. They have eaten nothing since early morning. They have been under the strain of battle, and have suffered heavy losses. Many officers have been killed or wounded. Thousands of faint-hearted men have drifted to the rear. Others think that the victory is already won.

Looking now at the Union line, we see it at two o'clock more compact than at any time during the morning. The line is much shorter. It, too, has suffered great losses. Down by the landing are thousands of fainthearted men, who would gladly cross the river if they could, and leave their comrades to finish the fight. Some are swimming Lick Creek and fleeing to Crump's Landing. But there are brave men in the lines who have no thought of yielding another inch, and every time the Confederates advance they drive them back. General Bragg says: "Hindman's command was gallantly led to the attack, but recoiled under a murderous fire. The noble and gallant leader fell severely wounded. The command returned to its work, but was unequal to the heavy task. I brought up Gibson's brigade, and threw them forward to attack the same point. A heavy fire soon opened, and after a short conflict this command fell back in considerable disorder. Rallying the different regiments by my staff-officers and escort, they were twice more moved to the attack, only to be driven back."

It was W. H. L. Wallace's division which withstood all these assaults.

It is half-past two. General Johnston is directing the movements of Breckinridge's troops down by Lick Creek, when a shell explodes above him, and a jagged piece of iron strikes his thigh, severing an artery. He grows faint, and reels in his saddle. Governor Harris, of Tennessee, lays him upon the ground, moistens his lips with brandy, but in a few minutes he ceases to breathe. The Confederate army has lost its commander, who, smarting under the disaster at Donelson and Nashville, determined to win a great victory.

An officer informs Beauregard of Johnston's death.

"Do not let the army know it. The battle may as well go on," he says.

Nearly at the same moment General W. H. L. Wallace, who has rolled back the Confederates, falls mortally wounded. It is a sad loss to the Union army. He has been cool and brave, and encouraged his men—inspired them with his own lofty valor. His troops give way. It exposes Prentiss's division. The Confederates gradually gain the rear of Prentiss, who is finally surrounded and obliged to surrender, with two thousand five hundred of his men.

A great shout goes up. Once more the Confederates take heart.

From morning till four o'clock in the afternoon the battle raged, the Confederates forcing the Union troops back nearly two miles, but were unable to drive them any farther for several reasons.

In a battle lasting many hours there comes a time when the troops break down through exhaustion. "This is hard pounding, but we will see which can stand it longest," said Wellington at Waterloo. "We shall hold them yet," said Grant to his chief of staff, General Webster, at five o'clock. He was taking note of the situation of affairs—the concentration of his troops, the line being hardly a mile in length, its position along the northern bank of Dill's ravine. In every army there are two classes of men: those who grow fainthearted, and who lose heart under disaster, those whose determination and courage rise under disaster. At five o'clock on that Sunday afternoon the troops standing along the bank of that ra-

14

vine are of the class who have no thought of final defeat. Whatever the outcome of the battle may be, they are there to fight. General Grant had lost at this hour between six and seven thousand; there was a great crowd of faint-hearted fugitives cowering along the river bank. Probably there are not more than ten thousand men in line, but Lew. Wallace is not far away with six thousand fresh troops. During the afternoon General Webster has been preparing a line of defence along Dill's ravine, which extends from the river nearly one mile towards the north-west. Bundles of hay, pork-barrels, boxes, anything that can be used, are placed along the northern bank. Men go to work with spades, and in a short time have a formidable breastwork. General Webster places all the cannon in position, between twenty and thirty in number.

The artillerymen who have lost their guns are eager to work the heavy cannon ranged along the ravine. Going up the road leading to Crump's Landing we see Sherman covering it with his two brigades. At his left are McClernand and Hurlbut's divisions, reaching down to the heavy guns. The shattered divisions of W. H. L. Wallace and Prentiss are in rear.

On the Confederate side Jackson's, Chalmers's, Gladden's, and Gibson's brigades are getting ready to make the last attack, which it is expected will drive Grant into the river, or compel his surrender. General Beauregard has not comprehended all the points of the situation, neither has any Confederate corps commander. Success thus far has crowned their efforts. They have driven the Union troops almost to the landing. One more attack and the victory will be complete; but the troops at this moment are nearly as much disorganized as the Union regiments. Many of them have left the ranks to secure the plunder in the captured camps. Others, weary with the march from Corinth, having wasted their rations, are searching for something to eat. At this sunset hour the enthusiasm and courage of the morning, through weariness and exhaustion, are wanting.

We saw the men of Nelson's division of Buell's army crossing Duck Creek with their knapsacks on their bayonets. They did not know what would come of it, but here they are being ferried across the Tennessee by the steamboats forming at the landing. They see the thousands of fugitives cowering under the bank. The Confederate cannon-shot and shells are whirring through the trees. Right above them the heavy guns, under General Webster, are thundering. The roll of musketry is like the crescendo of an orchestra as Ammen's brigade winds up the bank and comes into position between the heavy guns and the river, and pours its volleys down upon the Confederates in Dill's ravine. At the same moment there comes a roar from the great guns on the gunboats *Lexington* and *Tyler*, which send their shells up the ravine.

General Bragg, commanding the troops south of the ravine, directs Jackson and Chalmers and Gibson to charge across it, climb the northern bank, and finish the victory for the Confederates. They descend the southern slope, making their way through the chincopins and hazels. Instantly a line of fire runs along the northern crest. The heavy cannon flame upon them in front, the eleven-inch shells come tearing across their flank, a withering storm of bullets beats in their faces. In a moment the line in gray melts away; not a soldier gains the northern crest. The regiments are cut to pieces. With this last attack and repulse, the victory, so sure a few moments ago, becomes a defeat.

In the life of General Beauregard we find an account of this last attack: "General Beauregard, seeing that nothing but a concerted and well-supported attack, in heavy mass, could that evening strike a finishing blow, by which the enemy would be crushed, ordered the corps commanders to make a hasty reorganization of the troops for a combined onslaught. He caused all fragmentary bodies and stragglers to be gathered up, and they were carried forward to swell the line of battle. They were not pressed to the front, as ordered, in combined attack, but in a series of disjointed assaults, which were easily broken, and with slaughter, by the formidable weight of metal which girded the Federal position, supported by a still heavy force of infantry, while the shells of the gunboats swept the long ravine which our different commands had to cross. The troops were greatly disorganized; the commands were cut up and intermingled, and greatly confused. . . . General Hardee was bringing up two regiments, when one broke in disorder and fell back out of the fight. . . . Wood's brigade made no impression upon the artillery and the infantry supporting it. . . . Gladden's brigade was led under a heavy fire from the light batteries, siege-pieces, and gunboats across the ravine, ascended the ridge with bristling bayonets; it could go no farther. . . . Chalmers vainly endeavored to ascend the ridge. . . . Jackson saw that a farther advance was impracticable."

"Three different times," says Colonel Fagan, of Gibson's brigade, "did we go into that valley of death, and as often were forced back. All was done that could be done, as the heaps of killed and wounded give ample evidence."

The wearied soldiers of both armies lie down to sleep, with their loaded guns beside them, while the sentinels stand like statues along that valley of death, watching and waiting for the morning. There is little sleep for the Confederates, for through the night the gunboats send their shells through the forest in the direction of their bivouac fires.

When General Grant arrived at Pittsburg Landing in the morning, and learned the state of affairs, he saw that there was no danger of an attack at Crump's Landing, and sent an order to Lew. Wallace to march at once to the "right of the army," but did not specify by which road. General Grant had given a verbal order to the officer who carried it, but the order which General Wallace received at half-past eleven was written with a pencil upon a sheet of paper stained with tobacco juice, and bore no signature. The officer, fearing that he might not remember what General Grant had said, picked up a crumpled piece of paper and wrote it with a pencil. General Wallace started at once, with his cavalry in advance, towards the sound of the firing, taking the road towards the bridge which he had constructed across Snake Creek. General Wallace did not know that General Sherman had fallen back. While on the march a second officer came with an order for him to march rapidly, and who said, "We are repulsing them." At this moment the firing seemed to General Wallace to be getting farther away. Another messenger came. "Where are you going?" he asked. "To the right of the army," was the reply. "Don't you know that we are driven back almost to the landing, and the chances are that we shall be driven into the river?" General Wallace was astounded. General Rawlins, of Grant's staff, and McPherson, of the engineers, rode up, having been sent to ascertain his whereabouts, and to bring him with all possible haste to the landing. After conference with them, General Wallace ordered his division to countermarch and go back to the starting-point, and take the old road to the landing. We can see our mistakes after we have made them, but are not always clear as to what is best for us to do in emergency. General Wallace did not know the exact position of affairs at the landing, neither did General Grant know the exact position of General Wallace. Had either known just how things stood, it is altogether probable that Wallace, instead of countermarching, would have gone on. He was in rear of the Confederates with six thousand men—those who had swept up the slope of Donelson under General Smith. The Confederates at this moment in front of Wallace were very much disorganized; they had suffered severely from the fire of Sherman's, W. H. L. Wallace's, and McClernand's divisions. The appearance of such a body on their left flank and rear undoubtedly would have carried consternation along the demoralized and shattered ranks. Said Grant to General Wallace in 1864, "If I were to be in the same situation again I

THE BATTLE OF SHILOH.

should order you to go on." It was dark when the head of Wallace's column reached the lower bridge across Snake Creek. He crossed the creek and halted in the road, thus forming the right wing of the army for the battle of the next day.

General Beauregard's headquarters on Sunday night were about one mile in rear of the line of battle. General Bragg occupied General Sherman's tent near Shiloh Church. During the evening the Confederate corps commanders came together at Beauregard's headquarters and received their orders for the following day. They felt the loss of General Johnston, but were jubilant over what had been accomplished, and confident of success. They had no doubt that the victory would be made complete in the morning. General Beauregard sent a despatch to Richmond announcing that he had won a victory. He did not know that Buell at that moment was coming into position with his divisions on the north bank of Dill's ravine, where Chalmers and Jackson had been repulsed.

During the night General Grant is laying his plans for the morning. As at Donelson, he decides no longer to stand on the defensive, but issues orders to begin the battle at daylight. He leaves General Buell to make whatever disposition he pleases with his troops. Just as daylight breaks, Thompson's battery, of Lew. Wallace's division, sends its shells across the ravine through which winds Tillman's Creek towards Snake Creek, upon Pond's brigade of Confederates. At the same instant the batteries down towards the river begin to thunder, and a few moments later the firing opens all along the Union line. With returning daylight many of the stragglers of yesterday, cheered now by the knowledge that Buell's army has arrived, return to their regiments.

Beginning upon the right, between the road leading to Crump's Landing and Tillman's Creek, we see Lew. Wallace's division facing southwest, then Sherman facing south, then McClernand, and the remnant of W. H. L. Wallace, then Hurlbut, and what is left of Prentiss. Buell's three divisions—Nelson's, McCook's, and Crittenden's—occupy the ground from the main Corinth road to the river. Nelson's division is in Dill's ravine. It is twenty minutes past five when Nelson moves out from the ravine southward, followed by Crittenden, who comes into position on Nelson's right, followed in turn by McCook, who takes the right of Crittenden. The first musketry firing is between Nelson's skirmishers and the Confederates under Breckinridge. Almost at the same moment Wallace's skirmishers on the right advance upon Pond's Confederate brigade. Wallace crossed Tillman's Creek and pushed Pond from his position, then waited for the advance of Sherman on the edge of a large field. About

PITTSBURG LANDING.   (FROM A PHOTOGRAPH, MAY, 1862.)

seven o'clock Sherman and McClernand advanced to the left of Wallace's
division.   While this is going on, Buell's divisions are pushing the Confederates in front of them back over the ground where the fight was hot-
test on Sunday—"the hornet's nest," as the soldiers called it.   Through
the forenoon the battle goes on, but not with the terrific energy of Sunday.   The Confederates are no longer on the aggressive.   Two Union batteries, those of Mendenhall and Terrill, obtain a position from which they
send an enfilading fire upon the Confederate batteries in front of McCook.
General Sherman is upon the spot, and gives direction to the firing.   The
Confederate cannon are quickly silenced and driven.   This, together with
the folding back of Breckinridge and Bragg by Nelson and Crittenden on
the left, the aggressive energy of McCook, Hurlbut, and Sherman in the
centre, and the resistless advance of Wallace on the right, can have but one
result, the final defeat of the Confederates.

Early in the forenoon General Beauregard gave up all expectation of
winning the battle.   He knew that Buell had arrived, that the Union
army was now much larger than his own, that his army had lost its energy, and that sooner or later he must retreat; but he resolved to make a
show of resistance, and to fall back that he might save his troops from a
final rout, which would be the probable result if he were to attempt a
vigorous attack.   It was two o'clock when Governor Harris, of Tennessee,
serving on General Beauregard's staff, asked Colonel Jordan if the battle

was not going against them, and if there was not danger of a rout. Colonel Jordan expressed his fears to Beauregard for the safety of the army, and asked if it would not be well to get away as soon as they could. "I intend to withdraw in a few moments," was the reply; and officers were sent with orders to the corps commanders to retire from the field. At three o'clock the Confederate army, with disordered ranks, disheartened, defeated, having lost more than twelve thousand troops, began its weary march back to Corinth. The last roll of musketry died away—fired beyond the little log church, almost on the very spot where the struggle began.

General Beauregard reached Corinth, and sent this despatch to Richmond: "We have gained a great and glorious victory—eight to ten thousand prisoners and thirty-six cannon. Buell reinforced Grant, and we retired to Corinth, which we can hold. Loss heavy on both sides." On the same day he sent a flag of truce to Grant asking leave to bury his dead, with this message: "Sir,—At the close of the conflict yesterday, my forces being exhausted by the extraordinary length of time during which they were engaged with yours on that and the preceding day, and it being apparent that you had received, and were still receiving, reinforcements, I felt it my duty to retire, and withdraw my troops from the immediate scene of battle."

The Union army lost thirty-three guns on the first day; but on the second Sherman's division recaptured seven, McClernand's three, and the army of Buell twenty—in all thirty guns. The Union loss was about twelve thousand, of whom three thousand were taken prisoners. General Beauregard reported his loss at nearly eleven thousand, almost all killed and wounded. He reported the number killed at seventeen hundred and twenty-eight. General Grant says that it was much larger; that more than that number were buried in front of the divisions of Sherman and McClernand. The Confederates were the attacking party on the first day, and their loss was much greater than Grant's. On the second day the Union army began the attack, and quite likely their loss was equal to the Confederate. The battle was fought with great obstinacy on the part of the Union troops. Grant says: "Excluding the troops who fled, panic-stricken, before they had fired a shot, there was not a time on the 6th when we had more than twenty-five thousand men in line." Beauregard's force was nearly forty thousand. The troops on both sides were undisciplined. The battle decided nothing, except that Beauregard lost his prestige as a great commander. His despatch announcing a great victory aroused for the moment the enthusiasm of the Southern people, but when they learned that it was a defeat instead he was no longer looked upon as a hero.

CHAPTER X.

NEW ORLEANS AND MEMPHIS.

FROM the forests of Minnesota, in the heart of the continent, the Mississippi River pours its mighty flood to the sea. With its branches—the Missouri, Ohio, Tennessee, Cumberland, Arkansas, and Red rivers, and their thousands of smaller streams—it is the arterial system of the continent. The dead tree which falls into the stream five thousand miles away is borne to the Gulf of Mexico; the grains of sand washed from the summit of the Rocky Mountains is carried by the ever-sweeping current to the sea. When the Southern States seceded from the Union no river on the globe had a commerce so great as that of the Mississippi.

The people of New Orleans had great expectations. They thought that by the secession of the Southern States and the setting up of the Confederacy New Orleans would become the metropolis of the Western world; that St. Louis and Cincinnati would cease to grow; that New York would no longer control the commerce with England and Europe; that grass would grow in the streets of Boston. When the State seceded, cannon thundered on the levees and bonfires blazed. When troops were called for, the merchants opened their pocket-books and gave liberally to fit out the Washington Artillery, which took part in the battle of Bull Run.

On the low and marshy land thirty miles from the Gulf of Mexico the United States had built two strong forts — St. Philip, on the north bank, and Jackson, on the south. They were built of brick. The walls were thick, and there were one hundred and twenty-six guns in position to sweep the river. In addition to the forts, a great chain was stretched from shore to shore, resting upon eight old hulks anchored in the stream. Blacksmiths and carpenters were at work constructing a huge steam battery, the *Manassas*, carrying sixteen guns, and a steam ram, the *Louisiana*, shaped like a turtle, nearly all under water. Flat-boats were piled with pitch, pine-wood, and barrels of tar, to be sent adrift if a Union fleet should appear.

Such a fleet did appear. Its commander was David Glasgow Farragut, who was born near Knoxville, Tennessee. He went to sea when he was only ten years old, under Captain Porter, in the frigate *Essex*, and was in the terrible fight between that vessel and the British ships *Phœbe* and *Cherub* in the Bay of Valparaiso, in 1812.

His friends were mostly in the South, but he was true and loyal to the flag under which he had fought, and was selected to command the fleet sent to capture New Orleans. He had seventeen vessels—all wooden ships—besides twenty-one mortar-boats—schooners which had been purchased. In all, he had about two hundred cannon.

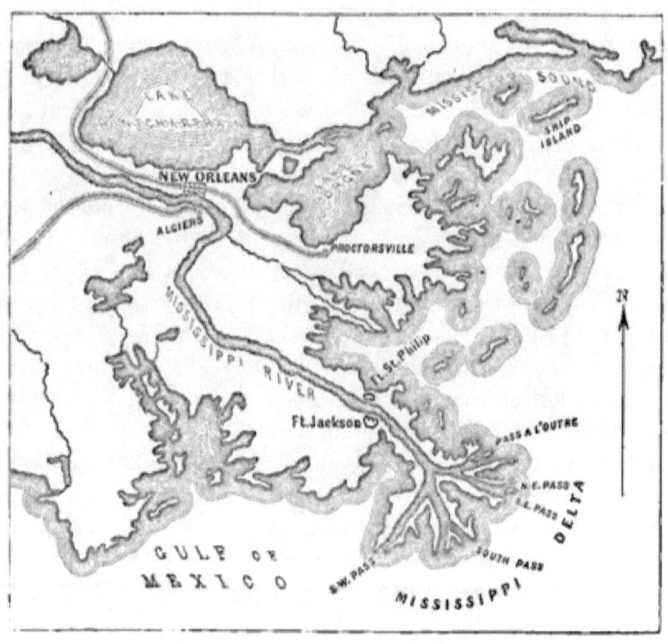

THE MISSISSIPPI BELOW NEW ORLEANS.

A fleet of steamers sailed from New York with fifteen thousand troops on board, commanded by General Benjamin F. Butler, to hold the city after its capture.

Admiral Farragut had much difficulty in getting the large vessels over the bar at the mouth of the river. It took two weeks, with the aid of tugboats, to get the *Pensacola* across; but one by one the vessels—all except the *Colorado*—were at last in the river.

"Dress all your rigging with green boughs," was the order of the admiral.

The soldiers went on shore with their axes, cut down branches of trees, took them on board, and lashed them to the masts and yard-arms. Below Fort Jackson the river turns, and the vessels dropped anchor under the shelter of the woods. Then the sailors saw why they had been ordered to dress the rigging. The Confederate soldiers in the forts would not be able to distinguish the vessels from the trees.

The mortar-vessels were drawn up beside the bank and tied to the trees. Mr. Gerdes, of the Coast Survey, went round the bend in a boat, sighted the fort with his transit instrument, and found out by triangulation just how far the distance was from the boats to the fort.

Commander Porter had charge of the mortar-vessels. The Confederates had a regiment of men prowling through the woods, up to their waists in water, who reported that the mortars were getting ready.

Colonel Duncan, commanding the Confederate gunboats, let loose a fire-boat. It was at daybreak, April 16th, when the Union sailors saw it sweeping round the bend, lighting up the river. They leaped into their boats, seized it with grappling-irons, and towed it to the shore.

The next morning the mortars began, and before night one thousand four hundred shells, each weighing two hundred and eighty-five pounds, had been thrown into the forts. Through the night, the next day, and for six days and nights, the shells swept up from the mortars high in the air, and fell, sinking deep into the mud, exploding, lifting cart-loads of earth into the air. The barracks were set on fire, killing fourteen and wounding thirty-nine men. It was terribly trying to the Confederate soldiers in St. Philip, who had little sleep. But they were brave, and though they could not see the mortar-boats, sent rifle-shot towards them, which crashed through the woods, sinking one of the schooners and disabling one of the Union steamboats. The thunder of the mortars rolled along the river, reverberating from shore to shore, stunning the fish, which floated to the surface, and breaking windows at the Balize, thirty miles away. ·

Admiral Farragut was getting out of patience. The mortars could not silence the forts, and he determined to run past them; but he must first cut the boom opposite Fort Jackson. In the night Captain Bell, with two gunboats, steamed up to it. He tried to blow up one of the hulks, but the torpedo did not explode. Men with hammers and chisels went to work upon the chain. Though all the guns in the fort were sending shot and shell upon them, they hammered till the chain snapped, leaving an opening for the ships.

Down the river came more fire-rafts; but the sailors knew how to manage them, and no harm was done, except that two of the vessels, in getting out of their way, ran against the steamer *Mississippi* and carried away her main-mast.

Admiral Farragut thought out in advance what part each ship was to perform. He divided his fleet into divisions. First division: *Pensacola, Mississippi, Cayuga, Oneida, Varuna, Katahdin, Kineo*, and *Wissahickon*. Centre division: *Hartford, Brooklyn*, and *Richmond*. Third division: *Sciota, Iroquois, Kennebec, Pinola, Itasca*, and *Winona*.

The *Hartford* was the flag-ship, a noble vessel, which sat as graceful as a swan upon the water. She was two hundred and twenty-five feet in

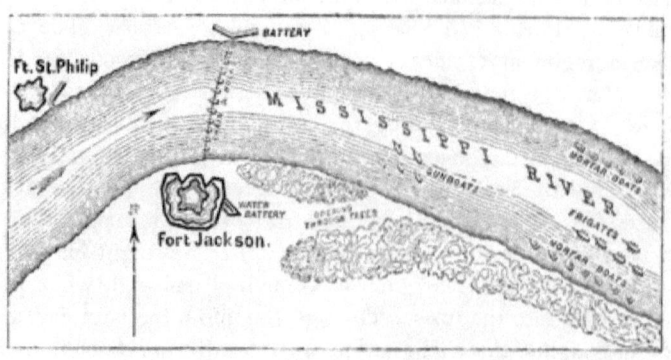

FORTS OF THE MISSISSIPPI.

length, and carried twenty-two nine-inch Dahlgren guns, two twenty-pounder Parrott's, and a rifled Sawyer gun on her decks; up in the main-tops were howitzers in iron houses. The forts were so low that the howitzers could pour grape and canister from the main-tops right down upon the men working the guns on the barbette of the forts.

Admiral Farragut planned what each ship was to do. The column under his command was to attack Fort Jackson, while the right column, under Captain Bailey, was to push on and pour their broadsides into Fort St. Philip, and attack the Confederate fleet.

The chain-cables were looped over the sides of the ships to protect them. The gun-carriages were whitewashed, so that the sailors might see how to handle the guns.

At midnight the boatswains piped their whistles, and the sailors on the ships leaped from the hammocks, which were stowed away, and the decks cleared for action. The sailors up at the mast-heads on the lookout, at five minutes before two, saw two red lanterns go up at the peak of the *Hartford*. It was the signal for sailing.

The Confederates knew that something was going on in the fleet, and they set great piles of wood on fire on both shores to light up the river, and sent down more fire-rafts, which came floating towards the ships.

Three o'clock. The crescent moon is rising in the east. The sky is clear. Scarce a breath of air disturbs the leaves of the forest. You hear only the swirling of the water. Suddenly the mortars open. The shells stream skyward, sail slowly for a moment through the air, and then descend upon the forts. Round the bend moves the line of ships, the *Cayuga*, of Captain Bailey's division, in advance. The guns of Fort Jackson flame, and a moment later those of St. Philip are thundering; also a battery near by. Just above St. Philip are the Confederate war-vessels, ready for action.

Five minutes — and the *Cayuga* has poured her broadsides into St. Philip, and has passed through the opening in the raft. Ten minutes more and five of the Confederate vessels are upon her like so many wolves upon a single deer that has outrun the rest of the herd.

It is to be a battle fought in the darkness, with a thick haze on the river, with the smoke of nearly four hundred guns hanging like a pall over the swirling stream, with only the light of the crescent moon low in the eastern horizon, and the lurid flame of the fire-rafts and the flashes of the cannon, with clouds of black smoke rolling up from the chimneys of the war-ships, and the air thick with shot, shells, grape, and canister. No one can tell just what takes place. The vessels, one after another, steam through the opening in the raft.

> "The way to the work was plain,
> Caldwell had broken the chain—
> (Two hulks swung down amain,
>   Soon as 'twas sundered)—
> Under the night's dark blue,
> Steering steady and true,
> Ship after ship went through—
> Till, as we hove in view,
>   Jackson out-thundered.

> "Back echoed Philip! Ah, then,
> Could you have seen our men,
>   How they sprung in the dim night's haze
> To their work of toil and clamor!
> How the loaders with sponge and rammers,
> And their captains with cord and hammers,
>   Kept every muzzle ablaze."

The *Pensacola* follows the *Cayuga*, steaming slowly, her gunners taking deliberate aim, sending eighty-pound rifled shot, and shells, eleven inches in diameter, into the fort. But the gunners in the fort do terrible execution on her decks, killing and wounding thirty-seven men.

Through the storm from both forts steams the *Oneida*, driving with all her force at a Confederate ship, striking it amidships and cutting it half-way through. Both broadsides flame at the same instant upon the Confederate vessels swarming around her.

Up past the forts comes the *Varuna*, unfortunately running aground. Down upon her sweep the Confederate ships *Governor Moore* and the *Manassas*, crushing holes in her sides, smashing planks and timbers into kindlings. The vessel begins to sink, but her guns keep up their thundering, sending three eight-inch shells into the *Governor Moore*, and riddling her sides with solid shot, making such terrible havoc that she pulls down her flag and surrenders.

From the cannon on the other side of the ship five shells smash through the sides of another Confederate vessel, making it a complete wreck. The *Varuna* sends still one more shell into the boilers of a third vessel. There is a rush and roar of steam, and the crew leap into the river to save themselves from being scalded. Lower settles the *Varuna*. The sailors leap from the deck into the rushing stream, to be picked up by the boats of the *Oneida*.

The *Mississippi* poured a broadside into Jackson, another into St. Philip. The *Manassas* comes down with a rush upon her, crushing a hole in her hull below the water-line, and disabling her machinery by the shock. But all the while her guns are roaring—sending eight-inch solid shot into the *Manassas*, riddling her iron plates, setting her on fire.

The *Katahdin* puts on all steam, runs close under St. Philip, and pours her fire into the iron-clad *Louisiana*. The *Kineo* runs close up to St. Philip, and then sends solid shot at the *Manassas*.

The *Wissahickon*, unfortunately, runs ashore in the darkness before reaching the fort, but floats again, runs past the forts, only to ground once more. These vessels belonged to the first division. They were to pay little attention to the forts, but to engage the thirteen Confederate vessels.

It was just half-past three in the morning when the *Hartford*, leading the second division, swept round the bend of the river. By the light of the fire-rafts and the blazing piles of pitch-pine wood on shore the Confederate gunners in Fort Jackson behold the beautiful outlines of the vessel, and the shot and shell begin to sweep her decks. The *Hartford* can only reply with her bow gun. But at five minutes before four, from the middle of the stream, her broadsides open upon both forts. Ten minutes, and she is past them, but in the darkness runs aground. The *Manassas* pushes a great raft of fire upon her. In an instant the flames are leaping up her sides and into the rigging. The steam-pumps are set to work; the sailors lower their buckets, dip up the water, dash it upon the flames, and all the while the cannon are thundering.

> "In a twinkling the flames had risen
> Half-way to main-top and mizzen,
> Darting up the shrouds like smoke.
> Ah, how we clanked at the brakes !
> And the deep steam-pumps throbbed under,
> Sending a ceaseless flow.
> Our topmen—a dauntless crowd—
> Swarmed in rigging and shroud.
> There ('twas a wonder !)
> The burning ratlins and shrouds
> They quenched with their bare, hard hands.
> But the great guns below
> Never silenced their thunder !"

The *Hartford* floats once more. A Confederate vessel crowded with men comes down to board her, but Captain Broome lets fly a shell, and she disappears.

The *Brooklyn*, in the darkness, runs upon one of the hulks of the raft. The *Manassas*, another Confederate vessel, fires upon her, but getting clear and running close up to St. Philip, the *Brooklyn* sends such a storm of grape and canister from her great guns that by the flashes the sailors can see the Confederates fleeing from the fort.

A Confederate vessel—the *Warrior*—comes down upon her, but the *Brooklyn* sends eleven shells into her, and the *Warrior* is a helpless wreck, on fire from stem to stern.

The *Richmond* steams slowly past the forts, firing steadily, the gunners watching the flashes from the fort and taking deliberate aim.

The *Sciota*, with Captain Bell on her deck, leads, steaming rapidly past the forts, engaging two Confederate vessels, and setting them on fire.

The *Iroquois* passes the forts. The Confederate vessel *McCrea* sweeps her decks with grape, but she sends one eleven-inch shell and a broadside of canister into the *McCrea*, driving her off, and opens her broadsides upon the rest of the Confederate vessels.

The *Pinola*—the last to pass the forts—receives the fire of the forty guns of St. Philip, but arrives in season to take part in the fight with the Confederate vessels.

A shell from one of the forts explodes in the boiler of the *Itasca*, and she drifts back below the hulk. The *Winona* is driven back, her decks slippery with the blood of her crew.

What a scene it is! Lurid flames, burning rafts, the flashing of three hundred guns, a storm of shells raining upon Fort Jackson, the air thick with solid shot, grape and canister, vessels rushing upon each other, black clouds of smoke rolling up from pitchwood smeared with tar, white clouds belching from the cannon's mouths!

Daylight is dawning—the uproar dying away. The Confederate fleet is destroyed. Some of the vessels have disappeared, like the *Varuna*, beneath the swirling waters; others are shattered wrecks drifting seaward. The *Manassas* is all aflame; the powder left in her magazine explodes, and she disappears forever.

Never before was there such consternation in New Orleans. Men lose their senses. At the levee is a great fleet of steamers loaded with cotton. In an instant they are ablaze—the people setting them on fire, cutting the cables, and sending them adrift in the stream. People run hither and thither, not knowing what to do or where to go. In an hour property worth millions of dollars is licked up by the flames.

Up the river steam the vessels, the *Cayuga* in advance. Three miles below the city the Confederates have erected a battery of twenty heavy guns, which open upon her, but the *Hartford*, *Pensacola*, and *Brooklyn* open with their broadsides such a stream that the Confederates flee in terror, and the vessels steam on, dropping anchor in front of the city at one o'clock in the afternoon of April 25th. On the ships the sailors swing their caps and hurrah. On the shore is a crowd of people cursing and swearing in impotent rage.

"Burn the city!" shout the ragamuffins, who have nothing to lose.

"Shoot the coward who commanded the forts!" they cry, not knowing how gallantly the Confederates in the forts had fought, nor that the Confederate flag is still flying above them.

But they could not hold them. The garrisons began to desert, and they were surrendered to General Butler, who took possession of New Orleans on the 1st of May.

In the battle the loss on the ships was forty killed and one hundred and seventy-seven wounded.

Let us see what has been accomplished in the Mississippi Valley. The first victory was at Fort Henry; the second, Fort Donelson. Then came the evacuation of Bowling Green and Nashville, the battle of Pittsburg

15

Landing, the taking of Island No. 10, the opening of the rivers down to Fort Pillow, fifty miles above Memphis. New Orleans has been taken, and the fleet of Admiral Farragut is at Vicksburg.

We come to the last week in May. Since the battle of Pittsburg Landing General Halleck has been gathering an army of nearly one hundred thousand men to advance upon Corinth. Beauregard has about half as many. He is exceedingly cautious, builds long lines of intrenchments, then advances a mile and builds another long line — sets the soldiers to work digging wells to supply the troops with water. He supposed that he would be compelled to besiege Corinth, and brought forward heavy guns and erected batteries. On the 28th of May he opened fire. But there were no Confederates at Corinth; they had marched silently away to Tupelo, fifty-two miles south of Corinth.

General Halleck was greatly surprised and chagrined, for he had lost an opportunity to strike a blow.

Fort Pillow, forty miles above Memphis, was no longer of any account, for the Union army could take it from the rear. The Confederates, therefore, spiked the guns, burned their barracks and what supplies they could not take away; and the Confederate gunboats went down the river to Memphis, where several of the boats had been built.

Commodore Montgomery commanded the fleet. He had eight vessels. They were: *General Beauregard*, four guns; *Little Rebel*, two; *General Price*, four; *Sumter*, three; *General Lovell*, four; *Thompson*, four; *General Bragg*, three; and *General Van Dorn*, four — total, twenty-eight guns.

Fort Pillow evacuated! It was astounding news to the people of Memphis. They learned it at noon, June 5th. The merchants closed their stores. Some of them began to pack their goods. Some of the citizens jumped on board the cars and fled from the city.

The Confederate fleet made its appearance.

"I shall retreat no farther," said Commodore Montgomery; "I shall fight a battle in front of the city, and to-morrow morning you will see Lincoln's gunboats sent to the bottom."

The dawn is breaking when I step from the *Benton*, the flag-ship of Commodore Davis, to the tugboat *Jessie Benton*. It is a bright summer morning. The woods are resonant with the song of birds, the air balmy. Light fleecy clouds, fringed with gold, float along the eastern horizon.

The Union fleet is at anchor three miles above the city.

"Drop down below the city and see if you can discover the Confederate fleet," is the order to the captain of the *Jessie Benton*.

FORT PILLOW.

We sweep around the majestic bend of the river and behold the city. The first rays of the sun are gilding the spires of the churches. A crowd of people is upon the levee—men, women, and children—who have come out to see the Union fleet sent to the bottom.

The *Jessie Benton* is a swift little craft, tender to the fleet to carry orders. As I stand upon the deck I can see all that is going on. Suddenly a vessel with a black cloud of smoke rolling from the chimneys shoots into the stream. It is the *Little Rebel*, Commodore Montgomery's flag-ship. One by one the other vessels follow, forming in two lines of battle.

In the front line, nearest the city, is the *Beauregard*, next the *Little Rebel*, then the *Price* and *Sumter*. In the second line, behind the *Beauregard*, is the *Lovell*, then the *Thompson*, *Bragg*, and *Van Dorn*.

The Confederate cannon are rifled, and of long range. They are pivoted, and can be pointed in all directions. The boilers of the vessels are protected by iron plates. Slowly they begin to move up stream, and the *Jessie Benton* turns her prow to the current, and we steam back to the fleet.

The boatswains are piping all hands to quarter. The sailors are throwing open the ports, running out the guns, placing shot and shell on deck, taking down rammers and sponges, and distributing cutlasses.

"Let the men have their breakfast," is the order from the flag-ship. Admiral Davis believes that the men will fight best on full stomachs. They eat the rations of beef and bread and drink their steaming coffee while standing beside the guns.

There are five gunboats in the Union fleet. The *Benton* is nearest the Tennessee shore, then the *Carondelet*, *Louisville*, *St. Louis*, and *Cairo*. There are also two rams—the *Queen City* and *Monarch*. The rams are river steamers, with thick oak sides; they carry no cannon, but on each boat are one hundred riflemen.

"Round to; head down stream; keep in line with the flag-ship," was the order which we on board the *Jessie Benton* carried to each boat of the line; then returned and took our position between the *Benton* and *Carondelet*.

I am on the top of the tug, beside the pilot-house. The sun is an hour high, and its bright rays lie in a broad line of golden light upon the eddying stream. Look down the river to the city and behold the house-tops, the windows, the levee crowded with men, women, and children. The flag of the Confederacy floats defiantly. The fleet is moving slowly towards us. A dense cloud of smoke rolls up from the chimneys of the steamers and floats over the city.

There is a flash, a puff from the *Little Rebel*, a sound of something in the air, and a column of water is thrown up a mile behind us. A second shot from the *Beauregard* falls beside the *Benton*. A third from the *Price*, aimed at the *Carondelet*, misses by a foot or two, and dashes up the water between the *Jessie Benton* and the flag-ship. It is a sixty-four-pounder. If it had struck us our boat would have been splintered to kindlings in an instant. Commodore Montgomery sees that the boats of the Federal fleet have their iron-plated bows up stream, and comes up rapidly to crush them at the stern, where there are no iron plates. A signal goes up from the *Benton*, and the mud-turtles, as the soldiers called them, begin to turn towards the enemy. The crowd upon the levee think that the Federal boats are retreating, and hurrah for Commodore Montgomery.

There has been profound silence on board the Union gunboats. The men are waiting for the word. It comes.

"Open fire and take close quarters."

The *Cairo* begins. A ten-inch shot screams through the air and skims along the water towards the *Little Rebel;* another from the *St. Louis;* a third from the *Louisville;* another from the *Carondelet;* and lastly from the *Benton*. The gunners cronch beside their guns to sight the shot. Some are too high, some too low. There is an answering roar from all the Confederate boats; the air is full of indescribable noises; the water boils and bubbles around us; it is tossed up in columns and jets. There are sudden flashes overhead, explosions, and sulphurous clouds, and whirring of ragged pieces of iron. The cannonade reverberates from the high bluff behind the city to the dark green forest upon the Arkansas shore, and echoes from bend to bend.

The space between the fleets is gradually lessening, for the turtles are advancing. A shot strikes the *Little Rebel;* one tears through the *General Price*, another through the *General Bragg*. Commodore Montgomery is above the city, and begins to fall back; he is not quite ready to come to close quarters. How fast one lives at such a time! All of your senses are quickened; you see everything, hear everything; the blood rushes through your veins, your pulse is quickened; you long to get at the enemy, to sweep over the intervening space, lay your boat alongside, pour in a broadside, and knock them to pieces in a twinkling! You care nothing for the screaming of the shot, the bursting of the shells. You have got over all that. You have but one thought—to tear down that hateful, flaunting flag; to smite the enemies of your country with all your might.

While this cannonade was going on, I noticed the two rams casting loose from the shore. I heard the tinkle of the engineer's bell for more fire and a full head of steam. The sharp-shooters took their place. The *Queen* came out from the shelter of the cotton-woods, crossed the river, and passed down between the *Benton* and the *Carondelet*. Colonel Ellet stood beside the pilot and waved his hand to me. The *Monarch* was a little later, and instead of following in the wake of the *Queen*, passed between the *Cairo* and the *St. Louis*.

See the *Queen!* Her great wheels whirl up clouds of spray, and leave a foaming path. She carries a silver train sparkling in the morning light. She ploughs a furrow which rolls the width of the river. Our boat dances like a feather on the waves. She gains the intervening space between the fleets. Never moved a queen so determinedly, never one more fleet—almost leaping from the water. The Stars and Stripes stream to the breeze beneath the black cloud unfolding, expanding, and trailing far away from her smoke-stacks. There is a surging, hissing, and smothered screaming of the pent-up steam in her boilers, as if they had put on all their energy for the moment, as if they had flesh, blood, bones, iron, brass, steel, and were nerved up for the trial of the hour!

Confederate officers and men behold her in astonishment. For a moment there is silence. The men stand transfixed at their guns, forgetting their duties; then, as if moved by a common impulse, bring their guns to bear upon her. She is exposed on the right, on the left, and in front. It is a terrible cross-fire. Solid shot scream past, shells explode around her. She is pierced through and through. Her timbers crack; she quivers beneath the shock, but does not falter. On, on, faster, straight towards the *General Beauregard*.

The commander of that vessel adroitly avoids the stroke. The *Queen* misses her aim; sweeping by like a race-horse, receiving the fire of the *Beauregard* on one side and the *Little Rebel* on the other. She comes round in a graceful curve, almost lying down upon her side, as if to cool her heated smoke-stacks in the stream. The stern-guns of the *Beauregard* send their shot through the bulwarks of the *Queen*. A splinter strikes the brave commander, Colonel Ellet. He is knocked down, bruised and stunned for a moment, but springs to his feet, steadies himself against the pilot-house, and gives his directions as coolly as if nothing had happened.

The *Queen* passes round the *Little Rebel* and approaches the *General Price*.

"Take her aft the wheelhouse!" shouts Colonel Ellet to the pilot. The commander of the *Price* turns towards the approaching antagonist. Her wheels turn; she surges ahead to escape the terrible blow. Too late. There is a splintering, crackling, crashing of timbers; the broadside of the boat is crushed in. It is no more than a box of cards or thin tissue-paper before the blow.

There are jets of flame and smoke from the loop-holes of the *Queen*. The sharp-shooters are at it. You hear the rattling fire, and see the crew of the *Price* running wildly over the deck, tossing their arms. The unceasing thunder of the cannonade drowns their cries. A moment, and a white flag goes up. She surrenders.

But the *Queen* has another antagonist—the *Beauregard*—which sweeps down with all her power. There is another crash; the bulwarks of the *Queen* are crushed. There is a great opening in her hull. But no white flag is displayed; no cries for quarter, no thoughts of surrendering. The sharp-shooters pick off the gunners of the *Beauregard*, compelling them to take shelter beneath their casemates.

We who see it hold our breaths, unmindful of the explosions around us. How will it end? Will the *Queen* sink with all her brave men on board?

NAVAL ENGAGEMENT AT MEMPHIS,
JUNE 6, 1862.

1. Federal gunboats; 2, 2. General Beauregard; 3, 3. Little Rebel; 4, 4. General Price; 5, 5. Sumter, 6, 6. General Lovell; 7, 7. General Thompson; 8, 8. General Bragg; 9, 9. General Van Dorn; Q. Queen City; M. Monarch.

But her consort is at hand—the *Monarch*—commanded by Captain Ellet, brother of Colonel Ellet. He was five or ten minutes behind the *Queen* in starting, but he has appeared at the right moment. He, too, has been unmindful of the shot and shell falling around him. He aims straight as an arrow for the *Beauregard*. The *Beauregard* is stiff, stanch, and strong, but her timbers, planks, knees, and braces are no more than laths before the powerful stroke of the *Monarch*. The sharp-shooters pour in their fire. The engineer of the *Monarch* puts his force-pumps in play and drenches the decks of the *Beauregard* with scalding water. An officer of the *Beauregard* raises a white cloth upon a rammer, the signal for surrender. The sharp-shooters stop firing. At this moment three boats are floating helplessly in the stream, the water pouring into the hulls through the splintered planking.

Captain Ellet saw that the *Queen* was disabled, and took her in tow to the Arkansas shore. Prompted by humanity, instead of falling upon the other vessels of the fleet he took the *General Price* to the shore.

The *Little Rebel* was pierced through her hull by a half-dozen shots. Commodore Montgomery saw that the day was lost. He ran alongside the *Beauregard*, and notwithstanding the vessel had surrendered, took the crew on board to escape. But a shot from the *Cairo* passed through the boilers of the *Little Rebel*. The steam rushed out like the hissing of serpents. The boat was near the shore, and the crew jumped into the water, climbed the bank, and fled to the woods. The *Cairo* gave them a broadside of shells as they ran.

The *Beauregard* was fast settling. The *Jessie Benton* ran alongside. All had fled save the wounded. There was a pool of blood upon the deck, warm from the heart of a man who had been killed by a shell.

"Help, quick!" was the cry of Captain Maynadier.

I rushed on board in season to assist in saving a wounded officer, lifting him to the deck of our boat, and the next moment the *Beauregard* disappeared.

"I thank you," said the officer, "for saving me from drowning. You are my enemies, but you have been kinder to me than those whom I called my friends. One of my brother officers, when he fled, had the meanness to pick my pocket and steal my watch, thinking it was the last of me."

There is no cessation of the cannonade. The fight goes on. The *Benton* is engaged with the *Lovell*. They are but a few rods apart, and both within a stone's-throw of the multitude upon the shore.

Captain Phelps stands by one of the *Benton's* rifled guns, runs his eye along the sights, and gives the word to fire. The steel-pointed shot enters the starboard side of the hull by the water-line. Timbers, braces, planks— the whole side of the boat, is torn out; the water pours in. The vessel settles to the guards, to the ports, reels, and with a lurch disappears, going down like a lump of lead. It is the work of three minutes.

Her terror-stricken crew are thrown into the current. A man with his left arm torn, broken, bleeding, and dangling by his side, runs wildly over the deck. He beckons now to those on shore, and now to his friends on board the boats. He looks imploringly to Heaven and calls for help, then disappears in the eddying whirlpool. A hundred human beings are struggling for life, buffeting the current, raising their arms, catching at sticks, straws, planks, and timbers. "Help! help! help!" they cry. It is a wild wail of agony mingled with the cannonade.

There is no help for them on shore; there, within a dozen rods, are their friends — their fathers, mothers, brothers, sisters, wives, children —

they who urged them to join the service, who all but compelled them to enlist. All are powerless to aid them! They who stand upon the shore behold those whom they love defeated, crushed, drowning, calling for help!

Commodore Davis beholds them. His heart is touched. "Save them, lads!" he says.

The crews of the *Benton* and *Carondelet* rush to their boats. So eager are they to save the struggling men that one of the boats is swamped in the launching. Away they go, picking up one here, another there—ten or twelve in all. A few reach the shore and are helped up the bank by lookers-on, but fifty or sixty sink to rise no more. How noble the act! how glorious! Bright amid all the distress, all the horror, will shine forever, like a star of heaven, such an act of humanity.

The *Price*, *Beauregard*, *Little Rebel*, and *Lovell*—one-half of the Confederate fleet — were disposed of. The other vessels attempted to flee. The Union fleet had swept steadily on in an unbroken line. Amid all the appalling scenes of the hour there was no lull in the cannonade. While saving those who had lost all power of resistance, there was no cessation of effort to crush those who still resisted.

A short distance below the *Little Rebel*, the *Thompson*, riddled by shot and in flames, was run ashore. A little farther down stream the *Bragg* was abandoned, also in flames from the explosion of a nine-inch shell thrown by the *St. Louis*. The crews leaped on shore and fled to the woods. The *Sumter* went ashore near the *Little Rebel*. The *Van Dorn* alone escaped. She was a swift steamer, and was soon beyond reach of the guns of the fleet.

The fight is over. The thunder of the morning dies away, and the birds renew their singing. The abandoned boats are picked up. The *Thompson* cannot be saved. The flames leap around the chimneys; the boilers are heated to redness. A pillar of fire springs upward in long lances of light. The boilers, beams of iron, burning planks, flaming timbers, cannon, shot, and shells, are lifted five hundred feet in air in an expanding, unfolding cloud, filled with loud explosions. The scattered fragments rain upon forest, field, and river, as if meteors of vast proportions had fallen from heaven to earth. There is a shock which shakes all Memphis, and announces to the disappointed, terror-stricken, weeping, humiliated multitude that the drama which they have played so madly for a twelvemonth is over, that retribution has come at last.

Thus, in an hour's time, the Confederate fleet was annihilated. Commodore Montgomery was to have sent the Union boats to the bottom; but his expectations were not realized, his promises not fulfilled. It is not

CLOSING SCENE OF THE NAVAL BATTLE BEFORE MEMPHIS. (FROM A SKETCH MADE AT THE TIME.)

known how many men were lost on the Confederate side, but probably from eighty to a hundred. Colonel Ellet was the only one injured on board the Union fleet. The gunboats were uninjured. The *Queen* was the only boat disabled. In striking contrast was the destruction of Montgomery's fleet.

The victory opens the Upper Mississippi from Cairo to Vicksburg.

CHAPTER XI.

THE PENINSULAR CAMPAIGN.

THE section of Virginia between James and York rivers is called by the people of that State "The Peninsula," and the military movement made by the Army of the Potomac in 1862 is known as the Peninsular campaign.

When the army under General McDowell marched to Bull Run it was a movement towards Richmond. The idea was uppermost in the mind of the people and of General McClellan that he must capture Richmond. It was the capital of the Confederacy. The Confederate Congress was in session there. It was thought that its capture would put an end to the rebellion. The people had cried, "On to Richmond!" but they did not see, neither did General McClellan, that Richmond was of little account. The strength of the Confederacy was in the armies under Johnston and Beauregard. They must be defeated before the rebellion could be crushed. In the Revolutionary War the British obtained possession of Philadelphia, but the Continental Congress moved to York, and the war went on. When General Howe got tired of holding it he undertook to march to New York, and was pounced upon by General Washington at Monmouth.

President Lincoln saw what General McClellan and the people did not see—that the Confederate army must be defeated first of all. Johnston was at Centreville. Why not attack him there, within a day's march of supplies?

President Lincoln became so dissatisfied with General McClellan's inaction that on Washington's birthday, February 22d, he issued an order for all the armies to move. The Western armies did move, and we have seen what they accomplished at Donelson, Island No. 10, and Pittsburg Landing. At the time the order was issued General McClellan had no plan as to what he would do. He was not willing to march to Centreville, which was strongly fortified, but wanted to go down the Potomac to the Peninsula, and march to Richmond.

"McClellan never intended to march to Centreville," says Prince De

Joinville, of France, who was on McClellan's staff, and who has written a history of the war. "For weeks and perhaps months this plan of going to the Peninsula had been secretly maturing."

The President was afraid that while McClellan was on his way to Richmond General Johnston would be on his way to Washington—for Jefferson Davis would have liked nothing better than to swap off Richmond for Washington. We now know that Davis and Johnston talked the matter over, and that one of the plans devised by Beauregard was to cross the Potomac below Washington, and another to cross above Washington, get between Washington and Baltimore and cut the railroad.

President Lincoln said that General McClellan and his corps commanders must decide upon a plan, but that enough troops must be left to protect Washington. There were five corps commanders—Sumner, McDowell, Heintzelman, Porter, and Keyes.

"A force of forty thousand should be left to protect Washington," said General Sumner.

"With the forts fully garrisoned, twenty-five thousand men will be enough," said Keyes, Heintzelman, and McDowell.

"Leave Washington entirely secure, and move the remainder of the force down the Potomac, choose a new base at Fortress Monroe or anywhere, but move in pursuit of the enemy by some route," was the order of Mr. Stanton, Secretary of War.

The day after the council of war General Johnston and Jefferson Davis knew all about it through spies; for there were still a great many men and women in Washington who sympathized with the Confederates, and who planned to find out all that was going on.

General Johnston saw that he must be in position to defend Richmond; it was of no use to stay at Centreville. He sent off his supplies, abandoned the batteries along the Potomac, evacuated Centreville, crossed the Rappahannock River, and waited to see what McClellan was going to do.

The army was to go by water, one hundred and eighty miles, to Fortress Monroe. Open your map of Virginia and you will see the James River coming down from Richmond. North of it is the York River, a short arm of Chesapeake Bay, with a railroad leading from West Point to Richmond.

Never before was there such activity in hiring vessels—113 steamboats, 188 schooners, 88 barges, which were obtained in Baltimore, Philadelphia, New York, and Boston, costing millions of dollars. In thirty-seven days 122,000 men, 15,000 horses, 1150 wagons, 264 pieces of field artillery, beside ambulances, thousands of tents, a mountain of supplies, were transported from Washington to Fortress Monroe.

The Confederate works at Yorktown were erected where the English fortifications stood in the Revolutionary War. When these were captured, the vessels could then go up York River to West Point and White-House, and the army, while besieging Richmond, could receive its supplies by the York River Railroad. General McDowell, with forty thousand men, was to move from Washington to Fredericksburg, covering Washington till the army was in front of Richmond, and then join him.

General McClellan could not go up James River, because the *Merrimac* was guarding it, with only the *Monitor* to keep her from destroying the Union fleet. Going now to Yorktown, we find Wormsley Creek emptying into York River, on the one hand, and Warwick River emptying into the James, on the other, with only a narrow strip of land between them. General Magruder, commanding the Confederates at Yorktown, built dams on the streams, making them wide and deep, and erected earthworks and mounted heavy guns. He had only eleven thousand men to hold a line thirteen miles in length. General Johnston, commanding the Confederate army at Richmond, thought that it would not be possible for him to hold Yorktown for any length of time, and instructed Magruder to make as much show and noise as he could with his troops. Magruder was ready to retreat at any moment, and was much surprised when he saw the Union army go into camp and begin to throw up intrenchments.

McClellan expected that the navy would attack the Confederate batteries at Yorktown, and open a passage up York River, but Commodore Goldsborough said he had not enough vessels to undertake it. McClellan expected that the forty thousand troops at Fredericksburg, under McDowell, would come down and threaten the rear of Magruder, but President Lincoln, not willing to leave Washington exposed, withdrew McDowell from McClellan, who complained that it overturned all his plans. He decided that he must have heavy cannon and begin a siege. The soldiers laid aside their muskets and began to construct earthworks.

In a field on the farm of Mr. Garrow stood three chimneys. General Magruder had burned the houses that they might not afford shelter to the Union troops. A Vermont soldier discovered that Warwick River was only about waist-deep at that point, and that there was not a large force of Confederates opposite. There was an earthwork with a twenty-four-pounder howitzer near the stream, and a quarter of a mile away two smaller cannon. The soldiers of the Vermont brigade could see that the Confederates were strengthening their works. General McClellan ordered the Vermont troops to make a reconnoissance across the stream.   On the morning of April 16th the Vermonters could hear the Confederate bands playing the tune of " Rosa Lee."   Just then the cannon of Mott's Union battery opened their brazen lips and sent their shells across the stream, and the band stopped playing.   The Third and Fourth regiments from Vermont opened fire.   The Confederate guns replied.   Through the forenoon the fusillade went on.   General McClellan and all the members of his staff rode down towards the three chimneys, and looked through their glasses at the Confederate works.   McClellan ordered General Smith, com-

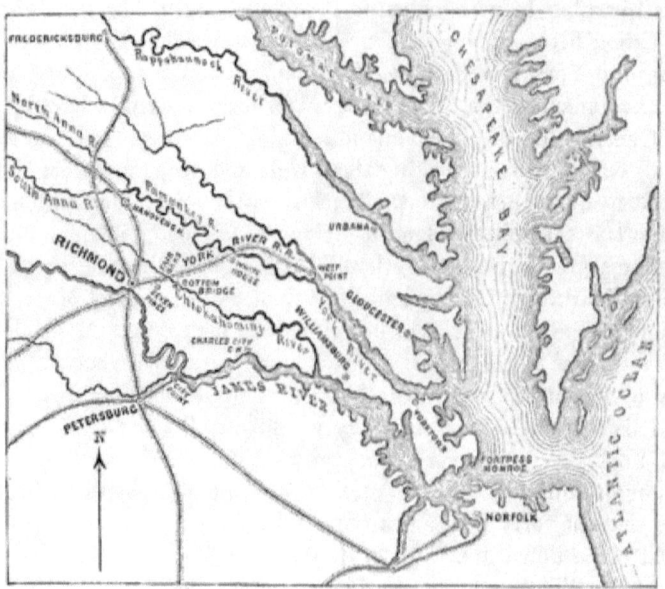

THE PENINSULAR CAMPAIGN.

manding the troops, to send a small force across the stream, but not to bring on a general battle.   Two companies of the Third Vermont, holding their guns and cartridge-boxes over their heads, crossed the river, while eighteen cannon rained shells upon the Confederate works.   The Confederate troops in the rifle-pits fled.   The Vermonters waited for reinforcements, but none were sent.   The Fifteenth North Carolina opened upon them, but its colonel was killed, and the regiment thrown into confusion. Two Georgia regiments came and opened a destructive fire, and a little later seven Confederate regiments came upon the run, and the Vermonters

were compelled to retreat. Of one hundred and ninety-two who crossed
the stream, nearly one-half were killed or wounded. Among the killed
was William Scott. In the month of November, 1861, while the regiment
was near Washington, he went on picket two nights in succession, the last
night to relieve a sick comrade. He fell asleep, was tried by court-martial,
and condemned to be shot. It was the evening before the day fixed for
his execution when a gentleman from Vermont came to my room greatly
distressed, and asking if there was not some way by which the life of William Scott could be saved. There was a minister in Washington for
whom President Lincoln had great regard—Rev. Mr. Smith. I hastened
to Mr. Smith's house and found that he had gone to bed, but when he
learned what I wanted, he quickly dressed and went with me to the White
House. I remained in the anteroom while he ascended the stairs to see
the President, and to intercede for the life of the boy. This was the reply of President Lincoln : " I shall take into consideration all extenuating
circumstances, and endeavor to do what is right." Others came to intercede for the boy. In the morning, instead of a file of soldiers, a volley, a
mangled corpse, President Lincoln jumped into a carriage and drove with
all haste to the regiment, arriving there just in season to put a stop to
his execution. On the bank of the river Warwick we see William Scott,
mortally wounded, offering, with his dying breath, his last prayer that God
will bless President Lincoln.

Through the month the soldiers were digging in the mud ; McClellan
was getting the two-hundred-pounder guns into position. When all were
ready he would open a terrific cannonade. On the night of May 1st a
negro came into the Union lines with the information that the Confederates were leaving Yorktown. McClellan did not believe the story. On
the morning of the 4th he would open fire.

"Keep up a heavy fire through the night, but spike the cannon at daybreak and retreat to Williamsburg," was General Magruder's order ; and all
through the night the Confederate cannon thundered, throwing shot and
shell at the Union earthworks.

Daybreak came, and suddenly the firing ceased. There was silence in
Yorktown ; and then General McClellan discovered that there was not a
Confederate soldier in the place ; all had gone.

"With five thousand men we had stopped and held in check over one
hundred thousand of the enemy," said Magruder. He carried off all his
light artillery, but left fifty-two heavy guns in the intrenchments.

It is twelve miles from Yorktown to Williamsburg. Three miles east
of the town you come to College Creek, which runs south to the James.

ARRIVAL OF THE COLUMN.

Another little stream, Queen's Creek, trickles north to York River. The old stage-road from Yorktown to Richmond runs along the narrow neck of land between the head-waters of the two streams. At this gate-way the Confederate engineers had laid out Fort Magruder. With the two streams protecting the flanks, it would be an easy matter for a small force in the fort and behind the breastworks to hold a much larger army at bay.

Early in the morning of May 4th the cavalry under General Stoneman left Yorktown in pursuit of Magruder. The mud was deep in the roads, the cavalry could not ride very fast, but before night they came upon the Confederates of General Longstreet's division. In a short time thirty of the cavalry went down before the Confederate rifles. The battery horses sank in the mire. The Confederates saw their opportunity, rushed upon them, and captured one of Gibson's guns. Stoneman was obliged to fall back. There had been a drizzling rain through the day, and at night a storm set in which drenched the weary troops of both armies, who had to lie tentless upon the water-soaked turf.

The morning of May 5th dawned; the rain had ceased. General Hooker's division of Heintzelman's corps had pressed on, following the cavalry, and at half-past seven was in line of battle, advancing towards Fort Magruder, south of the stage-road, while Smith's division came into line north of it. Longstreet's troops had greatly the advantage in position. Longstreet and A. P. Hill had gone as far as Williamsburg, but seeing how strong a place it was between the two streams, had turned back to hold it. When Hooker began the attack only a portion of the Confederates had arrived. Their cannon were in the fort, well protected, while the Union artillery was in the open field. While the Union batteries were wheeling into position, shells began to explode among the horses and cannoneers. When once in position, the Union artillerymen sent their shot and shells with such true aim that several of the Confederate cannon were silenced. Hooker's brigades came out of the woods along the eastern bank of the stream to find themselves in front of a formidable abatis. The soldiers crouched amid the fallen trees and poured in their fire. A desperate struggle begins. The Confederates advance, but are in turn driven. The Union men work their way almost up to the fort, but are compelled to fall back. Through the forenoon Hooker carries on the battle alone; not a musket is fired by Smith's division. General McClellan is at Yorktown, and does not know that a battle is going on. He has appointed General Sumner to take command at the front. There are nearly forty thousand men near at hand, but Sumner issues no order; not a brigade is ordered to Hooker's assistance.

General Kearney is far away with his division. He hears the uproar of battle. He is an old soldier, was in the Mexican War, and in Italy, at the battle of Solferino. The road is filled with teams, but he orders them aside and hurries on with his men. He waits for no orders from the commander-in-chief, nor from Sumner. His troops grow weary. He knows that they need to have their enthusiasm aroused, and orders the band to play. "Play 'Yankee Doodle,' or any other doodle you can think

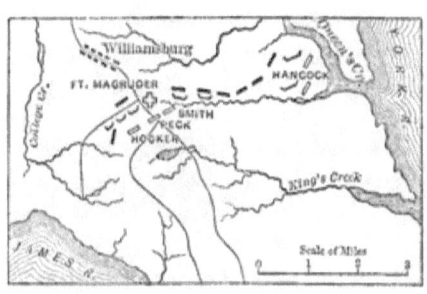

MAP OF WILLIAMSBURG.

of!" he shouts. The band strikes up, and the weary soldiers swing their caps and push on towards the battle-field.

Peck's brigade, of Couch's division, comes into position on Hooker's right on the stage-road. At the same moment Kearney's troops, which have marched past other divisions, come up and relieve Hooker, who has fought the battle alone through the day.

Berry's brigade is in the advance. It emerges from the woods, and comes into line in rear of Hooker. It has come at the right moment, for Longstreet is advancing. Hooker's troops file to the rear, the Confederates following with a victorious cheer; but suddenly a pitiless storm bursts upon them from Berry's line.

"Give them the bayonet!"

The order runs along the line. Kearney's men rush forward with a cheer, driving the Confederates back to the fort.

"You can get across Queen Creek down there," said a negro to Captain Stewart. "There is a dam, and the road crosses it and goes on to Williamsburg."

General Smith sent Captain Stewart with four companies to see about it.

"Infantry and artillery can cross," was the word sent back by Stewart; and General Hancock with his brigade moves up the road, crosses the dam, and takes possession of the deserted Confederate intrenchments on the west side. He has the Sixth Maine, Fifth Wisconsin, Forty-ninth Pennsylvania, Forty-third New York, and Wheeler's battery. He can see Fort Magruder across the plain to the south, smoking and flaming. He is almost in Johnston's rear.

"I can go to Fort Magruder if well supported," is his message to General Smith, his division commander. He is in a field near a farm-house. From the farm-house westward is a rail-fence. Wheeler's battery comes into position on a knoll close by the house. The Fifth Wisconsin and Forty-third New York are behind the fence; the Forty-ninth Pennsylvania behind the house; the Sixth Maine are behind the battery to support it. Out from a piece of woods come two Confederate brigades of Hill's division. Wheeler's guns flame. Hancock sees that the force in front of him is greatly superior to his own. He is too far out, and retreats towards the dam, to a better position on the east of a hill, all the troops in line.

On sweep the Confederates with exultant cheers; but the cheering suddenly ceases, for a terrible fire bursts upon them. They come to a stand-still.

Down the slope moves the Union line, and the Confederates flee across the field. More than five hundred are cut off by Hancock's advance, and find themselves prisoners. Night is settling down. The battle is over, the victory won.

During the night Johnston retreats, leaving several cannon, many wagons, and several hundred of his wounded. Of the Union troops two thousand two hundred were killed and wounded; of the Confederates, about one thousand.

There was a commotion in Richmond.

"In the President's mansion," writes Pollard, the Southern historian, "all was consternation and dismay."

Jefferson Davis's niece wrote a letter to a friend, but the mail-bag was captured. Thus read the letter: "General Johnston is falling back from the Peninsula, and Uncle Jeff thinks we had better go to a safer place than Richmond. He is miserable. He tries to be cheerful and bear up against such a continuation of troubles; but, ah! I fear he cannot live long if he does not get some rest and quiet."

The Confederate Congress adjourned hastily. A great many people left the city. The public documents were put in boxes and sent away. Mrs. Jefferson Davis took down her window-curtains, tore up the carpets, packed the pictures, and left the city. The Treasury Department, printing notes which passed for money, removed its presses to Georgia, and universal gloom settled over the Confederate capital.

To understand General McClellan's campaign on the Peninsula we shall have to study the map not only of the country around Richmond, but also take a look at Norfolk, the Shenandoah Valley, and Fredericksburg.

General McClellan wanted to capture Richmond. He was moving up the Peninsula for that purpose, expecting that General McDowell, who was at Fredericksburg, would move south, and join him on the north bank of the Chickahominy River.

Let us see the outlook now from the Confederate side.

"Richmond," said the *Despatch* of that city, "must be defended. If it is captured, in the eyes of Europe it would be like the taking of London or Paris by an enemy."

General McClellan did not want to attack the Confederate army at Centreville, because the fortifications were strong, but those around Richmond were a great deal stronger. Thousands of slaves had been working with spades and shovels throwing up intrenchments. To prevent the Union gunboats from ascending James River, piles were driven across the stream a few miles below the city, and heavy guns mounted at Drury's Bluff. The Confederate Government set itself to gather an army as large as that commanded by General McClellan, and troops were hurried up from North Carolina, South Carolina, and Georgia.

In the Shenandoah Valley there are two Union armies: one, under General Fremont, of ten thousand men, is in the upper Shenandoah; the other, under General Banks, who is at Harrisonburg with five thousand. They are not far apart. United, they can move upon Richmond from the west.

The Confederate Government sent General Jackson with twenty thousand men to capture or drive Fremont and Banks out of the Shenandoah Valley, which he did very quickly, driving Fremont west towards Kanawha, and compelling General Banks to retreat down the Shenandoah into Maryland. He accomplished it by rapid marches; by falling first on one and then on the other before they were aware of his presence. It was a very ably conducted campaign on the part of Jackson, and the world began to see that he was a remarkable man.

The Confederate Government had no troops to spare to hold Norfolk; it was decided to abandon the place. On the night of May 10th the buildings in the navy yard were set on fire. Commodore Tatnall, commanding the *Merrimac*, finding that he could not take her up James River, set her on fire. The flames reached the magazine, and at five o'clock in the morning there was an explosion heard far away. James River was open now to the Union gunboats, and the *Monitor* and the *Galena* went up to Drury's Bluff, almost to Richmond. The guns in the Confederate works were so much higher than the cannon on the vessels that the Confederates had the advantage, and the gunboats were repulsed.

The Union army was advancing along the banks of the Chickahominy, and a great fleet of steamers and schooners were unloading supplies at White House. General McClellan might have stopped where he was, sent the supplies round to James River, marched the army in that direction, and made Harrison's Landing his base of supplies. He had formed his plan, and did not change it, for he expected that McDowell with his troops would come down from Fredericksburg and join him; but McDowell was no longer under him; besides, General Anderson was at Bowling Green, near Fredericksburg, with fifteen thousand Confederate troops, and General Branch was at Hanover Court-house with nine thousand, confronting McDowell.

The Chickahominy is a small stream, not more than forty feet wide in August; but when the spring rains are on, it overflows its banks and spreads out over all the valley, which is nearly a mile wide. There are marshes, swamps, dense forests, and tangled thickets. The railroad as you go from West Point to Richmond crosses from the north to the south at Bottom's Bridge. The Confederates had destroyed all the bridges, but the Union army rebuilt them. Engines and cars were brought on vessels from Baltimore and Washington, and the railroad put in running order. The army was divided. Three corps—Sumner's, Porter's, and Franklin's—advanced up the north bank, Keyes's and Heintzelman's along the south bank, of the Chickahominy. It is less than forty miles from Williamsburg to Bottom's Bridge, but the movement was so slow that two weeks passed before the army reached the bridge, which gave General Johnston ample time to concentrate the Confederate troops. General Fitz-John Porter advanced to Hanover Court-house, had a brush with General Branch, captured one cannon and some prisoners, and tore up the railroad track on the line running to Gordonsville.

It is the last week in May. Johnston's opportunity has come. The Union army is divided. He will move out from Richmond with nearly all his force, and strike Keyes and Heintzelman, and crush them with an overwhelming blow. The Chickahominy, with its swirling flood, would be his ally; for a great rain flooded the lowlands and swept away all but one of the bridges. With the bridges gone, McClellan would not be able to send any troops to their assistance.

The planters of Virginia have a delightful custom of giving appropriate names to their homes. Going east from Richmond down the Nine-mile Road, we come to a farm-house with a grove of oaks around it, to which the owner has given the name of Fair Oaks. A short distance farther, across the railroad, at the junction of the Nine-mile Road with the stage-road leading from Williamsburg, we come to Seven Pines, so named because seven tall pines rear their stately trunks and wave their green plumes above a planter's home.

Mr. Echo lives in the house a few rods west of the junction of the two roads; Mr. Hilliard a little farther east; Mr. Tignor in the house south-west of Seven Pines. Going up the Williamsburg Road a short distance towards Richmond, we come to two houses just alike, standing south of the road. The soldiers of the Union army call them the "twin houses." General Couch's division of Keyes's corps is at Seven Pines, General Casey's at Fair Oaks. Going down the Williamsburg Road two miles, we find Kearney's division of Heintzelman's corps. Two miles farther brings us to Hooker's division of the same corps. Kearney and Hooker have been placed to guard the roads leading south across White Oak Swamp, so that the Confederates cannot come round upon their flank and rear.

Through Friday night the Confederate troops are on the march: Huger's division down the Charles City Road, with the intention of getting in rear of Couch and Casey; Longstreet's and D. H. Hill's divisions march down the Williamsburg Road, to strike Casey in front; Smith's and Magruder's divisions down the Nine-mile Road, to fall upon the right flank of Casey near Fair Oaks. General Johnston is with General G. W. Smith on the Nine-mile Road. Huger is to begin the attack. When Longstreet hears the roar of Huger's cannon he is to strike, and at the same moment Smith is to advance and fold back Casey's right. In all, between forty and fifty thousand men are advancing to the attack.

Eight o'clock—nine o'clock—ten. No sound from Huger. He is toiling in the mud. Longstreet is waiting impatiently; Casey's pickets capture Major Washington, one of General Johnston's aides, and bring him before General Keyes. There comes a sound of musketry from the picket line. The prisoner's countenance suddenly lights up, which leads General Keyes to think that something unusual is going on in the woods in front, and orders the troops under arms, and sets men to work with axes to cut down trees.

Noon—three o'clock. General Hill is out of patience waiting for Huger's advance. He hopes to surprise Casey, and instead of sending skirmishers in advance, sweeps on with his whole line. Casey's cannon open. Colonel Bailey directs the batteries, and lets fly canister and shells, which make havoc in Hill's ranks.

The assault is upon Naglee's brigade. Suddenly Longstreet appears upon the right of Hill, getting in rear of Casey's left flank. The Confederates outnumber the Union men four to one. The firing is quick and heavy. General Sumner, three miles away, hears it, and orders his men under arms.

Casey's soldiers are all new; this their first battle.

An aide rides through the woods to Heintzelman, but misses his way, and it is two o'clock before Heintzelman knows what is going on.

The Confederates under D. H. Hill come into an open field, and all of Casey's cannon open upon them. The fire is so destructive that they cannot face it, and they lie down, while Longstreet is folding round the left flank. For three hours Casey holds his ground, but the line crumbles piecemeal, the troops falling back towards Seven Pines. Colonel Bailey spikes the guns which cannot be dragged away, and is shot down while doing it. Casey's whole line retreats to that held by General Couch. Two regiments of Couch's division are moving up towards the railroad to support Naglee, when they see across a field towards the north-west long lines of Confederates—the troops of General Smith, who, seeing the gap between Couch and Casey, rush in and cut off four regiments, which are not captured, but which are driven towards the Chickahominy.

This is on the right of the Union line. Now, going down to the left, we find Longstreet driving all before him. Casey's troops are fleeing towards Seven Pines; but suddenly a regiment—the Tenth Massachusetts—which has been held in reserve advances. It requires nerve and muscle to go forward when all others are retreating; to be a breakwater when the flood sweeps all before it; but they hold Longstreet in check.

"Had the regiment," says Keyes, "been two minutes later they would have been too late to occupy that fine position, and it would have been impossible to have formed the next and last line of battle, which stemmed the tide of defeat and turned it towards a victory."

Casey has been driven a mile. His camp is in the hands of Longstreet. Couch's line has also been folded back.

Other actors came—General Kearney, with Jameson's and Berry's brigades. The soldiers lay their knapsacks upon the ground, move out upon the left of the Tenth Massachusetts, lie down behind the felled trees, and wait for the advance of the Confederates. They are sheltered by the trees, and pour in a deadly fire.

In rear of Seven Pines is the hospital. The sick men, down with fever, hear the tide of battle rolling nearer. A soldier rushes in.

"The rebels are sweeping all before them!" he shouts.

Lieutenant Rice, of the Eleventh Maine, hears it, springs to his feet, and grasps his gun.

"All of you who can hold up your heads follow me!" he cries. Men who have not been able to stand spring up at the word. Their cheeks are thin, fever is raging in their veins; but a dozen weak and tottering men follow him. They reach the front. Seven times Lieutenant Rice loads and fires, taking deliberate aim; then a bullet pierces his breast, and he falls dead.

An officer with one hundred men who have been out on picket come up the road.

"Where is my regiment?" he asks of General Heintzelman.

"I cannot tell you; but if it is fighting you want, just go in, for there is good fighting all along the line."

It is almost sunset; but now another actor comes to take part in the drama. When General Sumner heard the first roll of musketry, without waiting for orders from McClellan, he issued his own orders to his troops to be under arms. He knew that the water in the river was rising rapidly, and sent men down to the Grapevine Bridge, as his soldiers called one of the bridges which they had built, to tie it to the trees with ropes. He marched Sedgwick's division down to the water's edge. It was late in the afternoon before he received orders to cross the river. All the other bridges had been swept away by the rising flood. This was afloat, but the ropes held it in place. Into the water marched the troops, wading a long distance before they reached the bridge. Kirby's battery came, the horses sinking in the mud, and the wheels going almost to the hub. The horses floundered and splashed in the stream, but the soldiers put their shoulders to the wheels, tugged at the traces, lifted the axles, and with great exertion the battery reached the other side.

Gorman's brigade is in advance, followed by Dana's. They move towards the sound of the firing, facing south-west. At this moment the Confederates, under General G. W. Smith, are moving south-east towards Fair Oaks across the field, and through the woods between the Nine-mile Road and the railroad. The advance of Sumner compels Smith to change his line. The sun has gone down, twilight is stealing on, when Kirby wheels his cannon into position and sends his shells across the field into the Confederate lines. Gorman's brigade of five regiments charges across the field. There are two fences before them, and the Confederates are behind the farther one. With a cheer the Union troops dash down the first and rush towards the second. There are quick flashes—brighter now than before the sun went down. The Confederates are driven. General Johnston, while rallying his men, is struck by a piece of shell, and General Smith is placed in command of the army by Jefferson Davis, who has come

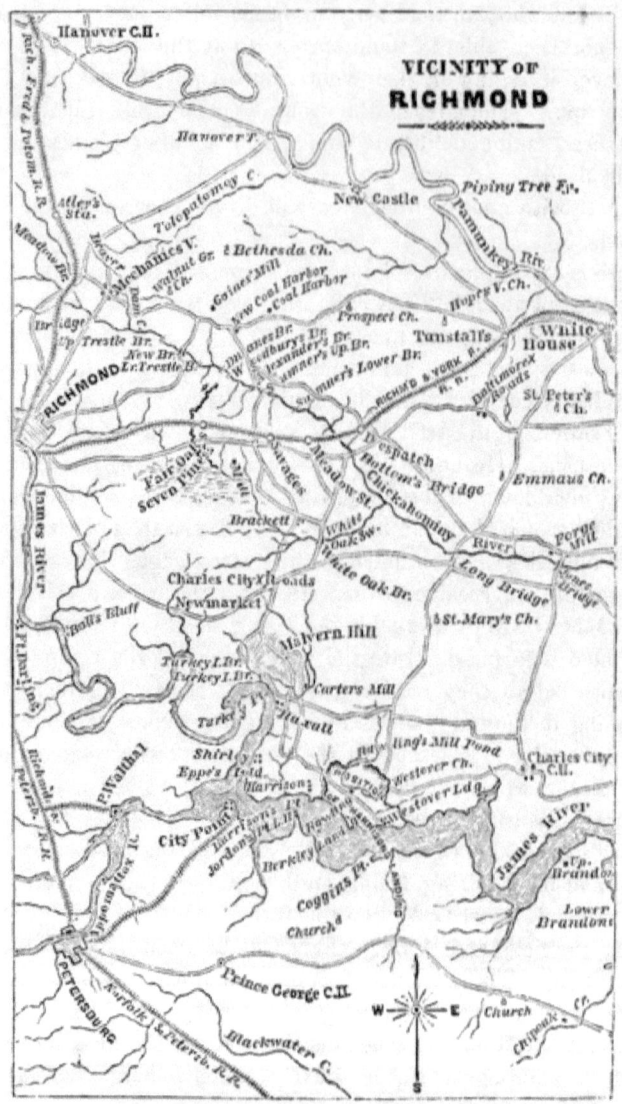

out with Mr. Mallory, Secretary of the Navy, and General Robert E. Lee, to see the battle. At nine o'clock the sounds of the conflict die away, and both armies prepare for the morrow.

The Confederates feel that they have won a victory. They have driven the troops of Casey's division nearly a mile, and are sleeping in the captured tents. They have captured ten guns, and are picking up more than five thousand muskets. General Johnston, however, has not accomplished all that he intended. He expected to crush Keyes's corps and drive Heintzelman's into the Chickahominy; but he has done neither. General Huger has disappointed him. This is what a Confederate soldier has written :

"As I rode down through the field I met Franks, one of Longstreet's aides, looking as blue as indigo. 'What is the matter? are you not satisfied with what we have done?'

"'Satisfied be hanged! Old Jeff, Mallory, Longstreet, and all the rest of them are as mad as thunder. Huger's slowness has spoiled everything. He had positive orders to begin the fight in the morning, and he hasn't fired a gun to-day.'"

Huger was not regarded as an officer of much energy, but he had been making a long, hard march through the mud, and his men were tired out. Had he been in position and attacked vigorously, things might have gone badly for the Union army.

Sometimes there are ludicrous as well as sad scenes on a battle-field. Captain Lawton was a Confederate officer on General Longstreet's staff. He saw a soldier coming out of the woods with his gun on his shoulder, and deliberately going to the rear. "You are going the wrong way," said the captain. The soldier did not notice him. "I say you are going the wrong way. Turn about, sir," said the captain, drawing his sword. The soldier levelled his gun and cocked it. "See here, you little man on that horse, I've been in thar. I know what is going on in thar, and if you think that you are going to send me in thar again you're mistaken." The captain saw the muzzle of the gun aimed at him, the look of determination on the soldier's face, and said, "Well, my good fellow, perhaps you will think better of it after you have got over your fright."

"You can go in thar, captain, if you want to; I haven't the least objection."

The soldier went to the rear, while the captain, the next moment, reeled from his horse, struck by a ball, which, however, only disabled him for a time.

At daybreak on Sunday morning an orderly belonging to the Confederate army rode out of the woods into the Union lines.

"Where is General Anderson?" he asked.

"He is here. What do you want of him?" said a colonel.

"I have a despatch for him from General Pryor."

"I will take it. You are my prisoner. Soldiers, guard this man."

The orderly was much astonished to find himself a prisoner. The despatch gave information of the disposition of the Confederate forces for the battle soon to begin again.

During the night the whole of Sumner's corps crossed the Chickahominy, and at daybreak the troops thus strengthened were ready to renew the battle. Sedgwick remained where he fought on Saturday. Richardson's division was in line on his left, and formed in two lines, with

FAIR OAKS.

French's brigade in front, on the railroad, and Howard and Meagher in the second line in his rear. Kearney, Couch, and Hooker, with the remnants of Casey's division, were in the vicinity of Seven Pines.

The battle began at five o'clock. At that hour the Confederates are discovered south of the railroad, in the woods, in front of Richardson. Pettit's Union battery opens with shells, and the stillness of the Sabbath morn is broken by deep reverberations rolling along the Chickahominy. From the woods where Pettit sends his shells there comes a volley— another—another—and the men begin to drop from Richardson's ranks. The Confederates advance and attack French's brigade at short range. For an hour the men stand in their places and deliver their fire upon the columns which pushed against them. Reinforcements come up from Longstreet's reserves, and Howard is brought up from the second line to meet them. His horse is shot, he is wounded in the right arm, and is forced to leave the field.

By the onset of his brigade the Confederate line is broken. Hooker comes up the railroad and falls upon the Confederates in front, breaking, dividing, and scattering them. Sickels is advancing along the Williamsburg Road. Berry and Jameson are moving over the ground of Saturday, between Seven Pines and White Oak Swamp. Richardson and Sedgwick are also in motion. From Fair Oaks to the swamp south of Seven Pines the Union line advances over the bloody field. It is like the swinging of a gate, with its hinges near Fair Oaks, and reaching past Seven Pines to White Oak Swamp.

The Confederates have failed in what they attempted, and are retreating, with broken, demoralized ranks, to Richmond. The road is filled with fugitives. Heintzelman and Sumner press on until they are within four miles of the city.

"I have no doubt but we might have gone right into Richmond," says General Heintzelman.

"I think that if the army had pressed after the enemy with great vigor we should have gone to Richmond," is the opinion of General Keyes.

"They (the Federals) missed an opportunity of striking a decisive blow. These opportunities never return," writes Prince De Joinville, of France, who was with McClellan when he recalled the troops from their pursuit and established his lines as they were on the morning of Saturday.

The loss on the Union side was five thousand seven hundred and thirty-seven. The Confederate loss, as reported in Smith's, Longstreet's, and Hill's divisions, was six thousand seven hundred and eighty-three. Whiting's division also suffered severely, so that the entire Confederate loss was nearly eight thousand.

There was consternation in Richmond. The city was full of stragglers. Long lines of ambulances came in filled with wounded. People hastening to the cars, expecting that ere long the Union soldiers would be marching into the city.

General McClellan had two corps north of the Chickahominy which he might have swung down upon the city while the victorious corps which had driven back the Confederates pressed on; but he had no plan except to besiege the city, and the great opportunity went by, never again to return to him.

After the battle of Fair Oaks a month passed before anything of importance happened around Richmond. General McClellan was building bridges across the Chickahominy and roads through the swamps. The soldiers were cutting down trees and throwing up intrenchments. There were rainy, hot, and sunshiny days. Sickness came. The hospitals were full of men down with the fever. General McClellan called loudly for reinforcements, and General McCall's division of Pennsylvania reserves was sent to him.

The Confederates had a large division of cavalry, commanded by General Stuart, who started north of Richmond on the night of June 13th, rode east, came suddenly upon a party of Union cavalry at Old Church, and captured it. He reached the Pamunky River, burned two schooners and fourteen wagons, and then pushed on to the railroad at Tunstall's Station and waited for a train, which came down the road, going east. The engineer saw the Confederate cavalry on both sides the track. What should he do? Should he stop? No; he would drive on faster. He pulled the throttle. The cars were filled with sick and wounded men. The cavalrymen began to fire. The bullets whistled past the engineer's head. A few of the men in the cars were wounded, but the train thundered past, and reached White House in safety.

General Stuart moved on, crossed the Chickahominy, came upon a Union hospital, captured and paroled the sick men, crossed White Oak Swamp, and made his way to Richmond. He had trotted round the Union army. It was a brave and daring ride, and won for General Stuart a great reputation. General McClellan saw that some morning he might find his communications with York River cut off, and began to think about doing what he might have done after the battle of Williamsburg — make the James River his line of communication.

The dividing of the army — having one portion south and another north of the Chickahominy — the failure to follow up the victory at Seven Pines, and the ride of Stuart, were unfortunate affairs for General McClellan. He was at the head of an army of volunteers — men who were accustomed to think for themselves, and who, before entering the army, had been in the habit of expressing their opinions, and who now discussed his generalship around their bivouac fires. It was mortifying to think that a body of cavalry could ride around an army of one hundred thousand men.

General Johnston having been wounded, Jefferson Davis appointed Robert E. Lee commander of the Confederate army. He was born in Virginia. His father was an officer under Washington during the Revolution. General Lee graduated at West Point in 1829, was chief engineer of General Wool's brigade in Mexico. He was a great favorite of General Scott. He was superintendent at West Point several years. Probably it was through the influence of General Scott that he was made a colonel in the United States Army in March, 1861, just before the war began. He commanded the marines at Harper's Ferry when John Brown was captured. When Virginia seceded, he resigned his commission, left the old

flag, went to Richmond, and on April 22d was appointed by the Governor
of the State to command the Virginia troops. In accepting the command
he said: "Trusting in Almighty God, an approving conscience, and the
aid of my fellow-citizens, I devote myself to the aid of my native State, in
whose behalf alone will I ever draw my sword." General Lee believed
the doctrine taught by Calhoun, that the supremacy of the State was superior to that of the Nation. He did not see that in the sequence of events
the sovereignty of the State would be swept away by the Confederacy.
He was sent by Governor Letcher to the valley of the Kanawha. He had
accomplished little there, and had been recalled to advise in military affairs
at Richmond. He had promised to serve his State only, but on June 3d
he was in command of the Confederate army. He was intimately acquainted with the whole country between Richmond and Washington, for
he was born on the banks of the Rappahannock, in Westmoreland County,
and was owner of the beautiful home, Arlington, overlooking the city of
Washington; had ridden time and again over the country between Washington and Richmond, and knew every stream and road. He was fifty-
three, in the maturity of all his powers; a refined, courteous, kind-hearted
gentleman, respected and beloved by all who knew him. Such the commander with whom General McClellan had to deal.

General Lee resolved to reinforce his army by bringing Jackson from
the Shenandoah; not to confront McDowell, who was at Fredericksburg, but to fall upon one wing of McClellan's divided army. The
Union army was not only divided by a river, but it reached from Hanover
Court-house to White Oak Swamp, a distance of more than twenty miles.

General Stonewall Jackson was at Port Republic, in the Shenandoah
Valley. On the evening of June 18th his troops began to move east.
They did not know whither they were going, for Jackson was accustomed
to keep his own counsels. On the same day the troops of General Whiting's division, at Richmond, received orders to be ready to move. They
were informed that they were going in the cars to reinforce Jackson.

On Belle Isle, in the river James, at Richmond, were a large number
of Union prisoners who were to be exchanged. The day before they were
to come north a train of cars filled with Confederate troops stopped a while
in front of the prisoners.

"We are going up to join Jackson," said the Confederates.

The same day a man who pretended to be a Frenchman came into
McDowell's lines at Fredericksburg. "Fifteen thousand men have left
Richmond to join Jackson," he said.

"A large body of troops have joined Jackson," was the despatch sent by General Sigel, out beyond Manassas, to Washington. What was the meaning of it? Was Jackson going to march upon Washington? General Halleck and Secretary Stanton knew not what to make of it.

Let us go with General Whiting, commanding the division of Confed-

GENERAL ROBERT E. LEE.

erates, on board the train, up to Lynchburg, where the cars are switched north; from thence we ride to Gordonsville, thence east to the town of Frederickshall, on the Virginia Central Railroad. It has been a round-about journey.

17

General Lee's headquarters were out on the Mechanicsville Road, north-east of Richmond. At noon on Monday, June 23d, the officers of Lee's staff saw a man covered with dust ride up and wearily dismount. He was in citizen's dress. It was Jackson, who had ridden fifty-two miles during the morning. He had laid aside his uniform and had come on a military pass, that none might know him. Although weary and exhausted, he would only drink a glass of milk. General Lee had called the command-ers of four divisions together to lay before them his plan for attacking McClellan. They were Jackson, Longstreet, A. P. Hill, and D. H. Hill. " Your four divisions are to make the attack upon the troops north of the Chickahominy. I have sent Whiting's division to reinforce Jackson, and have allowed the Richmond papers to announce that large reinforcements have been sent to enable Jackson to drive the Union troops out of the valley and to move on Washington. McClellan receives the Richmond papers regularly."

General Lee left the four commanders to settle upon a plan of attack. Jackson would have much the longest march to make. He would be ready, he said, to attack at daylight on the 26th. On June 25th Jackson, with Whiting's troops, is at Ashland, twenty miles north of Richmond. On the morning of the 26th General Lee starts with his whole army, ex-cept twenty-five thousand men, under Magruder, left to defend Richmond. General Branch's division marches due north up the Brook Turnpike; General A. P. Hill marches north-east over the Mechanicsville Turnpike; while Longstreet and D. H. Hill march east to strike the Chickahominy at New Bridge.

General Fitz-John Porter commanded the Union troops north of the Chickahominy. A little stream comes down from the north — a branch of the Chickahominy — upon which Mr. Ellison has a mill a mile south-east of the little cluster of houses called Mechanicsville. The road from Mechanicsville to New Bridge crosses the stream by the mill. General Seymour's brigade is standing on the east bank, facing west, near the mill; farther up the stream is General Reynolds's brigade; still farther up are Griffin's and Martindale's.

It is past noon when the cannon of A. P. Hill and Branch open fire in front of the Union line, but it is three o'clock before the Confederates are in position to begin the battle. General Porter has cut down trees and built breastworks. His line is well protected. All through the after-noon the artillery on both sides hurl shells and solid shot across the stream. In vain are all the efforts of Hill and Branch to move the Union troops from their position. They assault the Union lines, but are driven back with great slaughter. McClellan receives startling news—that Jackson is sweeping round to get in rear of Porter and cut off communications with York River. Porter must not only fall back, but the whole army must retreat to James River.

As you go east from the New Bridge Road you come to the farm of Mr. Hogan. Farther on you descend a steep hill and come to Powhite Creek, where the water is slowly turning the wheel of Dr. Gaines's grist-mill. Ascending the bank on the other side, and riding a short distance, we come to a cluster of houses which make up the hamlet of New Cold Harbor. A large gum-tree stands on the south side of the road. As you rest beneath the tree you are on the spot where General Lee stood during the battle fought on June 27th, and known as the battle of Gaines's Mills.

MECHANICSVILLE, 1862.

Going due south, and crossing another little stream which trickles west, then south, and south-east to the Chickahominy, a mile brings us to the farm-house of Mr. Watts, surrounded by a grove of trees, with a chimney at one end. Beneath the trees we find General Fitz-John Porter, who has been placed in command of the Union troops on the north bank of the Chickahominy. He has removed his own quarters to the south side. General Porter has cut down the trees along the bank of the little rivulet, and has thrown up rifle-pits and intrenchments. He is to hold the enemy in check while General McClellan makes preparations for a retreat to James River. He has thirty thousand men against nearly seventy thousand Confederates. Commencing on the creek near the Chickahominy, we see on our right hand General Morrill's division, with Butterfield's, Martindale's,

WATTS'S HOUSE.

and Griffin's brigades. Upon the other side of the stream are the divisions of Longstreet, A. P. Hill, and Whiting.

General Griffin's brigade is south of the road which comes down from Cold Harbor. North of the road is General Sykes's division of regulars, composed of Warren's, Chapman's, and Buchanan's brigades, confronted by Ewell's, D. H. Hill's, and Jackson's divisions. General Porter's second line at the beginning of the battle is composed of McCall's division, stationed near the centre, in rear of Griffin.

Late in the day Slocum's division of Sumner's corps crosses the Chickahominy and takes position in rear of Sykes's.

It is a hot, sultry day. General Lee is at Hogan's plantation, near New Cold Harbor, sitting beneath the portico of the farm-house absorbed in thought. He is neatly dressed in a gray uniform buttoned to the throat. Longstreet is sitting in an old chair at the foot of the steps, beneath the trees, eating a lunch, with his feet against a tree, his uniform faded and torn, buttons missing, and his boots old and dusty. Gregg, Wilcox, Pryor, Featherstone, and other generals are there waiting for Jackson, who has been marching hard all the morning to get into position. A

THE BATTLE OF GAINES'S MILLS.

courier comes down the Cold Harbor Road, delivers a message to Lee, who mounts his horse and rides away to New Cold Harbor.

It is just two o'clock in the afternoon when Lee is ready to begin the attack. There has been a cannonade all along the line north and south of the Chickahominy. Magruder, on the south side, has instructions to make a grand demonstration, as if he were going to attack McClellan. It is his intention to keep him from sending troops to Porter's aid.

Lee intends to make a grand onset and sweep Porter into the Chickahominy. Under cover of a fire from the artillery, A. P. Hill begins the attack upon Griffin and Martindale. The Confederate infantry advances

NEW COLD HARBOR, 1862.

through the belt of timber and descends the ravine. From the Union rifle-pits there are sudden flashes and quick spurts of flame, and the battle-cloud becomes thick and heavy.

It would require many pages to make a full record of the terrible combat. How Longstreet urged his men into the woods; how brigade after brigade marched against Martindale, Griffin, and Butterfield, only to fall back with broken and shattered ranks; how the ground became strewn with the dead and wounded; how men in the opposing armies fired into one another's faces and fell almost into one another's arms, mingling their life-blood in one crimson stream ; how Jackson pressed on over the plain, urging his men nearer and nearer; how the Pennsylvania Reserves went up to aid the regulars ; how couriers dashed through the woods over to General McClellan, asking for reinforcements; how Slocum's division went over, reached the field, and held in check the dark masses forming upon the flank of the regulars and reserves.

The hours hung heavily. Three o'clock—four o'clock—five o'clock— and no break in the line. Thirty-five thousand against seventy! But the pressure is terrible. French's and Meagher's brigades, of Sumner's corps, are ordered across the Chickahominy. Six o'clock; the struggle is fiercer than ever. Every regiment is brought to the front on both sides. The artillery still thunders, but the Union infantry are out of am- munition. Longstreet has been hurled back as often as he has advanced, and so have A. P. Hill and D. H. Hill; but Jackson is working towards the Chickahominy. Sykes's men, who have been facing north, are obliged to face east to meet Jackson's troops, coming from Old Cold Harbor. Union soldiers begin to leave the ranks and move towards the rear. There is a desperate rush from Jackson's brigades, and the Union line gives way.

If there were a fresh division, or a brigade even, at hand the tide might be stopped; but no reinforcements are at hand. There are fifty thousand men upon the southern bank of the river, but General McClel- lan is afraid that Magruder will make an attack, and sends no additional troops to Porter.

The regulars and Pennsylvania Reserves are worn out ; their ammuni- tion is nearly gone. They can have no more support, but at this mo- ment, after they have held at bay for four hours a superior force, they are called upon to withstand the last grand charge of Jackson.

Whiting's Confederate division advances ; he is received with grape and canister. His line halts, wavers, almost breaks; but Jackson, Whit- ing, Hood, and McLaws urge the men to push on. They leap across the ravine, halt a moment, sheltered by the bank above them from the fire of the Union batteries, and then storm the breastwork and seize the guns. There is a short struggle, a falling back of the Union troops, and the battle of Gaines's Mills is lost to General McClellan.

Meagher and French have reached the field, but are too late to save the day. Twenty guns have fallen into Lee's hands, and several hun- dred prisoners. Cook's cavalry, in the rear, drawing their sabres, dash upon the exultant foe, but it is an ineffectual charge. The retreating troops fall in behind French and Meagher, and form a new line nearer the Chickahominy as the darkness comes on. They have been driven from their first position, but Lee has not power enough to drive them into the Chickahominy. He decides to wait till morning before renewing the attack.

The morning dawns, and Porter is beyond his reach across the river, with all his siege-guns, ammunition, and supplies.

How near Lee came to losing the battle may be seen by the following extract from the account of a correspondent of the *Richmond Whig*:

"It was absolutely necessary that we should carry their line; and to do this, regiment after regiment, and brigade after brigade, was successively led forward. Still, our repeated charges—gallant and dashing though they were—failed to accomplish the end, and our troops, still fighting, fell steadily back. Thus for more than two mortal hours the momentous issue stood trembling in the balance. The sun was setting far in the west, darkness would soon be upon us, and the point must be carried. At this juncture—it was now five o'clock—the division of the gallant Whiting hove in sight. On reaching the field their troops rapidly deployed in line. The charge was made under the most galling fire I ever witnessed : shot, shell, grape, canister, and ball swept through our lines like a storm of leaden hail, and our noble boys fell thick and fast; and yet, still with the irresistible determination of men who fight for all that men hold dear, our gallant boys rushed on.

"Suddenly a halt was made; there was a deep pause, and the line wavered from right to left. We now saw the character of the enemy's works. A ravine deep and wide yawned before us, while from the other side of the crest of the almost perpendicular bank a breastwork of logs was erected, from behind which the dastard invaders were pouring murderous volleys upon our troops. The pause made by our troops was but a brief breathing-space. The voice of McLaws was heard : ' Forward, boys! Charge them!' and with a wild, mad shout our impetuous soldiery dashed forward."

There was not time to take away all the supplies which General McClellan had accumulated. Through the night teams were in motion, and the trains upon the railroad ran, carrying sick and wounded men and provisions to White House.

On the morning of the 28th, Keyes's and Porter's corps started across White Oak Swamp, followed by wagons, artillery—fifty heavy siege-guns —which McClellan had brought up from Yorktown. At White House

Landing, sloops, schooners, barges, and steamboats were departing for York River, hastening rapidly away, for no one knew how soon Jackson might appear.

At Savage's Station are barrels of pork, beef, sugar, coffee, boxes filled with bread, blankets, boots and shoes, which cannot be removed. They are set on fire, and the odor of burning bacon and leather is wafted on the summer air.

Far down the line a black cloud rises heavenward from the bridge across the Chickahominy, which has been set on fire. A railroad train loaded with cartridges, shot, and shell is standing on the track. The soldiers fire the cars. The engineer pulls the throttle and jumps from the engine, and the train whirls down the descending grade. It is two miles to the burning bridge. Faster and faster it flies, dashing along the fields, over the meadows, through the forest, a trail of fire, a streaming banner of flame and smoke. It reaches the bridge, leaps over the abutment, the engine going down into the stream, the flaming cars, one after another, piling upon it, while from the burning mass the exploding shells scatter the fragments far and wide.

It is Saturday—a joyful day in Richmond, for the word runs through the city that Lee has won a great victory, and that he is about to crush McClellan and compel his surrender. The multitude shout and swing their hats. But there are sorrowful scenes when the wounded are brought in. All the hospitals are filled. Lee has lost more than five thousand men.

McClellan could not take the thousands of his wounded in the hospitals to James River. His ambulances were filled, and the long line started on its weary journey. One of the chaplains, who was left with a corps of surgeons and nurses to care for those that could not be taken, gives this account of the heart-rending scene:

"The officers and soldiers who still lingered with their companions now prepared to leave. Many a manly cheek was wet with tears as they bade farewell to those whom they never expected to meet again. There were many sad partings. Up to this time the disabled had not known that they were to be left behind; when it became manifest that such was to be their fate, the scene could not be pictured in human language. Some wounded men who were left in their tents struggled through the grounds, exclaiming, 'I would rather die than be left in the hands of the rebels.' I heard one man cry out, 'O my God! is this the reward I deserve for all the sacrifices I have made, all the battles I have fought, and the agony I have endured?' Some of the younger soldiers wept like children, others turned pale, some fainted."

Among the wounded was Captain Reed, of Indiana. His company was out on the skirmish line. His son William, sixteen years old, with patriotic fire in his blood, had enlisted as commissary-sergeant. When the battle at Savage Station began, he seized a musket, went to the front, but was struck down by a bullet. The father wraps him in his blanket, pillows his head with his coat.

"Leave me, father, and take care of the men," are the words of the boy, and the captain returns to his place, soon to fall with a bullet through his shoulder. When darkness settles down, and the roar of battle dies away, they see the lines in blue move away in the darkness. They are prisoners. The captain surrenders his sword to Colonel

CAPTAIN REED AND SON.

Gorman, of the Fourteenth South Carolina, who generously returns it, and with great kindness does what he can to relieve their sufferings. They are taken to Libby Prison, where the boy gives his life to his country.

Sunday morning dawns. The Union troops still hold the breastworks in front of Richmond. Lee does not know what is going on in the Union lines.

Magruder sends out a small force to attack Sumner at the farm of Mr. Allen, but Hazard's and Pettit's batteries, with Sedgwick's division, quickly repulse the assault. Lee is reorganizing his ranks, and his soldiers are resting after the victory. He does not know how precious the moments are; he will learn to-morrow, when he finds that McClellan is on his way to James River.

It is only nine miles from Fair Oaks to Malvern Hills, but White Oak Swamp lies between, with only two narrow roads across it. There was no time to construct new ones. General McClellan must, in changing his

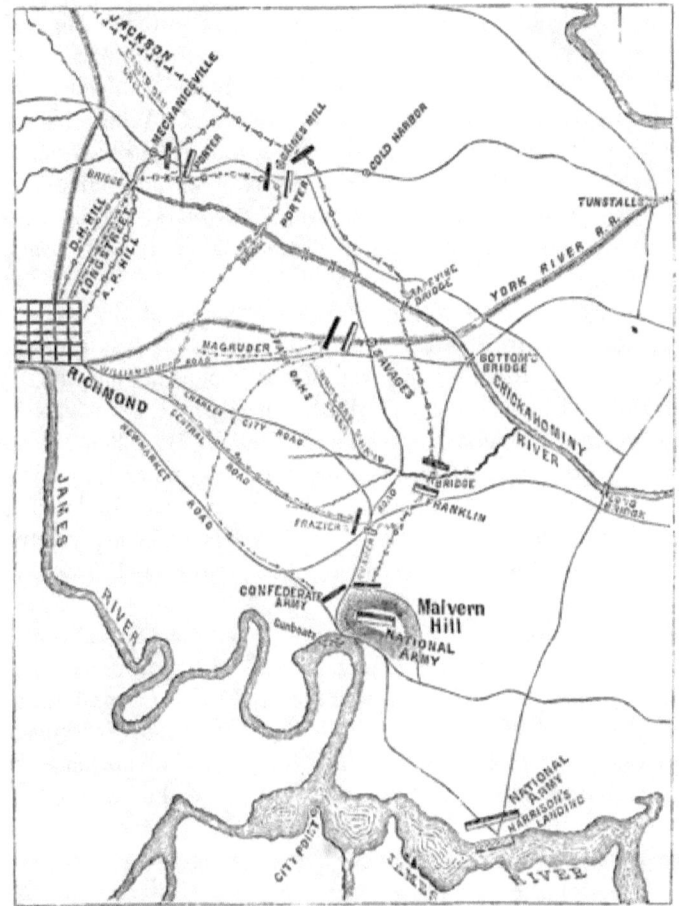

DIAGRAM OF THE RETREAT.

base, carry food sufficient to last him a week. The soldiers took three days' rations in their haversacks; three days' more were taken in the wagons, and twenty-five hundred cattle were driven in advance.

While the cannon were still playing on the north side of the Chick-

ahominy at Gaines's Mills, the wagons were in motion towards White
Oak Swamp. Strategy in war is not exactly like a game of checkers,
for in that game one side moves at a time; but in military operations
both sides move at the same moment. Strategy is to deceive your opponent, and so gain an advantage.

General Lee had made the movement from Richmond to crush the
section of the Union army north of the Chickahominy. He had sent
Jackson far round to strike the railroad and cut off communication with
York River. He expected to see McClellan abandoning his lines in front
of Richmond, and retreating towards Williamsburg. When the sun rose
on the 28th of June he discovered that the Union troops were still along
the Chickahominy. He was pleased. They were not thinking of retreating. He would let the soldiers rest a day, care for the wounded,
and then move east, get between McClellan and York River, and turn
the defeat into a rout.

General Lee had no suspicion of the movement of the Union army
to the James. Magruder, with twenty-five thousand, was south of the
Chickahominy, and thinking that the Union troops were retreating, ordered forward Kershaw's and Griffith's brigades. They came upon
French's brigade of Sumner's corps on the farm of Mr. Allen. The Confederates made two charges, but were repulsed with much loss. This was
about half-past nine in the morning. The army was withdrawing, and
Sumner fell back to Savage's Station to join Heintzelman; but through
some misunderstanding Heintzelman left his position and crossed White
Oak Swamp without informing Sumner.

Through the forenoon a mist had hung over the Chickahominy, but
now it lifted; and Magruder, finding that there were no Union troops
before him, pushed forward to strike a second blow. It was four o'clock
when McLaws's and Magruder's own division approached Savage Station.
Through the hours of this Sunday the troops of Sumner stood in line
motionless as statues, guarding the road leading to the swamp, covering
the retreating army. Brooks's brigade of Franklin's corps also remained.
With reckless impetuosity, without waiting for any co-operation from
Jackson, who was repairing the bridges across the Chickahominy, Magruder hurls his brigades upon Sumner. But instantly there comes a roll of
thunder from six Union batteries.

It was past five o'clock before Magruder opened the battle. An hour
passed of constant artillery firing; then the Confederates advanced across
the wide and level plain.

There was a stream of fire from Sumner's line—a steady outpouring of deadly volleys, with answering volleys from the Confederate lines. Sumner's batteries left off firing shell and threw canister, and the lines which had advanced so triumphantly were sent in confusion across the field. Longstreet and Jackson, under cover of the gathering darkness, once more pushed on their reluctant troops. Sumner brought up his reserve brigades. It was a short, sharp struggle — a wild night tempest — the roaring of fifty cannon and twenty thousand muskets. The evening was calm; not a breath of air stirred the leaves of the trees.

"Who are you?" asked an officer of the Fifth Vermont, dimly seeing a regiment in the darkness. There was a momentary silence, and then the question came back,

"Who are you?"

"The Fifth Vermont."

"Let them have it, boys!" were the words of command shouted by the Confederate officer. The Vermonters heard it. There was no flinching. Instantly their rifles came to their cheeks.

There were two broad flashes of light, two rows of dead and wounded. But the Vermonters held their ground, and the Confederates disappeared in the gloom of night.

Following the wagons were thousands of sick and wounded Union soldiers working their way towards the swamp, urged on by hope of escaping the hands of the Confederates. It was heart-rending to hear the words of those who were too badly wounded to be moved, or who could not be taken away.

General McClellan sent a last despatch to Secretary Stanton: "If I save this army now, I tell you plainly that I owe no thanks to you or to any other person in Washington. You have done your best to sacrifice this army."

It was regarded as very discourteous. It was a grave offence to charge President Lincoln and the Secretary of War with seeking to destroy the Union army.

We need not wonder that General McClellan felt very sore when, instead of marching towards Richmond, he was moving away from it. He had been defeated, and defeat is hard to bear.

"Glendale" is the euphonious name given by Mr. Nelson to his farm, located two miles south of White Oak Swamp. It is a place where several roads meet—from the north, the Swamp Road; from the east, the Long Bridge Road; from the south, the road leading to Malvern Hills; from the south-west, the Newmarket Road; from the north-west, the

Charles City Road, leading to Richmond. There are farm-houses, groves, ravines, wheat-fields waving with grain. There is a church upon the Malvern Road, and west of it a half-mile the mansion of Mr. Frazier, where the Confederate lines were formed on the 30th of June.

At sunrise all the divisions of the Union army were south of the swamp. Richardson and Smith, with Naglee's brigade of Casey's division, were guarding the road through the swamp; Slocum was on the Charles City Road, north-west of the church; Kearney was between that road and the Newmarket Road; McCall was on the Newmarket Road, with Hooker and Sedgwick behind him, near the church; Porter and Keyes were at Malvern with the trains.

Lee divided his army. Jackson, D. H. Hill, and Ewell followed McClellan across the Swamp Road, while A. P. Hill, Longstreet, Huger, Magruder, and Holmes made all haste down the Charles City Road from Richmond, to strike McClellan on the flank and divide his army. The President of the Confederacy went out with A. P. Hill to see the Union army cut to pieces.

Jackson reached the bridge across the sluggish stream in the swamp, but it was torn up, and on the southern bank stood Smith's and Richardson's divisions, with Hazard's, Ayers's, and Pettit's batteries. Jackson brought up all his guns. There was a fierce artillery fight, lasting through the day. Jackson succeeded in getting a small infantry force across towards evening, but it was not strong enough to make an attack, and nothing came of all his efforts to harass the rear.

During the afternoon the Union pickets on the Charles City Road discovered A. P. Hill's troops filing off from the road west of Frazier's farm towards the south. The Confederates went across the fields and through the woods to the Newmarket Road. While the main body was thus taking position, a small force of infantry and a battery opened fire upon Slocum; but he had cut down the forest in his front, forming an impassable barrier, so that he was secure from attack.

General McCall formed his division of six thousand men, with Meade's brigade north of the road, Seymour's south of it, and Reynolds's—commanded in this battle by Colonel Simmons—in reserve. He had five batteries in front of his infantry, pointing down a gentle slope upon an open field.

It was half-past two before A. P. Hill was ready to make the attack. He threw out two regiments as skirmishers, which advanced upon McCall's lines, but they were repulsed. Hill had twelve brigades: six of his own and six of Longstreet's. Magruder and Huger had not arrived.

Brigade after brigade advanced, but recoiled before the direct fire of the Union batteries, sustained by the infantry.

"The thunder of the cannon, the cracking of the musketry from thousands of combatants, mingled with screams from the wounded and dying, were terrific to the ear and to the imagination," says a Southern correspondent.

"Volleys upon volleys streamed across our front in such quick succession that it seemed impossible for any human being to live under it," writes another Confederate correspondent.

Five o'clock! The battle has raged two hours and a half, sustained wholly by McCall. The Confederates desist from their direct attack in front, and throw all their force upon Seymour's left, south of the road. McCall sends over the Fifth and Eighth regiments from his second line.

"Change front with the infantry and artillery," is his order.

Hill is pushing along his left flank to gain the rear of McCall, who orders a charge, which is executed with a promptness and vigor sufficient to check the advancing troops. But his line has become disordered by the charge. Hill hurries up his reserve brigades, which fire while advancing.

The gunners of the German batteries are seized with a panic and leave their pieces, while the drivers dash off to the rear, breaking through the infantry and trampling down the men.

The sun is still an hour and a half above the horizon. The Fifty-fifth and Sixtieth Virginia (Confederate troops) charge upon Randall's battery, shooting the few gunners who remain, and capture the cannon. McCall tries to rally the fugitives which break through Hooker's and Sumner's lines. Hooker has Grover's brigade on the right, Carr's in the centre, and Sickles's on the left. The Sixteenth Massachusetts and Sixty-ninth Pennsylvania, of Sedgwick's division of Sumner's corps, join Hooker on the right. They pour in a fire upon the left flank of the Confederates. Along Sumner's front are five batteries—thirty cannon in all.

On the side of the Union troops there are fifteen thousand infantry; on the Confederate side more than twenty thousand. But the Union troops have the advantage of position. They are compactly formed. The thirty guns, double-shotted, make great havoc in the Confederate ranks. Grover's brigade drives the Confederate troops and recaptures Randall's battery. It is an irresistible charge, made with such power that a portion of the Confederate troops flee in consternation towards Richmond. The officers try to rally them, but vain are their efforts.

"Many of the officers," writes a Southern correspondent, "wept like children. Everything seemed lost, and a general depression came over all hearts. Batteries dashed past in headlong flight. Ammunition, hospital, and supply wagons rushed along and swept the troops away from the field. In vain the most frantic exertions, entreaty, and self-sacrifice of the staff-officers. The troops had lost their foothold."

The arrival of General Magruder's division alone saved Hill from a disastrous rout, and the sun went down upon the gory field lost to Lee, for he had suffered a severe repulse. He had committed a great blunder in dividing his army. Jackson, with more than one-half of the troops, had been easily kept at bay along the sluggish stream winding through the swamp. Instead of crushing McClellan, Lee had suffered a signal defeat, dimming the glory of the victory at Gaines's Mills.

MALVERN HILL.

Two miles south of Glendale, overlooking James River, rise the Malvern Hills, a beautiful swell of land sloping towards the north. The Crewe house, built of red brick, surrounded by elm-trees, is on the hill. West of it are the Strawberry Plains, through which winds a little brook.

The north-west side of the hill is sharp and steep, and General Barnard places the batteries one above another, with the heavy siege-guns on the summit. East of the hill towards Harrison's Landing is the house of Mr. Binford.

18

General Fitz-John Porter was placed in command. On the west side, overlooking the plain, was Porter's corps; General Sykes's division on the extreme left, nearest James River. Behind these two divisions was Couch's, on the side of the hill.

Next in line was Heintzelman, with Kearney on the left and Hooker on the right. Beyond Heintzelman was Sumner's corps, reaching to Mr. Binford's house. Behind Sumner was Franklin, while Keyes was still farther east, near Mr. Carter's mill. Porter's troops faced west, Keyes's east, the army being a semicircle.

At daybreak Jackson, Ewell, and D. H. Hill, are in motion crossing White Oak Swamp. They are to attack the north-east side of Malvern, by the Binford house, while Magruder and Huger are to attack the north-west side. A. P. Hill and Longstreet's corps have suffered so terribly that they cannot go into the battle.

Through the forenoon the Confederate troops are marching to get into position. Lee intends, by a grand assault from all sides, to produce a panic in the Union lines, capture the cannon, and make a complete victory.

Four o'clock. Armistead's brigade, of Huger's division, leads the assault. The beginning of the cannonade is to be the signal for Jackson. Magruder's cannon open fire, but are soon silenced and driven from their positions by the superior fire from the semicircle of batteries on the slopes of Malvern. Armistead pushes on with spirit, but his brigade is cut to pieces by shells, by volleys from Howe's brigade, and his troops are hurled back, disorganized and broken. The flags of the Fourteenth Alabama are lost.

Magruder is angry. He was blamed yesterday for not being on hand when wanted; and now, without judgment, orders up regiment after regiment singly to attack Porter, but every attack is repulsed.

The wind is north-east, and the roar of the conflict does not reach Jackson. From four till six o'clock his troops wait. D. H. Hill is impatient. Lee wonders why Jackson does not begin. The wind lulls at nightfall, and the rattle of musketry and the reverberations of the cannonade fall on the ears of Hill.

The Confederate troops come out from the woods in which they have been standing, rush with a yell upon Kearney's division, only to be rolled back as the waves are broken upon the rocky ledges of the ocean shore.

There is little concert of action on the Confederate side. The plan has miscarried. Malvern is aflame with the flashes of more than one hundred guns, hurling solid shot and shell into the Confederate lines. General Hunt, commanding the Union artillery, keeps the batteries in constant play, while the gunboats in the river send shot and shell across Strawberry Plains. General McClellan is on the *Galena*, and each general manages his own corps as seems to him best.

The sun goes down, and night comes on. At nine o'clock the battle ends. Lee has suffered another repulse, with great loss.

"Retreat to Harrison's Landing," is the order from McClellan. It is six miles down the river, and during the night the army makes its way to that point, where steamboats are arriving with supplies.

"Although," says General McClellan, in his report, "the battle of Malvern was a complete victory, it was necessary to fall back still far-

THE GUNBOATS AT MALVERN HILL.

ther, in order to reach a point where our supplies could be brought to us with certainty."

That was not the opinion of some of his officers. General Martindale was so angry that he shed tears.

"I, Philip Kearney," shouted that general, "enter my solemn protest against this order to retreat. We ought, instead, to march into Richmond. In full view of all the responsibility of such a declaration, I say to you all, such an order can only be prompted by cowardice or treason."

In the morning the Union army is at Harrison's Landing, while the Confederate army is moving towards Richmond. During the seven days' fighting McClellan has lost about sixteen thousand, and Lee twenty thousand men.

The campaign for the capture of Richmond was over. It was undertaken against the judgment of President Lincoln, who could see with his plain common-sense what General McClellan did not comprehend—that the Confederate army would be stronger at Richmond than it possibly could be at Centreville; that it would be easier to strike a blow near Washington than at Richmond, far from the base of supplies, and in the enemy's country.

CHAPTER XII.

CONFEDERATE MANASSAS CAMPAIGN.

THE campaign of McClellan against Richmond had failed. The Union army was at Harrison's Landing, inactive, dispirited, wasting with sickness. There were rivalries and jealousies among the generals. The commander-in-chief gave much more of his confidence to Fitz-John Porter and Franklin than to Hooker, Heintzelman, and Kearney. Favoritism, wherever exercised, in a school or army, where obedience is required, impairs discipline. It was natural that the colonels, captains, lieutenants, and soldiers should also have prejudices either for or against the different corps commanders and the commander-in-chief. There was a marked decline in the discipline of the army, and a great deal of murmuring, especially on the part of some of the officers.

HARRISON'S LANDING.

Up to this time the military campaigns had been made at hap-hazard. There had been no head. It was seen that there must be some controlling mind, and General Halleck was called to Washington by President Lincoln to give direction to military movements.

On June 26th Major-general Pope was appointed by President Lincoln commander of an army along the Rappahannock. He had three corps: Sigel's, Banks's, and McDowell's—in all, about forty-nine thousand men. General Pope was educated at West Point, was in the battle of Buena Vista, and had rendered excellent service at New Madrid, on the Mississippi, and in the capture of Island No. 10.

When the war began, President Lincoln called for seventy-five thousand soldiers.

"Where will he get them?" everybody asked; but under that call ninety-one thousand offered themselves. In July, 1861, he called for five hundred thousand, and more than seven hundred thousand enlisted. More troops were needed, not only for Virginia, but on the Mississippi, in North Carolina, South Carolina, Georgia, Texas—in all the seceded States.

In July, 1862, he called for three hundred thousand more. The people, instead of being disheartened by the disasters that had come upon the Army of the Potomac, hastened to fill up the ranks. All over the North, in every town and village, once more was heard the drum-beat. Regiments were forming; men who had not thought of enlisting hastened to enroll their names, bidding farewell to friends, to give their lives for their country if need be. Not only three hundred thousand, but four hundred and twenty-one thousand enlisted. This was the song they sang, written by John S. Gibbons:

"We are coming, Father Abraham, three hundred thousand more,
   From Mississippi's winding stream and from New England's shore;
   We leave our ploughs and workshops, our wives and children dear,
   With hearts too full for utterance, with but a silent tear;
   We dare not look behind us, but stendfastly before—
   We are coming, Father Abraham, three hundred thousand more.

"If you look all up our valleys, where the growing harvests shine,
   You may see our sturdy farmer boys fast forming into line;
   And children from their mothers' knees are pulling at the weeds,
   And learning how to reap and sow against their country's needs;
   And a farewell group stands weeping at every cottage door—
   We are coming, Father Abraham, three hundred thousand more.

"You have called us, and we're coming, by Richmond's bloody tide,
   To lay us down for freedom's sake, our brothers' bones beside;
   Or from foul treason's savage grasp to wrench the murderer's blade,
   And in the face of foreign foes its fragments to parade.
   Six hundred thousand loyal men and true have gone before—
   We are coming, Father Abraham, three hundred thousand more."

Confederate troops were hastening to reinforce the army of Lee. Negroes who came into McClellan's lines had great stories to tell of the immense army in Richmond. He was calling for reinforcements, and blamed the authorities as having brought about the failure of the campaign by taking away McDowell from his control. He wrote this to Secretary Stanton: "If I cannot fully control all his troops I want none of them, but would prefer to fight the battle with what I have, and let others be responsible for results." From the beginning McClellan believed that Lee had two hundred thousand men.

There were three separate armies in Virginia besides McClellan's: one in the lower Shenandoah, under Banks; one in the upper Shenandoah, under Fremont; and one at Fredericksburg, under McDowell. There was no unity of plans, and on June 26th they were placed under the command of General Pope, who issued an unfortunate address.

"I have come," he said, "from the West, where we have always seen the backs of our enemies; from an army whose business it has been to seek the adversary, and to beat him when found; whose policy has been attack, and not defence."

The officers and men thought that he was drawing unjust comparisons between the soldiers of the East and those of the West. Such was not his intention, but he did not reflect how they would receive such an address. They knew that they were brave, and an imputation that they were inferior to Western troops was very offensive.

General Halleck directed General Pope to concentrate his army and cut the railroads leading west from Richmond. Such a movement would compel General Lee to send away some of his troops.

It had that effect. Lee sent Jackson with his own corps and other troops up to Louisa Court-house the day after Pope assumed command. On June 27th he sent A. P. Hill's division. In his letter to Jackson he said, "These troops will exceed eighteen thousand men. Your command ought certainly to number that amount." This made Jackson's army thirty-six thousand besides the cavalry under Stuart.

What should be done? It was a perplexing question at Washington. General McClellan was calling for reinforcements, but there were no troops to send him. His campaign had been a failure, and Secretary Stanton and General Halleck, and the country generally, had lost confidence in him as a commander. General Halleck saw that quite likely Lee would throw an overwhelming force on Pope, and a portion of the troops under Burnside were hurried from North Carolina to reinforce him. The

Confederate Government was conscripting men to fill up the ranks of the army. Something must be done.

On July 24th General Halleck went to Harrison's Landing to see McClellan, who asked for fifty thousand more troops. "I am not author-ized to promise you more than twenty thousand," said Halleck. "I will make the attempt to take Richmond with that number," was the reply. General Halleck returned to Washington. Upon his arrival, there came a despatch from McClellan that he must have thirty-five thousand. It was not possible to send that number.

There was only one thing to be done: to withdraw the army from the James to some position where it could co-operate with the army under Pope, and it was decided to bring it to Acquia Creek, on the Potomac, below Washington. "Send away your sick as fast as you can," was the despatch to McClellan July 30th. On August 3d Halleck ordered the withdrawal of the whole army, but McClellan, instead of at once obeying, sent a protest. "I fear it will be a fatal blow," he said. "Here, directly in front of this army, is the heart of the rebellion; it is here we should strike the blow which will determine the fate of this nation. A decided victory here, and the military strength of the rebellion is crushed," he said to Halleck. He thought that the Union army would be demoralized if withdrawn. Not till August 14th did the troops take up the line of march to Yorktown. Two weeks had been lost.

It is not strange that he did not like to retrace his steps. Few men like to take the back track. It was hard to recognize in any way the hu-miliating fact that the movement to Richmond was a failure.

About half-way between Orange Court-house and Culpeper Court-house, north of the Rapidan River, is Cedar Mountain, which stands by itself, one of the outlying hills of the Blue Ridge.

It is the first week in August. The telegraph informs General Lee that Pope is marching south from Culpeper Court-house. The Confeder-ate pickets down by Malvern Hill report that the Union troops are get-ting ready to leave Harrison's Landing; that there is a great bustle and stir — steamers and schooners departing with supplies, that camps are breaking up. General Lee has sent General Jackson north-west with twenty-five thousand men to confront Pope. On the 9th of August Jack-son is marching up the road leading north across Cedar Mountain.

General Banks, with about seven thousand five hundred Union troops, is marching south from Culpeper. Pope sends Colonel Marshall with this order: "General Banks is to move to the front immediately, assume command of all the force, deploy his skirmishers if the enemy advances, and attack him immediately as he approaches, and be reinforced from here."

It was not a written order, but General Banks required it to be written out by Colonel Marshall, for a military commander wants to know just what he is to do. Was he to advance and attack? No; but if Jackson advanced he was to attack him. General Pope sent General Roberts, an engineer officer, to select the ground Banks was to *hold*. General Pope ought to have written out exactly and explicitly just what General Banks was to do; but he did not, and it was the beginning of a series of mistakes.

It is past noon when General Banks forms his line, the troops facing south. They see the mountain before them, and General Augur, commanding a division, files out west of the road, and General Williams east of it. Crawford's brigade has the right of the line; General Geary's brigade stands next in line; then Prince's brigade. General Greene has only two small regiments. General Gordon's brigade is held in reserve half a mile in rear of Crawford.

The ground is a gentle slope rising towards the mountain. There are corn and wheat fields, clumps of trees, and out on the right, where Crawford forms his line, there are woods. The wheat has been cut, and is standing in shocks. Out in the woods, and far out on both flanks, General Bayard has his cavalry skirmishers keeping watch, for it is well known that Jackson is advancing.

It is eleven o'clock when General Jubal Early, commanding the First Confederate Brigade, comes out upon the north slope of the mountain and beholds Bayard's cavalry. He brings up four guns. He is on much higher ground than Bayard. The cavalrymen see white puffs of smoke amid the cedars, and hear the shells scream through the air. Bayard places Knapp's battery in position. Other batteries come up, and from one till half-past three o'clock the artillery firing echoes along the mountain sides.

It is a bold front which Banks presents—so audacious that Jackson thinks the whole of Pope's army is before him, and hesitates about making an attack. He has twenty-five thousand men, but supposes that Pope has double the number, not for a moment imagining that there is only one small division of less than eight thousand. He places Ewell on the east side of the road and Winder on the west, with A. P. Hill in the rear of Winder. The last-named officer is struck by a shell and killed, and General Taliaferro takes command of the division.

What shall General Banks do? Jackson has deployed his line. If the enemy advances he is to attack. Has Jackson advanced? Certainly he has advanced from where he was in the morning. General Roberts has selected the ground which Banks is to hold, but to attack he must necessarily advance. His nearest support is Ricketts's division, which is nearly

MAP OF CEDAR MOUNTAIN.

four miles in his rear. He does not know that with less than eight thousand he is confronted by twenty-five thousand.

It is half-past five, a sultry summer afternoon, when Geary and Prince, east of the road, and Crawford out in the woods, west of it, march forward with quick steps, firing rapidly. It is like the sudden outbreak of a storm. Jackson has not expected to be attacked, but has been getting ready to sweep down upon Banks like a hound upon its prey. Crawford's men rush through the woods and fall suddenly upon the left flank of Campbell's brigade. The First Virginia battalion is the first to feel the stroke and gives way in confusion.

"Change front!" is the order to the Forty-second Virginia; but the officer who gives it, Major Logan, falls mortally wounded, and the regiment breaks. General Garnett is wounded and Lieutenant-colonel Cunningham killed. Crawford's men, with a cheer, next rush upon Taliaferro's brigade, striking it in flank, while Geary and Prince are attacking in front, driving it in disorder.

"All the troops," says Early, "had fallen back; and the enemy was advancing up the slope of the hill." There is consternation in the Confederate lines. A great stream of fugitives is pouring down the road. The artillerymen of Winder's battalion are lashing their horses to a run to the rear to take new positions. Officers are riding with orders to Branch, Pender, and Archer, commanding the brigades of Hill's division. Ronald's brigade comes up to confront Crawford and Geary.

The fresh Confederate troops bear down upon Crawford and Geary, and drive them back. The Tenth Maine makes a charge to roll back the advancing Confederates. In a few minutes one hundred and seventy-three out of four hundred and sixty-one officers and men are killed and wounded. A half-hour too late, Banks orders Gordon to attack. His troops go upon the run across the little creek and through the wheat-fields. It is a brave assault, but a useless sacrifice of men. They are compelled to retreat.

It is a hard-fought, bloody, useless conflict. In an hour and a half 1661 Union troops were killed and wounded, and 1314 Confederates. It was so audacious a stand on the part of the Union troops that Jackson, who had expected to march on to Culpeper, turned back and retreated across the Rapidan. At Kearnstown, near Winchester, in the Shenandoah, in 1861, he had been defeated by General Shields and General Kimball, and here at Cedar Mountain he had come very near being defeated by an army not a third the size of his own. He saw that he could not go on to Culpeper, for Pope's entire army would confront him, so he retreated to wait for the arrival of reinforcements.

In June the theatre of war was before Richmond; in September it was to be in front of Washington, around and on the field where the first great battle of the rebellion had been fought.

Lee consolidated his army into two corps, making Jackson and Longstreet commanders. D. H. Hill, with a small force, was left to guard Richmond. Jackson had fourteen brigades and fourteen batteries—thirty-five thousand men; Longstreet had the divisions of Hood, Anderson, Walker, and McLaws—thirty-five thousand; Stuart commanded the cavalry—five thousand—giving Lee seventy-five thousand in all.

On the morning of the 15th the brigades of Longstreet were at Gordonsville. On the same day the retreating brigades of McClellan were marching east over the battle-ground of Williamsburg towards Yorktown to take steamers for Acquia Creek and Alexandria.

It was a very important letter which the Union cavalrymen, under General Bayard, captured from a Confederate officer on August 16th—a letter from Lee to Jackson, informing him of what he intended to do, and how many men he had. General Pope read it, and saw that he was to be attacked by an army numbering seventy-five thousand. General Reno, with two small divisions, had joined him; but, all told, he had only forty-nine thousand men. There was but one thing for him to do—fall back north of the Rappahannock and take a position to cover Washington, and await the arrival of McClellan's troops.

General Lee has conceived a brilliant movement. He will hold Longstreet on the south bank of the Rappahannock, make Pope believe that he intends to cross and attack him, while Jackson makes a swift and roundabout march to get in the rear of Pope, capture his supplies, and cut off his connection with Washington.

Jackson is on the west bank of the Rappahannock, at Sulphur Springs.

At daybreak, August 25th, his brigades march north-west away from the river. The Union cavalrymen guarding the other side see columns of dust rising in the west. What is Jackson up to? Whither is he going? He is heading towards the Blue Ridge. Is he intending to go through some of the gaps into the Shenandoah Valley? General Pope, who is at Warrenton, has his army well concentrated, but he does not know what to make of those clouds of dust far away in the west towards the Blue Ridge. A Union officer, Colonel Clark, is out on picket. He creeps through the woods close up to the road over which Jackson is marching, lies there all the morning and counts the regiments—thirty-six of them, with cavalry and batteries. When they have gone by, he hastens to General Pope at Warrenton with the news.

The Bull Run Mountains lie north-west of the old battle-field of Bull Run. General Pope does not mistrust that Jackson, although marching west, is aiming for Thoroughfare Gap; but before night Jackson has crossed the river at Harrison's Ford, and is at the little village of Orleans. His men have marched twenty-five miles in the broiling sun. They throw themselves down for a few hours' rest, but at daybreak are once more marching north towards the little town of Salem. Now they turn east, and in the evening, after another twenty-five-mile march, are in possession of the Gap.

How easy it would have been for Pope to have sent a division of troops up there by rail and taken possession of it in advance! But he did not suspect that Lee would divide his army and send Jackson to make such a roundabout movement.

In war it is very necessary for military commanders to keep a sharp lookout on the back door as well as on the front. Usually it is much easier to get in at the rear than at the front. The movement which Jackson was making was very hazardous, and if General Pope had divined what he was intending to do, and fallen back towards Manassas, he could have crushed him. If his cavalry picket had been out beyond the Bull Run Mountains keeping watch, he might have saved the army from the disasters that resulted from his want of care and foresight. But while Jackson is stealing round to his rear, Pope, joined by Heintzelman and Fitz-John Porter's corps, is planning to make a sudden dash across the Rappahannock and attack Longstreet. He knows nothing of what is going on in his rear.

It is eight o'clock in the evening of the 26th. Suddenly the telegraph between Pope's headquarters and Washington ceases ticking. General Stuart has pushed south-east from Thoroughfare Gap with his cavalry, and is at Bristoe Station, three miles west of Manassas Junction. Two empty trains, with the engines, are there, and he runs them off the track. Jackson is following Stuart, and at midnight his leg-weary soldiers, who have marched nearly sixty miles in a little more than two days, are at Manassas Junction, capturing three hundred Union troops, with forty-eight cannon, one hundred and seventy-five horses, ten locomotives, fifty thousand pounds of bacon, two thousand barrels of flour, thousands of bushels of oats, one thousand barrels of corned beef, with an immense supply of bread, two thousand barrels of salt pork, fruit, hospital stores, and ammunition. The Confederate cavalrymen mounted the fresh horses. The soldiers ate all they could, filled their haversacks, spiked the cannon, and set the sheds containing the stores on fire.

Union cavalrymen rode in hot haste to Warrenton, and General Pope soon comprehended the meaning of Jackson's movement. He was cut off from Washington; his supplies were destroyed. He must make a quick march towards Manassas, fall upon Jackson, and crush him before Lee could come to his aid. Officers ride with orders, and at daybreak, August 27th, every division is moving eastward. At the same moment Longstreet is moving over the same route that Jackson took for Thoroughfare Gap, to join Jackson before Pope can fall upon him.

General Halleck in Washington learned that something wrong was going on at Manassas. General Slocum's division of the Army of the Potomac was at Alexandria, and General Taylor's brigade of New Jersey troops hastened to the cars, and were taken out as far as Bull Run on Wednesday morning, August 27th. The troops filed out of the cars, marched across the bridge, and on to Manassas Junction. Suddenly the heavy guns which Jackson had captured opened on them, and then the Confederate infantry. General Taylor, seeing that Jackson's whole corps was in front of him, retreated towards Blackburn's Ford. Stuart, with his cavalry, dashed upon the surprised troops, capturing Taylor and nearly half the brigade. Those not captured fled through the woods towards Centreville utterly disorganized.

General Hooker at the same hour—three o'clock in the afternoon— is marching east from Warrenton Junction along the railroad.

A brook called Broad Run, which is crossed by the railroad near the station, comes down from the north-west, along which is posted Ewell's division of Confederates. Hooker deploys his men, outmanœuvres Ewell, makes a vigorous attack, and drives him across the run so rapidly that he cannot remove his wounded. It is a quick, sharp fight, in which Ewell loses between three and four hundred men, and Hooker nearly the same

number. General Pope arrives while the fight is going on, and at sunset
on this Wednesday night begins to comprehend the situation of affairs.
It is not a small force of cavalry and infantry that has gained his rear,
but half of Lee's army. He is of the opinion that Jackson is swinging
his whole corps south, to get between him and Alexandria, and sends orders to his own generals to move in the same direction—making the mistake of removing General McDowell's and Sigel's corps from Gainesville,
where the turnpike from Centreville to Warrenton crosses the railroad
running through Thoroughfare Gap. They were in the best place possible
to keep Lee from joining Jackson.

Leaving Pope now, let us go up to Manassas and see what Jackson's
plans are. He knows that Pope outnumbers him; that he cannot wait at
Manassas; that it will not do for him to get between Pope and Alexandria, but that he must retire to a position where Lee can join him. He
remembers the old field of Bull Run—knows every foot of the ground.
North of it is an unfinished railroad, excavations and embankments, along
which he will post his troops and hold the ground till Lee arrives. So,
while Pope is marching his troops south-east and south towards Manassas
Junction, Jackson is retreating north-east to this chosen position.

General McDowell, in obedience to Pope's orders, begins his march
eastward. He is at Gainesville, the point where the Manassas Gap Railroad crosses the Warrenton Pike. Suddenly a cannon on a hill north of
the turnpike flashes. There is a short fight, and the enemy disappear
from the hill, retreating north-east. McDowell thinks it is Stuart's cavalry that he has encountered, but it is General Bradley Johnson's brigade
of Taliaferro's division instead. McDowell does not suspect that he has
struck Jackson's right wing, and that if he continues his march east along
the pike he will find himself confronted by Taliaferro's and Ewell's divisions. He has orders to march to Manassas Junction. He turns south,
and marches away from the very spot which he ought to hold. If he
were to march a mile farther east he would find the enemy. The head
of the column turns south in obedience to orders, and the great opportunity to crush Jackson is lost.

It is half-past four in the afternoon when word comes to General Pope
that Jackson is at Centreville, east of Bull Run. It is a mistake. He has
been there, and A. P. Hill was there in the morning; but now Jackson
has his whole army along the line of the unfinished railroad south of Sudley Springs. Pope, accordingly, sends orders to his different corps to
march towards Centreville.

It is almost sunset. Kearney's division of Heintzelman's corps has

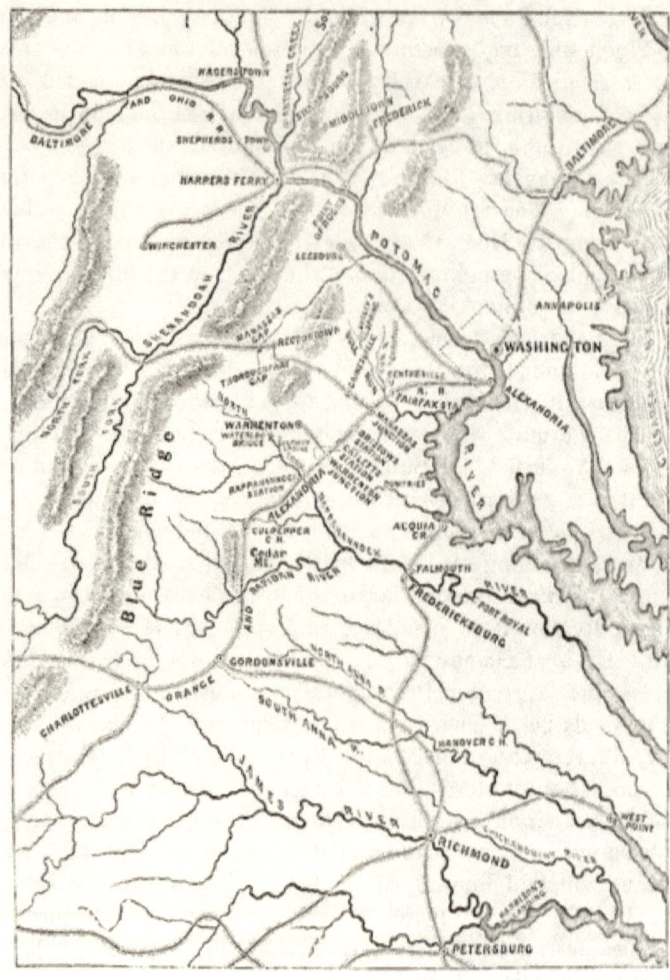

THE SORTIE OF LEE.

made a quick march, crossed Bull Run at Blackburn's Ford, and is nearly up to Centreville. Reno's division is behind him on the east bank; Hooker is on the west bank; Reynolds and Sigel are two miles south of the old battle-field; Porter's corps is at Bristoe Station; Banks is behind him, guarding the trains.

Ricketts's division is well up towards Thoroughfare Gap, just where it ought to be to keep Longstreet from coming through. King's division has been there, but has been ordered to Centreville. If he had been ordered to remain with Ricketts, far different, in all probability, would have been the history of the campaign.

Let us see the situation at the moment the sun is sinking behind the Blue Ridge. Kearney, at Centreville, has come up with the rear of A. P. Hill's corps. Thirteen miles away in the west Longstreet is coming through Thoroughfare Gap. Ricketts's guns are flashing in front of him. King is on the turnpike, his soldiers in column, marching at will. King has no expectation of being attacked. He does not know that Ewell and Taliaferro are ready to pounce upon him from a piece of woods across the open field north of the turnpike.

The sun is just sinking below the horizon, and the cool of the evening is delightful to the weary soldiers, who hear the boom of cannon far away in the east towards Centreville, where Hooker and Kearney are driving the rear of A. P. Hill from that place north-west towards Sudley Springs. Not a soldier in Gibbon's and Doubleday's brigades of King's division mistrusts that half a mile from the turnpike Taliaferro has his batteries in position, and that the gunners are taking aim.

There are flashes and white clouds of smoke along the edge of the woods; shells burst amid the astonished and startled troops. The column comes to a halt and waits for orders. General King is not there. Gibbon and Doubleday hold a quick consultation.

" Tear down that fence !" is the order, and the fence on the north side of the turnpike is thrown to the ground in a twinkling. The two generals resolve to know the meaning of this audacious cannonade.

Gibbon's brigade—the Second, Sixth, and Seventh Wisconsin, and the Nineteenth Indiana—advances across the field. A line of light fringes the dark-green foliage of the forest. A moment later they give their answer by a volley of musketry. The Union batteries gallop to a hill, wheel into position, and open fire.

Doubleday has the Fifty-sixth Pennsylvania, and the Seventy-sixth and Ninety-fifth New York regiments. They turn from the turnpike and move up a gentle slope. Gibbon marches through a piece of woods to an open field. The regiment holding the left of the line advances to Mr. Brawner's house, driving the Confederate skirmishers, coming upon Taliaferro's line, which is posted along the railroad-cut crossing Brawner's farm. The battle extends from the farm-house, out-buildings, and hay-stacks eastward to the woods, where Ewell's division is stationed. Doubleday advances across the open field north-west of the little cluster of buildings called Groveton, charging straight into the woods.

General Taliaferro has four brigades : Baylor's, Johnson's, Taliaferro's, and Stafford's. Two of Ewell's brigades are also engaged: Trimble's and Lawton's; in all, there are twenty-nine Confederate regiments against seven Union. It is nearly six o'clock when the battle begins; it is a terrific struggle. This is what General Taliaferro says of it:

"For two hours and a half, without an instant's cessation of the most terrible discharges of musketry, round shot, and shell, both lines stood unmoved, neither advancing, and neither breaking nor yielding, until at last, about nine o'clock at night, the enemy slowly and sullenly fell back and yielded the field."

General Taliaferro was wounded. General Ewell received a bullet in his knee and was carried to a farm-house, where his leg was amputated. Three Confederate colonels, one lieutenant-colonel, and four majors were killed or wounded.

"It was a fierce and sanguinary fight," said Jackson. Through the twilight hours the two lines faced each other—the Union troops mostly in the open fields, the Confederates in the edge of the woods—and fired sullenly in each other's faces, broad sheets of flame from musketry and cannon lighting up the lurid scene—one-third of the Union troops being killed or wounded.

Gibbon and Doubleday have fallen back to the turnpike. The soldiers are not in the least disheartened. They have lost one-third of their number. The field where they have fought is thickly strewn with killed and wounded, but they make the welkin ring with their cheers. They know that they have fought three times their own number.

Jackson hears the hurrahs sounding on the night air, and does not know what to make of it. A defeated army marches away in silence; but the Union troops, instead of marching away, are hurrahing as if they had won a victory. It must be that they have been reinforced. Instead of sweeping down and crushing King as he might have done, he consolidates his line.

General King is in a quandary. What shall he do? Pope has been marching to attack Jackson before Longstreet arrives. He has encountered Jackson's right wing: to stay where he is will be hazardous. He does not know where to find Pope, and resolves to march towards Manassas. The wounded are gathered, the long train of ambulances move away, and at one o'clock in the morning the two brigades which have fought so brave a battle retire from the spot which they ought to hold at all hazards.

With their marching away they put it out of the power of Pope to crush Jackson before the arrival of Longstreet; for Ricketts, who has been trying to hold Thoroughfare Gap against Longstreet, has been outflanked

19

by a division which crept over the mountains farther north, and is marching south towards Bristoe Station. In the morning McDowell and Sigel
were in the best possible position, but now there is nothing to prevent the
union of Longstreet and Jackson.

It is August 29, 1862, and the sun is rising. General Pope is at Centreville. He has made the mistake of thinking that Jackson is retreating,
but is glad to hear that he has halted. He does not know that Longstreet's troops are pouring through Thoroughfare Gap. He has been in
pursuit of Jackson, has found him, and now will crush him. Couriers
ride with orders to the commanders of the different corps and divisions.
Heintzelman, with Hooker's and Kearney's, are at this hour between
Centreville and Bull Run. Crossing Stone Bridge and riding west, we
come to the field of the first Bull Run battle. One mile beyond it, south
of the turnpike, near Groveton, we find Reynolds's division of Pennsylvania Reserves, Sigel's corps, and Milroy's independent brigade. Now,
turning south, and riding along a country road through woods and fields,
we come to the railroad near Manassas, where we find the troops of Fitz-
John Porter. He is three miles distant from Sigel and Reynolds. McDowell is near him. Banks is three miles farther south, at Bristoe Station,
guarding the trains, moving slowly, when he ought to be moving rapidly,
towards Bull Run.

The army under Pope is not a compact body; the troops have very
little confidence in him as a commander. His own troops have not forgotten the unfortunate order which he issued when he took command, and
are beginning to suffer for want of the provisions which Jackson destroyed.
The troops which have been serving under McClellan are prejudiced
against him. There is want of harmony among the corps and division
commanders. Under such circumstances General Pope proposes to fight
a great battle. He will crush Jackson, and then fall back towards Washington and reorganize and revictual his army.

Reynolds is near Groveton, within a mile of the field where King
fought so bravely the night before. East of him, next in line, are
Schenck's and Schurz's divisions, and then Milroy's brigade, facing north-
west.

With the rising of the sun the battle begins. The Confederate troops
are the same that fought the previous night—Taliaferro's division, commanded now by Starke, and Ewell's, commanded now by Lawton. The
Confederates drive back Schurz's division, but are driven in turn. One
of Schurz's brigades gains the railroad embankment and holds it.

At half-past five in the morning, General Porter receives an order to march at once to Centreville; but it is half-past seven before he is ready to move. Then he receives an order to march towards Gainesville. The troops turn north-west and march along the railroad leading to Gainesville. At half-past eleven they are at Dawkin's Branch, a little stream running south. They can see the shells bursting in the air two miles north of them; the rattle of musketry falls upon their ears. Porter has twelve thousand men. An officer comes to him with this despatch from General Buford, commanding the cavalry, who is near Gainesville, on the left flank of Reynolds: "9.30 A.M.—Seventeen regiments, one battery, and five hundred cavalry passed through Gainesville three-quarters of an hour ago on the Centreville road. I think this division should join our forces, now engaged, at once."

What should Porter and McDowell do? The order from Pope was to march to Gainesville; but Longstreet was already at Gainesville. His advance had joined Jackson, according to this despatch. Should they turn off from the road, strike through the woods, and find a route due north to Reynolds?

Porter and McDowell rode out a little distance and saw that the ground was uneven, that the troops would find it difficult marching. Farther east is the road leading to Sudley Springs. King's and Ricketts's divisions are already on it, and at noon they take up their line of march towards the sound of the cannonade.

General Porter's skirmishers are in the woods west of Dawkin's Branch, his cannon are planted along the east bank, and his troops are in line. He sees a cloud of dust west of him. What is the meaning of it? Is Longstreet swinging his troops south to attack him?

The Confederate pickets immediately in front of Porter are Rosser's cavalrymen who have been sent by Longstreet to raise a great dust in front of Porter, to make him think that his whole force is moving towards Manassas. The cavalrymen have tied bundles of brush to the tails of the horses, and are riding up and down the road.

General Porter did not like to receive orders from Pope, and his prejudice is seen in his despatches to McClellan.

"We are working," he writes, "to get behind Bull Run, and I presume will be there in a few days, if strategy does not use us up. The strategy is immense, and the tactics in the inverse proportion. . . . I believe the enemy have a contempt for the Army of Virginia. I wish myself away from it, with all our old Army of the Potomac, and so do our companions."

Through the afternoon Porter waits. The order directing him to move to Gainesville was a joint order to himself and McDowell. McDowell has moved up the road to Sudley Springs, and reaches the field of battle in season to be of service, but Porter does not follow. He is but two miles from the conflict; a fleet horse would take him to Pope's headquarters in half an hour; no messenger is sent to obtain instructions. Through the afternoon Porter remains motionless. Pope the while supposes that Porter is obeying the order already sent.

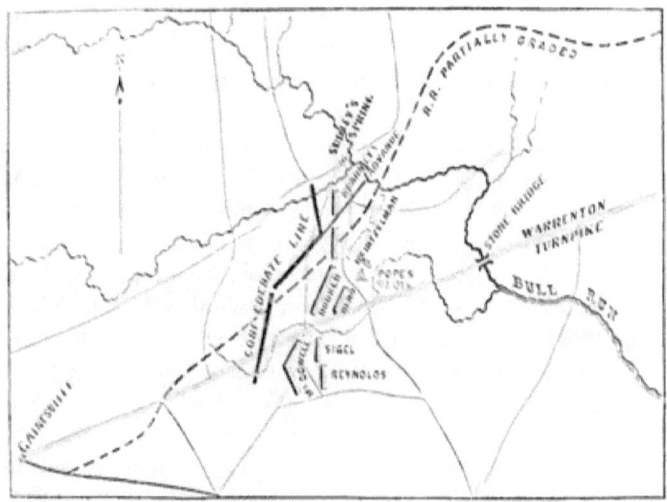

MAP OF GAINESVILLE.

It is four o'clock before Heintzelman is in position to attack A. P. Hill, who holds the left of the Confederate line. He selects Grover's brigade of Hooker's division to lead.

"Advance till you receive the fire of the enemy; deliver your own, then charge bayonets!" are the orders.

The brigade, which has been in all the battles of the Peninsula, moves across the fields towards the woods and the railroad embankment, behind which the Confederates are lying. First a rattle, then a roar of musketry and of Confederate cannon. The line in the field comes to a halt; the muskets fall to a level; a line of light runs the entire length. With a hurrah they go up to the embankment, driving the Confederates back upon the second line.

Now is the time to hurl in the reserves, break the Confederate line at the centre, fold it back, and crush the divided wings. But no troops come to their support. For twenty minutes they struggle, and then are compelled to fall back, leaving more than six hundred killed and wounded on the field.

Kearney was to advance at the same moment that Grover attacked, but for some reason he did not till later, when he rolled back the Confederate line.

"For a while victory trembled in the balance," are the words of Hill.

Gregg's Confederate brigade loses six hundred and thirteen killed and wounded, including every field-officer excepting two. Hill's troops are protected by the railroad embankment. He orders up Lawton's and Early's brigades, and Kearney is driven from the position which he has gained.

It was noon when King's division started from Dawkin's Branch to march north; and now, at six o'clock, just as the sun is going down, the troops which in the last night's gloaming turned from the turnpike west of Groveton and attacked Jackson's right wing, once more advance to attack, not the worn and wearied troops of Jackson, but Hood's division of Longstreet's corps — the troops which Buford saw pouring through Gainesville at half-past nine. Here they are, with three batteries lining the edge of the forest. Darkness once more is coming on when King's troops move to the attack. General King is not able to sit in his saddle, and General Hatch commands the division. For three-quarters of an hour they struggle, when, outnumbered, they are obliged to retire, leaving one cannon in the hands of the enemy. Night closes upon a bloody scene. The Union troops have attacked, have driven the enemy from his chosen position.

General Pope believed that the tarrying of Porter at Dawkin's Branch was the cause of all his subsequent failure and disasters, and that officer subsequently was relieved of his command, was tried by court-martial, and dismissed from the army, to be reinstated again by Act of Congress in 1886. History doubtless will acquit Fitz-John Porter of being disloyal; but as the years go by, and as the secret history of the war is unfolded, it will be seen that the prejudices engendered in the Army of the Potomac by undue favoritism on the part of General McClellan had much to do with the train of disasters on the field of the second Manassas.

How easy it is to make mistakes, and in war how terrible sometimes are the consequences! General Pope is confident that the enemy is retreating, when, instead, Lee is posting his troops to renew the battle. On this Saturday morning Pope, instead of attacking, might have had his whole army east of Bull Run, on the heights of Centreville, resting his wearied

soldiers and obtaining fresh provisions; but, on the contrary, at midnight
he issues his orders for an advance "*in pursuit*" of the enemy.   Porter
had arrived, and the army, with the exception of Banks's corps, was at last
concentrated.

On the ground occupied by the Confederate army in the first battle of
Bull Run are the Union troops.   There are woods with cleared fields;
two swells of land—that on which stands the house of Mr. Henry, and
west of it, a mile distant, Bald Hill and Mr. Chinn's house.   On the north
side of the turnpike were the troops of Generals Heintzelman, Reno, Sigel,
King, and Porter.   General Pope knew that Jackson was still along the
line of the railroad embankment, and massed his troops to attack him,
not suspecting that Lee was moving Longstreet south of the turnpike to
turn his own right flank.

Through the forenoon both armies have been getting ready for the
conflict.   Just before Porter advances to attack Jackson, Reynolds and
Ricketts discover the troops of Longstreet creeping round the left flank,
and Reynolds forms his division to meet him.

The brigades of Barnes and Butterfield, of Porter's corps—fresh troops
that have had no part in the battle since they came from the Peninsula—
are first engaged.   King's division, a great deal smaller than it was forty-
eight hours ago, also advances.

"I am hard pressed, and must have reinforcements," is Jackson's message to Lee.

An officer rides to Longstreet with Lee's message: "Jackson needs
assistance.   Send him what troops you can spare."   The troops will have
to march nearly three miles to get there.   Longstreet has a better plan.
The Union troops advancing against Jackson face north-west.   Longstreet
is south of Groveton.   He sees that he can bring his artillery into position to fire north-east, and that the shot and shells will enfilade Porter's
line.

"I saw that if I were to open fire the attack against Jackson could
not be continued ten minutes.   I made no movements with my troops,"
said Longstreet to me after the war.

A battery wheels into position and the shells scream through the air,
bursting in Porter's ranks, and doing such execution that in ten minutes
Butterfield and Barnes are falling back.   Had not Longstreet opened at
the very moment, Jackson would without doubt have been driven from
the position.

General Pope has not yet discovered what Lee is about to do, and
makes the mistake of ordering Reynolds to cross the turnpike and assist

in the attack upon Jackson. McDowell is still on the south side of the pike.

Longstreet sees the mistake which Pope has made. His whole line advances — five divisions — Evans, Anderson, Kemper, Jones, and Wilcox. They have been concealed in the woods. They come into the open field west of Mr. Chinn's house. Pope quickly sees his mistake, and Sigel and two brigades of Ricketts's division, under General Tower, with twelve cannon, go upon the run across the turnpike to join McDowell. General Sykes, with two brigades of regulars, hastens to the Henry house hill, and also Reynolds, with the Pennsylvania Reserves. McLean's brigade of Schenck's division is on Bald Hill. Sigel, seeing how hard pressed they are, sends Schurz's division to help them. The conflict rages around the Chinn house. Colonel Koltes and Colonel Fletcher Webster, son of Daniel Webster, the great statesman, are killed and General Tower wounded.

Passing over to Longstreet's lines, we see Hood's division cut to pieces, one-fourth of the troops killed or wounded. Anderson's is almost annihilated. In one brigade of five regiments every field-officer except one is killed or wounded. The ground is slippery with blood. Sigel's and McDowell's troops hold Bald Hill, despite all the efforts of Longstreet to drive them from the position by a direct attack, but the Confederate troops are creeping round towards the Henry house.

General Pope sees at last that the battle is going against him. He must hold his ground till the trains can get across Bull Run. The retreat begins, the troops in front of Jackson slowly falling back. The Henry house hill must be held to the last, and there, on the very spot where the final struggle in the first battle of Bull Run took place, comes the last struggle of the day. Longstreet advances, but all of his attempts to drive the regulars under General Sykes ends in failure. The sun has gone down, darkness is coming on, but there are still flashes on the Henry hill, where the cannon and muskets flame.

The cannon are silent at last, the battle over. Lee has won a victory and the Union troops are retreating across Bull Run. Lee has suffered so severely that his tired troops can make no quick pursuit.

There had been a great mistake made by General McClellan at Alexandria, in not co-operating as heartily as he might with Pope. The Army of the Potomac, when it landed at Alexandria and passed beyond the fortifications, was no longer under his command, but received orders from Pope. We need not wonder that he keenly felt the change. He had been commander-in-chief of all the armies, had issued orders to generals in the Far West as well as along the Atlantic shore. That power had been taken away; and now his army, which he had led so near Richmond that he could hear the church-bells toll the hour, was being transferred to Pope. Instead of being at the head of a great army he was at Alexandria, sending his troops to another commander. Pope needed supplies. This the answer of McClellan: "Wagons and cars will be loaded and sent as soon as a cavalry escort is sent to bring them out." Pope sends this to Halleck in reply: "Such a despatch, when Alexandria is full of troops, and we are fighting the enemy, needs no comment." Pope has this to say in his report: "I do not see what service cavalry could have rendered in guarding a railroad train. I did not feel discouraged till I received this letter." To Pope's request for ammunition this McClellan's reply: "I know nothing of the calibre of his guns." On the afternoon of the 29th, with the booming of cannon at Manassas rolling across the Potomac, he telegraphs to President Lincoln as to the course to be adopted: "To leave Pope to get out of his scrape and at once use all means to make the capital safe."

September 1st. It is a rainy morning, but Jackson is on the march, crossing Bull Run at Sudley Ford, where McDowell forded it when he marched to the first Bull Run battle. He marches north, then north-east, along a country road till he reaches the Little River turnpike, and then turns south. He is north-east of Centreville, and is aiming for Fairfax Court-house to get once more between Pope and Washington. It is a hazardous moment, for Longstreet is far behind, and Pope has been reinforced by Sumner and Franklin, who have twenty thousand men.

Pope discovers Jackson's movement, and orders the army to fall back towards Fairfax. At Germantown is the junction of the Little River and Warrenton pikes. Hooker and Reno and Kearney are there, when Jackson, just at dark, comes down the Little River pike, files into the woods and fields south of Chantilly, near Ox Hill. It is nearly dark when A. P. Hill begins the attack with Branch's, Hay's, Trimble's, and Gregg's brigades, which are hurled back by Reno and Kearney, with severe loss to Jackson; but the Union army suffers a great loss in the death of General Stevens and General Kearney. Once more night comes on, closing the battle.

It has been a period of disaster and defeat to the Union army, and of victory to the Confederates. General Pope, in his retreat, has been obliged to leave a large number of his wounded on the field. There was one very pathetic scene. In an orchard lay six Union soldiers near one another, not under the sheltering shade of the trees, but in the broiling sun. Each of the six had lost a leg, and one, Corporal Tanner, had lost both legs. Near by them was a soldier with a ghastly wound in his side, made by an exploding shell. They were hot with fever and parched with thirst. The surgeon who had been left in charge of them had taken too much liquor, and was incompetent, through intoxication, to care for them.

The suffering soldiers could see the apple-trees near by loaded with luscious fruit—so near, and yet so far away! The ripening apples were dropping to the ground. "Oh that we had some of them!" said one. The soldier with a wound in his side, hearing the exclamation, dragged himself towards the trees, stretching out his arms, clutching the long grass, gaining inch by inch until he could reach the apples and toss them back to the others. It was a supreme effort. He did not know the names of his suffering comrades; they were not members of the same regiment, but they wore the blue, and were giving their lives for their country; that was enough. A few moments later he who had made this sacrifice breathed his last breath, and was motionless evermore. His last work had been one of love, good-will, and devotion.

The army was out of provisions. Sumner's and Franklin's corps had reached Centreville, but they had very little to eat. It is possible that if there had been any controlling mind a stand might have been made at that point and Lee, in turn, defeated; for the Confederates, although they had destroyed Pope's provisions, were needing supplies, and would have been compelled to make a second attack, or retire towards Manassas. General Pope saw that the troops had no confidence in him, that the army was disorganized, and that the best course would be a falling back to the fortifications at Arlington and Alexandria.

General McClellan was there, and the troops which had temporarily been turned over to Pope once more came under his command, and the work of reorganization began.

Lee's plan for crushing Pope, and bringing about the withdrawal of McClellan from the James, had been crowned with success. There was great rejoicing in the South, and much despondency throughout the North. General Lee had lost many men; but having crushed Pope, and compelled the withdrawal of the Army of the Potomac from the James to Washington, he determined to carry the war northward, across the Potomac, in a new and aggressive campaign.

CHAPTER XIII.

INVASION OF MARYLAND.

IT was universally believed in the South that the sympathies of the people of Maryland were with the Confederacy. The song "My Maryland!" had been sung in every hamlet of the seceded States. It was believed that if General Lee were to cross the Potomac and enter that State
thousands of young men would flock to his ranks; that Baltimore would
welcome him with open arms; and that the possible result might be the
capture of Washington, or a movement into Pennsylvania. He would be
in a rich and fertile country. The harvest had been gathered, and he
could obtain all needful supplies. Such a movement would terrify the
Northern States. If he could fight another battle and win a great victory
north of the Potomac, England and France would recognize the Confederacy and break the blockade. The soldiers were ready and eager to invade
the North. Had they not driven McClellan from Richmond? Had they
not defeated the combined armies of McClellan and Pope?

On September 5th the Confederate army crossed the Potomac at No-
land's Ford, General Jackson leading the column. The water was only
knee-deep, and the soldiers swung their hats, cheered, and sung "Maryland! my Maryland!"

General Lee issued a strict order against plundering private property.
He regarded Maryland as a Southern State, and the army must not do
anything to offend the people. It was harvest-time; the orchards were
loaded with fruit, the barns filled with hay and grain, and there were
thousands of acres of corn ripening in the golden sunlight.

At ten o'clock on September 6th General Stuart's cavalry entered
Frederick. There were Marylanders in the Confederate army, who
were warmly welcomed by their friends. A few women waved their
handkerchiefs, but most of the people gazed in silence upon the troops.
The soldiers were well supplied with Confederate paper-money, and
they paid liberally for boots, shoes, flour, bacon, cattle, and horses. The
people did not dare to refuse the money, although they knew it was
worthless.

CONFEDERATES CROSSING THE POTOMAC.

General Lee issued an address, which read as follows: "The people of the South have seen with profound indignation their sister State deprived of every right and reduced to the condition of a conquered province. Believing that the people of Maryland possessed a spirit too lofty to submit to such a government, the people of the South have long wished to aid you in throwing off this foreign yoke, to enable you again to enjoy the inalienable rights of freemen."

The people of Maryland did not feel, however, that they were under a foreign yoke, or that they were a conquered province. They did not swing their hats and hurrah, but on the contrary made up their minds to stand by the Union.

All the Confederate troops in and around Richmond were hurried forward to reinforce General Lee. General Walker joined him at Frederick with two brigades. On the afternoon of September 7th General Lee unfolded his plans to General Law. "There are," he said, "between eight and ten thousand stragglers between here and Rapidan Station. Besides these we shall be able to get a large number of recruits who have been accumulating at Richmond for some weeks. They ought to reach us at Hagerstown; we shall then have a very good army. In ten days from now, if the situation is then what I confidently expect it to be after the capture of Harper's Ferry, I shall concentrate the army at Hagerstown, effectually destroy the Baltimore and Ohio Railroad, and march to Harrisburg, Pennsylvania. That is the objective point of the campaign. I wish to destroy the railroad bridge over the Susquehanna, which will disable the Pennsylvania railroad for a long time. With the Baltimore and Ohio in our possession, with the Pennsylvania broken, there will remain to the enemy but one route of communication with the West—that by the lakes. After that I can turn my attention to Philadelphia, Baltimore, or Washington. General McClellan is an able general, but a very cautious one. His army is in a very demoralized and chaotic condition, and will not be prepared for offensive operations, or he will not think it so, for three or four weeks. Before that time I hope to be on the Susquehanna."

There were eleven thousand Union troops at Harper's Ferry and Maryland Heights, where there were strong works, with heavy cannon. Maryland Heights are higher than all the other summits in the vicinity and commanded Harper's Ferry and London Heights, on the south side of the river. General Lee saw that it would not do to leave so large a force in his rear to pounce upon his trains. Harper's Ferry must be captured. We can now see just how General Lee laid his plan, and what considerations led to his adopting it. His whole army is near Frederick. He

issues his orders on Wednesday evening, September 9th. He will divide
it into five sections. He will send Jackson, who has so drilled and disciplined his troops that they can march thirty miles in a day with ease,
over South Mountain westward, through Boonesboro', through Sharpsburg,

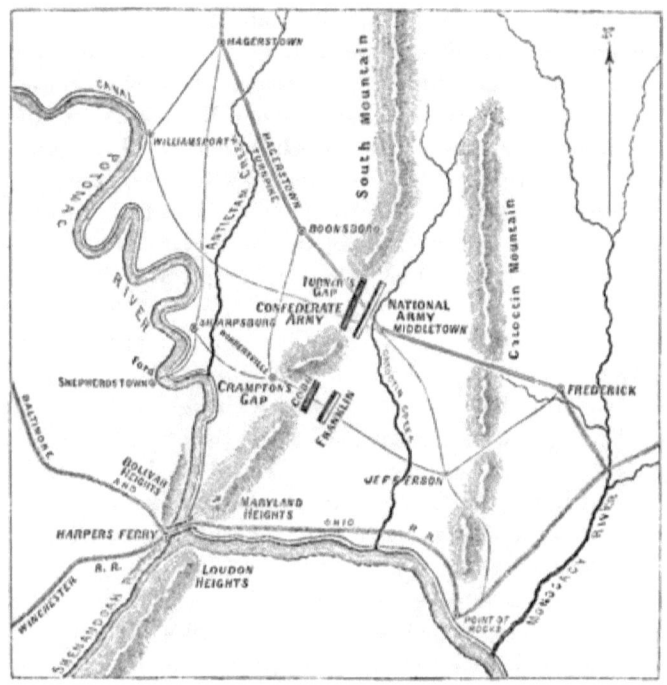

SOUTH MOUNTAIN.

to cross the Potomac at Shepardstown, marching south to Martinsburg, in
Virginia, seizing the Baltimore and Ohio Railroad, and pushing east to
Harper's Ferry. Jackson is to be at Martinsburg on Friday evening, and
at Harper's Ferry on Saturday morning. While he is making this wide
circuit of nearly sixty miles, in as many hours, McLaws's division is to
march south-west, and close upon Maryland Heights. At the same time
Walker's division is to cross the Potomac opposite Frederick, turn west,
and seize London Heights, on the east bank of the Shenandoah, overlooking Harper's Ferry. These simultaneous movements will cut off the eleven
thousand from McClellan.

While these three sections of the army are thus employed, D. H. Hill
is to hold the passes at South Mountain, and Longstreet is to move on to

Hagerstown. General Lee understands the qualifications of McClellan to command an army. He saw the commander of the Army of the Potomac remaining at Alexandria through the winter; saw him sit down before Yorktown with more than one hundred thousand men, with only eleven thousand Confederates in front of him. He knows how long he was in advancing from Yorktown to the Chickahominy; how he lingered at Harrison's Landing while he himself was hastening northward to crush Pope. His scouts give him information every evening of the slow movement of McClellan towards him. He can count upon McClellan's slowness as a permanent factor in all his plans and calculations. On the other hand, he can count upon Stonewall Jackson's swiftness. If he orders Jackson to be at Harper's Ferry on Saturday morning, he will be there without fail. General Stuart is to send a squadron of cavalry with each division to pick up all stragglers. When Harper's Ferry falls, all are to hasten northward towards Sharpsburg. It is a bold, hazardous plan, based on the known slowness of McClellan. Lee will have time to strike the blow and concentrate his army before McClellan will be in position to attack him.

The Union army had been reorganized with right and left wings and a centre. The right wing was commanded by General Burnside, and consisted of the First Corps, commanded by General Hooker, and the Ninth, under General Reno. Each corps had three divisions: the First Corps, King's, Ricketts's, and Mead's divisions; the Ninth Corps, Wilcox's, Sturgis's, and Rodman's.

The centre was commanded by General Sumner, who had the Second Corps, with Richardson's, Sedgwick's, and French's divisions; and the Twelfth Corps, under General Mansfield, composed of Williams's and Greene's divisions.

The left wing, commanded by General Franklin, contained the Fifth Corps, under General Porter, and the Sixth, under Franklin.

On Sunday afternoon, September 7th, General McClellan left Washington, establishing his headquarters near Rockville, fourteen miles from Washington, where he remained till the following Friday. The army was moving less than six miles a day towards Frederick.

On the morning of the 10th the Confederate troops began to move away from that town. Two days later, on the 12th, General McClellan wrote: " From all I can gather, Secesh is skedaddling, and I don't think I can catch him unless he is really moving into Pennsylvania. In that case I shall catch him before he has made much headway towards the interior. I am beginning to think he is making off to get out of the scrape by re-crossing the river at Williamsport, in which case my only hope of bagging him will be to cross lower down, and cut into his communications near Winchester. He evidently don't want to fight me, for some reason or other."

While McClellan was writing this on Saturday evening, the Union cavalry and the Ninth Corps, under Burnside, were marching into Frederick. A soldier brought a very important paper to McClellan, picked up in the house which had been occupied by General D. H. Hill—a copy of Lee's orders, giving all the details of the proposed movements of the Confederate army.

It is not often that a general commanding a great army comes into possession of a document revealing all the plans of his opponent, making him master of the situation. Longstreet at Hagerstown would be thirty miles away from the divisions at Harper's Ferry. The old National Road, over which the stages rattled before the railroads were constructed, leads north-west from Frederick; first over the Catoctin range of hills to the little village of Middletown, then over the South Mountain Range, through Turner's Gap, to Boonesboro', and on to Hagerstown. Another road leads south-west, crosses the South Mountain Range through Crampton's Pass, six miles south of Turner's Gap, and descends into Pleasant Valley. It would be an easy matter for McClellan to move with half or two-thirds his army through Crampton's Pass, while the remainder marched up the old stage-road. By such a movement he could thrust himself between the two wings of Lee's army, and at the same time relieve Harper's Ferry. There would be few Confederates to confront him at Crampton's Pass; and once in Pleasant Valley, he would be in rear of D. H. Hill, who was holding Turner's Gap, and who would be compelled to fall back towards Hagerstown. Instead of doing this, General McClellan decided to send Franklin's corps and General Couch's division of the Fourth Corps through Crampton's Pass, and to move with the bulk of the army—more than sixty thousand men—up the old stage-road. It would not be a flanking movement, but following a retreating army, and attacking its rear-guard in a strong position.

At twenty minutes past six on Saturday evening he wrote the order to Franklin to move at daylight on Sunday morning. Quickness and resolute energy were the all-important considerations. The army had moved slowly. The troops were fresh, and well supplied with provisions. Franklin's troops had taken no part in the battles under Pope at Manassas. They were in superb condition. The weather was delightful, the roads excellent. Why have Franklin wait till morning? Why not make the march in the night? There were no Confederates to confront him east of Crampton's Pass. Little did McClellan comprehend that the great issues of the campaign were enfolded in those words: "You will move at daybreak." If the Confederates under McLaws held Crampton's Pass, Franklin was to form his troops for attack, and half an hour after hearing the opening of battle at Turner's Gap he was to fall upon McLaws. These the closing words of McClellan's order: "I ask you at this important moment to use all your intellect and the utmost activity a general can exercise." With this injunction were these words: "If you find the Pass held by the enemy in large force, make all your dispositions for attack, and commence it about half an hour after you hear severe firing at the Pass on the Hagerstown Pike, where the main body will attack."

With so much depending on quick and energetic action, the order for Franklin to wait for the opening of the battle at Turner's Gap is an enigma which General McClellan never explained.

It is a twelve-mile march which Franklin has to make. His troops start at daybreak to climb the Catoctin Range and then descend into the valley beyond. The Confederate pickets at the Pass see the winding column of men in blue coming down the slope at ten o'clock, and send word to McLaws, who is three and a half miles away, directing his cannon upon the Union intrenchments on Maryland Heights, and who hastens with his troops to hold the Pass. If Franklin had moved at sunset he would have been at the foot of the Pass a little past midnight, unseen by the Confederates. While Franklin is thus advancing, let us see what is going on at Turner's Pass, on the old stage-road.

Early in the forenoon of Sunday, the 14th of September, General Burnside, leading the Union army, ascended a high hill a few miles west of Frederick, and looked down upon one of the loveliest valleys in the world. At his feet was the village of Middletown; beyond it, in the bottom of the valley, the Catoctin Creek winds through ever-verdant meadows, past old mansions surrounded with well-filled barns; north and south, far as the eye can reach, are wheat and clover fields, and acres of corn putting on its golden hues. Beyond the creek the road winds along the mountain-side, past the little hamlet of Bolivar. There are ledges, loose stones, groves of oak, and thickets of mountain shrubs. There is a house on the summit, at Turner's Gap, once a tavern, where the teamsters and stagemen of former days watered their tired horses and ate a lunch. It is old and dilapidated now. Standing there and looking east, it seems as if a strong-armed man might hurl a stone upon Middletown, hundreds of feet below. Twelve miles away to the east are the spires of Frederick, gleaming in the sun. Westward from this mountain gate-way we may

20

behold at our feet Boonesboro' and Keedysville and the crooked Antietam; and still farther westward the Potomac, making its great northern sweep to Williamsport. In the north-west, twelve miles distant, is Hagerstown, at the head of the Cumberland Valley. Longstreet is there on this Sunday morning, sending his cavalry up to the Pennsylvania line, gathering cattle, horses, and pigs.

General D. H. Hill, from Turner's Gap, beholds the Union army spread out upon the plains before him, reaching all the way to Frederick City; dark-blue masses moving towards him along the road, through the fields, with banners waving, their bright arms reflecting the morning sunshine. He is a native of South Carolina, and was educated by the Government at West Point. He was a teacher at the North Carolina Military School, and before the war did what he could to stir up the people of the South to rebel. He told them that the South had won nearly all the battles of the Revolution, but that the Northern historians had given the credit to the North, which was a "Yankee trick." He published an algebra in 1857, which Stonewall Jackson pronounced superior to all others. His "problems" were expressive of hatred and contempt.

"A Yankee," he states, "mixes a certain number of wooden nutmegs, which cost him one-fourth of a cent apiece, with real nutmegs, worth four cents apiece, and sells the whole assortment for $44 and gains $3.75 by the fraud. How many wooden nutmegs are there?"

"At the Woman's Rights Convention, held at Syracuse, New York, composed of one hundred and fifty delegates, the old maids, children, wives, and bedlamites were to each other as the numbers 5, 7, and 3. How many were there of each class?"

"The field of Buena Vista is six and a half miles from Saltillo. Two Indiana volunteers ran away from the field of battle at the same time; one ran half a mile per hour faster than the other, and reached Saltillo five minutes and fifty-four and six-elevenths seconds sooner than the other. Required, their respective rates of travel."

General Burnside formed his lines along the Catoctin Creek. General Cox's division was south of the turnpike, on the old road over which General Braddock and Washington marched in 1755, which winds up the mountain to Fox's Gap, one mile south of Turner's. General Reno's division advanced along the turnpike. It is seven o'clock in the morning when Scammon's brigade of Ohio troops moves into position. Robertson's battery is south of the turnpike, in a field, throwing shells up the mountain into the woods, where Hill's men are lying sheltered from sight by the foliage.

There is a reply from the Gap. Solid shot and shells fly from the mountain to the valley. Hayne's battery joins Robertson's. Simmons opens with his twenty-pounder, and McMullin with four heavy guns; and while church-bells far away are tolling the hour of worship, these cannon in the valley and on the mountain-side play the prelude to the approaching strife.

Scammon's brigade leads the way by the old Sharpsburg Road, the men toiling slowly up the hill, through the fields and pastures, over fences and walls, sometimes losing foothold and falling headlong or sliding downward. The brigade was preceded by a line of skirmishers, and was followed by Crook's brigade. Cox was moving to gain possession of Fox's Gap, where Hill has stationed Garland's brigade and Pelham's battery. General Colquitt is to hold Turner's Gap. Hill has five brigades, which have great advantage in position.

The Union troops toil up the mountain-side, and a little past nine o'clock the first ripple of musketry breaks upon the morning air. Lieutenant Crome, of McMullin's battery, runs up two cannon and opens fire, but the skirmishers of the Twentieth North Carolina pick off the gunners. Lieutenant Crome is killed, and the cannon stand there with no one to load them. The Confederates do not dare to run down and capture them. Scammon slowly works his way round upon Garland's flank. A storm of bullets sweeps through the woods from the Union muskets. General Garland is talking with Colonel Ruffin, of the Twentieth North Carolina, who is urging him to go to a safer place. He will not go, and the next moment falls mortally wounded.

The Confederates are behind a stone wall. The Union troops charge upon them, the Twelfth Ohio rushing upon a battery, but the gunners are quick to limber up their pieces and make their escape. Then the Thirtieth Ohio, with fixed bayonets, charge upon the Twenty-third and Twelfth North Carolina, and the Confederate line gives way. Cox is in possession of Fox's Pass. Hill sends G. B. Anderson's brigade to attack him, but Anderson is repulsed. An onset as vigorous as that which overthrew Garland at that hour of the morning doubtless would have whirled D. H. Hill's whole force from the mountain; for Longstreet, who had started from Hagerstown, was several miles distant, and there were no other Confederate reinforcements at hand. The Union troops on the old stage-road were slowly advancing. The mountain is steep; it rises one thousand feet above the valley. It took the Union engineers a long while to decide which was the best point to attack, and it was mid-afternoon before the troops were in position. We see Hooker's corps filing along a narrow country road, past Tabor Church, north of the stage-road, to attack Hill's left flank. The other three divisions of the Ninth Corps follow Cox's advance. Burnside, who is in command, has waited for Hooker to arrive. Hooker has made a rapid march, but it is past three in the afternoon before he is in position. Burnside supposed that Longstreet and Hill together confronted him, but when Cox opened the battle Longstreet was ten miles away; and now, as Hooker is getting ready to advance, Longstreet's troops are panting up the western slope of the mountain.

Hooker's corps is composed of Ricketts's and King's divisions and the Pennsylvania Reserves. The artillery—all the batteries which can be brought into position—send their shells up the mountain. Steadily onward moves the long line across the fields at the foot, up the pasture-lands of the slope, into the woods.

Hood's division of Confederates is the first to reach the ground which Colquitt has held through the day. There is a rattling of musketry, then heavy rolls, peal on peal, wave on wave, and a steady, constant roar. Not yielding an inch, but advancing slowly or holding their ground, the veterans of the Peninsula continue their fire. The mountain is white with the rising battle-cloud; there are shouts, yells, outcries mingling with the cannonade, echoing and reverberating along the valleys.

"Please open upon that house with your battery," was the order of Colonel Meredith, of the Nineteenth Indiana, commanding a brigade in King's division, to Lieutenant Stewart, of the Fourth United States Artillery. The house was filled with Confederate sharp-shooters. Lieutenant Stewart sights his guns. A shell crashes through the rooms, and the Confederates swarm out from doors and windows, like bees from a hive, in hasty flight. The men from Indiana give a lusty cheer.

Gibbon's brigade moves up the old stage-road; Longstreet's troops are arriving; and as the sun goes down the volleys of musketry are like the grinding of the pebbles washed by the waves of the sea. The battle dies away as the darkness comes on. General McClellan has lost at Turner's Gap fifteen hundred and sixty-eight men, all but twenty-two of them killed or wounded. Among the killed was General Reno, commanding the Ninth Corps. He was a native of Virginia, but, unlike General Lee, and most of the officers from the Southern States who had sided with the Confederacy, felt that he was in honor bound to fight for the old flag. General D. H. Hill, author of the "Algebra" and commander of the Confederate troops in this battle, in his account of it speaks of him as a "renegade Virginian who was killed by a happy shot from the Twenty-third

BATTLE OF SOUTH MOUNTAIN. FRANKLIN'S CORPS STORMING CRAMPTON'S PASS.

North Carolina." The Confederate loss was between two and three thousand, more than fifteen hundred of them prisoners.

Going down to Crampton's Pass, six miles from Turner's, where we saw Franklin forming his lines at ten o'clock, we see the battle opening at noon, with Slocum's division on the right and Smith's on the left. The Confederates are under General Howell Cobb, of Georgia, who bankrupted the United States Treasury during Buchanan's administration—one of the conspirators who brought about the Rebellion. He holds the Pass with three brigades. The battle goes on for three hours, when Cobb is compelled to flee, losing one cannon and four hundred prisoners, with nearly as many more killed or wounded.

The troops at Harper's Ferry heard the cannon, the roll of musketry at Crampton's Gap. Colonel Miles knew that the Army of the Potomac was fighting its way to his relief, but at eight o'clock on Monday morning, September 15th, against the remonstrances of his officers and soldiers, he raised a white flag in token of surrender. A moment later he was mortally wounded. Harper's Ferry was lost, with its eleven thousand men and seventy-three cannon, through the incapacity of Colonel Miles; through the postponement by McClellan of the hour of marching for Franklin from sunset on Saturday till daybreak on Sunday; through the movement of the main body of the army to Turner's Gap instead of Crampton's. The troops were indignant at the surrender, with so little resistance on the part of Miles; some of them shed tears over the disgrace.

The Union cavalry, numbering twenty-five hundred, made their escape under cover of the night. They followed winding forest-paths through the woods, avoiding the roads till they were north of Sharpsburg. While crossing the Williamsport and Hagerstown road, they came upon Longstreet's ammunition-train.

"Hold!" said the officer commanding the cavalry to the forward driver. "You are on the wrong road. That is the way."

The driver turned towards the north as directed, not knowing that the officer was a Yankee.

"Hold on there! You are on the wrong road. Who told you to turn off here, I should like to know?" shouted the Confederate officer in charge of the train, dashing up on his horse.

"I gave the order, sir."

"Who are you, and what right have you to interfere with my train, sir?" said the officer, coming up in the darkness.

"I am colonel of the Eighth New Jersey Cavalry, and you are my prisoner," said the Union officer, presenting his pistol.

One hundred wagons and seventy-four men were thus quietly cut out from the trains.

At the head of this company of prisoners marched a man with down-cast eyes, sunburned, dusty, dressed in gray, with a black feather in his hat, Fitz-Hugh Miller. He was a Pennsylvanian. It was he who arrested Cook, one of John Brown's accomplices in 1859, and delivered him over to Governor Wise. Cook was tried, found guilty, and hanged. When the war broke out Miller went South, and was a captain in Lee's army. The people of Chambersburg knew that he was a traitor. "Hang him!" they shouted. "A rope!—get a rope!" There was a rush of men and women towards him. They were greatly excited. Some picked up stones to hurl at him ; others shook their fists in his face ; but the guards closed round him, and hurried the pale and trembling man to prison as quickly as possible, and saved him from a violent death.

General Lee had defeated Pope at Bull Run, had entered Maryland and pushed north to Hagerstown. Jackson had captured Harper's Ferry, and there was now no Union army to cut off his retreat, threaten his rear, or intercept his communication with the Shenandoah Valley. His officers and soldiers were expecting that he would lead them into Pennsylvania ; but General Lee knew that he could not move farther north, now that he had been driven from South Mountain, for the Union army was pouring over the mountain, and would soon be upon him. He must select a field where he could concentrate his army and fight a defensive battle. If he could once more defeat McClellan he could then invade Pennsylvania. But his troops had made long and swift marches ; they were weary and worn. He had lost a great many men. Thousands had been killed and wounded, other thousands had straggled. All told, he had not more than fifty thousand. General McClellan, however, believed that he had nearly one hundred thousand.

General Lee, after capturing Harper's Ferry, could have recrossed the Potomac, but he preferred to fight a battle north of the Potomac, and selected a field where it would be impossible for General McClellan to turn either of his flanks or get in his rear.

In western Maryland is the little town of Sharpsburg, with a turnpike leading north to Hagerstown, and another running east to Boonesboro', and across the South Mountain Range to Frederick. Three miles west is Shepardstown, on the Potomac, which can be forded at low tide. A mile east of Sharpsburg is Antietam Creek, which rises north of Hagerstown, runs south between high, steep banks, and empties into the Potomac three miles south of Sharpsburg. It can be forded in many places.

Daybreak, September 15th, McClellan's troops are in possession of South Mountain, seven miles from Antietam. Thirty-five brigades are ready to advance. Lee has fourteen brigades, under Longstreet and Hill, which at that hour are making their way westward across Antietam River.

The cannon have been at work all the morning at Harper's Ferry, but at eight o'clock the reverberations die away. The white flag has been flung out and the place surrendered.

The Union cavalry under Pleasanton are at that moment dashing upon the Confederate cavalry, Lee's rear-guard at Boonesboro', capturing two cannon and two hundred and fifty prisoners. At the same hour General McClellan issued orders for the army to move on; but at half-past twelve the Ninth Corps had not started. Late in the afternoon, after a march of seven miles, Richardson's division of Sumner's corps reached the eastern bank of the Antietam to find Longstreet and Hill upon the western bank. Far different the marching of Stonewall Jackson's men. They have made the sixty-mile march from Frederick to Harper's Ferry, have captured the eleven thousand Union troops, and now are making the twenty-five-mile march back again to Sharpsburg. Through the afternoon, through the night of the 15th, they are pushing on, and at eight o'clock on the morning of the 16th are at Shepardstown. Before sunset on the 16th Jackson's whole force, except A. P. Hill's division, together with McLaws's and Walker's, are at Sharpsburg.

Through the forenoon of the 16th General McClellan, with his staff, is riding up and down the eastern bank of the Antietam, looking at the position of the Confederates, receiving the cheers of his troops. Not till afternoon does he decide what to do. Before noticing the movements of the army, let us walk up the turnpike towards Hagerstown. It is a beautiful country of rolling fields, patches of woodland, and farm-houses. We look down over the slopes to the winding Antietam beyond. Ten miles away is the South Mountain Range, with the white houses of Boonesboro' nestling at its western base. Nearer is the village of Keedysville. Everywhere there are beautiful fields, waving with ripening corn.

Just out from the village we look to the right upon a great barn and a small cottage, the home of Mr. Piper, a quarter of a mile from the turnpike. Farther up the pike, three-quarters of a mile from Sharpsburg, we see a lane turning off to the right which leads down to Mr. Muma's and Mr. Rulet's farms. We turn east through their farms to the turnpike, which runs east from Sharpsburg to Keedysville. The rains have washed it, and it is lower than the surrounding fields. Keep this road in mind, for we shall see it again by-and-by.

Going back to the Hagerstown turnpike we come to a low, square brick building on the left—a little church where the Dunkers meet for worship. Behind the church, and north of it, is a beautiful grove of oaks. East of the church is a cornfield, with another grove of oaks. Another half-mile brings us to Dr. Miller's house, on the east side of the turnpike, with his barn west of the road. There is a cornfield behind the barn. A little farther we come to Mr. Poffenburger's house, on the east side. If we were to walk down the narrow lane which branches off from the turnpike in front of Poffenburger's towards the north-west, a mile would bring us to the Potomac. Turning south-west from Poffenburger's, and walking down another narrow lane, we come to a large white house owned by Mr. Nicodemus. Going through his door-yard, and walking west fifty rods, we come to a beautiful swell of land. We see that a cannon planted there can throw shells in every direction—that it has the sweep of all the country.

It is only two miles from the Potomac to the Antietam. General Lee sees that by forming a line from the hill on Mr. Nicodemus's farm to the Antietam he will have a great advantage of position, and will not be under the necessity of protecting his flank and rear. It is a strong line of swells of land, hollows, groves, ledges, rail-fences, cornfields, orchards, stone walls. These are the natural defences. In addition, the soldiers dig a trench and build a breastwork from the stone ledges west of the Dunker church to the turnpike south of it. Lee throws out his advanced line to the ridge east of Joseph Poffenburger's house, extending it south through the east grove of woods to Mr. Muma's field. This front line is half a mile east of the church.

It was two o'clock in the afternoon of September 16th when the Pennsylvania Reserves, under General Meade, crossed the Antietam. They encountered Jackson's pickets on Mr. Hoffman's farm. There was a sharp skirmish and a cannonade, which lasted till dark, the Confederates being driven back to Mr. Poffenburger's. At dark the Pennsylvanians lay down upon their arms in a cornfield.

General Mansfield's corps crossed the Antietam during the night and halted a mile in rear of General Hooker, while General Sumner's troops remained east of the Antietam. General Burnside, with the Ninth Corps, moved south on the east bank of the stream and bivouacked at the base of Elk Ridge, to be in position to cross by a stone bridge which now bears his name.

General McClellan's plan was to attack Lee's left with Hooker's and Mansfield's corps, supported by Sumner, and as soon as matters looked favorable there, to have Burnside cross and attack south of Sharpsburg. He held Porter east of Antietam in reserve.

The morning of the 17th was threatening, and heavy clouds hung upon the summits of South Mountain. At five o'clock Hooker's men rise from the furrows in the cornfield, shake the dew-drops from their hair, roll their blankets, kindle their fires, and eat their breakfasts.

In the field west of the Dunker church the soldiers of Hood's Confederate division were kindling their fires, breaking open barrels of flour, wetting it with water, and baking cakes in the ashes. General Hood had held the line in the east woods till midnight, when Lawton, Law, and Trimble relieved him.

The Union pickets began the battle, aiming at the dusky forms stirring amid the corn-leaves. Then the batteries opened. A shell from a Confederate cannon burst in the Sixth Wisconsin, disabling eight men, before the regiment made any movement.

Doubleday's brigade, north-east of Poffenburger's house, held Hooker's extreme right. Then came Meade's division, with Ricketts's division in rear. Mead was to lead the advance, and his troops pressed on after the skirmishers towards the woods east of Dr. Miller's house.

On the Confederate side Lawton's division of Jackson's corps held the position. Ripley's brigade, of D. H. Hill's division, was between the woods and Mr. Munna's house. McClellan's batteries—thirty cannon— east of the Antietam, opened fire, sending solid shot and shell upon Lawton, Ripley, and Hill.

"It enfiladed my line, and was a damaging fire," said Jackson in his report.

But Jackson's batteries replied, and the cannonade rolled along the valleys, announcing to the people of Hagerstown, Boonesboro', and Sharpsburg that a great battle had begun.

General Ricketts advanced with Christian's and Duryea's brigades, and with the Pennsylvania Reserves moving towards the cornfield south of Miller's house, driving the Confederates. They reached the middle of the field, but were met by a withering fire from Lawton's, Hays's, Trimble's, Walker's, and Douglas's brigades of Jackson's command.

The men dropped thick and fast on both sides, some killed instantly, others hobbling away: the Confederate wounded towards the woods by the Dunker church, the Union wounded towards the east woods. The Confederate cannon planted around the church hurled shells from the front, while the batteries on the hill behind the house of Mr. Nicodemus enfiladed the Union line.

Hooker had, in all, about ten thousand men—ten brigades. Double-day was reaching out west of the turnpike by Poffenburger's house. If Hooker had known just how Jackson's line was formed—if he had known that the hill behind Nicodemus's house commanded the entire field as far south as Muma's house—he would not have advanced towards the Dunker church, but would have reinforced Doubleday and carried the hill. But he could not see how commanding a position it was; so from that hill the shot and shells came with terrible effect.

In the cornfield, in Mr. Miller's orchard, all over the ground between the east and west woods, the struggle went on, Jackson bringing in all his troops, with the exception of Early's brigade, and all his artillery, and sending in haste for Hood to help him. General Starke, commanding the Stonewall division, was killed; also Colonel Douglas, commanding Law-ton's brigade. Lawton, commanding Ewell's division, and Walker, commanding a brigade, were wounded. More than half of Lawton's and Hays's, more than one-third of Trimble's, and all the regimental commanders in these brigades, except two, went down.

On the Union side Ricketts loses one hundred and fifty-three killed and eight hundred and ninety-eight wounded. Of Phelps's brigade nearly one-half were killed or wounded.

By half-past seven o'clock the first act of the drama is over. The musketry dies away, but the cannonade goes on—Battery B, Fourth United States Artillery, Cooper's and Easton's Pennsylvania batteries, and Edget's New Hampshire, on the ridge by Poffenburger's, sending a continuous storm of shells into the woods beyond Nicodemus's house, whence came another storm, riddling Poffenburger's house and barn, upsetting his bee-hives, ploughing the ground in his garden, exploding in the rail-fences, and whirring away over the heads of the worn and weary men lying upon the ground. Hooker's batteries kept up the fire to prevent Jackson from assuming the offensive, and the Confederate guns replied—possibly to prevent a renewal of the attack, which had all but succeeded.

The cannonade dies away, and the gunners throw themselves upon the ground to rest a while, kindle their fires, and drink a cup of coffee.

At early morn I mounted my horse in Hagerstown, where I had arrived on the preceding evening, upon its evacuation by Longstreet. The people of the town were at the windows and in the streets, listening to the reverberations rolling along the valley. The wind was from the south-west, a gentle breeze; the clouds were sweeping the tree-tops of South Mountain. I had a seven-mile ride before me to reach the field, and half resolved to go down the turnpike to Sharpsburg, gain the rear of the Con-

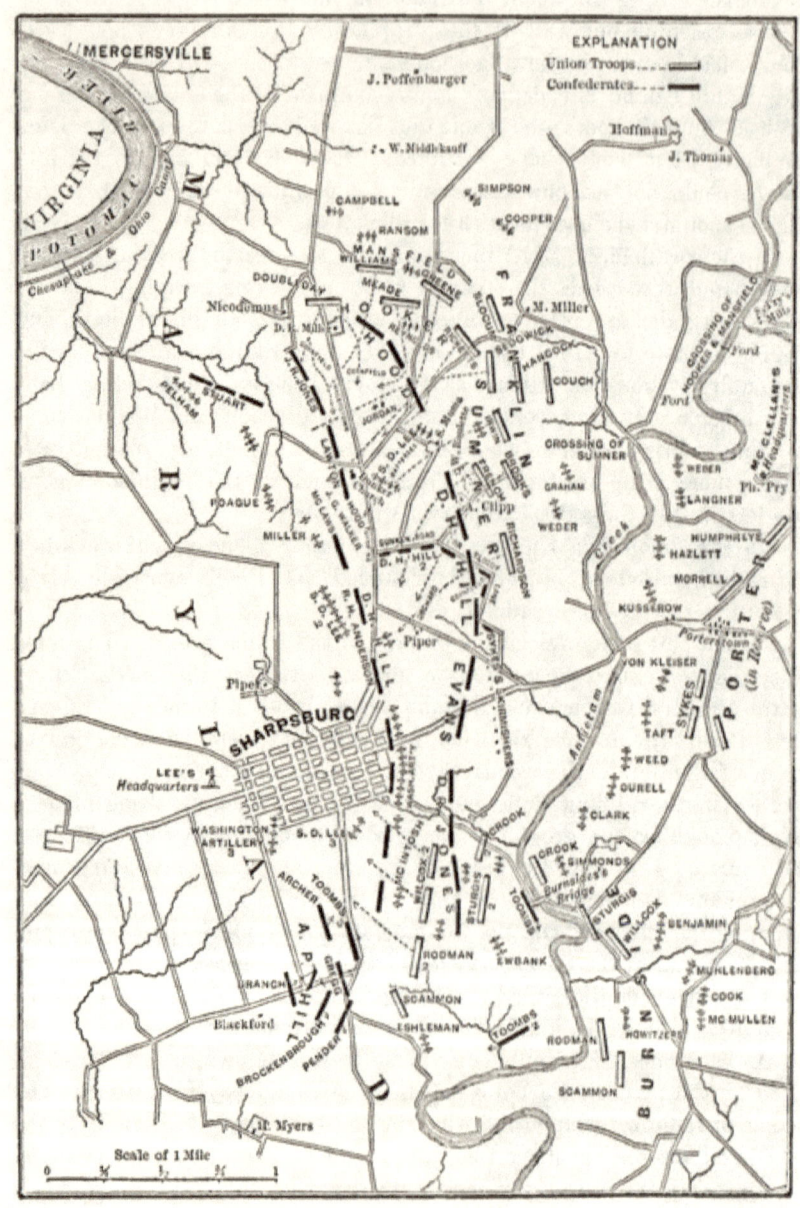

MAP OF ANTIETAM.

federates, and see the battle from that side. I was in citizen's dress, and might not be turned back by the Confederates; but the people of Hagerstown dissuaded me from attempting it.

The uproar begins again, and a rattle of musketry, like the pattering of the first drops of rain upon a roof, then a roll, crash, roar, and rush like a mighty ocean billow. Riding rapidly down the Boonesboro' Road, I came upon a Confederate soldier who was lying beneath a tree, wrapped in his blanket. He doubtless thought that I was a Union cavalryman, and raised his hand imploringly, as if to ask me not to shoot him. He was thin and pale, had dropped in the retreat, and had not strength enough to move on. There was fever in his hollow cheeks, and I left him with the conviction that he never again would see his Southern home, and that ere many days he would be at rest forever—life's battle ended.

Another mile, and I came upon the drift-wood of the Union army. Every army has soldiers faint of heart in battle. I came upon one group in bright, new uniforms—fresh soldiers, who were fleeing from this their first battle.

"Where does this road lead to?" one asked, with white lips.

"To Hagerstown; but where are you going?"

"Our division has been ordered to Hagerstown, and we are going there to join it."

I knew that he was not telling the truth. They hastened on, cowards for the moment.

Striking across fields towards the white powder-cloud rising above the trees, I came upon the hospital, on the farm of Mr. Hoffman, where, at that early hour, there were long rows of wounded. Turning from the sickening scenes I ascended a hill, and came upon the men of Hooker's corps, who had opened the battle, learned the story of their conflict, and then rode on to Joseph Poffenburger's house, behind which were thirty cannon, and their muzzles pointing south-west. At the moment their brazen lips were cooling. There was a lull in the battle. All was quiet in the oak grove along the Hagerstown Turnpike. I could see no gleaming bayonets amid the trampled corn-rows west of D. R. Miller's barn. I did not know that the line of men in blue lying on the ground by Poffenburger's was the foremost line of the Army of the Potomac. I rode down through the door-yard, where the hollyhocks were opening their white and red bell-shaped flowers to the morning sun. The flower-beds in the garden were trampled. A Confederate shell had exploded among the beehives; the Union soldiers had gathered the honey, and the swarms were angrily buzzing in the air. I went down the turnpike towards Miller's house, and came upon a Union soldier crouching beneath the wall.

"Where are you going?" he asked.

"I thought that I would go to the front."

"The front! You have passed it. I am on the skirmish line; you had better get out of here mighty quick. The Rebs are in the corn, right there."

I acted upon the timely advice and turned back; none too soon, for a moment later solid shot and shells were screaming through the air. Going south, I came upon the Twelfth Corps, General Mansfield's. It had bivouacked a mile in rear of Hooker's, and did not arrive at the east woods till after eight o'clock.

General Mansfield was an old man, white-haired, but his eye was keen, and he had a resolute will. He deploys his line from Dr. Miller's house south through the garden—the cornfield beyond. He has only two small divisions—Crawford's and Greene's. He rides along the line, his long, white hair streaming in the wind. He does not stop to consider that he is a conspicuous object; that Confederate sharp-shooters are crouching in the corn west of the turnpike; that some are but a few rods distant behind Dr. Miller's barn. He rides forward into the orchard south of the house. A minie-bullet comes from the cornfield, and he falls from his horse mortally wounded. General Williams succeeds to the command. Many of the soldiers of the Twelfth Corps are new, and this is their first battle; but they are brigaded with veterans who have been through all the battles of the Peninsula and Bull Run, and move resolutely to the attack.

At the word of command the line moves down the gentle slope, past Miller's house, across the turnpike, through the cornfield beyond, to the west woods. Suddenly they come upon sharp-shooters crouched behind the trees, who retreat as the line advances. On through the woods moves the line to the western edge, to come upon Hood's division, posted behind limestone ledges and a rail-fence. Sheets of flame burst from the hill, where Stuart's cannon hurl canister upon the men in blue under Crawford. The Confederates are well protected, the Union troops wholly exposed.

In the thick of the fight General Hooker is wounded, and the command of the right wing devolves upon General Williams. He has no force in reserve. Hooker's corps is too much broken to come to his support. Hartsuff's and Gibbon's brigades have joined in the attack, but there are no others at hand. Mansfield expected that Sedgwick's divis-

SCENE BY RAIL-FENCE, ANTIETAM.

ion of Sumner's corps would attack by the Dunker church, but that division is nearly a mile in the rear, moving slowly. If it were present,
D. H. Hill would not be rushing from the field south of the church to
roll back Greene's division. The Union lines are melting away, and are
gradually forced back over the field, thickly strewn now with their fallen
comrades.

The second act in the terrible drama is over—badly managed on the
part of the Union commanders, but admirably by Jackson, who has shift-
ed his troops to meet every emergency. He has had all the advantage
of position, and nearly, if not fully, as many troops as Hooker in the
first attack, and more than Mansfield in the second. General McClellan,
by sending in a corps at a time, frittered away his strength. Only Hooker's and Mansfield's had been ordered across the Antietam to attack the
Confederate left. It was twenty minutes past seven in the morning when
Sumner received his orders to cross the stream. He had been in position
on the eastern bank for thirty-six hours, and might have opened the attack before sunset on the 15th, but no orders had come to him.

Through the morning the men of this corps have heard the deafening
cannonade and the rolls of musketry. They meet wounded men, and hear
doleful stories of disaster. Sumner forms Sedgwick's division in a column of brigades, Dana's in front; close behind it Gorman's, and then

Howard's. General Sumner is between sixty and seventy years of age, a brave and grim old man, who has seen a great deal of hardship on the Western plains with the cavalry, but who, till the breaking out of the war, had but little experience with infantry. He makes a mistake in thus forming his line, and not holding a portion of the troops to protect his left flank. Possibly he thinks that General French, who is to attack by Muma's house, will shield him on the left; but French's division is far behind, just turning into the fields south of Mr. Hoffman's house.

General Sumner does not mistrust that there are ten Confederate brigades lying concealed in the hollow and behind the fences between the Dunker church and Muma's house, ready to swing upon his rear as Sedgwick moves towards the church; but there they are, waiting their great opportunity.

Hot blasts from the Confederate guns behind the church beat upon Dana's line as it moves across the turnpike. Gorman is on the turnpike, Howard just east of it, when suddenly the men in gray rise from the hollows in Muma's field. Sumner is talking with Colonel Kimball, of the Fifteenth Massachusetts, when Major Philbrick of that regiment shouts, "See! the Rebels!"

"My God! We must get out of this!" Sumner exclaims. He is in front of the church, between Gorman's and Dana's brigades, and rides back to Dana's advancing line. "Change front!" he shouts. The line comes to a halt. Officers run hither and thither. The men have been advancing south-west; they must get into position to face south-east. General Howard, commanding the rear brigade, sees the Confederate line folding round his left flank. The regiment on the extreme left of his line is the Seventy-second Pennsylvania, and is the first to feel the blow. The bravest men in the world, standing as they find themselves, would be no more than sticks and straws in a whirlwind at that moment. Five minutes ago Sedgwick's brigades were advancing over the smooth and level field; now all is confusion. Howard and Dana swing as best they can to meet the onset. Gorman, instead of pushing on, begins to fall back, not over the ground where he has advanced, but northward towards Miller's and Poffenburger's.

The struggle is short, but the loss fearful. In a very few minutes more than two thousand of Sedgwick's men are killed or wounded, and the whole division driven back to the east woods. But the Union batteries open with canister, and the ten Confederate brigades are driven in turn to the shelter of the hollows in Muma's fields, and into the woods by the church.

21

When the Fifteenth Massachusetts regiment advanced towards the church it numbered five hundred and eighty-two; in twenty minutes three hundred and forty-three had been killed or wounded. Very severe were the losses of the Confederates in this short mêlée.

"Here I witnessed," says General Hood, "the most terrible clash of arms by far that has occurred during the war."

The disaster to Sedgwick had come about through the formation of the entire division as an assaulting column, with not even a skirmish line of flankers. Had Sumner waited till French's and Richardson's divisions were in line, far different would have been this story of the battle.

General French's division of Sumner's corps followed Sedgwick, crossing the Antietam, turning to the left, and marching through the fields towards the house of Mr. Muma. Richardson filed to the left, moved along the bank of the river, crossed a little brook which springs from the hill-side near Rulet's house, encountered Hill's skirmishers, drove them up the ravine, and formed his line under cover of a hill.

French is in the ravine, with half of his division north of the brook, the other half south. He has Weber's, Kimball's, and Morris's brigades, and forms them as Sedgwick did his, in three lines — Weber in front, Morris in the second, and Kimball in the third line.

Morris's men have never been under fire. They are new troops, they have heard the roar of battle through the morning; and now, as they advance across the fields, the batteries on the hills all around Rulet's house open upon them, gun after gun, battery after battery. The hill-side grows white; a silver cloud floats down the ravine and enfolds them; there are flashes, jets of smoke, iron bolts in the air above, tearing up the ground below or cutting through the ranks; they feel the breath of the shot, the puff of air in their faces, and hear the terrifying shriek. A comrade leaps into the air, spins round, or falls to the ground. They behold his torn and mangled body, but they see not the shot that wounded him.

D. II. Hill has his front line in the ravine by Muma's. The Confederate soldiers have an opportunity to fill their canteens from the cool water bubbling up from the spring-house. The sharp-shooters are in Muma's chambers, firing from the windows at French's troops as they advance over the field east of the house. The skirmishers in the burial-ground near the house rest their muskets upon the white head-stones.

French arrives while Sedgwick is having the great struggle in front of the church. Kirby's, Bartlett's, and Owen's batteries, of Sedgwick's division, are on the hill-side east of Miller's field, raking the Confederate lines.

ANTIETAM.

The illustration is an accurate representation, drawn by William Ward during the engagement. The battery in the foreground was stationed north of Roulette's house, near the centre of General Sumner's line. French's and Richardson's divisions are seen in the middle of the picture, and the Confederates, under D. H. Hill and Longstreet, beyond. Mumma's house and barn are in flames, in the centre of the picture.

The sharp-shooters occupying Muma's house and barn, finding the place too hot for them, apply the torch to the buildings, and retreat to Rulet's orchard. The dark pillar of cloud, the bright flames beneath, the constant flashing of the artillery, and the hill-sides alive with thousands of troops, their banners waving, their bayonets gleaming, is a terrible scene of grandeur.

Weber's brigade advances steadily, throwing down the fences, scaling the stone walls, preserving a regular line. Not so with Morris's, which is thrown into confusion. The time has come to strike a great blow.

"Tell General Kimball to move to the front and come in on the left of Weber," is French's order to General Kimball.

The brigade swings towards the south, past Morris's brigade, enters the ravine, and pushes on towards Rulet's.

Far up the hill-side, in Rulet's, Muma's, and Dr. Piper's cornfields, are the Confederates of Longstreet's and D. H. Hill's reserve brigades. On the hills south of Sharpsburg is A. P. Hill, just arriving from Harper's Ferry. All of the hills are smoking with artillery. Jackson's batteries by the church are still firing upon Howard, who, now that Sedgwick has been carried from the field, commands that division of Sumner's corps.

Just beyond Muma's the road is sunk below the surface of the ground. It has been used many years, has been washed by rains, forming a natural rifle-pit, in which D. H. Hill posts his first line. Between this pathway and the pike is a cornfield, in which he stations his second line, with his artillery planted on the knoll higher up, near the turnpike.

It is but a few rods from Muma's to the road—"Bloody Lane" since the battle. There is an apple orchard west of Rulet's house, beyond which the ground rises sharp and steep—a rounded knoll, sloping towards the west into the sunken path.

The line of advance taken by Weber carries him directly towards the smoking ruins of Muma's buildings, while Kimball passes between Muma's and Rulet's.

Weber's troops move over the mown field, past the burial-ground, leaping the fences. Some of the men pause a moment, rest their rifles on the rails and tombstones, and take a long shot at the dark line in the corn-field. They cannot see the nearer line of Hill's division lying in the hidden road.

Kimball, a little farther south, joining his right to Weber's left, sweeps on in splendid order past Muma's spring-house, his left wing touching the apple-trees around Rulet's. The Union batteries east of the Antietam—the twenty-pounder Parrotts—Richardson's batteries on the hillocks beyond the ravine—Kirby, Owen, Thompson, and Bartlett, are all at work.

Smith's division of Franklin's corps—the Sixth—which has arrived from Crampton's Gap, advances to protect the right flank of French, confronting the Confederate troops that have driven Sedgwick from the field.

Under cover of this fire French moves up the hill. His men reach the crest and behold a rail-fence between them and the road. Suddenly thousands of men seem to rise out of the ground. The work of death begins. French's men, instead of fleeing from this unexpected foe, intrenched in so strong a position, rush with a loud hurrah towards the fence. The lines are not ten paces apart. Hill's is consumed like a straw in a candle's flame, it melts like lead in a crucible; officers and men go down, falling in heaps. The few who are left after the tremendous volleys flee into the cornfield beyond. French's men tear away the rails, leap over the fences, plunge into the road, trampling down the dead and dying, rush upon the second line with uncontrollable fury, scattering it in an instant.

I am in rear of the line, upon a knoll, with the scene like a panorama before me. French's men come to the house and spacious barn of Rulet. The lines divide, but unite once more beyond. I see the blue uniforms beneath the apple-trees in the orchard. The sunlight glints from barrel and bayonet. There comes a crash of musketry—lightning flashes, white powder-clouds. Above the uproar I hear the Union cheer, the Confederate yell.

There are turning-points in the lives of men. A parting of ways has come to McClellan. He is sitting in an arm-chair across the Antietam, beholding the scene through a telescope, but does not see the golden moment. Fitz-John Porter's corps is there, eleven thousand men. Were he to hurl them upon the discomfited Confederates he would divide Lee's army at the centre.

While French was thus dealing with General D. H. Hill, Richardson was engaging Longstreet. General Meagher, with his Irish brigade, was on the right, the tip of its wing touching Rulet's garden. Caldwell's brigade was on the left, reaching down nearly to the Boonesboro' Turnpike. Brooke's brigade was in reserve.

Longstreet's batteries were on the hills around Dr. Piper's, and his troops—a part of them—in the road, the upper end of which was held by D. H. Hill. His line was so formed, and such was the ground, that Caldwell, instead of swinging round upon Sharpsburg, was obliged to fall in rear of Meagher, and became a second line instead of a part of the first.

French was pouring in his volleys north of Rulet's, and Meagher, climbing the knolls and rushing up the ravines, came upon the enemy in the road. It was a repetition, or rather a continuation, of the scene then enacting a few rods farther north. The Irish brigade fought till their ammunition was exhausted. They drove the Confederates from the road, and held it. Again and again Longstreet endeavored to recover it. General Richardson was wounded, and carried from the field. General Meagher was bruised by the falling of his horse. His men, worn, exhausted, half their number killed and wounded, retired by breaking ranks and filing to the rear, Caldwell's troops filing to the front at the same moment, and taking their places. It was done as deliberately as if it were a dress parade.

The ground towards the Boonesboro' pike is very much broken. There are numerous hillocks and ravines, cornfields, stone walls, and fences. Under shelter of these Longstreet stealthily moved a division to attack Caldwell's right flank in the cornfield west of the sunken road. It was a part of the force attacking French. Brooke's brigade went upon the run up the ravine, and filled the gap between Caldwell and Kimball, and held it against all the assaults of the enemy.

On Caldwell's left the sunken road winds among the hills. Longstreet still held that ground. Colonel Barlow reconnoitred the situation. He commanded the Sixty-first and Sixty-fourth New York regiments, and ordered them to march by the left flank. They pushed out into the fields towards Sharpsburg, gained the flank of the enemy still holding the road, and forced three hundred to surrender. He also captured their colors.

There is once more a lull in the battle. Longstreet is making preparations to regain his lost ground. Having failed on French's right, by Rulet's, he renews the attack on the left. But Colonel Cross, of the Fifth New Hampshire, who has fought the Indians of the Western plains, who has tracked the grisly bears of the Rocky Mountains, discovers the movement. It is the same which has been successful against Sedgwick. The left of Caldwell is far advanced towards Dr. Piper's when Colonel Cross sees Longstreet's troops making a rapid movement to gain a hill in his rear. He changes front, and his regiment goes upon the run to gain the hill. The two lines are within close musket-range. They make a parallel movement, firing as they run. It is an exciting race. Colonel Cross cheers his men, inspires them with his own untamable enthusiasm, gains the hill, faces his troops towards the enemy, and delivers a volley. It checks their advance a moment, but, rallied by the officers, they rush on, charging up the hill. Cross, reinforced by the Eighty-first Pennsylvania, which has followed him, gives the word, "At them, boys!" He leads the countercharge. The Confederates break in confusion, leaving a stand of colors and three hundred prisoners in Cross's hands.

Again Longstreet tries to drive back the centre and regain the road, and again Barlow repulses him, charging through the cornfield, almost up to the Hagerstown Turnpike, and gaining Dr. Piper's house. Vin-

cent's and Graham's batteries gallop to the hills south of Rulet's, wheel into position, and reply to the batteries on the hills along the turnpike north of Piper's. Hancock, who now commands Richardson's division, can hold his ground, but he cannot advance.

Thus, by one o'clock, Lee has been pushed from his advanced lines on the right and on the left. He still holds the rocky ledges in the woods behind the church, and main-

THE SUNKEN ROAD.

tains his position along the turnpike and holds the lower bridge, where Burnside is endeavoring to force a crossing.

It was past one o'clock when Franklin's corps, with Smith's and Slocum's divisions, arrived. It had marched twelve miles. The soldiers were weary. Slocum's division relieves Sedgwick, while Smith occupies the ground near Rulet's house. There is a consultation of officers in the woods in rear of Slocum's position. Franklin wishes to attack with all his force. Irwin's brigade and the Vermont brigade are already engaged. General McClellan rides across the Antietam, comes upon the field, directs the commander to hold his position, but to make no attack. He rides bareheaded on his favorite horse along the lines. The troops cheer him. He takes a hasty look at the field, directs the commanders to hold their ground, but issues no other order, and rides back to his headquarters east of the Antietam.

I went in that direction, and reached the headquarters, the house of Mr. Pry, a large, square mansion surrounded with trees. McClellan was seated in an arm-chair on the lawn, his staff were near by, their horses saddled and bridled. Stakes had been driven into the ground to support the telescopes through which McClellan and Fitz-John Porter and other officers were surveying the battle-field.

Four stone bridges cross the Antietam. Hooker and Mansfield had crossed the two upper ones. The next one is on the road leading west from Keedysville to Sharpsburg; the fourth, farther south, is twelve feet wide and one hundred and fifty in length. General McClellan had ordered General Burnside to carry the bridge, cross the stream, and attack Lee's right flank. The west bank is steep. There is a grove of oak-trees, a limestone quarry, and a stone wall, where General Toombs had placed his brigade, to pour deadly volleys upon the bridge. He had four pieces of artillery.

Burnside places a line of batteries along the eastern bank, and all the morning the cannon throw solid shot and shell at the Confederates, making a great noise, but doing little damage. He forms his troops with Sturgis's division on the right, Wilcox's in the centre, Rodman's on the left, with Cox's division, commanded by Crook, in reserve.

"You are to carry the bridge, gain the heights beyond, and advance along their crest to Sharpsburg, and reach the rear of the enemy," was the order of McClellan to Burnside.

There was no imperative need for such an order. It was not necessary that the bridge should be carried. The water in the Antietam was low, and it could be forded in many places; but neither McClellan nor Burnside thought of having the troops ford the stream.

Several messengers were sent by McClellan to Burnside in the early morning, directing him to assault the bridge.

"McClellan appears to think that I am not trying my best to carry the bridge. You are the third or fourth one who has been to me with similar orders," said Burnside to Major Sackett.

The men must wind down a hill, cross a level plateau, and rush upon the bridge, climb the steep bank beyond, with cannon vomiting canister and shrapnel, and the riflemen of Toombs's command picking them off from their place of concealment and protection in the stone quarries. Again and again the head of the assaulting column melted away.

General Sackett says: "General Burnside ordered assaults to be made upon the bridge which were for a long time unsuccessful. I had been at his headquarters for fully three hours, when Colonel Key arrived from

McClellan's headquarters with positive orders to push across the bridge and to move rapidly upon the heights; to carry the bridge at the point of the bayonet, if necessary, and not stop for loss of life, as sacrifices must be made in favor of success."

The Second Maryland and Sixth New Hampshire troops, in column, charged upon the bridge. Instantly the west bank was a sheet of flame. The head of the charging column melted away, and the troops fell back

BURNSIDE BRIDGE.

under cover of the ridge on the eastern bank. It was one o'clock before Burnside was ready for a second attack. Then the Fifty-first New York, Fifty-first Pennsylvania, Thirty-fifth and Twenty-first Massachusetts, and Seventh Connecticut rushed upon the bridge, carried it, drove Toombs from the stone quarry and walls, and the divisions, one by one, crossed the stream and deployed along the western bank.

There had been a fearful sacrifice of life. After the bridge had been carried a large portion of the troops forded the stream, which they might have done during the attack, if such an order had been issued.

At three o'clock the whole Ninth Corps advanced. Jackson and Hood were sending men upon the run southward to help Longstreet to resist Burnside's attack. It is a critical moment with Lee, but his heart is cheered by the arrival of A. P. Hill from Harper's Ferry. His soldiers go on the run across the fields. They have marched seventeen miles in seven hours. The brigades of Pender and Brockenbrough hold the extreme right. Then come the brigades of Branch, Gregg, and Archer, joining Toombs and D. R. Jones. From three o'clock till late in the afternoon the battle rages in the fields south of Sharpsburg.

Burnside almost reaches the town, but his left flank, Rodman's division, is exposed. A. P. Hill attacks it sharply, and the troops fall back towards the Antietam.

The sun is going down, red and large as seen through the murky battle-cloud. One of the Union batteries from my position seems to be in the sun. All of the Confederate cannon are in play. The whole landscape is flaming and smoking, but as darkness comes on the flashes cease, the thunder dies away. Groping my way amid the bivouac fires and along the lines, I come upon a group of soldiers who have eaten their supper of hard bread, and are whiling the hours away with song and story. Tender thoughts come as they think of comrades who never more will march with them or stand by their side in battle, and thoughts of loved ones far away. This the song I hear:

"Do they miss me at home? do they miss me?
'Twould be an assurance most dear
To know at this moment some loved one
Were saying, 'I wish he were here.'"

Through the night the troops rested on their arms. With the rising of the sun on the 18th the cannonade began. General Couch's division had arrived. McClellan had twenty-five thousand troops that had taken no part in the battle, yet no orders were issued to renew the struggle. He had eighty-thousand men, and more troops were on their way.

"Whether to renew the attack on the 18th or to defer it, even with the risk of the enemy's retirement, was a question with me," says General McClellan. He decided to wait. He believed that Lee had one hundred thousand, but at no time during the battle of the 17th were there fifty thousand Confederates on the field.

A white flag came out from the Confederate lines asking for an armistice to gather up the wounded between the two armies. It was granted. I walked over the field in front of the Dunker church, where

the conflict had been so fierce. The dead were there in blue and gray.
Upon the breast of one in blue lay a pocket Bible, open at the Psalms.
Looking at the page, I read, "Yea, though I walk through the valley of
the shadow of death, I will fear no evil: for thou *art* with me; thy rod
and thy staff they comfort me." Upon the fly-leaf the sentence, written,
doubtless, by a loving mother, "We hope and pray that you may be permitted by a kind Providence, after the war is over, to return"—a prayer
never to be granted. The son had given his life to his country.

The day passed, neither army renewing the attack; but through the
night the Union pickets could hear the tramping of feet, the rumble of
cannon-wheels growing fainter in the distance, and mistrusted what the
morning revealed—that the Confederates were retreating. When the sun
rose once more not a Confederate was to be seen; all were south of the
Potomac. McClellan gave orders for the army to advance. The various
corps pushed on to Sharpsburg. General Porter's corps hurried down to
the Potomac, forded the river, and formed on the southern shore, but
found itself confronted by the Confederate artillery. The soldiers advanced, but were driven with great loss. When they could have done
great good they were not used; when they were used they could accomplish nothing. So the great battle was fruitless of results.

The Union army has greatly outnumbered the Confederate, but it has
attacked by divisions and frittered away its strength; has lost between
twelve and thirteen thousand in killed and wounded. How great the
Confederate loss was will never be known. General Lee estimated the
number at less than eleven thousand; but from the crossing of the Potomac at Frederick to the recrossing after the battle, nearly twenty thousand had been lost from his ranks.

Riding up the hill-side to the sunken road, I came upon the line of
men who had gone down under the onslaught of French and Richardson,
lying as the grass lies in the swathe of the mowers. They were in rows,
like the ties of a railroad, in heaps like sticks of wood. The hot blast
which had flamed in their faces had shrivelled Hill's lines as the simoom
blasts the verdure of the forest. There were prostrate forms which in
the full vigor of life had gone down with resolution and energy still lin-
gering on their pallid cheeks. There was one with a cartridge between
his thumb and finger, the end bitten off, and the paper between his teeth,
when the fatal bullet pierced his heart, and all the machinery of life
came to an instant stand-still. A young lieutenant had fallen while
trying to rally his men, his resolute energy was still on his face. In the
cornfield beyond, fourteen Confederate dead were lying in a heap, the

SCENE AT THE SUNKEN ROAD.

stalks and broad green leaves trampled and stained with the crimson life-flood.

By the Hagerstown Turnpike the body of a Confederate sharp-shooter was hanging on the limb of a tree. He had climbed into it for a commanding position, and had been picked off by a Union soldier. The horses of a Confederate battery had gone down in a heap in the public square in Sharpsbur

General McClellan was there. The troops were passing through the town. The complacent look which illuminated his countenance on the day of battle was no longer there. Those who had cheered him when he rode along the lines in front of Muma's burning buildings no longer swung their hats. That Lee had escaped when he might have been crushed was the manifest conviction. The unexplained inaction of the 18th had brought about a marked change of sentiment among men and officers alike towards General McClellan.

CHAPTER XIV.

INVASION OF KENTUCKY.

WE have followed the Army of the Potomac during the summer of 1862, and now turn towards the west to see what the armies in that section of the country have been doing.

The battle of Pittsburg Landing was fought in April. In June the Confederate army under Beauregard retreated to Tûpelo, in Mississippi, where Beauregard was succeeded by General Bragg.

On the Union side, General Halleck, who had commanded all the Union armies west of the Alleghanies, was called to Washington and made general-in-chief. He made the mistake of dividing the army which had fought the battle of Pittsburg Landing, and scattering it in detachments all the way from Memphis to Chattanooga. The army under General Grant, which had fought during the first day at Pittsburg Landing, held the country between Memphis and the little town of Iuka, twenty-five miles east of Corinth, on the Memphis and Charleston Railroad. The army under General Buell was farther east. Opening the map, we see Huntsville, in Alabama, a very pretty place, north of the Tennessee, where Buell's right wing was stationed. It is one hundred miles from Iuka. Going east from Huntsville in a straight line sixty miles, we come to the little hamlet of Jasper, north of Chattanooga, where we find the left wing of his army. Some of the divisions are at Dechard. Buell is obliged to receive his supplies either from Memphis or Nashville, where there are depots filled with flour, beef, and pork.

The army is not so large as it was in June, for the time of the soldiers who enlisted for a year has expired. They have gone home, and their places have not been filled by new recruits.

General Bragg planned a movement of the Confederate army from Tupelo to Chattanooga. The troops went in the cars south to Mobile, then north the entire length of Alabama to Chattanooga. The wagons moved across the country. By this movement he was in a position to strike General Buell's left flank.

His ranks, which had been thinned by the battle of Pittsburg Landing, were once more filled up; not by volunteers, but by men who had been forced into the army under the Conscription Act passed by the Confederate Congress.

The people of the South seceded from the Union in defence of State Rights, but they were beginning to see that State Rights were not regarded by the Confederate Government; that the government set up by the Confederate Congress was a despotism. If a conscript resisted, he was seized by force. If he secreted himself, he was hunted down.

General Lee was moving north in Virginia, and General Bragg resolved to march north and invade Kentucky, which would compel General Buell to fall back to the Ohio River. At the same time General Kirby Smith was to march from East Tennessee due north into Eastern Kentucky, to Lexington, Frankfort, and on towards Cincinnati. Such movements, it was thought, would transfer the theatre of war to the banks of the Ohio. It was believed that there were thousands of young men in Kentucky who would join the Confederate army. Bragg hoped to capture Louisville and invade Ohio.

Kentucky was rich in horses. The harvests had been gathered; he could live upon the country. He would create terror in the Western States just as General Lee was creating consternation at Washington by his invasion of Maryland.

The Confederate cavalry was far superior to the Union cavalry. At the beginning of the war the Union Government did not encourage the formation of regiments of cavalry because the outfit was so costly. On the other hand, the Confederates saw that cavalry, by making rapid movements, could be used with great effect.

At Murfreesboro' was a brigade of Union troops: the Third Minnesota, Colonel Lester, and Ninth Michigan, Colonel Duffield, with four pieces of artillery and a company of cavalry. General Crittenden commanded the post. The officers disagreed; there was little discipline, and things generally were at loose ends. The officers forgot that "eternal vigilance is the price of liberty." General Forrest, commanding a brigade of Confederate cavalry, learned from his spies how things were: that the Third Minnesota Regiment was encamped east of the town, and six companies of the Ninth Michigan west of it—they were three miles apart —and that one company of the Ninth was quartered in the court-house.

It is not known how the negroes around Murfreesboro' discovered what Forrest intended to do, but it is certain that a negro came into town and said, " Massa Forrest is coming with a big army, sure."

"It is a nigger story," said the officers, who paid no attention to it.

Daylight is streaming up the east on July 12th when the Union pickets south of Murfreesboro' hear a clatter of hoofs upon the turnpike, and discover a long line of cavalry coming like the wind. The pickets fire their guns. The guards in town hear the clatter of the two thousand horses, and give the alarm. The soldiers in the court-house bar the doors. With a whoop and yell the Georgians and Texans galloped through the streets, capturing the Union guards and taking possession of the town. Two of the Confederate regiments dashed upon the camp of the Ninth Michigan, but the regiment rallied and drove them. Forrest attacked the Third Minnesota, but Colonel Lester formed his troops and opened fire. Forrest dashed round to Lester's rear and attacked the camp, but was again driven. He went back to the Ninth Michigan, dismounted two of his regiments, sent the Second Georgia to get in rear of the Union troops, then hoisted a white flag, and sent a message to Duffield, demanding his surrender, and Duffield complied with this demand. Having captured these, he turned about and made the same demand upon Lester, who was too weak to resist. So seventeen hundred men, four cannon, six hundred mules and horses, and a million dollars' worth of supplies were lost. Forrest carried away what he could and burned the rest.

General Nelson, commanding the nearest troops, started to capture Forrest; but as he had no cavalry, Forrest trotted away eastward to McMinnville, then rode north fifty miles to Lebanon, then dashed west nearly to Nashville, captured one hundred and fifty guards along the railroad, burned four bridges, and rode back to McMinnville.

John H. Morgan, who was born at Lexington, Kentucky, and who had served in the Mexican War, was brave and daring. He had joined the Confederates, and raised a regiment of young men who were ready for any adventure. They were mostly Kentuckians acquainted with the country. General Bragg sent him to destroy the railroad between Louisville and Nashville over which General Buell received his supplies. He started from Knoxville, in East Tennessee, July 4th, with one thousand men, mounted on good horses; crossed the Cumberland Mountains north-west, reached Tompkinsville, in Kentucky, one hundred and fifty miles from Knoxville, and captured four companies of Union cavalry. Not stopping, he pushed on to Glasgow, forty miles north of Tompkinsville, and captured some supplies. He issued a proclamation calling upon all true Kentuckians to join him. A few wild and restless fellows enlisted. His horses were tired, and he rested one day, and then rode north to the railroad near Mammoth Cave, and destroyed a bridge across Barren River.

General Morgan had a very skilful telegraph operator, George Ellsworth, who had an instrument in his pocket, which he quickly attached to the wires. On July 10th Morgan and Ellsworth, with a body-guard of fifteen men, reached the Louisville and Nashville Road. Ellsworth climbed the telegraph-pole, took down the wire, and put on his instrument. Pretty soon he read a message from General Boyle, who was in Louisville, to General Brown at Bowling Green. It was raining, but all through the evening Ellsworth read off the messages, learning all the news of the day, besides a great deal about military affairs. Morgan found out that Stanley Matthews was provost-marshal of Nashville, and so sent a despatch

CAVALRY ENGAGEMENT.

to Henry Dent, who was provost-marshal at Louisville. Thus it read: "General Forrest attacked Murfreesboro', routing our forces, and is now moving on Nashville. Morgan is reported to be between Scottsville and Gallatin, and will act in concert with Forrest."

On the 12th Morgan reached Lebanon, and Ellsworth took possession of the telegraph-office at half-past three in the morning. He waited till half-past seven, when the instrument began to click. He found that the operator, whoever he was, was calling B, which he discovered from the book was the Lebanon office, and was signing himself Z. Ellsworth answered the call. Then came the questions and answers:

22

" What news ?   Any skirmishing after your last message ?"

" No ; we drove what little cavalry there was away."

" Has the train arrived yet ?"

" No.   About how many troops will there be ?"

" Five hundred."

Ellsworth did not know what office he was talking with, but determined to find out, and sent this message : " A gentleman has bet the cigars that you cannot spell the name of your station correctly."

"Take the bet.   L-e-b-a-n-o-n J-u-n-c-t-i-o-n.   How did he think I would spell it ?"

" He gives it up.   He thought you would put in two b's in Lebanon."

" Ho ! ho !   He's a green one."

" Yes, that's so.   What time did the train with soldiers pass ?"

" At half-past eight last night."

" Very singular where the train is."

" Yes ; let me know when it arrives."

But the train did not arrive. A few minutes, and Ellsworth heard from the Union operator that it had gone back to Lebanon Junction, and that the soldiers on the train had had a skirmish with some of Morgan's cavalry.   General Morgan went to Midway, where Ellsworth again telegraphed. For several days he used the wires, sending a great many messages, and intercepting all the Union despatches.   The Union officers in Louisville, Nashville, and everywhere else were greatly mystified over the orders which they received.   Morgan upset all their plans.

From Somerset, on July 22d, he sent this despatch to General Boyle, the Union commander at Louisville — his old friend : " Good-morning, Jerry.   This telegraph is a great institution.   You should destroy it, as it keeps me too well posted.   My friend Ellsworth has all your despatches since the 10th of July on file.   Do you wish copies ?"

He sent this to Hon. George Dunlap, another old friend : " Just completed my tour through Kentucky.   Captured sixteen cities, destroyed millions of dollars' worth of United States property, paroled fifteen hundred Federal prisoners.   Passed through your county, but regret not seeing you."

Morgan went north to Cynthiana, only fifty miles from Cincinnati ; but finding Union troops were closing around him, he retreated to Tennessee.

A month passes.   Bragg is getting ready to move, and so is Kirby Smith, who is at Knoxville, and who is to invade Eastern Kentucky.   He sends Colonel Scott, with nine hundred cavalry and several pieces of artillery, in advance ; he passes through Monticello, and crosses the old battle-ground at Mill Springs. On the 29th General Smith approaches Richmond, only thirty miles south of Lexington.

General Nelson, who commands the Union troops in this section of the State, has stationed Manson's and Cruft's brigades at Richmond. The troops numbered nearly seven thousand, but they were new recruits. There was a skirmish and battle, with bad management on the part of Manson. His army was thrown into confusion, and he ordered a retreat. The Confederates pressed on and captured many prisoners. General Nelson arrived from Lexington, and rallied the fugitives at Richmond, but was wounded. Manson was captured, and all the artillery, with three thousand of the Union troops. In a day the only Union force that could oppose General Smith was swept away.

With banners flying and drums beating, the victorious Confederates marched on to Lexington, the most important town in central Kentucky. Many of the soldiers in his army are Kentuckians, and the sympathies of a large portion of the people are for the Confederacy. Ladies wave their handkerchiefs from the windows; little girls pick flowers from the gardens and strew them in the streets; women stand in their door-ways with baskets of provisions; merchants present the soldiers with boots and shoes.

No Union force confronts General Smith. He can move on towards Louisville, cut off Buell from that city, and take possession of it, perhaps. At any rate, he will be in position to join General Bragg, who is advancing from Chattanooga. General Smith can move due north, and strike a blow at Cincinnati. Which shall he do? If he can threaten Cincinnati, it will frighten the people of Ohio and prevent the forwarding of troops to Louisville to head off Bragg. He decides to move north. He will be in a rich and fertile section, and besides, he has another object in view—the setting up of a Confederate government in Kentucky. Jefferson Davis believes that if a government favorable to the Confederacy can but be established the people of the State will rally round it.

Young men are flocking to Lexington to join Kirby Smith's ranks; and with a civil government to direct affairs, he indulges the belief that the State can be saved to the Confederacy. He little comprehends how deep is the attachment of the majority of the people for the Union. He marches north, keeping his cavalry in advance. On September 15th he is so near Cincinnati that he can hear the whistles of the steamboats. But if he ever seriously thought of capturing Cincinnati, he discovers that it will not be an easy task. In a night strong fortifications have risen on all the hills around Covington. An energetic man is in com-

mand— General Lew. Wallace. All the shops and stores in Cincinnati
are closed, and forty thousand men are at work with axes and shovels,
and are mounting cannon. Troops have come from all parts of Ohio
and Indiana. The steamboats have howitzers mounted on their decks to
patrol the river. Before capturing the city the Union troops must be
driven from the fortifications; the river must be crossed before the Confederate troops can seize the spoils. General Smith is too good a soldier
to attempt such an enterprise. He can threaten, but not attack. He
waits for General Bragg.

On August 21st General Bragg began to cross the Tennessee River at
Chattanooga. The mountains lie in ridges, and run from the north-east
to the south-west. Chattanooga is in the valley of the Tennessee River.
By moving his troops to Chattanooga, General Bragg had placed himself
east of one of the ranges, while the Union army under General Buell was
west of it.

General Bragg determined to mask his movement by sending out his
cavalry to annoy Buell. General Forrest started with his brigade and
reached Short Mountain Cross-roads, where Captain Miller, with a portion
of the Eighteenth Ohio, was stationed. Miller had built a stockade.
His men had just eaten dinner, and were a short distance away, when they
heard the clattering of hoofs and saw the Confederate cavalry charging
down the road. Miller got into the stockade with a portion of his men,
while those who were cut off by the cavalry fled to the woods. The men
of the Eighteenth Ohio fought so resolutely that Forrest was obliged to
retreat, with a loss of twelve killed and forty-one wounded. The next day
he came upon the Twenty-sixth Ohio, under Colonel Fyffe, nine miles
west of McMinnville. Fyffe formed his regiment in line of battle, and
attacked the Confederates so suddenly and vigorously that they fled in
every direction.

General Morgan was more successful. He crossed the Cumberland
River at Hartsville and rode rapidly to Gallatin, twenty-five miles north-
east of Nashville, where he captured two hundred Union troops, burned a
railroad bridge, captured a train of freight-cars, ran it into a tunnel north
of Gallatin, set the cars on fire, and loosened the timbers which supported
the roof of the tunnel, which came down with a crash, filling the excavation with great masses of rock. No trains could pass, and Nashville was
cut off from Louisville.

General Buell sent General R. W. Johnson with six hundred and forty
cavalry of the Second Indiana, Fourth and Fifth Kentucky, and Seventh
Pennsylvania regiments to attack Morgan, but after a hard fight near

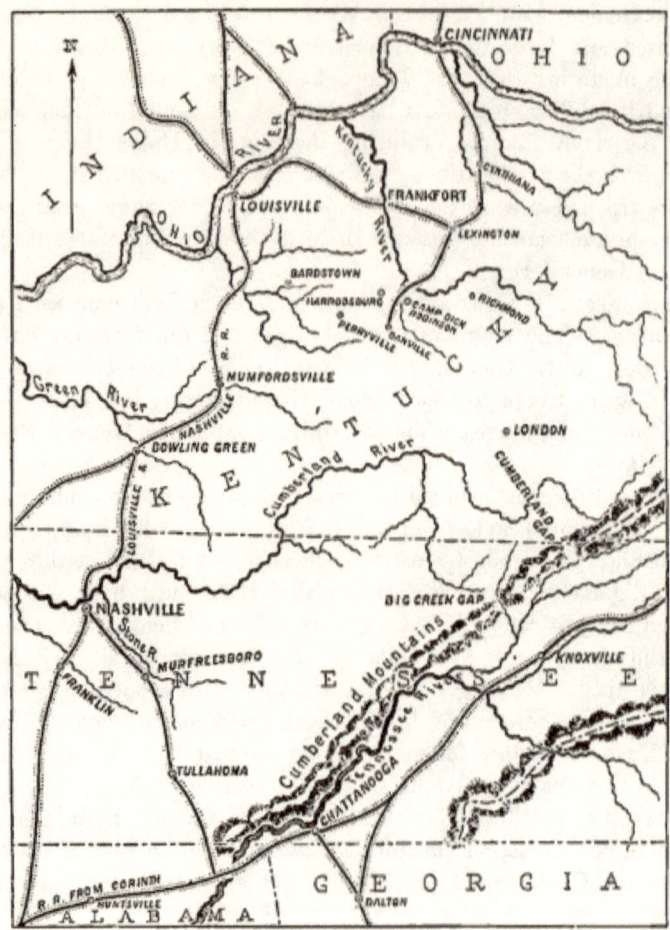

THE SORTIE OF BRAGG.

Gallatin, Johnson was defeated and captured, with a portion of his command, while the remainder were put to flight.

The women of the town rejoiced over the defeat of the Union troops. They waved their handkerchiefs, and provided nice things for the Confederate soldiers.

Over the mountain-range called Waldron's Ridge marched the Confederate army of forty thousand men, and thence to the Cumberland River, crossing it at Carthage, forty miles east of Nashville. General Bragg was nearer Louisville and Cincinnati than General Buell, who was south of Nashville. His plan was to compel Buell to fall back to the Ohio River, and he hoped thus to secure Kentucky to the Confederacy.

Northward along the turnpike leading from Carthage to Munfordsville pressed the Confederates, the cavalry, under Colonel Scott, burning the bridges spanning Salt River. The roads were dry and dusty. The summer heat had dried the streams; the rivers could be forded anywhere. The troops suffered for want of water. The secessionists of Kentucky welcomed them with hurrahs, while those who stood up for the Union saw their cornfields stripped and their hay-stacks disappear.

On September 13th General Bragg's advance, under General Chalmers, reached Munfordsville, where there was a fort garrisoned by Union troops, under Colonel Wilder, of the Seventeenth Indiana. A Confederate officer approached the fort with a white flag, and called upon Wilder to surrender. "I decline to do so," was the reply.

Chalmers opened fire, and his skirmishers advanced, but were driven back, and he waited for reinforcements before attacking in earnest.

Reinforcements meantime arrived in the fort—Colonel Dunham, with one thousand men and Konkle's battery. Colonel Dunham, being Wilder's senior officer, assumed command. Again the white flag appeared, with a demand to surrender, and Colonel Dunham declined.

Chalmers had six regiments, twelve cannon, a brigade of cavalry, and a battalion of sharp-shooters. He deployed his line and opened fire. The cannon thundered, and there were volleys of musketry, but Chalmers did not dare to risk a charge. General Bragg arrived with the main body of the army. A third time the Confederates displayed a white flag, and an officer brought a note from Bragg, who informed Dunham that the fort was surrounded by an overwhelming force. Again Dunham refused to surrender. He sent the answer by Colonel Wilder, who saw that what Bragg had stated was true—that the whole Confederate army was drawn up around the fort. Dunham thereupon called his officers together, and they decided that it was better to surrender than to have a battle, with the prospect of great loss and almost certain defeat. So at two o'clock on the morning of September 17th the fort was surrendered, the officers to retain their swords, the troops to be paroled, and to have four days' rations.

At daylight on the 17th — the hour when Hooker was advancing through the cornfield in front of the Dunker church at Antietam—this force of fifteen hundred men at Munfordsville—the only troops in front of Bragg — was swept from his path. By a rapid march he could get to Louisville before Buell could overtake him; but he did not attempt it. At the moment when he ought to have marched swiftly and struck a

great blow, he hesitated. He waited at Prewitt's Knob till Buell was
close upon him, deploying his troops to attack; then, instead of fighting
a battle, pushed north-east to Bardstown, while Buell, instead of following, and forcing him to fight, marched to Louisville. Bragg had accomplished what he intended — forced the Union army to fall back from
northern Alabama to the Ohio. He issued this proclamation to the people of Kentucky:

"Kentuckians! we have come with joyful hopes. Let us not depart in sorrow, as we
shall, if we find you wedded in your choice to your present lot. If you prefer Federal
rule, show it by your frown, and we shall return whence we came. If you choose rather
to come within the fold of our brotherhood, then cheer us with the smiles of your wom-
en, and lend willing hands to secure yourselves in your heritage of liberty.

"Women of Kentucky! your persecutions and heroic bearing have reached our ears.
Let your enthusiasm have free rein. Buckle on the armor of your kindred, your husbands, sons, and brothers, and scoff to scorn him who would prove recreant in his duty
to you, his country, and his God."

Some of the people of the State were ready to welcome General
Bragg. A few young men were eager to join the Confederate ranks. A
great many of the women hailed the Southern army with joyful looks and
sparkling eyes, but the great heart of the State was beating loyally and
true for the Union. Far-seeing men knew that Bragg would soon be
driven by the great army gathering at Louisville—thousands of soldiers
from Ohio, Indiana, Michigan, and all the West—to join Buell.

Jefferson Davis and the Confederate authorities at Richmond were in-
dulging in the delusion that if a Confederate government could be set up
at Frankfort, the capital of Kentucky, the people would recognize it, and
yield allegiance to the Confederacy.

They did not comprehend that the people of the State were farther
than ever from yielding allegiance to the Confederate Government. Not
only did Davis believe that he could secure Kentucky, but that Illinois,
Indiana, Missouri, and Iowa could be induced to abandon the contest
against the South by offering to them the free navigation of the Mississippi to the Gulf of Mexico. On the day that Bragg issued his proclamation a committee of the Confederate Congress reported in favor of
making such an offer. Instead of that, the soldiers of the North-west
were pouring in, and on October 1st Buell had an army of nearly one
hundred thousand men.

The women of Frankfort and many of the men had given a welcome
to the Confederate army. Mr. Richard Hawes was to be inaugurated
governor at noon October 4, 1862. Major-general Kirby Smith was de-

tailed by General Bragg to arrange the military escort. Thus read the order:

> "The governor will be escorted from his quarters by a squadron of cavalry, and accompanied by the commander of the Confederate States forces, Major-general Buckner, Brigadier-general Preston, and their respective staffs. The commanding general will present the governor to the people, and transfer in behalf of the Confederate States the civil order of the State and public records and property."

Nearly all the Confederate generals are present at the inauguration—Bragg, Kirby Smith, Buckner, Stevenson, Cleburne, Heath, Churchill, Preston Smith, William Preston. They gather in the Capitol Hotel for a banquet. The landlord brings out his wines and liquors. The ladies keep open house, feasting the officers of the army.

Mr. Richard Hawes is escorted to the Capitol, and takes the oath of allegiance to the Confederate States. The flag of the Confederacy waves above the Capitol.

It is six o'clock in the evening, and General Bragg is taking tea with an accomplished lady, Mrs. Preston, when a cavalryman dashes up to the door with the startling news that the Union troops are close at hand. Governor Hawes, six hours a governor, suddenly packs his carpet-bag. The Confederate generals leap into their saddles. The ladies who hung out Confederate flags in the morning hasten to take them in. There are only two Confederate infantry regiments in Frankfort, with some cavalry. The officers do not stop to take ceremonious leave of the ladies who are entertaining them, and before they are out of the streets on the south side of the town the Union cavalry are dashing across the bridge and entering upon the other side. The new governor is riding southward—governor only in name. The ladies who have smiled so graciously upon the Confederates, entertaining them, and looking forward to a new order of things in Frankfort under the administration of a Confederate governor, in grief and anger contemplate the sudden change which has taken place, while those who have stood by the old flag—whose husbands and brothers are fighting for the Union—open wide their doors and spread bountiful repasts.

The true history of the war comprises something more than fighting —more than the thunder of cannon, the rattle of musketry, the advance and retreat, the victory and defeat. It includes the hardships, trials, and endurance, the sympathies, hopes, griefs, sorrows, passions, and actions of men and women who heard nothing of the uproar of battle, who saw little of the grandeur and nothing of the horror of a battle-field.

In Kentucky, Tennessee, Missouri, Virginia—in all the Border States, as they were called, the war was around the hearth-stones—in the homes of the people. People distrusted their old-time friends; near neighbors were often bitter enemies, a sad state of affairs, paralyzing society, engendering feuds and animosities so bitter that many years must yet pass before they will wholly disappear.

We have seen General Bragg, by his movement northward from Chattanooga, compelling General Buell to hasten from northern Alabama to Louisville, and now we will go down to the vicinity of Corinth and look at a second part of Bragg's programme.

Corinth was an important military point, because there the railroad running from Columbus, Kentucky, to Mobile crossed the Memphis and Charleston Road. When General Albert Sidney Johnston was forced back from Bowling Green by the taking of Fort Donelson, he selected it as the next position to be held, and it was from thence that he marched to attack General Grant at Pittsburg Landing, to fight a great battle, in which he was defeated, and in which he lost his life. We have already seen how General Halleck, in May, 1862, with Grant's and Buell's armies combined, advanced upon Corinth, building long lines of intrenchments; that when he was ready to open fire with his heavy siege-guns he found the Confederates had slipped away under Beauregard to Tupelo, in Mississippi.

We have also seen Buell holding the country east of Corinth, and Bragg conceiving the plan of putting his troops on the cars, sending them to Mobile, and thence north to Chattanooga, to gain Buell's flank and rear, and then marching into Kentucky, compelling that general to march back to Louisville.

General Grant was commander of the Department of West Tennessee. He had two small armies: the army of the Mississippi, under General Rosecrans—the troops which Pope commanded before he was ordered to Virginia (Hamilton's, Stanley's, Davies's, and McKean's divisions)—twenty-two thousand men, and the Army of the Tennessee (Sherman's, McPherson's, Ord's, and Hurlburt's divisions), eighteen thousand men.

The Confederate Army of the South-west was commanded by Major-general Earl Van Dorn, composed of the divisions of Breckinridge, Maury, and Little—thirty-eight thousand men. Van Dorn was left to hold Grant in check, while Bragg, by his march into Kentucky, transferred the theatre of war to the Ohio River.

Van Dorn sent General Armstrong with his twenty-five hundred cavalry north from Grand Junction to attack the Union troops at Bolivar.

The Confederate cavalry rode swiftly through the woods, expecting to surprise Grant's cavalry, but the movement was discovered.

Colonel Crocker, with nine hundred men, advanced from Bolivar to meet Armstrong. He formed his brigade of cavalry and mounted infantry in the woods. Skirmishing began, and continued till night. The cavalrymen dashed at each other. A few Confederate and a few Union men went down in the mêlée. Crocker slowly drew off his men and fell back, crossing the Hatchie River to Bolivar. Armstrong did not dare to attack, but turned off, crossed the river, and made a dash at the railroad at Medon Station. The Seventh Missouri and Forty-fifth Illinois were there.

" Pile up the cotton-bales and make a fort," shouted the officers when the alarm was given. The soldiers rushed to the station and piled the bales into a breastwork, with openings through which they could fire.

The Confederate cavalry dismounted and advanced, but were glad to leap into their saddles again and retreat towards the Hatchie River. Colonel Dennis, with seven hundred infantry and two cannon, followed, and came upon them. Armstrong turned about, saw how small a force it was, and deployed his men, sending them out on each flank. The Confederates charged and captured the two cannon, but the Union infantry rallied and poured in so hot a fire that the Confederates retreated, leaving the guns, which they could not take away, and losing one hundred and seventy-four men. Van Dorn gained nothing by the movement.

The Confederate commander thought that this movement to Bolivar would make Grant think that the whole Confederate army was intending to attack his right flank, and that he would hurry up the troops from Corinth ; but that commander saw that it was only a feint to cover some larger movement. He discovered that the troops under Van Dorn and Price were leaving Grand Junction.

At Iuka, twenty-six miles east of Corinth, are mineral springs. Before the war the planters of northern Alabama and Mississippi used to gather there in summer to drink the refreshing waters, lounge on the broad piazza of the hotel, and talk about raising cotton and the secession of the Southern States.

Colonel Murphy, commanding a brigade of Stanley's division, was there, but abandoned the town, retreating to Corinth, and making no effort to save or destroy the beef, flour, pork, and other supplies intrusted to his care, which fell into the hands of General Price, and which he was very glad to get.

General Price had fourteen thousand men at Iuka. Grant planned a movement which he hoped would result in the defeat of that force. He sent General Rosecrans with Stanley's and Hamilton's divisions — nine thousand men — south to the little town of Rienzi, on the railroad; from there the troops were to turn east, march along the country road to Jacinto, and come upon Iuka from the south. He sent General Ord to attack from the north-west, but who was to wait until he heard Rosecrans's guns before attacking.

General Rosecrans reached Jacinto on the 18th of September. The wearied troops kindled their bivouac fires, drank their coffee, and threw themselves on the ground, weary and worn, after a hard day's march. He had promised General Ord to be ready to fall upon Price early on the 19th, but he was yet twenty miles from Iuka. Heavy rains had fallen, the roads were deep with mud, the streams were swollen, and it was slow getting on.

Before daybreak the troops took up once more their march. At one o'clock in the afternoon the cavalry in advance came upon the Confed-

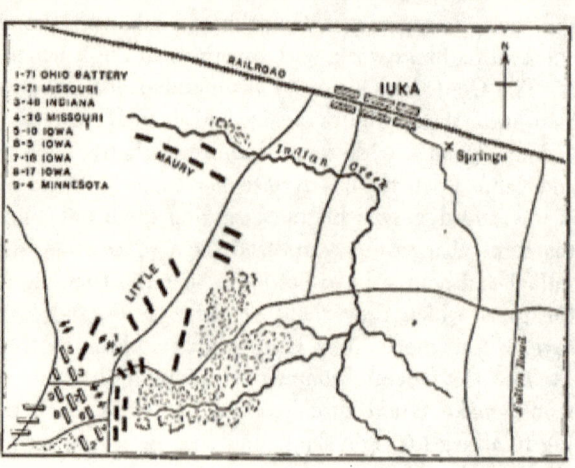

MAP OF IUKA.

erate outposts at Barnett's Corner. They were on the road leading from Jacinto to Iuka, marching north-east. There was still another road farther east, leading south to Fulton. General Rosecrans intended to sweep his right wing round upon that highway and attack from the south and east, while Ord was to assail Price from the north-west. His column was strung out — a long line of infantry, artillery, ammunition, and baggage-wagons. The woods were thick on both sides of the highway. He was nearly up to a cross-road, along which he could march to gain the Fulton Road, and his skirmishers were ascending a hill, when there came a sharp rattle of musketry in their faces.

General Price had discovered the movement, and laid a plan to fall upon Rosecrans with nearly all his force. With fourteen thousand men he would make quick work of the nine thousand strung out in a long col-

umn. He was acquainted with the ground; Rosecrans was not. Price
had forty-four cannon, and chose his position on a hill two miles south of
Iuka, deploying General Little's division, consisting of Gates's, Colbert's,
Green's, and Morton's brigades, in front, holding Maury in reserve to confront General Ord.

At Barnett's house a battalion of the Fifth Iowa deployed as skirmishers and drove the Confederates. At Miss Moore's house, five miles from
Iuka, the fight was sharp. The skirmishers, from the brow of a hill, discovered the enemy in line along a ravine. General Hamilton, commanding the division, was close behind the skirmishers, and saw that the time
for quick action had come; for suddenly a strong force of Confederates
rushed upon the Twenty-sixth Missouri, driving it back upon the head
of the column. His troops were in the road. The woods on both sides
were very thick. He knew nothing of the ground. Shells were bursting
around him, and bullets cutting the twigs. The Eleventh Ohio Battery
with great difficulty wheeled into position in the thick underbrush. The
leading regiment, the Fifth Iowa, went out upon the right, and the Forty-
sixth Missouri beyond it. The Forty-eighth Indiana went up the road
upon the run, and swung out to the left of the battery. It was after four
o'clock, and the sun well down towards the horizon, when, with these
three regiments and one battery in line, began the battle, which burst out
in an instant with great fury. Up the hill came other regiments—the
Fourth Minnesota and Sixteenth Iowa—which formed on the right in the
rear, and the Tenth Iowa and the Twelfth Wisconsin Battery on the left.
The Eightieth Ohio formed in reserve in rear of the Forty-eighth Indiana.

The ground was so rough and the woods so dense that Hamilton could
only have a front line of three regiments, while General Price had deployed one entire division. On the right of the Confederates was the
Texas Legion, which with a yell rushed forward, pouring volley after
volley into the left flank of the Fifth Iowa. Many Union soldiers went
down, but the regiment held its ground and gave deadly volleys in return.

The Eleventh Ohio Battery was commanded by Lieutenant Sears, who
worked his guns with great rapidity. The Confederates were within canister range, and he made great gaps in their lines. The Confederate cannon, on the other hand, were aimed too high, and the shot cut the twigs
of the sassafras-trees over the heads of the Union troops.

The Confederates determined to capture the Union battery, and came
on with a rush upon the Forty-eighth Iowa, which gave way, and then
came the shooting of the gunners and the horses. The frightened ani-
mals dashed through the ranks of the Twenty-sixth Missouri, which rushed

into the gap in the line, pouring a deadly fire into the faces of the exultant Confederates.   "Lie down and load; then rise and fire!" shouted
Captain Brown to the men of Company C.   The men obeyed, sheltering
themselves while loading, and then rising for an instant and firing.

"Fire low!" shouted a Confederate officer to his men, who saw the
Twenty-sixth Missouri sheltering themselves.   The Confederates fired low,
and then the Union men began to drop very fast.

This the scene at sunset: the Confederates charging upon the battery,
horses and men going down in a heap, dead and wounded piled one upon
the other, the air thick with bursting shells and leaden rain, the men firing
in one another's faces.

The Confederates had captured the battery, but could not hold it.
They retreated, rallied, rushed once more upon the guns, took them a
second time, but to hold them only a moment, for the Union troops came
on with a cheer and regained them.   For two hours the tide of battle
surged backward and forward over the same ground.   General Little, on
the Confederate side, fell mortally wounded.   General Price narrowly
escaped.   He brought up brigade after brigade, but could drive the Union
men only a few paces before his own lines were swept back in turn.

Night came at last, putting an end to one of the fiercest contests of
the war, brief but bloody, fought with unsurpassed bravery and obstinacy
on the Union side—seven regiments and two batteries (two thousand eight
hundred men in all) defeating nearly the whole Confederate force.   Darkness settled down upon the field, thickly strewn with killed and wounded;
the Union soldiers lay down where they stood, sleeping on their arms all
night long, with the rain pouring upon them.

General Price was uneasy.   He had attacked and been defeated.   His
ablest officer, General Little, had been killed.   There was a mournful scene
in Inka at his midnight burial.   The Confederate officers stood around;
torches threw their flickering light upon them as they heaped the earth
above the brave commander.   There was no drum-beat, no volley of musketry, a funeral very much like that of Sir John Moore on the battle-field
of Corunna, in Spain—

"Not a drum was heard, not a funeral note."

General Price was thinking what he should do, for the Union troops
under Rosecrans were sleeping on their arms, ready to renew the battle in
the morning.   North-west of the town were the troops under General Ord,
ready to advance.   There was but one road open to him, that leading
south to Fulton, and Rosecrans was ready to seize it in the morning.

A man to be a successful general must be able to make a retreat, if need be, as well as to win a battle. General Washington won the admiration of the British generals when he slipped away in the night from a superior force at Trenton, made an all-night march, fell upon the British at Princeton, and won a victory. General Price showed his good-sense and his ability to escape capture by giving instant orders for a retreat.

Morning dawned. The Union troops were ready for battle, but no Confederates confronted them. They were gone, escaping by the Fulton Road. Rosecrans entered Iuka, to find the houses full of Confederate wounded.

Hamilton's division had done nearly all the fighting. It contained less than three thousand when the battle began; but one hundred and thirty-seven had been killed, five hundred and twenty-seven wounded, and twenty-six had been captured.

The wind had blown from the north, and no sound of the conflict had reached the ears of General Ord, who had been waiting to hear the cannonade. If he had heard it, it is quite probable that Price's army would have been ground to powder, as corn is crushed between the revolving mill-stones.

When the Confederate soldiers saw that they were to evacuate the town they broke open the houses, helping themselves to whatever pleased them most. The people had welcomed them a few days before with open arms, but now they saw their property ruthlessly taken by the men from Missouri and Arkansas. They had espoused secession as a sovereign right, and had voted to secede, little thinking how bitter would be the turn of events. Price made a rapid march, sending his wagons in advance, the drivers urging on the mules, so that by daylight they were beyond the reach of Rosecrans's cavalry.

General Grant had failed in his plan to crush Price simply because he had relied upon General Ord's hearing the cannon of Rosecrans. So we see how small a matter in war will sometimes defeat the best-laid plans.

General Van Dorn determined to attack Corinth, the key to all the surrounding country. If it could be captured, the Union troops would be compelled to abandon West Tennessee. He had thirty-eight thousand troops, while Rosecrans, in command at Corinth, had only about twenty thousand.

There was a Confederate spy in the town, Miss Burton, who sent a letter to Van Dorn which fell into the hands of Rosecrans's detectives, who carefully unsealed it, made a copy, then resealed it and allowed it to go to Van Dorn. Miss Burton in her letter told Van Dorn how many

Union regiments Rosecrans had, the number of cannon, and informed him that the town could be best attacked from the north-west, between the two railroads. Rosecrans did not have Miss Burton arrested; he was too shrewd for that. But the detectives had their eyes on her so sharply that she could not send a second letter to let Van Dorn know that the negroes and soldiers were building redoubts and breastworks.

North and east of the town there are swamps, with knolls and thick woods—not a good place to deploy troops in line of battle. On the north-west, however, the ground is high and rolling, with no natural obstructions. Over this plateau Van Dorn intended to make his attack. The Memphis and Charleston Railroad comes into the town from the north-west, the Mobile and Ohio from the north.

Walking out over the Memphis Railroad, we see Fort Williams south of the road on a knoll, and the three twenty-pounder Parrott guns inside of it to sweep all the plateau. North of the railroad, on another knoll, is Fort Robinett, close by the county road leading to Bolivar. Walking north-east, and crossing the county road leading to Chewalla and the Mobile and Ohio Railroad, we come to the county road leading to Purdy, and beyond it we see Fort Powell, and farther on Fort Richardson. These are all the points we need keep in mind.

General Rosecrans had his cavalry out on all the roads—north, east, south, and west. The scouts brought word on the 2d of October that Van Dorn was making a rapid march. Rosecrans stationed Hamilton's division on the Purdy Road, its right extending to a swamp, its left reaching to Fort Powell. Davies's division was next in line, with General Stanley's division behind it in reserve, while General McKean's division held the left, south of the Memphis Railroad.

General Powell led the advance of the Confederates in the march to Corinth along a road south of the Memphis Railroad, and came into position, with the brigades of Rust, Villepigue, and Bowen in front, his left touching the Memphis Railroad, and Jackson's cavalry reaching south beyond the seminary, south-west of the town. General Price had two divisions: Maury's and Hebert's. Hebert had succeeded General Little, killed at Iuka. Maury's line began at the Memphis Railroad, in front of Fort Robinett. Moore's and Phifer's brigades made up the front line, with Cabell's in reserve. Hebert's division extended north-east, with Green's, Gates's, and McLean's brigades in front, and Colbert's in reserve.

General Rosecrans thought it best to begin the battle some distance from the town, beyond the line of the forts. By so doing he would develop the plans of the Confederates. Davies's division, in the centre was between the railroads, while McArthur's brigade went out on the south-west side of the Memphis Road. In front of Davies was an old breast-work built by Beauregard, held by Oliver's brigade.

It was half-past ten in the morning when Lovell's division (Confeder-ate) advanced and began the battle by falling upon Oliver. General McKean, on the left, saw that Oliver was going to be flanked, and sent McArthur's brigade to his assistance. The Confederates greatly outnum-bered the Union troops. After firing a while, the Confederates rushed, charged the breastwork, capturing two cannon, and driving Oliver back towards Fort Robinett, which uncovered Davies's flank. Moore's Confed-erate brigade sprang into the gap between Davies and McArthur, which compelled Davies's whole division to fall back.

The Tenth Ohio Battery, out on the Chewalla Road, had hurled shells upon the Confederates, but the time had come when it must go to the rear, for there were no regiments at hand to support it. The gunners limbered up the pieces and seized the sponges and rammers.

"Get bucket No. 2," shouts a corporal. The Confederates are not one hundred feet distant; but G. S. Wright, a boy of eighteen, runs and picks it up, with the bullets whistling about him, and brings it safely away.

Going up the Purdy Road, we see Hamilton's troops on the knolls north of the town, and the Confederate troops under Hebert in the woods west of him. Van Dorn has ordered Hebert to keep out of sight until the right moment comes, thinking that Hamilton will rush in to help Da-vies; but Hamilton makes no such movement. His troops in the morn-ing faced north-east, but he sees that Van Dorn is not going to attack from that quarter; and while the battle is raging west of him he is changing his line, so that at noon it faces north-west. His skirmishers have discov-ered the seven thousand Confederate troops under Hebert in the woods.

There has been a lull in the battle. The Confederates, elated by the success of the morning, are getting ready for a grand attack. Van Dorn plans to hurl his troops upon Davies's division and drive them on, brigade after brigade, over the ground between the two railroads.

In battle a general must be quick to see what the enemy intends to do, and be ready to receive the blow and strike one in return. Rosecrans comprehends Van Dorn's plan, and orders McKean to fall back to another ridge to join his right to Davies. Stanley, who has been near the town, is advanced, to be close to Davies, while Hamilton is to be ready to swing to the west and strike the Confederates in flank.

It was nearly three o'clock before Van Dorn was ready. First the cannon opened; then the brigades, one after another, fell upon Davies.

General Hackleman, commanding a Union brigade, was mortally wounded. General Oglesby, commanding another brigade, was also wounded. The troops began to waver, when up came Stanley's batteries, the horses upon the run. The gunners leaped from the limbers, wheeled the cannon into position, and poured canister into the Confederate ranks. General Mower's brigade came on the double-quick, and went into the thick of the fight.

Through the afternoon the battle rages. Sullivan's brigade, of Hamilton's division, comes to take part. At six o'clock the contest ceases. Van Dorn has driven, as it were, a wedge almost through the Union lines. To-morrow he will finish the work. He sends this exultant telegram to Richmond: "Our troops have driven the enemy from their positions. We are within three-fourths of a mile of Corinth. The enemy are huddled together about the town—some on the extreme left trying to hold their position. So far all is glorious."

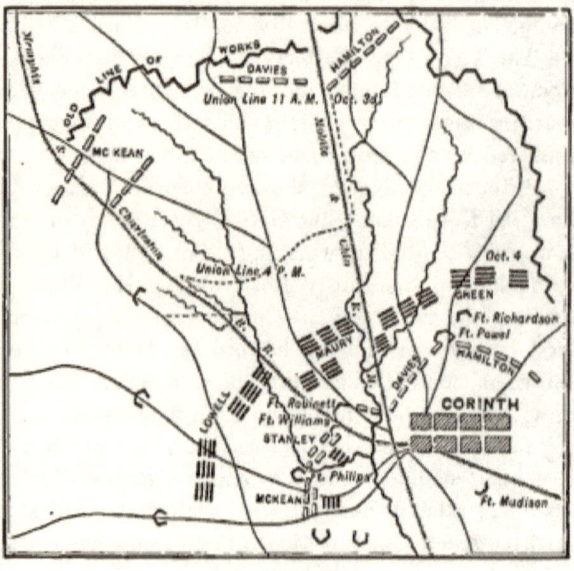

MAP OF CORINTH.

About the time the war began, an Indian named Chief Sky, in Wisconsin, captured a young eagle on the banks of the Flambeau River, a branch of the Chippewa. The company from Eau Claire brought the bird with them when they went into camp at Madison, and Captain Perkins named him "Old Abe," for Abraham Lincoln. The soldiers became fond of him, and he of the soldiers. He had a perch on the color-staff, and always sat there in battle, flapping his wings, as if in ecstasy, when the battle was wildest. The regiment is in Mower's brigade, and Old Abe on his perch, looking out over the scene. Cannon are thundering around him; there are long rolls of musketry; the air is thick with bullets. From the flank comes a fearful volley, enfilading

23

the line, cutting down scores of men, and severing the cord which holds Old Abe to the staff. He flaps his wings, rises above the two armies, circles out over the Confederates, then back again to his friends, and lights once more on his perch. The regiment is in retreat, and Old Abe goes with it, to be in a score of battles, and to come out of them all unharmed.

Night settles over the scene, and General Rosecrans prepares for the morrow. Several hundred negroes are set to work with axes, picks, and shovels, building breastworks north of Fort Powell. Rosecrans reforms his line, resting the left on Fort Robinett, the centre on the ridge between the two railroads, and the right on the high ground on the Purdy Road. McKean's division still holds the left; Stanley stands next in line; then Davies, then Hamilton on the right. Rosecrans calls all these officers to his headquarters—a white cottage with a portico, the home of Hampton Mark—explains his plans, and the officers post their troops accordingly.

Fort Robinett and Fort Williams were what military men call the keys to the position, so situated that their cannon could sweep all the field. If Van Dorn could get possession of the forts he could turn the guns upon other parts of the Union line. Being so important a position, we may expect Van Dorn to try his best to capture them.

The first brigade of the Second Division of Rosecrans's army (General Stanley) is called the Ohio Brigade, Colonel Fuller commander, composed of the Twenty-seventh, Thirty-ninth, Forty-third, and Sixty-third Ohio regiments. About ten o'clock at night the troops file into position. The pickets hear noises in front of them, and discover that the Confederates are planting a battery. Captain Brown, of the Sixty-third, goes out with two companies. Creeping along the Chewalla Road, he comes suddenly upon a Confederate officer, Captain Tobin, commanding a Tennessee battery, and takes him and his bugler prisoners.

At four o'clock in the morning the Union soldiers were astir. Rosecrans ordered that no fires should be kindled, but the soldiers wanted a cup of hot coffee, and disregarded the command. The Confederate artillerymen, aiming at the light, opened fire and sent their shells into Corinth. Sutlers, teamsters, and negroes hastened to the rear, but the soldiers ate their breakfast, and were ready for work. Captain Williams waited till in the dawning light he could see just where the Confederate batteries were, and then opened with his thirty-pounder Parrott guns. His aim was sure, the shells destructive, and the Confederate gunners made haste to get away, taking all but one gun, which was captured by the soldiers of the Sixty-third Ohio.

The skirmishers began as soon as it was daylight. The Confederate batteries joined in, and sent a shell crashing into the Tishomingo Hotel, filled with Union wounded, killing a soldier.

It was half-past nine when Hebert's Confederate division came out from the woods and advanced against Davies. The long lines of men in gray came into the clearing. Gates's brigade led the movement upon Fort Richardson. A storm beat in their faces; men dropped, but the column pressed on up the gentle ascent, rushing at last up to the line of breastworks, and leaped over them. Captain Richardson, for whom the fort was named, goes down, and his gunners are shot. The infantry supporting the battery are driven. The troops retreat towards the town, followed by the Confederates. McLean's Confederate brigade captures Fort Powell. Gates's men rush on into the town, charging up almost to Rosecrans's headquarters; but they are confronted by the Tenth Ohio and Fifth Minnesota and Immell's battery. Mark Hampton's house is riddled with bullets. Seven Confederates go down in front of it; but the wave which has rolled so far and so triumphantly has spent its force.

Going up the Purdy Road, we come to Hamilton's division. His batteries are sending shells westward, and we see Sullivan's brigade falling upon the Confederates, the Fifty-sixth Illinois sweeping them out of Fort Powell and recapturing it.

The Confederates under General Maury advanced against Forts Robinett and Williams. The thirty-pounder Parrotts opened upon them, but still the Texans and Mississippians pressed on.

"Forward! Charge!"

It was Colonel Rogers, of Texas, commanding a brigade, who gave the order. He had a battle-flag in his hand and led his men. Canister mowed them down, but they reached the ditch in front of the fort, and halted to take breath. Just so, at the battle of Buena Vista, the Mexicans halted when they should have advanced, and were mercilessly cut down. There are times in battle when moments are priceless. Such a crisis had arrived at Corinth. It was but a moment that they stood irresolute, but in that brief instant the Confederates lost a possible victory. Down into the ditch leaped the brave Rogers, his men following; climbing the parapet, but all to tumble headlong, pierced by bullets.

Little did Colonel Rogers suspect what a tempest would burst upon him; that the Ohio Brigade was close at hand biding its time, and that the Eleventh Missouri also was there.

For a few moments only can such a contest last—men firing into one another's faces, scores going down at every volley; men stabbing at one another with their bayonets and striking with the butts of their guns.

The contest was soon over, the Confederates fleeing over ground thickly strewn with killed and wounded. A few moments ago the Sixty-third Ohio numbered two hundred and fifty, now only one hundred and twenty-five. In front of Fort Robinett fifty-six Confederates are lying, piled one upon another.

The defeat was so decisive that Van Dorn ordered the instant retreat of his army. Before noon the shattered columns were gone, with Rosecrans in pursuit. General Ord was at Bolivar. He had started for Corinth while the battle was raging, intending to attack Van Dorn in the rear. He had four thousand men—Hurlbut's division. Van Dorn hastened west to get beyond the Hatchie River. Ord met him at the river. Confederate cavalry held the bridge, but Ord took possession of a hill and commanded the approach to the bridge with his cannon.

The Confederate troops charged upon the hill, but were driven by Ord, who was wounded in the mêlée. General Hurlbut then assumed command of the Union troops, and the battle went on, Hurlbut trying to get possession of the bridge.

Van Dorn saw that a net was closing around him. The cavalry scouts brought word that another body of Union troops under General McPherson was coming from the west. No time was to be lost. He turned his train into a narrow road leading south along the east bank of the river, towards Crum's Mill, and made a show of fighting till they were well under way, then withdrew his troops, losing in the battle of Hatchie eight cannon and three hundred men. He reached Ripley, but with a sadly demoralized army. Of his soldiers, more than fourteen hundred had been killed, and he had lost altogether more than eight thousand men. He had failed in what he set out to accomplish—to capture Corinth and compel the Union troops to abandon West Tennessee. It was the last effort of the Confederate army to regain that section of country.

October has come. Buell is at Louisville. He has reorganized his army, and begins a movement against Bragg, who is at Bardstown. Kirby Smith, with the Confederate troops which came from Knoxville, is at Frankfort. Buell advances, and Bragg sullenly falls back to Chaplin Hills, near Perryville. It is a beautiful country, a region of smooth fields, corn-lands, farm-houses, woods, and pastures on the Chaplin River, a small stream winding in graceful curves. Bragg has sixty thousand men. He intended to choose his ground and fight a defensive battle, but half of his troops are under Smith, thirty miles away. He suddenly changes his plan. He sees McCook's and Gilbert's divisions of Buell's army approaching

THE BATTLE OF CORINTH.

Perryville, and resolves to attack McCook and annihilate him before the other division can come to his aid.

On the 7th of October Daniel McCook's brigade of Sheridan's division, Gilbert's corps, is approaching Perryville on the road leading to Springfield. The roads are deep with dust, the ground parched, the springs dry, the men and horses suffering for want of water. The videttes reach a little stream, Doctor's Creek, and stop to fill their canteens, when there comes a rattling fire upon them from Confederate skirmishers sent out by Bragg. Sheridan brings Hiscock's and Barnet's batteries to the front, and after a brief cannonade the Confederates retire.

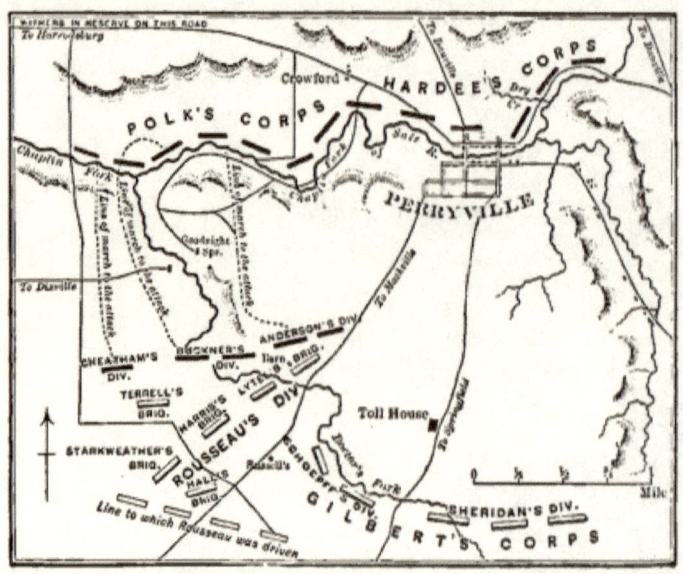

MAP OF PERRYVILLE.

General Buell and staff ride to the top of the ridge overlooking the country towards Perryville, and dismount in front of Carlin's brigade, looking over the ground with their glasses. No Confederate troops are in sight, but they are aware that a battle is imminent. "Well, Carlin, to-morrow you will have all the fighting you want!" is the remark of Colonel Fry. "Have you confidence in your troops?" Buell asks. "I will trust them anywhere," is the reply.

The rising sun of October 8th shines through the morning haze. The soldiers know that a battle is at hand, but it is nearly ten o'clock before the cannon open their lips.

This the formation of the Union line : Going west one mile to the road leading to Mackville, we come to the house of Mr. Russell, where we see Rousseau's division of McCook's corps coming down the road. Suddenly, from the woods along the creek, the Confederate cannon open fire. Rousseau brings Loomis's and Simonson's batteries into position, and the conflict begins. The Thirty-third Ohio deploys as skirmishers, followed by McCook's brigades, which come into line in the fields north-west of Russell's house.

Going out through the field where the corn is standing in shocks, we come to Terrell's brigade of Jackson's division—new troops which have never been in battle, with Starkweather's brigade in the rear. To the right of Starkweather is Harris's, and then Lytle's. Webster's brigade is in the rear, near Russell's house. Going east, we find Schoepf's division of Gilbert's corps, with Sheridan beyond.

Walking now over to the Confederate lines, we discover Polk's corps on the right and Hardee's on the left. Polk has charge of the attack. He has his own corps, with Cheatham's division, on the right, which is to strike Terrell. Buckner's division is in the centre, which is to advance through the fields and strike McCook's line, while Anderson's division is to crush Lytle's troops.

Cheatham advances so rapidly that almost before Terrell knows it the storm bursts upon his untried troops, who see three times their own number bearing down upon them. The line begins to waver. Jackson and Terrell try to rally the faint-hearted, but a moment later Jackson is killed and Terrell mortally wounded. The Union troops retreat in confusion, while the Confederates rush upon Parson's battery and seize the guns. At a blow McCook's right has been crushed.

McCook makes a mistake at the outset in not sending at once to Buell the information that he is attacked and needs reinforcements. He sends instead to Gilbert, who refers him to Buell, who is a strict constructionist. Everything must go by rule. Gilbert waits for orders, but none come. Carlin is eager to advance. General Mitchell, commanding a division, is anxious to sweep down upon Polk's flank, and asks permission of Gilbert to do so, but they wait for an order from Buell.

Having scattered Terrell's brigade, Cheatham advances upon Starkweather. The strife is getting hot all along the line, for Buckner is in front of Harris, while Anderson is opening upon Lytle. McCook brings forward Webster's brigade, but its commander is killed, and the Union troops are driven. The Confederates advance with jubilant yells. Loomis's Union battery is by Russell's house. The gunners have fired away

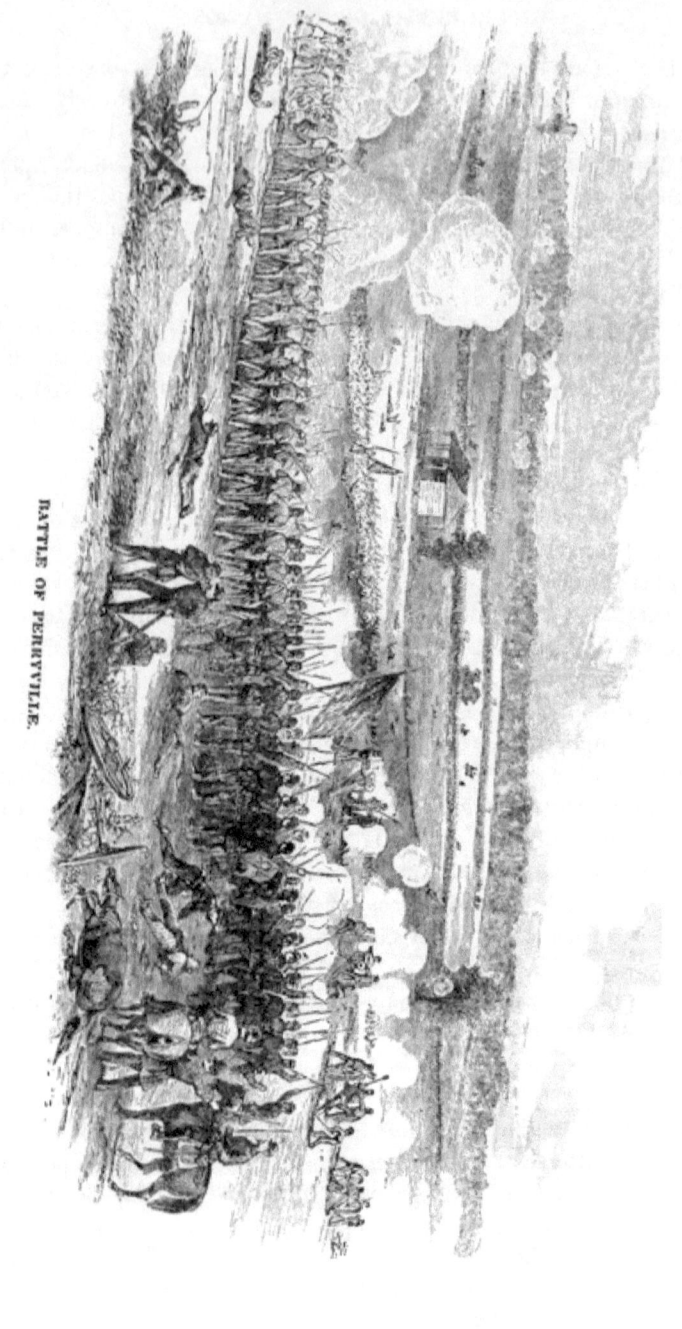

BATTLE OF PERRYVILLE.

all their long-range ammunition, and stand beside their pieces wiping the
sweat from their brows, biding their time. On rush the Confederates to
seize the cannon, but a storm of canister bursts upon them. Pinney's
battery, Fifth Wisconsin, comes upon the gallop, wheels into position, and
pours in its fire. The Confederates come to a halt, for at this moment
Gooding's brigade of Gilbert's corps comes across the field. Gilbert has
resolved to wait no longer for orders from Buell. The struggle is terrific.
In a few moments four hundred and ninety of Gooding's men are killed
or wounded. Steedman's brigade attacks with such vigor that the Confederates, who a few moments ago were sweeping all before them, are
driven in confusion back to Russell's house.

Sheridan the while, without any orders from Buell, advances Carlin,
who captures one hundred and thirty-three men and several wagons and
caissons. General Thomas is out on the right. He hears the uproar, waits
for orders from Buell, but none reach him, and he takes no part in the
struggle. He is in a position to sweep round and fall with resistless force
upon the Confederates. Night comes; the battle is over, fought almost
wholly by McCook, who has lost nearly four thousand men. No one will
ever know Bragg's loss; but as he brought on the fight, and was the attacking party, it probably exceeded the Union casualties. Bragg intended
to crush McCook, and then the other corps in succession; but had been
defeated instead. Through the night his trains were rumbling along the
roads; when morning came, his whole army was moving south. On the
11th Buell came upon Bragg's rear at Harrodsburg, and pressed him so
hard that the Confederate commander abandoned his sick and wounded.
Bragg had reaped a rich harvest of supplies in Kentucky, and was sending
his trains into Tennessee. Buell, instead of following, gave up the pursuit
and turned west towards Nashville, fearing that Bragg would swing round
in that direction. But the Confederate general was busy sending his trains
south. "The wagon-train," said the *Richmond Examiner*, "was 40 miles
long, and brought 1,000,000 yards of jeans, a large lot of clothing, boots
and shoes, 200 wagon-loads of bacon, 6000 barrels of pork, 1500 horses
and mules, and 8000 cattle and swine." Bragg had not captured Louisville or Cincinnati, but he had pushed Buell from northern Alabama back
to the Ohio River, had lived on the fat of the land for a month, and secured a vast amount of food. He had discovered, too, that Kentucky had
cast in her lot irrevocably for the old flag. He expected to obtain many
recruits for the Confederates, but few had joined him. Buell had shown
so little energy in the campaign that he was relieved of his command, and
Rosecrans, with the victory at Corinth in his favor, succeeded him.

CHAPTER XV.

CRUMBLING OF THE CONFEDERATE CORNER-STONE.

WE are ever to keep in mind the fact that behind all the noise and carnage of battle there were great ideas : the maintenance of the authority of government, the preservation of the Union, and that it was a struggle between two systems of labor, between two civilizations—the supremacy of ideas and institutions.

A great change was taking place in the opinions of the people of the United States in regard to slavery. In the first chapter we have seen how slavery was planted in this country, how it became a political power, and how it was at the bottom of all the troubles besetting the nation. When the Confederate cannon opened fire upon Fort Sumter it was from earthworks which had been constructed by slaves. The fortifications around Richmond from which McClellan had been driven, those at Donelson and at Columbus—all had been built by slave labor. The people of the North were beginning to see that while the white people were in the field fighting to destroy the Union, the slaves were tilling the soil and raising corn and cotton ; that slavery was giving great strength to the Confederate arms.

On the 22d of May, 1861, General Butler, at Fortress Monroe, declared that slaves which had been employed in building breastworks for the Confederates were contraband of war. In August, 1861, General Fremont, commanding in Missouri, issued a proclamation making free the slaves of all citizens in the State who were enemies of the Union.

He had no authority to issue such a proclamation, and President Lincoln declared it of no effect. General Halleck, who succeeded him in command, forbade negroes to come into his camp, and ordered the soldiers to drive them away ; but the troops saw that slavery was behind the Confederacy, and disregarded the order. They divided their rations with the negroes. They were rapidly becoming abolitionists. They could see with clearer vision than the politicians that slavery gave strength to the Confederacy. They talked it over by their bivouac fires. Why should they fight to maintain an institution which was at war with free labor ? Why

EFFECTS OF THE EMANCIPATION PROCLAMATION.

should they peril their lives for that which was at the bottom of all these troubles?

John Cochrane, of New York, was a member of Congress before the war. He had always been conservative; but when South Carolina fired upon Fort Sumter he forgot his conservatism in his zeal for the preservation of the Union. He commanded a regiment called "United States Chasseurs," from New York. He held a review, and the Secretary of War, Simon Cameron, was present. After the review Colonel Cochrane made a speech to his soldiers. He said that to put an end to the war the Government had a right to confiscate property, seize cotton, and as slaves were an element of power, it was the duty of the Government to seize them; and not only that, but to put arms in their hands to aid in suppressing the rebellion and to secure their freedom! Any general who should fail or refuse to do this was as unfit for service as he who should decline to explode a mine which had been prepared for the destruction of the enemy!

Up to this moment his men had stood mute and motionless, with arms at rest, but in an instant, as if all had been moved by an electric impulse, they burst into enthusiastic applause. This, the colonel said, was not abolitionism; it was only using the means at hand for suppressing the rebellion and saving the country.

At the close of the speech Mr. Cameron was called upon. He said that he fully indorsed every word Colonel Cochrane had said, and lest he should be misunderstood he would repeat that the sentiments of Colonel Cochrane upon this subject were his own, and he was glad to hear them.

This declaration, so straightforward and explicit, was received with great demonstrations of delight by the troops, and when Mr. Cameron descended from the platform they gave him three hearty cheers.

On December 2, 1861, I learned that there was a large number of negroes in Washington jail who had been arrested by the police, not for the commission of crime, but because they were slaves, and had run away from their masters. I visited the jail to see about it. Ascending the stone stairs and passing along a dark corridor to a great iron door which the jailer unlocked, we entered a room where there were sixty negroes—old men bending with age and young boys. There was no bed, no mattress or straw on the stone floor, not even a blanket to protect them from the cold. They were in rags, vermin were creeping over them, and the room was reeking with filth. They had been arrested under the slave laws of Maryland.

The statutes affecting the men in prison were passed when Maryland was a colony. If a slave went abroad at night without leave he could be punished by whipping, cropping, and branding with the letter R. If a slave were convicted of treason, arson, or murder, he was to have his right hand cut off, and then he was to be hanged, his head. severed from his body, the body divided into four quarters, and the head and quarters set up in the most public place in the county. It was lawful for any one to shoot and kill a runaway slave.

Under an Act passed 1820 a slave breaking a street lamp, or tying a horse to a tree in the street, flying a kite, attending a religious meeting, unless led by a white man, was to be whipped. A free negro must prove his freedom and enter into bonds with five good bondsmen to obey the laws. If he could not obtain them he must pay a fine of one thousand dollars or be sent to the workhouse. A free colored person found in the streets after ten o'clock at night was to be arrested and sent to jail. The police suspecting a negro of being a runaway slave were to put him in jail, and the negro must prove his innocence or be sold to pay the fees.

The poor creatures in the jail looked up wonderingly when I entered. Had I come to sell them into slavery? I asked them questions, and here are the notes written at the time:

"James Munroe, sixteen years old; belongs to Captain Demmington, who was captain of the police at the Capitol during Buchanan's administration, but who is now captain of a Confederate battery. When he went to Virginia he left James behind, who has been arrested because he has no master.

"Charles Jackson, from Fairfax County, Virginia; owned by William Dulin; lived near Fairfax Court-house; fifty years old. When the Union army entered Virginia his master sold his wife and children. Charles fled to the Union lines, was arrested by the police, and has been in jail three months.

"'You see, sir,' he said, 'when master sold my wife and children it broke me all up. I am sick; I can't eat. I sha'n't live long, but I don't want to die here. Oh, sir, can you do anything to get me out?' There were tears upon his cheeks as he knelt in supplication at my feet.

"George Washington (the slave-masters frequently named their slaves for the great men of the country); belonged to Benjamin Walker, near Oak Grove, Orange County, Virginia. He ran away and reached Washington. He thought the Union soldiers would be his friends. 'Liberty is sweet to me,' he said.

"Joe Curtis. He is a free negro; always has been free. He lived in Alexandria, was arrested by the police on the supposition that he was a slave. There is no one to pay his jail fees. Under the law he must be sold."

It was profitable business for the police to arrest negroes and put them in jail. They had a fee for every arrest, which was paid by the Government of the United States. Under the old law, if no one claimed them, free negroes were sold into slavery to pay the fees. The jailer and sheriff made a great deal of money.

"Robert Paine; owned by George Silkman, near Occoquon Mills, Virginia. His master is in the Confederate army. Robert took a boat, made his way up the Potomac to Washington to find freedom. He has been at work on the fortifications around Washington for forty days. Government owes him for his labor. He was arrested one night by the Georgetown police, and had been in jail ten weeks."

When the poor creatures saw me making notes of their answers they did not at first know what to make of it. Were they to be sold? Was I about to do something to help them? Their eyes kindled, their countenances became eloquent with hope. They crowded around me, begging me to aid them. My blood was boiling, and I determined that they should be free, and that the law under which they had been imprisoned should be wiped from the statutes.

"Please put down my name, sir," each said, crowding around me. Some of them had caught cold from sleeping on the stone floor, and were fast going in consumption.

"God bless you, massa!" was the chorus that fell upon my ears as I walked away. Fifteen minutes later I was in the Capitol reading my notes to Henry Wilson, Senator from Massachusetts. Together we returned to the jail.

"My God! Is it possible!" he said, as he gazed upon the poor creatures. "We will have this thing ripped up as sure as there is a God in heaven."

I called upon Charles Sumner, Senator from Massachusetts, read to him what I had written, and he too visited the jail and came out of it with his blood at fever heat.

The next day Senator Wilson introduced a resolution into the Senate "directing the discharge of all persons claimed as fugitives from service or labor confined in the jail in the District of Columbia."

"I have visited the jail, and have found such a scene of degradation as I never before witnessed," said Mr. Wilson.

"There are persons there," said Senator Sumner, "almost entirely naked, some of them without even a shirt. Some of them are free persons. Most of them have run away from disloyal masters. Some have been sent there by their masters for safe-keeping till the war is over."

"I think," said Senator Hale, of New Hampshire, "that when the Northern States find out that they are supporting here in jail the slaves of rebels who are fighting against us—that we are keeping, at the public expense, their slaves for them till the war is over—it will have a tendency to enlighten the minds of some of them in answering the question, 'What has the North to do with slavery?'"

24

Senator Grimes, of Iowa, visited the jail. "I think," he said, "that there never was a place of confinement that can be compared to the Washington jail, except the French Bastile or the Dungeon of Venice. I found one negro who had been there fourteen months—arrested on suspicion of being a runaway."

The resolution was passed, and the sixty negroes set at liberty. I had the satisfaction of seeing them breathe the fresh air of heaven, never more to be arrested as runaway slaves. It was the first step taken by Congress towards abolishing slavery. A few weeks later a bill was introduced for the emancipation of the slaves in the District of Columbia, which became a law in April, 1862.

There was rejoicing throughout the Northern States. Those who saw that slavery was the cause of the war hailed it as forecasting its doom. John G. Whittier, whose soul was set on fire for freedom thirty years before, wrote of the event :

> "I knew that truth would crush this lie—
> 　Somehow, some time the end would be;
> 　Yet scarcely dared I hope to see
> The triumph with my mortal eye.

> "But now I see it. In the sun
> 　A free flag floats from yonder dome,
> 　And at the Nation's hearth and home
> The justice long delayed is done."

It was a very small matter, seemingly, the pronouncing of the slave who had used a shovel in building a Confederate fort "contraband of war" by General Butler, but its influence was far-reaching. How I happened to go to Washington jail—what set my feet in that direction on the morning of December 2, 1861, I do not know. I had heard that negroes who had committed no crime were there ; that was all. I went, and great results came from it—the immediate liberation of those within its walls, followed by the quick introduction of the bills into the Senate for the emancipation of the slaves in the Territories and the District of Columbia where Congress had jurisdiction.

William Tillman was a negro cook on a schooner, the *S. J. Waring*, of New York. The schooner sailed from that port in June, 1861, just after the battle of Bull Run, for South America. The vessel was off the coast of South Carolina when the Confederate privateer *Jeff Davis* ran alongside, capturing the schooner, taking off all the crew except a German, a Yankee sailor, and the cook, and putting a Confederate captain, mate, and four sailors on board. The Confederate captain put the Yankee sailor in irons and told the German that he must mind the wheel.

"You are to cook for us, and when we get to Charleston I will have you sold," he said to William.

The schooner was headed towards Charleston, and the *Jeff Davis* steered away for other prizes.

William Tillman was a free man, but if the schooner were to reach Charleston he would be sold into slavery. Perhaps he never had heard the song written by Rouquet de Lisle—the Marseillaise of France—

"O Liberty! can man resign thee,
    Once having felt thy glorious flame?"

He felt it, however, and determined to strike a blow to secure his freedom.

Night comes. The white sails are set and the vessel is gliding towards Charleston. William is laying his plans. At midnight he steals softly on deck. The German is at the wheel; the mate has swallowed a glass of grog, and is sitting half asleep on the quarter-deck; the captain has gone to bed, and is sound asleep in the cabin. He goes back, opens the cabin door, swings a club with the strength of a giant, killing the captain at a single stroke. No cry is heard. He feels the pulse till it ceases to beat, creeps on deck, strikes the mate a blow, wounding but not killing him. "Help! help!" the mate cries, drawing his revolver; but before he can use it another blow comes, and he falls dead upon the deck. The four sailors are rushing aft, but are confronted by the negro with the revolver.

"Stop, or I'll shoot every one of you. Go down and take the irons off that man, or I'll kill you every one," he shouts, following them to the hatch. They release the Yankee sailor.

"Now it is your turn," he says to the four; and in a few minutes all of the Confederate sailors are in irons.

"I am captain. About ship!" The German and Yankee shift the sails, and the schooner, which a few moments before was gliding towards Charleston, is heading for New York. A storm comes on; more men are needed. The Confederates are released.

"If you obey orders you will be kindly treated; if not, you will be shot," are the words of Captain Tillman. Five days more, and the schooner, with the Stars and Stripes at the mast-head, sails into New York—William Tillman captain.

Great the wonder. A negro do this! The newspapers told the story. Barnum, the great showman, read it, and hastened on board the schooner. He must have the hero to exhibit in his museum. Crowds come to see the man who devised and executed the plan of recapturing a vessel from the Confederates, and who had exhibited courage and manly qualities as great as that of William Tell or any other hero of history. He had re-captured the vessel, and was entitled to the prize-money—five thousand dollars, which Congress voted him.

It set people in the Northern States, who thought of the negro as a weak and cowardly race, to thinking. What white man had done braver things? What white man had laid a plan more skilfully, or executed it more deliberately? Would not the time come when the slaves would strike a blow for freedom?

"To this colored man," said the *New York Tribune*, "is this nation indebted for the first vindication of its honor on the sea. It is an achieve-ment which alone is an offset to the defeat of the Union troops at Bull Run."

The Confederate privateer, after capturing the *S. J. Waring*, went cruising over the sea, capturing other vessels, among them the *Enchant-ress*, off the shoals of Nantucket. It had left Boston the day before, and was pointing its prow for St. Jago. The cook on the *Enchantress* was a colored man, who alone was kept on board by the captain of the *Jeff Davis*. He, too, was to be sold when the vessel reached Charleston. The privateer went on her cruise, and the *Enchantress*, with a Confederate crew on board, set her sails for that port. There was no chance for the one colored man to strike a blow for liberty such as William Tillman had given. He saw no way of escape. In a few days he would be sold into slavery.

The vessel was near Cape Hatteras. United States blockading vessels were off Hatteras Inlet. The captain of the gunboat *Albatross* saw a ves-sel steering south, and ran alongside. The sea was calm; there was little wind.

"What ship is that?" shouted Captain Prentice of the *Albatross*.

"The *Enchantress*."

"Where are you from?"

"Boston."

"Whither bound?"

"St. Jago."

Captain Prentice, satisfied with the answer, was ready to steer away, when the sailors saw a negro spring up from the hatchway of the *En-*

chantress like a jack-in-a-box, and leap over the taffrail into the sea and swim towards the gunboat.

"They are a privateer crew from the *Jeff Davis*, bound for Charleston," shouted the negro.

"Pick up that man; down with the boats!" was the order of Captain Prentice. Down went the boats.

"Heave to," was his order to the *Enchantress*, and that vessel came round, obedient to the command. The negro told his story, and a few minutes later the Confederate crew were in irons, and the recaptured vessel steering for Hampton Roads.

Going down now to Charleston, we see a blockading fleet, the Confederate flag flying defiantly above Fort Sumter, and a Confederate gunboat, the *Planter*, cruising in the harbor. It is used by General Ripley, commanding at Charleston, as a despatch-boat, going nearly every day down to the fort, and sometimes running past it to take a look at the Union war-ships. She has a 32-pounder pivot-gun and a 24-pounder howitzer.

The pilot of the *Planter* is a colored man, Robert Small. He knows all the shoals, shallows, and channels of the harbor, and all the inlets along the coast. He sees the Union war-ships, and knows that the flag waving at their mast-heads is the emblem of freedom. He believes that the Yankees, of whom he has heard a great deal, are the true friends of his race. While piloting the *Planter* around the harbor and through the intricate passages of the coast, he is turning over a plan which he resolves to put into execution.

Monday night comes, May 12, 1862. The *Planter* lies at her wharf in Charleston. The captain and officers are on shore. The fires are out. Robert is in charge of the vessel. If the police of Charleston had been sharp-eyed they might, perhaps, have seen at midnight several negroes gliding along the streets towards the wharf where the *Planter* was moored, but they did not discover five women and three children, the wives and little ones of the colored crew of the steamer.

For more than six weeks Robert Small has turned over his plan. For three days he has been secreting things in the hold of the vessel. The night is wearing away. It is two o'clock in the morning when one of the firemen strikes a match and sets the kindlings on fire under the boilers. The *Planter* is getting ready for a great day's work. At four o'clock the steam is hissing from the escape-valve.

"Cast off!" It is lowly spoken by Captain Robert Small, self-appointed to command the steamer. The vessel swings, the paddle-wheels plash the water. The flags of South Carolina and of the Confederacy are flying

above the decks.   Down the harbor glides the vessel as on other morn-
ings.   Passing Fort Johnson, Captain Small pulls the cord, and two puffs
of steam escape through the whistle.   It is the customary salute.   Little
does the sentinel, pacing his beat on the parapet of the fort, mistrust that
there has been a change of commanders on the *Planter* during the night;
that the man who stands in the pilot-house with the cord in his hand has
assumed a great natural right, and is about to deal the Confederacy a powerful blow.

On towards Fort Sumter, past it, saluting as on other days, glides the
Planter.   The sentinel on Sumter gazes at her, wondering what the
captain is doing, steering straight down the channel towards the nearest
Union war-ship, the *Onward*.

The sun has not risen.   It is the dim gray of the morning.   There is
a commotion on board all the Union gunboats.   The boatswains pipe their
whistles.   "All hands to quarters!" shouts Captain Parrott, of the gunboat
Augusta.   The cannon are loaded.   "Stand ready there!"

The gunners aim at the advancing vessel, and are ready to open fire,
when suddenly they see the Palmetto and Confederate flags come down
the halyards, and a white flag go up.   The vessel runs alongside the *Augusta*.   Captain Parrott is astonished when Captain Robert Small informs
him of his exploit.   He has brought out a vessel worth twenty thousand
dollars, and presents it to the United States Government, together with
four cannon and a large quantity of ammunition, which was to have been
delivered to the Confederate commander in Fort Ripley.   There are nine
colored men on board who have come over to the side of the Union.

It was a thrilling despatch which Admiral Dupont, commanding the
fleet, sent to Washington announcing the event.   Negroes do this!   The
people read it in amazement.   The newspapers opposed to the war, and
which were declaring it a failure, and had all the while been denouncing
the negroes as a race that could not take care of themselves, did not know
what to make of it.

Congress voted that Robert Small and his crew were entitled to the
prize-money, just the same as if he had been captain and they the crew
of a naval vessel.

We are to remember that the war as begun was for preserving the
Union by maintaining the Government; but the nation was marching
towards freedom.   Three days before Robert Small brought out the
Planter, Major-general Hunter, commanding at Hilton Head, issued a
proclamation.   He said: "Slavery and martial law in a free country
are incompatible.   The persons in these States—Georgia, Florida, and

South Carolina—heretofore held as slaves, are therefore declared to be free."

President Lincoln revoked this order for the same reason that he had revoked General Fremont's. He had sent a message to Congress urging the gradual abolishment of slavery by compensating the masters.

Ralph Waldo Emerson, the thinker, had this to say about it:

> " Pay ransom to the owner,
>   And fill the bag to the brim.
> Who is the owner ? The slave is owner,
>   And ever was. Pay him."

Congress was ready to pay for the slaves, and so were the people of the Northern States, but the conspirators who had brought about the war were fighting to establish a government with slavery for its corner-stone.

In his message to Congress President Lincoln appealed to the Border States—Maryland, Delaware, Kentucky, and Missouri, which had declared for the Union—to emancipate the slaves. "The change," said Mr. Lincoln, "would come as the dews of heaven—not rending or wrecking anything."

The people of the North were slowly coming to the conviction that, to preserve the Union, slavery must be destroyed, and were watching Mr. Lincoln's attitude with great solicitude. Public men, ministers, and religious bodies called at the White House urging him to issue a proclamation abolishing slavery. People in England sent memorials hoping that he would take such action. "If it is done, no foreign nation will dare to espouse the cause of the South. You will have the sympathy of the people of England," they said.

The "Peace Democrats," as they called themselves, men who opposed the war, were loud in their denunciations of any interference with the institution. General McClellan while at Harrison's Landing, forgetting his relations to the President, who was commander-in-chief, wrote a letter to Mr. Lincoln. He said: "Neither confiscation of property, political execution of persons, territorial organization of States, nor forcible abolition of slavery, should be contemplated for a moment. . . . Military power should not be allowed to interfere with the relations of servants. . . . A declaration of radical views, especially upon slavery, will rapidly disintegrate our present armies."

General McClellan was at the head of the army—a subordinate to obey orders, to prosecute the war, but in this letter he was instructing the President of the United States as to what he ought, or ought not, to do in political affairs. It brought quick replies from the newspapers. Horace Greeley, of the *New York Tribune*, Mr. Lincoln's earnest friend, published an open letter to the President, entitled the "Prayer of Twenty Millions," to which President Lincoln replied, August 22, 1862. He said: "My paramount object is to save the Union, and not either to save or destroy slavery. If I could save the Union without freeing a slave, I would do it. If I could save it by freeing all the slaves, I would do it. If I could save it by freeing some and leaving others alone, I would also do that."

The hearts of the people were greatly stirred. They sent the ministers who preached to them to Washington to plead with the President. Slaves were raising corn and wheat for the South. "They are doing the work, while the white men were fighting," said a delegation of ministers from Chicago.

"What good," Mr. Lincoln said to them, "would a proclamation of emancipation do as we are now situated? I do not want to issue a document which the whole world will see must necessarily be like the Pope's bull against the comet. Would my word free the slaves when I cannot even enforce the Constitution?"

There were warm debates in Congress. Senator Crittenden, of Kentucky, had voted against Mr. Lincoln, but had come to honor and respect him. Mr. Crittenden loved the Union. His son Thomas was a major-general in the Union army, his son George a major-general in the Confederate army.

"There is a niche in the temple of fame," he said, "near to Washington, which should be occupied by him who shall save the country. Mr. Lincoln has a mighty destiny. It is for him, if he will, to step into that niche. Mr. Lincoln is no coward. His not doing what the Constitution forbade him to do, and what our institutions forbade him to do, is no proof of cowardice."

Mr. Owen Lovejoy, from Illinois, whose brother had been shot by a pro-slavery mob at Alton, in 1837, was also Mr. Lincoln's earnest friend. Springing to his feet, he said:

"The gentleman from Kentucky says he has a niche for Abraham Lincoln. Where is it?" Mr. Crittenden raised his hand and pointed upward. "He points towards heaven. But should the President follow the counsels of that gentleman, and become the defender and perpetuator of human slavery, he should point downward to some dungeon in the Temple of Moloch, who feeds on human blood, and is surrounded with fires; where are forged manacles and chains for human limbs; in the crypts and recesses of whose temple women are scourged and men tortured. That is a suitable place for the statue of one who would defend and perpetuate human slavery. . . . I, too, have a niche for Abraham Lincoln, but it is in freedom's holy fane, and not in the blood-besmeared temple of human bondage; not surrounded by chains and fetters, but with the symbols of freedom; not dark with bondage, but radiant with the light of liberty. If Abraham Lincoln pursues the path evidently pointed out for him in the Providence of God, as I believe he will, then will he occupy the fond position I have indicated. That is a fame worth living for; ay, worth dying for, though that death led through the blood of Gethsemane and the agony of the accursed tree. That is a fame which has glory and honor and immortality and eternal life. His name shall not only be enrolled in the earthly temple, but it shall be traced on the living stones of the temple which rears itself amidst the thrones and hierarchies of heaven, whose top-stone is to be brought in with shouting of ' Grace, grace unto it.' "

The world did not then know that long before the beginning of this debate in Congress, before Horace Greeley wrote his letter, before the people began to call upon him at the White House with petitions and memorials, President Lincoln had resolved upon his course of action. To intelligently understand his action we must go back over the years to that day when he stood, a flatboatman, in the market in New Orleans, and saw a slave auction, his great and noble soul revolting at the sight. From that moment he hated slavery with all the intensity of his nature. We are not to forget the address on genius which he made in 1837, before a Lyceum in Illinois : " Towering genius disdains a beaten path. It thirsts and burns for distinction, and will seek it by emancipating slaves, or in regions hitherto unexplored."

Through the weary months of the war, while the loyal people thought him dilatory, halting, and almost doubted his sincerity, he was marking out his own course. There were influences that came to him that others did not take into account. He had seen the mighty hosts, with glistening arms, march past the Executive mansion, swinging their hats to him as the representative, the federal head of the great republic of free labor. He had heard their prophetic evangel—

> "John Brown's body lies mouldering in the grave;
> His soul is marching on."

Those whom he had loved best had laid down their lives for the Union. Before the outbreak of the war he had declared that the nation could not exist half slave and half free. On the banks of the Chickahominy were lying in their graves thousands who had saluted him with their cheers. Every newspaper that he opened had some story of service rendered to the army by slaves, or pathetic descriptions of their kindness, their praying for freedom. During the month of June, while the cannon were thundering at Gainesville and Malvern Hill, he was thinking about writing a proclamation of emancipation, and early in July prepared a rough draft. In his own private chamber he asked God to direct him. The proclamation lay in his desk through the month, unseen by any human being. We come to the first week in August. The members of the Cabinet have assembled—specially called. President Lincoln enters with a paper in his hand, but instead of telling the members of the Cabinet what it is, begins to read aloud a funny story from a book written by the humorist "Artemus Ward." He laughs heartily. His spirit has been chafed and worn through the weary days and restless nights by tidings of disaster to the great army on the James, by the aspect of affairs in the West, where Buell is in retreat. For a moment his spirit throws off all care, then the book is tossed aside, and the man who a moment ago was convulsed with laughter, is so grave and serious that the members of this great council of the nation, themselves grave and honorable, gaze in awe upon the dignity and greatness of the wonderful man.

"I have resolved to issue a proclamation of emancipation. I have not called you together for advice in regard to issuing it, but for suggestions in regard to the subject-matter."

He reads, and the members of the Cabinet listen. Mr. Blair objects to saying anything about arming the slaves, because it will repel many Northern people, and affect the result of the approaching elections. Mr. Chase, on the contrary, wishes the language about arming the slaves made much stronger.

"Mr. President," said Secretary Seward, "I approve of the proclamation, but I question the expediency of its issue just now. The depression of the public mind consequent upon our repeated reverses is so great that I fear the effect of so important a step. It may be viewed as the last resource of an exhausted Government—a cry for help—the Government stretching forth its hands to Ethiopia, instead of Ethiopia stretching forth her hands to Government—our last shriek on the retreat. I suggest its postponement until the army wins a victory."

President Lincoln accepts the suggestion. The Cabinet dissolves, the proclamation is laid away, the public does not know that it has been written. General McClellan, thinking that a proclamation may be issued, writes to the President a letter opposing such action. Stonewall Jackson falls upon Pope. Then come the disasters at Manassas, the falling back of the army to Washington like the drift of a wreck upon the shore, and the march of the Confederates into Maryland.

In the silent night Abraham Lincoln is communing with God, uttering a solemn vow that the proclamation giving freedom to the slaves shall be issued the moment a victory has been won.

On Wednesday, September 17th, comes the battle of Antietam. On Friday Lee recrosses the Potomac to Virginia. On Sunday President Lincoln is weighing each word of the great charter of freedom, and on Monday, September 22d, it is issued to the world. Thus it read: "All persons held as slaves on the 1st of January, 1863, in any States, or parts of States, then in rebellion should be then, thenceforth, and forever free."

"It is an invitation to the blacks to murder their masters," wrote the editor of the Boston *Courier*, who opposed the war. The next day the editor said, "The slaves will fight for their masters," which was not quite consistent with what he said the day before.

The newspapers which opposed the war were bitter in their denunciations. "It will destroy the Union," said one. "It is harmless and impotent," wrote another. "The slaves will cut their masters' throats," said a third.

Slave-holders from Kentucky and Maryland who professed to be for the Union hastened to Washington, asking the President to revoke it, but all over the North loyal men rejoiced.

There were many old planters who clung to slavery with a tenacity like that of barnacles to a worm-eaten hulk. The *Louisville Journal* condemned the proclamation, giving utterance to the voice of the slave-holders, declaring that the proclamation would have no binding force in that State; but the soldiers hailed it with joy. They felt that slavery was the cause of the war, and were longing to see it overthrown. General Bragg having left the State, many masters began to look up their slaves, some of whom had fled to the Union lines for protection.

One wing of the army was resting at Williamstown, about twenty-five miles south of Cincinnati, in which was a division commanded by General Q. A. Gillmore. When the army began a forward movement in pursuit of Bragg, General Gillmore issued an order known as General Orders No. 5, which reads as follows: "All contrabands, except officers' servants, will be left behind when the army moves to-morrow morning. Public transportation will in no case be furnished to officers' servants. Commanders of regiments and detachments will see this order promptly enforced."

Among the regiments of the division was the Twenty-second Wisconsin, commanded by Colonel Utley, an officer who had no sympathy with slavery. He had a cool head and a good deal of nerve. He had read the proclamation of President Lincoln, and made up his mind to do what was right, recognizing the President as commander-in-chief, and not the State of Kentucky. He did not turn out negroes accompanying his regiment. Three days later he received the following note:

"COLONEL,—You will at once send to my headquarters the four contrabands—John, Abe, George, and Dick—known to belong to good and loyal citizens. They are in your regiment, or were this morning.   Your obedient servant,
"Q. A. GILLMORE, Brigadier-general."

Colonel Utley, instead of sending the men, replied:

"Permit me to say that I recognize your authority to command me in all military matters pertaining to the military movements of the army. I do not look upon this as belonging to that department. I recognize no authority on the subject of delivering up contrabands, save that of the President of the United States.

"You are, no doubt, conversant with that proclamation, dated September 22, 1862, and the law of Congress on the subject. In conclusion, I will say that I had nothing to do with their coming into camp, and shall have nothing to do with sending them out."

The note was despatched to division headquarters. Soon after an officer called upon Colonel Utley, who, when the war began, was editor of a newspaper in Wisconsin, a man of convictions, and ever ready to stand by them, no matter what it might cost. His regiment was known as the "abolition" regiment.

"You are wanted, sir, at General Gillmore's quarters."

Colonel Utley made his appearance before General Gillmore.

"I sent you an order this evening."

"Yes, sir, and I refused to obey it."

"I intend to be obeyed, sir. I shall settle this matter at once. I shall repeat the order in the morning."

"General, to save you the trouble, let me say that I shall not obey it."

The colonel departed. Morning came, but brought no order for the delivery of the contrabands to their former owners.

The regiment marched the next morning with loaded muskets. The citizens beheld their negroes sheltered and protected by a forest of gleaming bayonets, and concluded not to attempt the recovery of the uncertain property.

While the regiment was near Lexington a negro came into the brigade. The colonels of three regiments would not permit him to remain in their camps, but the soldiers of Company A in the Twenty-second Wisconsin gave him food and shelter. He told a tale of brutality that stirred their blood. He had been half-starved, whipped, and pounded. He knew by instinct that the South was fighting to keep him in slavery, that the North was fighting for freedom.

The day after the arrival of the regiment at Nicholasville a large, portly gentleman, lying back in an elegant carriage, rode up to the camp, and making his appearance before the colonel, introduced himself as Judge Robertson.

"I am in pursuit of one of my boys, who, I understand, is in this regiment," he said.

"You mean one of your slaves, I presume?"

"Yes, sir. Here is an order from the general, which you will see directs that I may be permitted to enter the lines and get the boy," said the judge, with great dignity.

"I do not permit any civilians to enter my lines for any such purpose," said the colonel.

The judge sat down, not greatly astonished, for the reputation of the Twenty-second Wisconsin as an abolition regiment was well established. He began to argue the matter. He talked of the compromises of the Constitution, and proceeded to say: "I was in Congress, sir, when the Missouri Compromise was adopted, and voted for it; but I am opposed to slavery, and I once wrote an essay on the subject, favoring emancipation."

"Well, sir, that may all be so. If you did it from principle, it was commendable; but your mission here to-day gives the lie to your professions. I don't permit negro-hunters to go through my regiment; but I will see if I can find the boy, and if he is willing to go I will not hinder him."

The colonel went out and found the negro, Joe, a poor, half-starved, under-sized boy, nineteen years old. He told his story. He belonged to the judge, who had let him to a brutal Irishman for fifty dollars a year. He had been kicked and cuffed, starved and whipped, till he could stand it no longer. He went to the judge and complained, but had been sent back, only to receive a worse thrashing for daring to complain. At last he took to the woods, lived on walnuts, green corn, and apples, sleeping among the corn-shucks and wheat-stacks, till the army came. There were tears in Joe's eyes as he rehearsed his sufferings.

The colonel went back to the judge.

"Have you found him?"

"I have found a little yellow boy, who says that he belongs to a man in Lexington. Come and see him."

"This man claims you as his property, Joe. He says that you ran away and left him," said the colonel.

"Yes, sah, I belongs to him," said Joe, who told his story again in a plain, straightforward manner, showing a neck scarred and cut by the whip.

"You can talk with Joe, sir, if you wish," said the colonel.

"Have not I always treated you well?" the judge asked.

"No, massa, you hasn't," was the plump reply.

"How so?"

"When I came to you and told you I couldn't stand it any longer, you said, 'Go back, you dog!'"

"Did not I tell you that I would take you away?"

"Yes, but you never did it."

The soldiers came round and listened. Joe saw that they were his friends. The judge stood speechless a moment.

"Joe," said the colonel, "are you willing to go home with your master?"

"No, sah, I isn't."

"Judge Robertson, I don't think you can get that boy. If you think you can, there he is; try it. I shall have nothing to do with it," said the colonel, casting a significant glance at the soldiers.

The judge saw that he could not lay hands on Joe. "I'll see whether there is any virtue in the laws of Kentucky," he said, with great emphasis.

"Perhaps, judge, it will be as well for you to leave the camp. Some of my men are a little excitable on the subject of slavery."

"You are a set of nigger-stealers," said the judge, losing his temper.

"Allow me to say, judge, that it does not become you to call us nigger-stealers. You talk about nigger-stealing—you who live on the sweat and blood of such creatures as Joe! Your dwellings, your churches are built from the earnings of slaves, beaten out of them by brutal overseers. You hire little children out to brutes; you clothe them in rags; you hunt them with hounds; you chain them down to toil and suffering! You call us thieves because we have given Joe food and protection! I would rather be in the place of Joe than in that of his oppressor!" was the indignant outburst of the colonel.

"Well, sir, if that is the way you men of the North feel, the Union never can be saved—never! You must give up our property. The President's proclamation is unconstitutional. It has no bearing on Kentucky. I see that it is your deliberate intention to set at naught the laws," said the judge, turning away, and walking to General Gillmore's headquarters.

"You are wanted at the general's headquarters," said an aide soon after to Colonel Utley.

The colonel obeyed the summons, and found there not only Judge Robertson, but several other gentlemen; also Colonel Coburn, the commander of the brigade, who agreed with General Gillmore in the policy then current.

Colonel Coburn said, "The policy of the commanding generals, as I understand it, is simply this: that persons who have lost slaves have a right to hunt for them anywhere in the State. If a slave gets inside of the lines of a regiment, the owner has a right to enter those lines, just as if no regiment were there, and take away the fugitive at his own pleasure."

"Precisely so. The proclamation has no force in this State," said the judge.

"I regret that I am under the necessity of differing in opinion from my commanding officers, to whom I am ready at all times to render strict military obedience; but" (the colonel raised his voice) "*I reverse the Kentucky policy!* I hold that the regiment stands precisely as though there were no slavery in Kentucky. We came here as free men, from a free State, at the call of the President to uphold a free government. We have nothing to do with slavery. The Twenty-second Wisconsin, while I have the honor to command it, will never be a regiment of nigger-catchers. I will not allow civilians to enter my lines at pleasure; it is unmilitary. Were I to permit it, I should be justly amenable to a court-martial. Were I to do it, spies might enter my lines at all times and depart at pleasure."

There was silence. But Judge Robertson was loath to go away without Joe. He made one more effort.

"Colonel, I did not come to your lines as a spy, but with an order from your general. Are you willing that I should go and get my boy?"

The colonel reflected a moment.

"Yes, sir; and I will remain here. I told you before that I should have nothing to do with it."

"Do you think that the men will permit me to take him?"

"I have no orders to issue to them in the matter; they will do just as they please."

"Will you send the boy into some other regiment?"

This was too much for the colonel. He could no longer restrain his indignation. Looking the judge squarely in the face, he vented his anger in scathing words.

The judge departed, and at the next session of the court Colonel Utley was indicted for man-stealing. A quarter of a century has passed since then, but he has not yet been brought to trial, and the case is postponed forever.

The judge returned to Lexington, called a public meeting, at which he made a speech denouncing the Twenty-second Wisconsin as an abolition regiment, and introducing resolutions declaring that the Union never could be restored if the laws of the State of Kentucky were thus set at defiance. This from the judge, while his son was in the Confederate service fighting against the Union!

But the matter was not yet over. A few days later the division containing the Twenty-second Wisconsin, commanded now by General Baird, was ordered down the river. It went to Louisville, followed by the slave-masters, who were determined to have their negroes.

A citizen called upon Colonel Utley, and said, "Colonel, you will have trouble in going through the city unless you give up the negroes in your lines." The regiment was then on its march to the wharf. "They have taken all the negroes from the ranks of the other regiments, and they intend to take yours."

The colonel turned to his men, and said, quietly, "Fix bayonets!"

The regiment moved on through the streets and reached the Gault House, where the slave-holders had congregated. A half-dozen approached; one, bolder than the rest, sprang into the ranks and seized a negro by the collar.

A dozen bayonets came down around him. He let go his hold and sprang back again as quickly as he had entered the lines. There was a shaking of fists and loud curses, but the regiment passed on to the landing just as if nothing had happened.

General Granger, who had charge of the transportation, had issued orders that no negro should be allowed on the boats without free papers.

General Baird saw the negroes on the steamer, and approaching Colonel Utley, said, "Why, colonel, how is this? Have all of these negroes free papers?"

"Perhaps not all, but those who haven't have declared their intentions!" said the colonel.

The Twenty-second took transportation on the steamer *Commercial*. The captain of the boat was a Kentuckian, who came in great trepidation, saying, "Colonel, I can't start till those negroes are put on shore. I shall be held responsible. My boat will be seized and libelled under the laws of the State."

"I can't help that, sir; the boat is under the control and in the employ of the United States Government. I am commander on board, and you have nothing to do but to steam up and go where you are directed. Otherwise I shall be under the necessity of arresting you."

The captain departed, and began his preparations. But now came the sheriff of Jefferson County with a writ. He wanted the bodies of George, Abraham, John, and Dick, who were with the Twenty-second Wisconsin. They were the runaway property of a fellow named Hogan, who a few days before had figured in a convention held at Frankfort in which he introduced a series of secession resolutions.

" I have a writ for your arrest, but I am willing to waive all action on condition of your giving up the fugitives which you are harboring contrary to the peace and dignity of the State," said the sheriff.

" I have other business to attend to just now. I am under orders from my superiors in command to proceed down the river without any delay, and must get the boat under way," said the colonel, bowing politely.

" But, colonel, you are aware of the consequences of deliberately setting at defiance the laws of a sovereign State?" said the sheriff.

" Are you ready there?" shouted the colonel to the officer in charge of shipping the quartermaster and commissary supplies.

" Yes, sir."

" Then cast off!"

The warp which held the *Commercial* was thrown loose, the swiftly running current sweeping under the keel lifted the bow, and the boat began to swing from the shore.

The game was finished. Colonel Utley and the Twenty-second Wisconsin had won. If the sheriff had not leaped on shore he would have been compelled to take a trip down the Ohio against his will.

Judge Robertson had lost his slave, but the courts were open to him, and he brought suit against Colonel Utley and obtained judgment, attaching the property of the colonel and compelling him to pay for the abduction of the slave.

Revolutions never go backward. The conflict of ideas was sweeping the nation to a higher and loftier appreciation of the meaning of this government of the people. The past, the old system, the conception that the Government was for white men alone, was giving place to the idea that every man, irrespective of race, lineage, color, or condition, was entitled to equality before the law. Men who had learned their lessons in the public-schools were thinking for themselves upon the great questions which underlie a government of a free people. In the great conflict of ideas free thought, free speech, free action were to win the victory.

25

CHAPTER XVI.

FREDERICKSBURG.

IT was an orderly and well-managed retreat which General Lee made from the battle-field of Antietam across the Potomac to the vicinity of Winchester. General McClellan was satisfied with what he had accomplished. He had driven Lee out of Maryland. Two days after the battle he wrote: "Our victory is complete, and the disorganized rebel army has rapidly returned to Virginia, its dream of invading Pennsylvania dissipated forever. I feel some little pride in having, with a beaten and demoralized army, defeated Lee and saved the North."

The people of the Northern States rejoiced that Lee had been defeated at Antietam, but when they read the accounts of the battle they saw that McClellan had missed the chance of utterly crushing the Confederate army. For the future McClellan proposed to remain in the vicinity of Harper's Ferry, and rest, recruit, and reclothe the army. This his plan on September 27th: "My present purpose is to hold the army about as it is now, rendering Harper's Ferry secure, and watching the river closely, intending to attack the enemy should he attempt to cross to this side. . . . In the last battles the enemy was undoubtedly greatly superior to us in number, and it was only by very hard fighting that we gained the advantage we did."

He still believed that the Confederates greatly outnumbered the Union troops, and called for reinforcements.

On October 1st President Lincoln visited the army. General McClellan thus writes in regard to the visit: "His ostensible purpose is to see the troops and the battle-field; I incline to think that the real purpose of his visit is to push me into a premature advance into Virginia. I may be mistaken, but I think not. The real truth is that my army is not fit to advance. The old regiments are reduced to mere skeletons, and are completely tired out. They need rest and filling up. The new regiments are not fit for the field."

General McClellan did not like the Proclamation of Emancipation.

EXCHANGING RAGS FOR U. S. ARMY CLOTHING.

His friend Mr. Aspinwall came to see him. He writes this relative to his coming: " Mr. Aspinwall is decidedly of the opinion that it is my duty to submit to the President's proclamation, and quietly continue to do my duty as a soldier."

Finding that General McClellan had no plan, President Lincoln, upon his return to Washington, instructed General Halleck to direct him to " cross the Potomac and give battle to the enemy or drive him south. Your army must move now while the roads are good. If you cross the river between the enemy and Washington, and cover the latter by your operation, you can be reinforced by thirty thousand men. If you move up the valley of the Shenandoah, not more than twelve or fifteen thousand can be sent you." Though thus directed, the army did not move.

General J. E. B. Stuart, commanding the Confederate cavalry, was a very able officer. When McClellan was on the Chickahominy he had ridden round the Union army, destroying a railroad train, burning a large amount of supplies. He obtained permission from General Lee to make a very bold and hazardous movement into Pennsylvania. He knew that there was a large amount of clothing and supplies at Chambersburg. He is at Charlestown, his brigades encamped on Mr. Dandridge's farm. He selects eighteen hundred of his best men, and Major Pelham with four cannon. At daylight on the morning of October 10th he crosses the Potomac at McCoy's Ferry. A fog conceals his movements. General Kenly is at Williamsport with a brigade of Union infantry. A messenger informs him at seven o'clock of what Stuart is doing, but Kenly has no cavalry, and Stuart hastens on to Mercersburg, seizing what boots and clothing they can find in that town. Nothing is taken in Maryland, but once in Pennsylvania, the soldiers seize all the horses they can find. General Stuart has issued strict orders against plundering. Were he to permit it, his troops would soon be demoralized and beyond control. On the evening of the 10th the people of Chambersburg are surprised to see a company of Confederates dash into the town, rush to the buildings where the supplies for McClellan's army are stored, and exchange their worn-out suits of gray for the bright-blue clothing worn by the soldiers of the Union. They drink for the first time in many months delicious coffee. A few help themselves to private property, but are instantly arrested and punished by Stuart.

At daylight Stuart is moving south-east towards Gettysburg, setting the railroad buildings on fire as he leaves the town. Rain is falling in torrents, but he cannot wait for clearing skies. He knows that every effort will be made to prevent his return. No walking of horses now, but

25*

there must be hard riding. Horses break down, but the riders help themselves to others at the first farm. At sunset on the 11th Stuart is at Emmettsburg, in Maryland. The sympathies of the people in that town are with the South, and they welcome him with open arms. He cannot stay to enjoy their hospitality, but through the night the column moves on, avoiding Frederick, where there is a Union force, reaching the Potomac at the mouth of the Monocacy, and escaping to the Virginia shore just as two bodies of Union troops were closing upon him. The Union cavalry sent to cut him off, by false information had gone west, when it should have gone east, and had lost so much time in retracing its steps that Stuart escaped, losing only three men, carrying twelve hundred horses into Virginia, besides destroying the supplies at Chambersburg. It was mortifying to General McClellan and irritating to the people of the North. New regiments had been sent him, and the army on October 20th numbered one hundred and sixteen thousand. We now know that Lee's army numbered about sixty thousand, though General McClellan believed it to be as large as his own.

The President wrote a letter to General McClellan. Thus it read:

"You say that you cannot subsist your army at Winchester unless the railroad from Harper's Ferry to that point is in working order; but the enemy subsists his army at Winchester at a distance nearly twice as far from railroad transportation as you would have to do. He wagons his supplies from Culpeper Court-house. You dread his going into Pennsylvania, but if he does so in full force he gives up his communications to you absolutely, and you have nothing to do but to follow and ruin him. If he does so with less than full force, fall upon him and beat what is left behind.

"If he should move northward, I would follow him closely. If he should move towards Richmond, I would press closely to him, if a favorable opportunity should present, and at least try to beat him to Richmond on the inside track. We must beat him somewhere. If we cannot beat him where he now is, we never can, he being again within the intrenchments of Richmond."

On October 26th three pontoon-bridges were laid across the Potomac, and the army began to cross, but not until November 2d was the whole body of troops on the other side. Fifteen thousand men were left to guard Harper's Ferry, but twenty thousand were sent out from Washington to join McClellan. The roads were in excellent condition, the days delightful, the army in good spirits.

General Lee knew all that was going on, and when the army began to move south along the base of the Blue Ridge, Longstreet's corps passed through one of the gaps and took position at Culpeper, leaving Jackson's corps in the valley.

There were engagements between the cavalry of the two armies.

BURNING ENGINE-HOUSE AT CHAMBERSBURG.

Stuart was covering the falling back of Longstreet. There was a sharp fight at the little town of Markham; another at Barbee's Cross-roads, in which the Confederates were driven. The Union cavalry for the first time had been organized in brigades, and was doing effective work.

This was General McClellan's plan: "It was my intention if, upon reaching Ashby's or any other pass, I found that the enemy were in force between it and the Potomac, in the Valley of the Shenandoah, to move into the Valley and endeavor to gain their rear. I hardly hoped to accomplish this, but did expect that by striking in between Culpeper Court-house and Little Washington I could either separate their army and beat them in detail or else force them to concentrate as far back as Gordonsville, and thus place the Army of the Potomac in position either to adopt the Fredericksburg line of advance upon Richmond or to be removed to the Peninsula if, as I apprehended, it were found impossible to supply it by the Orange and Alexandria Railroad beyond Culpeper."

It was not a very definite plan. It looked once more towards a removal of the army to the Peninsula.

General McClellan was sitting in his tent at eleven o'clock in the evening, November 7th. Two officers entered — General Buckingham, bringing a letter from Washington, and General Burnside. General McClellan opened the letter and read:

"By direction of the President of the United States, it is ordered that Major-general McClellan be removed from the command of the Army of the Potomac, and that Major-general Burnside take command of the army.

"By order of the Secretary of War."

General Burnside did not wish to be commander-in-chief. He felt that he was not competent to command an army numbering one hundred and twenty-seven thousand. Twice he had refused the offered command, and accepted it only because he felt it to be his duty.

He reorganized the army, creating three grand divisions. The right wing was commanded by General Sumner, and included the Second Corps, commanded by Couch, and the Ninth, by Wilcox. The left wing was commanded by General Franklin, and included the First Corps, under Reynolds, and the Sixth, under General Smith. The centre was commanded by General Hooker, and included the Third Corps, under Sickles, and the Fifth, under Butterfield. General Burnside thought that it would be easier to handle the army by such an organization. At Antietam, when he was making his attack, he called upon General Porter for help, but Porter could not assist him without orders from McClellan; but under this arrangement a grand division commander could always have two corps at his disposal.

General Burnside determined to make a rapid march south-east along the north bank of the Rappahannock to Fredericksburg, cross the river and move on towards Richmond, establishing a new base of supplies at Acquia Creek, on the Potomac.

Why not attack where he was? General Halleck visited the army and endeavored to persuade Burnside to attack Lee at Gordonsville. They had long consultations. Halleck returned to Washington and laid the matter before President Lincoln, who assented to what Burnside proposed. It was to make Lee believe that he was going to attack him at Gordonsville, at the same time make a rapid march with Sumner's grand division down the north bank of the Rappahannock to Fredericksburg, and cross the Rappahannock on pontoons which General Halleck agreed to have there.

At eleven o'clock on the morning of November 14th General Burnside issued his orders for the right wing, under Sumner, to move at daylight the next morning. A strong party of pioneers with axes started in advance to cut bushes from the path. On Monday afternoon the troops were on the Falmouth Hills overlooking Fredericksburg; the other grand divisions followed.

The Confederate force in Fredericksburg consisted of the Fifteenth Virginia Cavalry, four companies of Mississippi infantry, and Lewis's battery — only six or seven hundred — who were surprised to see the men in blue swarming upon the opposite side of the river. Captain Lewis, of the Confederate artillery, wheeled his battery into position and sent a shell which struck a wheel of one of Captain Pettit's cannon, who the next moment opened fire with his ten-pounder Parrott guns, firing with such sure aim that the Confederate gunners drew off their pieces.

General Lee, in his report of operations, states that Sumner "was driven back by Colonel Ball with the Fifteenth Virginia Cavalry, four companies of Mississippi infantry, and Lewis's light battery." There was no driving back, for General Sumner made no attempt to cross. There was no fighting, except the brief cannonade and the retirement of the Confederate battery.

The pontoons had not arrived; the railroad to Acquia Creek had not been repaired; the part which General Halleck had promised to see to had not been done. While the troops are standing there they see a herd of cattle feeding in the pastures along the south bank of the Rappahannock, just above the town. A steer goes down to drink, steps into the stream, keeps wading till it reaches the Falmouth side.

Colonel Brooks, commanding a brigade, sees how high on the animal's side the hair is wet, and that the water is only three and a half feet deep. A messenger rides from Sumner with a letter to Burnside, asking permission to cross and seize the hills on Mr. Taylor's farm, north of the city.

"Wait till I come," is Burnside's reply. Burnside arrived and looked over the ground. Sumner had forty thousand men, which he could cross at once.

"The risk is too great; wait for the pontoons," he said.

Before morning Sumner's whole corps could have been securely intrenched on the hills opposite. In a few hours the partly destroyed railroad bridge could have been repaired. The rest of the army was close at hand. It would have been easy for the other corps to have crossed.

The next day the Confederates—McLaws's and Ransom's divisions—arrived, seizing the hills on Mr. Taylor's and Marye's farms, throwing up intrenchments and planting their cannon.

Perhaps it will never be known who was responsible for the delay of the pontoons, which did not leave Washington till November 19th, three days after Sumner's arrival, and which did not reach Burnside till the 25th. A great mistake had been made in Washington by somebody—a fact which we must keep in mind in judging of General Burnside's plans, movements, and failure. Twelve more days pass, the army reposing the while on the Falmouth and Stafford hills, over which General Washington rode in his boyhood.

The whole of General Lee's army was encamped on the hills behind Fredericksburg. Standing on the Falmouth side, I could see white tents in the distance. At night there was the glow of innumerable camp-fires. Morning, noon, and night I could hear the bugle-call of the cavalry and artillery, and the rataplan of the drum and the rumbling of wagons. There were but few people remaining in the town. The Confederate pickets patrolled the southern bank of the stream; the Union the northern.

"When are you going to Richmond?" asked the Confederate.

"We'll let you know by-and-by," was the answer.

What should General Burnside do? On the Upper Rappahannock he had been confronted by only two-thirds of Lee's army; now the whole Confederate force was on the hills before him. Every day the intrenchments were becoming stronger, and the Confederate batteries were all in position. On the Upper Rappahannock no pontoons were needed, but here they must be laid under a heavy fire. The Army of the Potomac had marched directly away from the Confederate army, opened a new base of supplies, expecting to take up its march towards Richmond;

but the Confederate army, behind unassailable intrenchments, blocked the
way. Burnside thought of making a second move down the river towards
Belle Plain, lay the pontoons there, and cross; but somehow General Lee
knew all about it, and sent D. H. Hill's division to occupy the ground
opposite the place selected for crossing. Winter had come; the river was
rising. That plan would not do. The army must not, however, go into
winter-quarters. The Northern people wanted to hear that Richmond
had been captured. From the beginning of the war the cry had been,
"On to Richmond!"

On the 10th of December General Burnside called his officers together
and laid his plan before them. It was to plant all the heavy artillery
along the hills (nearly one hundred and fifty guns), lay pontoons in five
places, and cross the army at night. Franklin's grand division was to
attack on the left; Sumner's on the right.

Soon after dark on the night of the 10th the Engineer Brigade, with
the pontoons on wheels, came down from the Stafford hills. Two bridges
were to be laid near the railroad; two more a third of a mile down the
stream, opposite the lower end of the town; two more a mile and a half
farther down, almost to Mr. Burnard's house. Sumner and Hooker were
to use those opposite the town, and Franklin those near Burnard's. The
engineers took the boats from the wagons, anchored them in the stream,
and commenced laying the timbers and planks. A dense fog hung
over the river, which concealed their operations, and before daybreak the
bridges were half completed. The Seventeenth and Eighteenth Mississippi, of Barksdale's brigade, and the Eighth Florida, of Perry's brigade,
were on picket along the river, while the Thirteenth and Twenty-first
Mississippi and Third Georgia were in reserve in the town. The Confederate sentinels walked the bank through the long night, peering into the
darkness, and listening to catch the meaning of the confused hum which
floated to them across the stream.

At five o'clock in the morning two signal-guns were fired on the
heights of Fredericksburg, rousing the troops of both armies. As the day
dawned there came a rattling of musketry along the river. Barksdale's
pickets opened fire. The gunners at the batteries were quick to respond,
and sent grape and canister across the stream. The Confederate pickets
opposite the lower pontoons soon disappeared, and the engineers completed their work. But in the town the Mississippians took shelter in
the buildings, and poured a deadly fire upon the bridge-builders. Almost
every man who attempted to carry out a plank fell, and the work came to
a stand-still.

"The bridge must be completed," said General Burnside.

Once more the engineers attempted it. The fog still hung over the river. Those who stood on the northern bank could only see the flashes on the other shore. The artillerymen were obliged to fire at random, but so effective their cannonade that the engineers were able to carry the bridge within eighty or ninety feet of the shore; and then so deadly was the fire of the Confederates that it was murder to send men out with a plank.

General Burnside stood on the piazza of the Philips' house, a mile from the pontoons, with Sumner and Hooker. Aides and couriers came and went with messages and orders.

"My bridge is completed, and I am ready to cross," was Franklin's message at half-past nine.

"You must wait till the upper bridge is ready," was the reply.

Two hours passed. A half-dozen attempts were made to complete the upper bridge, but it could not be done. Brave men, not belonging to the engineers, came down to the bank, surveyed the scene, and then, volunteering their services, seized a plank, ran out, but only to fall before the sharp-shooters concealed in the cellars of the houses not ten rods distant. Captain Brainard, of the Fiftieth New York, with eleven men, volunteered to finish the nearly completed work. They went out upon the run. Five fell at one volley and the rest returned. Captain Perkins led another party himself, and fell with a ghastly wound, while half of his men were killed or wounded. These were sacrifices of life with nothing gained.

The forenoon wore away. It was past one o'clock. General Burnside sent for General Woodbury, commanding the engineers, and for General Hunt, commanding the artillery, and talked over the situation.

"It is impossible to complete the bridge. It is murder to send men out to be shot down by the Confederates concealed in the cellars of the houses and firing from the windows," said General Woodbury.

By the code of war it would be allowable for Burnside to bombard the town, although there were women and children and non-combatants in the houses. He gave the order, and then one hundred and forty-seven cannon rained shot and shell upon the city. Nearly nine thousand missiles were fired. The air became thick with powder-clouds; the earth shook beneath the cannonade. The shells set fire to a block of buildings, and a dark column of smoke rose heavenward.

Few persons were injured, however, and the Mississippians were still in the cellars, ready to fire upon the bridge-builders. The first man who went out with a plank fell headlong into the water. One thing was plain

—the Mississippians must be driven from their hiding-places before the work could go on. A force must be sent over in the boats, charge up the bank, and drive them from the houses. It would be a hazardous undertaking.

"Who will go?" Colonel N. A. Hall, who was a lieutenant in Fort Sumter when Beauregard opened fire upon it, but now commanding a brigade, asks the question. He is colonel of the Seventh Michigan, one of the regiments of his brigade. The other regiments are the Nineteenth and Twentieth Massachusetts and Forty-second New York. They have fought at Fair Oaks, Savage's Station, Glendale, Malvern, and Antietam. The blood of Colonel Hall's own soldiers is up.

"We will go!" they shout.

The fog has floated away, the air is clear. The Mississippians are sending their bullets across the stream, but at a signal the men of the Seventh Michigan go down the northern bank upon the run, lift the boats from the wagons, push them into the river, and leap in. The paddles dip the water; the men are a fair mark for the enemy. One by one they drop, but on they go, faster and faster, towards the southern shore. The boats ground; the soldiers leap into the water and form under the shelter of the bank.

The boats recross the river, take on board portions of the Nineteenth and Twentieth Massachusetts, who join the Seventh Michigan. Together they charge up the bank, rush upon the houses, batter down the doors, driving out or taking prisoners the Confederates within.

> "They leaped into the rocking shallop;
>   Ten offered where one could go;
> And the breeze was alive with laughter
>   Till the boatmen began to row.
>
> "Then the shore where the rebels harbored
>   Was fringed with a gush of flame,
> And buzzing like bees o'er the water
>   The swarm of their bullets came.
>
> "But yet the boats moved onward—
>   Through fire and lead they drove,
> With the dark, still mass within them,
>   And the floating stars above.
>
> "Cheer after cheer we sent them,
>   As only armies can—
> Cheers for old Massachusetts,
>   Cheers for young Michigan.

"They formed in line of battle,
  Not a man was out of place:
Then with levelled steel they hurled them
  Straight in the rebels' face."

History furnishes but few records of more daring exploits than this. In fifteen minutes they cleared the houses in front of them, and took more prisoners than their party numbered!

It was half-past four in the afternoon—one of the shortest days of the

ATTACK ON FREDERICKSBURG.—THE FORLORN HOPE SCALING THE HILL.

year. The sun had disappeared in a dull gray bank of clouds ; darkness was coming on. Quickly, now, the bridge-builders finished their work, and the other regiments of Hall's brigade crossed, filed right and left, followed by Owens's brigade.

The Confederate batteries through the afternoon had been silent, but now from Taylor's Hill, north-west of the town, came solid shot and shell aimed at the bridge. The band of the One Hundred and Twenty-ninth Pennsylvania, standing on the north bank, began to play to cheer the men while crossing, but there was a sudden stop to the music not put down in the score when a shell burst close by them.

General Howard, commanding the division, formed his men on the southern shore—Hall's brigade on the right, Owens's on the left, and Sulley's in reserve by the river. The fighting was to take place in the streets. The Confederates could choose their positions. They knew every hiding-place whence they could fire and not be seen.

I stood on the river-bank and beheld through the gloaming the deployment of the troops. First in the fight was the Massachusetts Twentieth advancing up a street, receiving a fearful volley from the Mississippians, losing in a few moments nineteen killed and eighty-one wounded. I could see single flashes from doors and windows where the Confederate sharp-shooters had secreted themselves, and then sheets of flame from the men in blue in the streets. Captain Macy was directed to clear the street leading straight up from the river. The soldiers advanced, but the head of the column melted quickly away. Platoon after platoon went down. Ninety-seven officers and men were killed or wounded in the distance of one hundred and fifty feet. Though so many fell, the column did not falter, but with loud cheers rushed on, driving the Confederates from the houses.

The skirmishers rushed up a side street, gained the flank of the Confederates, and captured nearly one hundred prisoners.

"Old man," said one of the prisoners to Colonel Moorhead, commanding the One Hundred and Sixth Pennsylvania, "you are safe. I have tried four times to hit you, but somehow didn't do it."

Owens's brigade received a pattering fire from the sharp-shooters in the churches, but his men, sheltering themselves in door-ways, watched the flashes, and gave answering shots.

One of the men killed was Rev. Arthur B. Fuller, chaplain of the Sixteenth Massachusetts. He had rendered faithful service through the Peninsular campaign, working hard in the hospital day and night till his health had given way. He had been honorably discharged the day before, but knowing there was to be a battle had waited; so intense his patriotism he could not leave. He took a musket, became a volunteer, and joined the regiment as a soldier.

"I must do something for my country. Where shall I go?" he said to Captain Dunn.

"Now is a good time for you, if you wish to fight. Fall in on the left," was the reply.

The bullets were flying thick and fast. He exposed himself needlessly, standing in the middle of the street, and fell dead.

Gradually the flashes ceased, and the quick, sharp rattle of musketry became like the last drops of a summer shower.

Barksdale withdrew his troops to the outskirts of the town. They had made a determined resistance. At the next pontoon below the Confederates had prevented its construction. Burnside ordered Colonel Hawkins, commanding a brigade, to send over men in boats. Four boats were launched, and one hundred men of the Eighty-ninth New York crossed, captured sixty prisoners, and held the ground till reinforced.

In one of the warehouses was a quantity of tobacco. When the Confederates saw that the town was likely to be captured they threw it into the streets; but the Union soldiers quickly gathered it up, smoked their pipes round the camp-fires, and rehearsed the events of the day.

There were stringent orders against plundering; but as the Confederates had fired upon the advancing columns, and as Burnside had bombarded the town, the soldiers reasoned that the command was inoperative, and so appropriated to their own use whatever pleased their fancy. They cooked bacon and eggs, made hot cakes in the kitchens, eating them with sugar and molasses. They carried mattresses and beds into the streets, spreading them upon the sidewalks for a luxurious night's repose; dressed themselves in old-fashioned, antiquated clothes, danced and sang, and played upon the pianos. I saw a soldier throw away his cap and put on a tall hat, taking his place in the ranks, his comrades making fun of him for wearing a "stove-pipe" hat.

Those who laid themselves down to sleep upon the mattresses and carpeting were soon compelled to give them up to the surgeon for the use of the wounded. Only the buildings nearest the river were entered. As the army had scrupulously regarded the order against plundering up to this hour, it is probable that the houses would not have been ransacked had they not been used for concealment by the Mississippi sharp-shooters. From that hour on to the close of the war the soldiers paid little heed to orders against appropriating private property for their comfort.

26

Let us cross the Rappahannock at the village of Falmouth, above Fredericksburg, and view the position of the Confederates. Opposite the village we see a canal winding along the base of Stansbury's Hill, and carrying water to a grist-mill in the town.

Beyond Mr. Stansbury's house we see Mr. Taylor's house on another hill, and beyond that the house of Mr. Marye. Between Taylor's and Marye's is the plank-road leading from Hanover Street in the town westward to Orange Court-house. A sunken road runs along the base of the hill, with bank-walls on both sides. A brigade of men can lie there and find sure protection. Following this we come to another called the Telegraph Road, which crosses Hazel Run and leads to Spottsylvania.

General Longstreet's corps occupied the ground from the Rappahannock to Hazel Run. He had forty cannon on Taylor's Hill to sweep the fields behind the town with an enfilading fire, and fifteen guns to send a plunging fire straight down upon the fields. Out on Lee's Hill, to the right of Marye's, were thirty guns, to sweep a deep cut in the unfinished railroad winding up Hazel Run. The cannon were all behind breastworks which slaves had constructed during the three weeks that Burnside waited.

"I have one gun that I cannot find a place for," said Captain Alexander of the Confederate engineers, who had the placing of the cannon in charge.

"Put it in somewhere," said Longstreet.

"Why, general, you cannot comb your head with a fine-tooth comb any cleaner than I can rake the field with the artillery," Captain Alexander replied.

Nearly two miles below Fredericksburg, near the river, stood a large and stately mansion, surrounded by a beautiful grove—the house of Mr. Alfred Burnard. The Englishmen who settled in Virginia were fond of giving pleasant names to their estates. This one was known as Mansfield, which General Franklin used as his headquarters. Mr. Burnard was a slave-holder, and the cabins of his negroes stood across the field south of his house.

Going past the cabins, we cross a level field to the Bowling Green Road, lined with dark-green cedars. Looking south-east, we see a large house in the distance, the residence of Mr. Hamilton. The railroad leading to Richmond makes a curve just before reaching Hamilton's, rounding the foot of a wooded hill. Were we to go down a little beyond Hamilton's we should come to the river Massaponax. This wooded point of land is the right of the Confederate line held by Jackson's corps, extend-

BURNARD'S HOUSE, FREDERICKSBURG.

ing along the ridge to Hazel Run, which has its rise up in the ravines among the hills.

General Lee knew that Burnside must attack one or both of his flanks, and had cut a road along the ridge, through the woods, so that he could move his troops quickly from right to left or from left to right.

The 12th of December was foggy; all day long the clouds hung low upon the hills. The army began its crossing—Sumner's troops into the town, Franklin's by Burnard's house. Sumner took over one hundred and four cannon, Franklin one hundred and sixteen. Hooker's grand division remained on the north bank, to be sent over if needed. The army was on the south bank, but at sunset Burnside had not devised any plan for further action.

"On the night of the 12th," said Burnside, in his report, "the troops were all in position, and I visited the different commands with a view to determine as to future movements."

Burnside had one hundred and thirteen thousand men; Lee seventy-eight thousand, behind strong intrenchments. Lee could use every piece of artillery; of the Union cannon, only those belonging to Franklin's grand division could be used with any effect. Burnside visited Franklin, and then rode back to his headquarters and thought over what he would do. In the morning he ordered Franklin "to send out at once a division, at least, to seize, if possible, the heights near Captain Hamilton's."

He directed General Sumner to move out on the plank-road leading to Marye's Hill and seize the heights. These were the words of the order: "Holding these heights, with the heights near Captain Hamilton's, will, he hopes, compel the enemy to evacuate the whole ridge between these points."

There was probably not a division of the Union army that contained ten thousand men; while Jackson, in front of Franklin, had nearly forty thousand, Longstreet, in front of Sumner, had nearly as many more. Yet the order contemplated the easy brushing away of the Confederates on both flanks and the holding of the heights, which shows that General Burnside, honest and loyal, wanting to do great things, had really no adequate comprehension of the situation. He had twice refused to accept the command of the army; had declared again and again that he was not competent; but he had accepted the position, as a duty, when it was thrust upon him. His first plan had been thwarted by the inefficiency of somebody in Washington; his grand opportunity for getting possession of the heights had gone by; the people of the North were clamoring for a movement of the army somewhere, and here he was with his army in position, not knowing what he ought to do, yet doing just what he ought not to do—sending out two divisions, to be overwhelmed piecemeal. It would require very little generalship on the part of General Lee, or anybody else commanding the Confederates, to win a victory under such circumstances.

The First Corps held the left of the Union line. Going down the bank of the Rappahannock below Burnard's house, we see Doubleday's division extending from the river, at right angles with it, along the road leading to Richmond. The troops face south-east. Meade's division is next in line, facing south towards Hamilton's house; then Gibbon, Sickles, and Birney, also facing south. In rear, near the river, are the divisions of the Sixth Corps—Howe and Brooks in front, Newton and Stoneman in rear.

Walking down the Richmond road we come to the Confederates, A. P. Hill's division, with Archer's brigade on the extreme right, reaching down to the point where the railroad curves round the hill. Next in line are Lane's and Pender's brigades. Behind Hill are the troops of Early's and Taliaferro's divisions, and behind all D. H. Hill's. It is about thirty rods from the railroad, up a gentle slope, to the line of intrenchments, where Jackson's batteries are planted to sweep the whole field from the ridge to the Rappahannock. The cannon, and the divisions in rear of them, are concealed in thick woods.

Looking east, we see Stuart's cavalry and artillery drawn up on the level plateau, flanking Meade's position. One of his guns is a long-range rifled piece. From his position he will pour an enfilading fire upon the Union lines whenever they advance.

It was nine o'clock when Meade began to move. The sun was just beginning to clear away the fog. Meade moved towards the Bowling Green Road, but was obliged to halt while the pioneers cut away a hedge and bridged a ditch so that the cannon could cross.

DOUBLEDAY'S SKIRMISHERS, FREDERICKSBURG.

Suddenly there came the roar of a cannon breaking the stillness of the morning.

I looked at my watch, and saw that it was just half-past nine. Meade, apprehending an immediate attack on his left flank, halted. He had three brigades—Sinclair's, Magilton's, and Jackson's—and four batteries.

Sinclair's brigade was in the front line, Magilton's six hundred feet in rear, followed by Jackson's—in all, six thousand men.

When Stuart's solid shot came along the lines Meade halted Sinclair and swung Magilton up to his left, forming two sides of a square.

"Plant your cannon there," said Meade, pointing to a knoll, and three batteries sent their shells across the level fields.

Doubleday, seeing the flashes of Stuart's cannon, pushed down the river, extending his line towards Meade, his troops facing Stuart. His batteries opened fire.   With Meade's batteries it made a cross-fire, which was so uncomfortable that Stuart was obliged to withdraw his guns.

While this was going on the Confederate skirmishers crept along the hedges and opened fire, but two companies sent out by Meade drove them back.   Stonewall Jackson, seeing Doubleday's movement, and thinking that it was Franklin's intention to turn his left flank, sent D. H. Hill's division to Stuart's aid.

I rode out upon the plain and had a full view of the scene.   Doubleday was well advanced towards Stuart, his batteries in full play.   Meade was across the Bowling Green Road, in the open field, marching towards the railroad.   Gibbon was forming his division along the Bowling Green Road.   Nearly all of Franklin's batteries had advanced towards the road, and were sending solid shot and shells into the woods upon Jackson's troops.   Sixty heavy cannon were sending missiles over the army, across the plain into the Confederate lines.

Jackson's guns were thundering in response — Latham's, Johnson's, McIntosh's, Pegram's, and Crenshaw's batteries.

The cavalry, under General Bayard, is by Burnard's house.   The men stand by their horses, waiting orders.   Their commander is sitting beneath a tree, gazing upon the scene, smoking his pipe.   I salute him, and he returns it with a smile of recognition.   A solid shot comes across the field, and he who a moment ago was bidding me good-morning is speechless evermore.   He lives but a few moments.

As Meade's troops marched they came to a hollow before reaching the railroad, halted a moment, and then moved on.   It was a clear field to the railroad embankment, behind which they could see the sunlight glistening from the bayonets of the Confederates.

The direction of Meade's advance brings him against Lane's and Archer's Confederate brigades along the railroad.   There is a gap between the brigades, and there Meade drives his entering wedge.

It is a fierce and bloody contest.   The fourteen cannon on the hill pour their shells into the advancing Union line, firing over the Confederates; but up to the railroad, over it, rush the Pennsylvanians, capturing two hundred prisoners and several standards.   Archer and Lane are driven up the hill, followed by the Pennsylvanians.   Archer shifts the Fifth Alabama from his right to his left, but is not able to stop Meade.   He sends to General Gregg, who is in the woods, for help, and to Ewell, who is near Hamilton's house, and Trimble's and Lawton's brigades come upon the run.

It was Sinclair's brigade which had struck the first blow, and now

Jackson's and Magilton's came in against Gregg's South Carolina brigade, pouring in a fire which struck down nearly three hundred South Carolinians, among them General Gregg, who clung to a tree and waved on his men till he dropped unconscious upon the ground. Lawton's brigade came, followed by Trimble's, Hays's, Field's, and Walker's — an overwhelming force — which curled around Meade's flank, capturing a large number of his men, and driving him back over the railroad.

General Gibbon was to support Meade. He advanced to the railroad. The embankment was a breastwork, behind which the Confederates were lying. The fight was so severe that Gibbon, instead of supporting Meade, could not even hold his ground. Some of his regiments gave way, but the Ninety-seventh New York, the Eighty-eighth Pennsylvania, and the Twelfth Massachusetts made a brave fight. Root's brigade came up, charged with the other regiments upon the embankment, captured some prisoners, and drove the others into the woods; but Meade was being driven. Gibbon was wounded, and compelled to leave the field. Together the two divisions fell back, the Confederates following with exultant cheers; but Birney advanced to meet them, while General Ayre, commanding the artillery, wheeled thirty guns into position and hurled canister into the faces of the Confederates, sending them in turn back to the woods.

It was mid-afternoon when the troops returned from the unsuccessful attack on the left. Meade had struck a vigorous blow, and had lost more than one-third of his men. It was a brave and energetic charge across the open field, over the railroad, into the woods, sweeping back Archer and Lane, and striking a blow upon Gregg.

Of the sixty thousand men at Franklin's disposal, only from twelve to fifteen thousand had been engaged. Franklin had obeyed Burnside's order, but his own judgment would have put forty thousand in at the outset.

While the sun was going down the Confederates advanced upon Howe's and Newton's divisions; but it was a feeble attack. The artillery fire was too destructive for them to face; besides, Lee, secure in his position, was standing on the defensive.

I rode up to the right to see the movements there. The order issued to General Sumner was to move out on the Orange Court-house plank-road with a division and seize Marye's Heights. General French's division of the Second Corps was selected to make the attack, to be supported by General Hancock's division.

Let us survey the ground, that we may see the difficulties and obstacles to be overcome. Walking up Princess Anne Street, we reach the outskirts of the town, descend a hill, and come to the canal, filled with water. We are on the road leading to Orange Court-house. We cross a piece of marshy ground to a bank which, in the coming battle, is to be

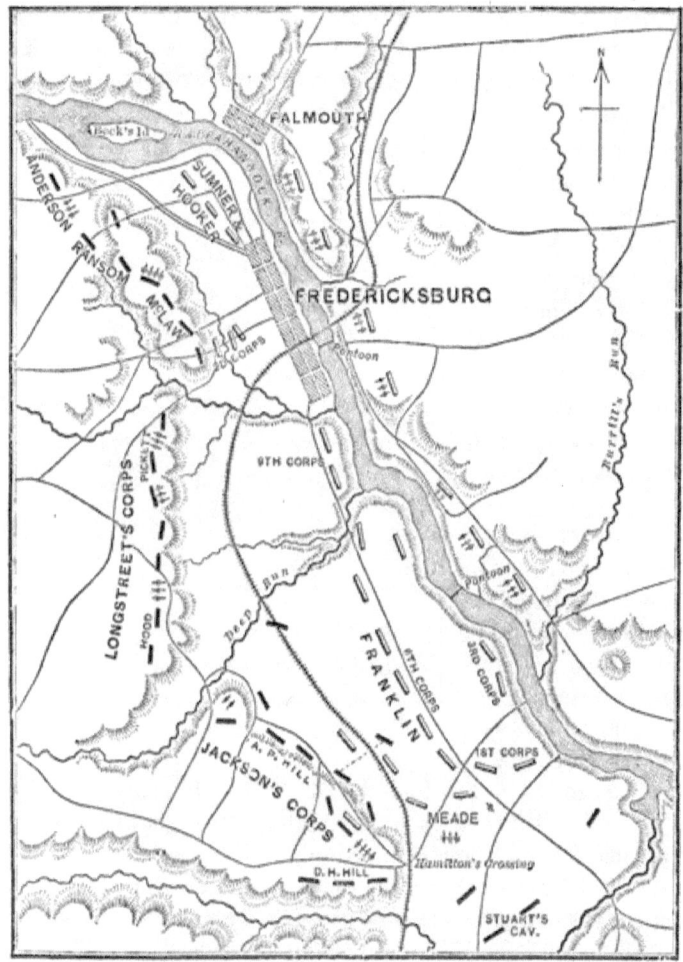

MAP OF FREDERICKSBURG AND VICINITY.

a blissful resting-place and shelter to thousands of Union troops. There are fences dividing the meadows into fields and pastures. Fifty rods up the turnpike brings us to the foot of Marye's Hill, to the road which leads off to the left, sunken three feet below the surface of the field.

The skirmishers advanced. Through the forenoon the Confederate cannon on the heights had been for the most part silent, but when the head of the column appeared, solid shot and shell came from the heights. The Eighth Ohio, marching up Hanover Street, was the first to feel the tempest, but without faltering it crossed the bridge and filed left into the meadow. At the same moment the First Delaware appeared on Princess Anne Street. At the instant most of the Confederate cannon were aimed at the Eighth Ohio, and the First Delaware was crossing the bridge before the storm came. It filed right, and went on with little loss. Not so fortunate the Fourth Ohio.

MARYE HOUSE.

There were one hundred and fifteen of this regiment detailed as skirmishers, and in a very few minutes five officers and forty-three men were killed or wounded; but they cleared the ground, driving the Confederates from their hiding-places, advancing across the meadow, halting beneath the ridge, there finding partial shelter from the storm.

General Nathan Kimball, the commander who defeated Stonewall Jackson at Kearnstown, in the Shenandoah Valley, is selected to lead the attack. He forms his brigade in Caroline Street, which runs parallel with the canal. I see the columns as they cross the bridges and deploy on the west bank of the canal in the meadow. The cannon which have been aimed at the skirmishers are turned upon the brigades, firing more rapidly than before. And now the Union cannon on the Stafford hills—the long-range guns—begin to send solid shot and shells with long-time fuses over the town. Some of the shells burst high above the Confederates, throwing out handfuls of white cloud upon the clear blue sky, or, striking the embankments, toss cart-loads of earth into the air.

General Cobb's Confederate brigade is in the sunken road, the men lying down close behind the stone wall. They bide their time.

Up from the shelter of the bank on the western verge of the meadow rises the advancing Union brigades. I see the men drop—a whole platoon—where a shell does its fearful work. The green grass is dotted with men in blue suddenly stricken down, but onward rolls the wave towards the heights. A line of light, and a white sulphurous cloud bursts out from the base of the hill. The men in blue come to a stand-still; those on the right gain the shelter of a house and barn, but those on the left are in the open field, with more than one hundred cannon on the right, the left, and in front, all raining shells upon them, and the thousands of muskets blazing in their faces.

The brigade commanded by Colonel Andrews, of the First Delaware, formed behind Kimball's. It was composed of the Fourth and Tenth New York and the Thirteenth Pennsylvania. Palmer's brigade was composed of the Fourteenth Connecticut, One Hundred and Eighth New York, and One Hundred and Eighth Pennsylvania.

The Confederate artillerymen had secured the exact range, and opened upon each regiment successively, but with the same steadiness that had marked those preceding them they deployed in the meadow, moved over the field, advanced almost to the base of the hill, only to be driven back with fearful loss to the shelter of the ridge.

General Sumner had obeyed Burnside's order by sending out a division. It had inflicted little damage upon the enemy. He now ordered Hancock's division to advance. There were three brigades—Zook's, Meagher's, and Caldwell's. It was mid-afternoon before the troops could be gotten into position. All the while Confederate shells were bursting in the air above the men lying close upon the ground beneath the bank.

Out from the two streets came Hancock's columns. To cover in part their advance, General Sumner directed all the batteries which could obtain the range of the Confederate position to open fire, but it was very little they could do. Again Marye's, Taylor's, and Lee's hills are all aflame. Out on the left the men in blue are almost up to the sunken road, standing there and delivering their fire with deliberate aim. In the conflict the Confederate commander, General Cobb, is killed while rallying his men. On the Union side General Kimball has been borne to the rear. Nearly all the commanders of brigades have been wounded. General Caldwell is disabled. Sixty-two of his officers and nine hundred and thirty-two men are killed or wounded. Colonel Cross, of the Fifth New Hampshire, is wounded. The next in rank takes command, to be wounded the next moment, followed by the third and the fourth officer in seniority. One hundred and sixty-five men are cut from the ranks, yet the survivors stand in line and deliver their fire, but are compelled at last to retire. A little over five thousand men marched up the slope, but in a few minutes two thousand and thirteen are stricken from the ranks.

General Sumner ordered up Howard's division. The troops were in the fight when the streets were cleared. They have been under arms through the day with nothing to eat, but they advance with the same intrepidity that drove Barksdale from the streets; but the volleys which they fire do little harm to the Confederates, while their own ranks are decimated by the continuous fire of the Confederates. General Ransom, commanding a Confederate division, respects the bravery of the men who exhibit such endurance. "They advanced with the utmost determination," he said.

The troops of the Second Corps were exhausted, and Sturgis's division of the Ninth Corps—Ferero's and Naglee's brigades—moved out between the Telegraph Road and the railroad. The Twenty-first Massachusetts has been in several battles; it was at Roanoke Island and Newbern, at South Mountain and Antietam. The regiment is almost up to the sunken road, when Sergeant Collins, carrying the flag, goes down. Sergeant Plunket, who was born in Ireland, who came to America when he was a little boy, who from the age of ten has earned his living, who was making shoes in West Boyleston, Massachusetts, when the thunder of the cannon at Sumter startled the nation, who left his shoemaker's bench, bade farewell to the girl who had promised to be his wife, to become a soldier, seizes the flag and shouts, "Come on!" and the regiment, catching his inspiration, goes on. A shell explodes and Sergeant Plunket is down. Both hands are gone, but with his bleeding arms he clasps the flag to his heart, staining it with his blood. To him there is nothing on earth so dear.

If there are brave men yielding their lives for a great idea in front of Marye's Hill, there are equally brave spirits behind the stone wall. General Edward Cobb, of Georgia, commanding the troops, is standing beneath the trees in Mrs. Stevens's garden when a cannon-shot crashes through the house, through bedroom and parlor, through the door, striking the brave man to the earth. Up on yonder hill stands Mrs. Stevens beholding the scene, shells exploding around her, solid shot tearing up the earth. She has been ministering to the Confederate wounded, and now dashes down the hill, tears off a portion of her skirt, and seeks to stay the flowing of the blood from the ghastly wound. So this woman's devotion shines like a star above the carnage and desolation of that dark December day.

General Burnside ordered Hooker to cross the river and join Sumner.

General Hooker reconnoitred the ground, and saw how vain would be any attempt he might make. "I do not think that we can carry it," he said, reporting in person to General Burnside.

"The attempt must be made," was the reply.

General Humphreys's division crossed the bridges of the canal.

SERGEANT PLUNKET.

"You are to charge bayonets and drive them from the sunken road," was the order.

The men fix their bayonets. I behold them as they leap up the bank on the western edge of the meadow. It is a rapid movement, which quickens to a run. They are almost up to the Confederate lines when again the line of light gleams along the brow of the hill. The front rank of men in blue melts instantly away. Of the four thousand that advanced, one thousand seven hundred have fallen.

The sun is setting. At this hour a great number flee to the railroad excavation for shelter, but a battery on Lee's Hill sweeps it with a direct fire. The Confederate artillerymen bide their time, waiting till it is crowded with men in blue; then the shells burst among them. General Lee beholds the slaughter from Marye's house.

"It is well that this is so terrible; we should grow too fond of it if it were not," he said to one of his officers.

In battle there is usually little pity for those whom you are fighting; you are there to kill men. The Confederates were fighting for an idea—for what they believed to be just and right—as were the Union men. They know that a half-dozen Union men are going down to one Confederate; know that they have an impregnable position, and wonder at the attempt to take it. Their pity is awakened as they behold the terrible slaughter.

General Burnside determined to renew the attempt in the morning with the Ninth Corps; he would lead it in person. He issued his orders, but General Sumner, General Hooker, and General Franklin remonstrated. It would be a horrible and useless sacrifice of men.

Sunday morning dawned beautiful and clear. General Burnside was thinking what he would do. On the left, where Meade had fought, and in front of the heights, were thousands of wounded. Humanity demanded that fighting should cease, and that they should be cared for. White flags were displayed; the soldiers on both sides stacked their guns and talked with each other, the Confederates trading tobacco for coffee.

"I am tired of fighting, and this war would soon be over if it were not for our officers," said a Confederate.

Twelve thousand three hundred and twenty-one Union soldiers had been killed or wounded; five thousand three hundred Confederates.

There was but one thing to be done—withdraw his army. It must be done at night and in silence; no sign of withdrawal must be made till darkness came.

On the left there had been no fighting since the repulse of Meade and Gibbon. Stonewall Jackson was eager to attack.

"We will make a night attack and drive them into the river," he said. He issued his orders. At dark his troops began to move into position. He sent word to General Lee of what he intended to do, but General Lee sent back word that he must not make any movement.

Little did General Lee mistrust as to what was going on in the Union lines — that the artillerymen were winding wisps of straw around the wheels of the cannon so that they would make no rumbling; that the divisions were moving rapidly away—the officers issuing their orders in a whisper. The wind is blowing from the south, the clouds are hanging low, a storm approaching.

It is just midnight when an officer reaches Colonel Williams, in command of the pickets on the left.

"Call in your pickets; we are to take a new position. Make no noise," are the orders.

The whisper runs along the line; the men move silently away. Morning dawns, and Lee beholds with astonishment the Union troops once more well within their camps on the north side of the river.

CHAPTER XVII.

FROM NASHVILLE TO STONE RIVER.

ON October 24, 1862, the Secretary of War issued an order creating the territory in Kentucky and Tennessee east of the Tennessee River as the Department of the Cumberland, relieving General Buell and appointing General Rosecrans in his place, who assumed command at Louisville on the 30th. He reorganized the army, appointing General McCook to command the right wing, General Crittenden the left wing, and General Thomas the centre. There were three divisions in each wing and five in the centre.

A month had passed since the battle of Perryville. During the time the army had been waiting to obtain clothing. The long march across the States of Tennessee and Kentucky from the Tennessee River, in northern Alabama, to Louisville on the Ohio, and the march from the Ohio to central Kentucky, and thence to Nashville, had worn out boots, shoes, and uniforms. The first thing to be done by General Rosecrans was to obtain fresh supplies and repair the railroads, which had been badly broken up by the Confederate cavalry. He saw that his own cavalry in comparison with that of the enemy was weak, but did not receive any reinforcements in that branch of the service, for the reason that the Government during the first year of the war did not see the need of cavalry. On the other hand, the Confederates from the outset saw what valuable services could be rendered by a body of horsemen moving rapidly from place to place, and made preparations accordingly.

General Rosecrans set a large number of men at work repairing the railroad, but it could not be reopened till the 26th of November. During the month the army near Nashville could receive its supplies only by wagons transporting the provisions thirty-five miles.

The Confederate cavalry all the while were on the move, tearing down and destroying, while the Union troops were repairing previous damages. While the army was refitting, the Confederates, under John Morgan, December 7th, dashed upon the town of Hartsville, on the Cumberland

River, where there were three Union infantry regiments, a battalion of cavalry, and two cannon, all under the command of Colonel Moore. The alarm was given. Moore sent out a company of skirmishers and formed a line on a hill overlooking a ravine. Morgan advanced his infantry to the ravine and opened a destructive fire in front, while his cavalry swept round to the rear. The Union troops were thrown into confusion, and, being nearly surrounded, Colonel Moore raised a white flag and surrendered. It was a notable victory for Morgan, who thus captured nearly two thousand men, with all the camp equipage, wagons, horses, and two cannon. Jefferson Davis was at Murfreesboro' consulting with General Bragg, and was so well pleased that he appointed Morgan a brigadier-general.

Morgan's success made him famous, and there was a great desire on the part of the young men of Tennessee and Kentucky to enlist in his command. He soon had seven regiments and between four and five thousand men. He divided his command into two brigades—one of three regiments, commanded by Colonel Basil W. Duke, with four cannon, and one of four regiments and three guns, under Colonel W. C. P. Breckinridge. Each regiment had a supply of axes, crow-bars, and sledge-hammers to destroy railroads and bridges.

General Bragg came to the conclusion that General Rosecrans intended to go into winter-quarters at Nashville, and he determined to compel him to fall back to Louisville—not by fighting a battle, but by breaking up the railroad so that he could not furnish his army with supplies. To carry out his plan he sent Morgan from Murfreesboro' to make a raid into Kentucky, Morgan's native State. He would still have a large force of cavalry left with his army.

On December 22d Morgan started with his two brigades. The cavalrymen were in high spirits. Many of them were from Kentucky, and well acquainted with all the roads. They would visit their friends, and would be warmly welcomed by those who sympathized with the Confederates. The harvests were gathered, and they would live upon the fat of the land. There were full cribs of corn for their horses, and good cheer for themselves. It would be glorious to swoop down upon the small bodies of Union troops posted to guard the railroad, take them prisoners, and then destroy the bridges which Rosecrans had reconstructed. Two days after starting, the Confederates came upon a battalion of Michigan troops, who fought so bravely that Morgan lost two officers and seventeen men. The next day, December 25th, he had a second skirmish near Munfordsville, in which he lost nearly fifty men. He came to Bacon Creek, where there were one hundred Union troops in a stockade ten feet high built of logs of wood set in the ground. He opened with his artillery, sent an officer demanding a surrender, which was refused. After another hot fire, he himself called upon the garrison to surrender, and promised such fair treatment that the offer was accepted.

Morgan pushed on to Elizabethtown, where there were six hundred Union troops, under Lieutenant-colonel Smith, who fought six hours, but were obliged to surrender. He had reached what he was after—the long, high trestle-bridges near Muldraugh's Hill, on the Louisville and Nashville Railroad. There were two, each nearly five hundred feet in length, and between eighty and ninety feet high. Fires were kindled, which ran up the great timbers, and in a few minutes the lofty structures were heaps of smouldering ruins. He moved so rapidly that it was useless to send infantry to intercept him. He met with a defeat, however, at Rolling Fork and Salt River from Colonel Harlan's brigade, and at Lebanon lost one hundred and fifty men.

Before Morgan began his advance, General Carter, with three regiments of Union cavalry, started from Lebanon, moved south-east, took a mountain road which wound through deep ravines, crossed the Cumberland Mountains forty miles north-east of Cumberland Gap, descended the Virginia side, and astonished the Confederates by appearing at Carter's Station, on the railroad leading from East Tennessee to Virginia, burning bridges, tearing up several miles of track, and returning to Kentucky by the same route. Morgan's raid was far more damaging than that of Carter's; but if General Bragg supposed that he was going to compel Rosecrans to fall back to Louisville, or that he could paralyze the Union army by cutting off its supplies, he was mistaken. Before Morgan started, Rosecrans had decided to march southward from Nashville, find Bragg, and attack him. It was a bold plan, for Bragg had an army larger than his own, and could choose his own ground. He could fight a battle when and where he pleased close to his base of supplies, with his troops all fresh, while Rosecrans must make a long and weary march, expose his troops to the rain and snow of winter, endure great hardship, and fight at a disadvantage. We must keep this in mind while we study the movement of Rosecrans upon Bragg at Murfreesboro', and the battle of Stone River, and what came of it.

We must not lose sight of political affairs while we follow the movements of armies. The political situation was a very grave one. In September, after the battle of Antietam, President Lincoln issued his first proclamation of emancipation, which gave great offence to those people in

27

the North who opposed the war. On the first week in November elections had been held in all the Northern States for members of Congress, and in most of them for Governor. New York, Pennsylvania, Illinois, and Indiana had elected Legislatures opposed to the war, and a majority of those elected to Congress were opposed to its continuance. In the Democratic political meetings resolutions had been passed demanding the withdrawal of the troops. It was said that the war was a failure, that the South never could be conquered, and peace was demanded at any price. General Rosecrans saw that a battle must be fought and a victory won. Although he had fewer troops than Bragg, though he must march thirty miles and attack the enemy on ground of Bragg's own choosing, he did not hesitate an instant, nor was he to be turned from his purpose by anything which Morgan might do. When he heard of Morgan's movement he was getting ready to move, and his orders were issued promptly and decisively.

Of the five divisions under General Thomas, that commanded by General Reynolds and two brigades of Fry's were detailed to guard the railroad. General Mitchell was left to hold Nashville. This assignment took away half of General Thomas's command, leaving him the First Division of Rousseau's, Negley's, and Walker's brigade of Fry's division. General McCook had the divisions of Johnson, Davis, and Sheridan; Crittenden the divisions of Wood, Palmer, and Van Cleve. The entire force was about forty-three thousand four hundred men; but it was necessary to detail a large number of men to guard the trains from the attacks of the Confederate cavalry, reducing Rosecrans's force to less than forty thousand.

Bragg had fifty-one thousand and thirty-six men, but the cavalry, under Morgan and Forrest, was away, reducing his force to forty-six thousand six hundred and four. On Christmas-day Rosecrans issued his orders to advance. For many a soldier it was the last Christmas on earth.

In an account of the operations at Island No. 10 I told the story of the exploit of Colonel Roberts, of the Forty-second Illinois, in spiking the guns of a Confederate battery during a terrific thunder-storm. He had been through several battles, and was now commander of the Third Brigade of Sheridan's division. We shall see him on the battle-field. On Christmas-day he invited three friends to dinner. After dinner they drank a glass of wine.

"Success to our arms," was the sentiment to which Colonel Roberts replied. He spoke of the Union, of liberty, of the army.

"I will take all the chances of rebel bullets," he said.

"So will I," said Colonel Harrington, of the Twenty-seventh Illinois.

"So will I," were the words of Lieutenant-colonel Swanwick, of the Twenty-second Illinois.

"And I," added Lieutenant Talliaferro.

Before the week closed all four were numbered among the slain.

At six o'clock on the morning of December 26th the Union troops began to move. Before noon Bragg, thirty miles away, at Murfreesboro', knew it, and issued his orders for the concentration of his troops. He selected a line about two and a half miles north of Murfreesboro', and ordered the construction of intrenchments. He directed the cavalry to make a show of fighting, and retard the advance of the Union troops as much as possible, while he strengthened his position.

ON THE MARCH IN A STORM.

Murfreesboro' was once the capital of Tennessee. It is not a very large town, but roads radiate from it in all directions. The Nashville turnpike and the railroad run north-west; Stone River rises among the hills twenty miles south of Murfreesboro', and runs due north, winding over a rocky bed. There was but little water in the stream at the time of the battle, but the troops could not readily get down to cross it without smoothing the banks.

Half way from Murfreesboro' to Nolensville is Stewart's Creek, a small stream emptying into Stone River, flowing through a deep ravine. It would have been a strong line of defence. General Rosecrans thought it possible that Bragg would select it for his line, and his movements were directed accordingly; but Bragg chose to fight nearer his supplies at Murfreesboro', and so make the Union troops do all the marching.

On Friday morning the left wing, under Crittenden, marched down the Nashville pike three miles, and, Palmer's division in advance, came upon Wheeler's Confederate cavalry, which fell slowly back, skirmishing all day. The division camped at night near La Vergne, having marched fifteen miles.

General Crittenden had been ordered to move slowly, because General McCook with the right wing was marching south towards Triune, where General Hardee was supposed to be. General Rosecrans intended to keep his army well in hand. It was eleven o'clock Saturday before Crittenden started from his bivouac, with General Wood's division in the advance. The head of the column reached the little village of La Vergne when there came a scattering volley from Confederate skirmishers. General Maury, with a brigade of Cheatham's division and Wheeler's brigade of cavalry, was there—not, however, to make a bold stand, but to delay the advance of the Union troops.

General Wood ordered General Hascall to form his brigade in two lines and charge upon the enemy. The order was obeyed and the Confederates fled, reaching Stewart's Creek, and setting the bridge on fire, but the Union troops hastened forward and extinguished the flames.

The Jefferson turnpike crosses Stewart's Creek five miles farther north. General Hazen sent Captain Maxey with ninety men of the Fourth Michigan Cavalry to seize that bridge. They proceeded down the road and came upon a company of cavalry. The Confederates retreated, and there was an exciting race down the pike and across the bridge. The saving of the two bridges was of great importance, for it enabled the army to move on without fording the creek.

It was a march through rain and mire, the wheels of the cannon sinking in the mud, the horses toiling, the men becoming weary; but on the evening of the 30th most of the divisions had arrived upon the ground where they were to fight a desperate battle.

Bragg had formed his line of battle on Sunday, the 28th, and for two days had been throwing up intrenchments. Breckinridge's division was on the east side of Stone River, in a forest; Cleburne's division was behind it. Bragg suspected that Rosecrans might cross the river and attempt to seize the town from the north-east. The main part of the Confederate army was on the west side of the river, in the edge of a cedar grove. This line was nearly three miles in length, with the cavalry out upon the left flank. We see fields, fences, ravines, knolls, roads, and farm-houses. Bragg knows every foot of the ground; Rosecrans knows noth-ing, except what he can discover as he rides hastily here and there. Un-fortunately he does not ride along the line occupied by the right wing. He does not see the ground, nor the faulty position of the troops under General McCook.

General Rosecrans's headquarters were in a grove of cedars on the west side of the Murfreesboro' and Nashville turnpike, which runs straight as an arrow from that point into the town. His division commanders, at nine o'clock on the evening of December 30th, came to headquarters to receive their orders.

General McCook, commanding the right wing, is to await an attack from Bragg, or if Bragg does not attack he is to advance and engage the force in front of him. If attacked in large force he is to hold his ground, while the centre, and especially the left, perform the work assigned them.

The centre, under Thomas, is to open with skirmishing, and engage the enemy with Negley's division, assisted by Palmer's division of the left wing. Rousseau's division is to be in reserve behind Negley's.

The left wing is to do the main work. Van Cleve's division is to cross Stone River at the lower ford, Wood's is to cross at the upper ford, and together they are to sweep Breckinridge from his position, move on and take possession of Murfreesboro'. The artillery of the two divi-sions, as soon as Breckinridge is driven, is to be planted upon a hill whence can be poured a destructive fire into the Confederate lines west of Stone River. It was a movement to turn Bragg's right flank, to hurl two strong divisions upon Breckinridge's single division and crush it. When that was done, Thomas in the centre and McCook were to press on and complete the work. Rosecrans knew that there was a large force in front of McCook, and the success of the plan would depend in a great degree upon the ability of McCook to hold his ground, or to fall back slowly if compelled so to do.

Let us walk down the turnpike just two miles. We come to Bragg's headquarters, close by the turnpike, on the east side. He has been in po-sition two days behind his intrenchments, waiting for Rosecrans. He is restless and impatient. Although he has chosen his position to fight a defensive battle, he decides to change his plan, and instead of waiting to receive a blow to give one. He will give two—he will not only attack Rosecrans but will cut off his supplies. Morgan with his cavalry is one hundred and thirty miles away in Kentucky, destroying the Louisville and

Nashville Railroad. He has still five thousand cavalry left, and resolves to send Wheeler's brigade to capture Rosecrans's supply trains.

Wheeler had five regiments, two battalions, and two cannon. At midnight on the 29th he moved north from Murfreesboro', crossed Stone River several miles from the town, reached Jefferson at daylight, and captured and destroyed a large number of wagons. He moved towards La Vergne, over the road along which Crittenden marched, captured another train, reached La Vergne at noon, destroyed all the supplies which Rosecrans had ordered to be forwarded to that town, pushed on to Rock Springs and destroyed another army train, reached Nolensville before night, and set the fifth train on fire. All the teamsters and soldiers ac-

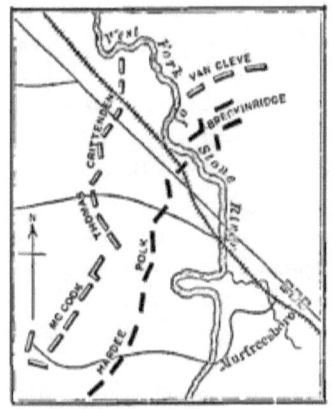

BEGINNING OF THE BATTLE.

companying the trains were captured and paroled, and the horses taken for use. Leaving Nolensville, he returned to Murfreesboro' to take part in the battle in the afternoon of December 31st.

It was a bold stroke, and Bragg was able to accomplish it because Rosecrans had no adequate cavalry force to cope with him. Bragg's first blow was in all respects successful. It was mortifying to Rosecrans to learn that his supplies were cut off; it was disheartening to the soldiers. Bragg's plan, besides the cutting off of Rosecrans's supplies, was to attack with his left wing, to turn Rosecrans's right flank, drive McCook back east of the Nashville turnpike, cut Rosecrans off from Nashville, and put the Union army to rout. It is not probable that Bragg had any idea as to what Rosecrans intended to do; but his plan was an exact counterpart of Rosecrans's. Bragg intended to keep his right wing under Breckinridge east of the river, where it was, and to advance his left wing and centre. Rosecrans intended to keep his right wing where it was, and to swing forward his left wing and centre. Bragg decided to make his left wing very strong, in order to strike a crushing blow. We see Cleburne's division, which was on the east side of the river, starting at midnight, crossing the river, the turnpike, and the railroad, marching west and taking position in rear of McCown's division, having gone from the rear of the extreme right to the rear of the extreme left.

General Sill commanded a brigade in the Union right wing. He was on the front line, very near the Confederate troops. He could hear the tramping of men and the rumble of artillery. It was two o'clock in the morning when he went over to General Sheridan's headquarters. "Something is going on; I can hear troops in motion. I think they are getting ready to attack us," he said.

General Sheridan hears the commotion, and together they go to General McCook. Sheridan thinks that the Union line is too long, and that the reserve—Baldwin's brigade—is too far in the rear. McCook does not make any change of position, nor does he notify Rosecrans that something is going on in his front.

General Thomas holds the centre, with Negley's division in the front line and Rousseau in the rear, extending to the turnpike. Between the turnpike and the river are the brigades of the left wing, which are to cross the river and fall upon Bragg's right flank, as planned by Rosecrans.

Bragg has placed McCown's division in front of McCook, with Cleburne's in his rear. They compose Hardee's corps, and are to swing around the Union right flank and drive McCook back to the turnpike. Wither's and Cheatham's divisions form Bragg's centre. Breckinridge holds the right east of the river.

The advantages are on the side of the Confederates. They outnumber the Union army, are acquainted with the ground, have had no long and weary marches, have three days' cooked rations in their haversacks, have been in their tents during the rain of the 29th, are on ground of their own choosing, behind breastworks.

The Union troops have marched, some of them between forty and fifty miles, through mud and rain, have bivouacked at night, have scant rations, are weary and footsore, have forded rivers, are chilled with the winter cold. They know nothing of the ground before them; the Confederate cavalry have cut off their supplies; they are to fight superior numbers in the open field; they have had little sleep, and the hospitals are already filling with soldiers broken down by the exposure and hardship.

General Rosecrans ordered the troops to be ready at seven o'clock. He could not well have fixed the time at an earlier hour, for some of the troops did not reach their positions till late on the evening of the 30th. Bragg, with his troops fresh and eager for battle, ordered McCown and Cleburne to advance at daylight.

It is the last day of the year 1862. The war has been going on since April, 1861. Kentucky has taken sides for the Union, yet there are twelve thousand Kentuckians in the Confederate ranks. If Bragg wins in the approaching conflict he will advance into that State. If victory is his, if he can defeat and rout the army under Rosecrans, Nashville will fall into his hands, Tennessee and Kentucky be redeemed to the Confederacy. The defeat of Rosecrans will be disastrous beyond measure to the Union, but glorious to the Confederacy.

Daylight is dawning when the Confederates of Rains's and Ector's brigades, followed by McNair's—their breakfast eaten, muskets loaded, knapsacks and blankets left behind—move to the attack. They throw down a fence, cross the road which runs west from the house of Mrs. Smith, the right of McNair sweeping west of the house, and the three brigades making a half-wheel towards the north.

The Union pickets open fire. General Kirk hears the musketry and leaps into his saddle. His brigade has eaten breakfast and is in line. He rides towards the pickets, and sees the long line of Confederates coming into the open field and wheeling north.

"Forward, Thirty-fourth Illinois!" is his prompt order. "Tell General Johnson that the enemy is advancing in force," was his message to that officer, sent by an aide.

The Thirty-fourth Illinois advances to the support of the pickets and fires volley after volley. If General Bragg thought to surprise the Union troops he was mistaken; they were awake, under arms, and getting ready. Edgarton's battery was in position, but the drivers had gone to the creek in rear to water the horses. General Kirk rode to Colonel Willich, commanding a brigade, for help, but could not find him. The colonels of the regiments thought that they ought not to advance without orders from their own commander. Kirk rides back. The Thirty-fourth Illinois is holding the whole of Ector's brigade in check. Kirk encourages them. He is in the thick of the fight, conspicuous on his horse. A Confederate singles him out and he falls mortally wounded.

The Confederates, brought to a stand-still for the moment by the prompt and resolute action of the Thirty-fourth Illinois, press on once more. Men fire into one another's faces. The color-bearer from Illinois waves his flag. Right in front of him is the color-bearer of the Tenth Texas, who jumps forward and grasps it. The Illinoisian seizes at the same moment the Confederate standard. The soldiers in both regiments see the struggle, and fire. Both men go down. Other men seize the banners. Again the rattle of musketry, and both color-bearers fall—the Confederates outnumbering the Union men. In the mêlée the Thirty-fourth loses its flag and is driven.

So near now were the Confederates that Edgarton's cannoneers had only time to fire two rounds before they charged upon and captured the guns.

THE BATTLE OF STONE RIVER.

General Kirk had fallen. General Willich was at Johnson's headquarters a mile away. Willich's men were eating breakfast when the storm burst. There was no one to command. A few companies fire upon the Confederates, but all is confusion. With a yell the Confederates rush forward and Willich's men flee. Captain Goodspeed sends two of his cannon to a knoll for a better position; but the Confederate cavalry under Wharton, out beyond the infantry, quickly capture them.

The Twenty-ninth and Thirtieth Indiana, of Kirk's brigade, are exposed by the flight of Willich's men, and are obliged to retreat, but it is in good order.

Only one regiment of the two brigades—the Seventy-seventh Pennsylvania, of Kirk's brigade—holds its ground. The Confederates under McNair have swept past it. It is a small regiment, only three hundred in all. It changes position, facing west. The soldiers see a battery come up behind them and wheel into position, and suppose it to be Union, but it is Douglas's battery of Ector's brigade instead. Its captain sees that the Union troops are laboring under a mistake, and he will profit by it. He unlimbers towards the west.

"Double canister," is the order, and the double charge is rammed home into the six pieces, less than five hundred feet distant from the Union line.

"Action to the right!"

The six pieces are trained upon the regiment, and the next moment the air is thick with leaden rain. The regiment is cut through, but faces about, gives an answering volley, and then the few that are left fall back in order.

McCook's right has crumbled—two brigades been put to rout, eight cannon lost: so quickly is it done that General Johnson knows nothing of the disaster till Willich's troops come straggling past his headquarters. He orders Baldwin's brigade to advance.

The first success of the Confederates had been accomplished by McCown, who had swept far out to the left, leaving a gap in the Confederate line, into which Cleburne's division moved, his right marching over the ground from which Willich and Kirk had been driven, his left coming against Post's and Carlin's Union brigades. Colonel Post saw that the Confederate line extended far beyond his left flank, and changed his position, falling back through the woods, forming on both sides of the cross-road leading from the Franklin Road to the Wilkinson Pike, posting Pinney's battery on the north side of the road. While he was doing this, Carlin's skirmishers were keeping up a galling fire upon Cleburne's advancing line.

General Carlin was in a cedar grove and a rocky glen, where his troops could shelter themselves behind the boulders. They were in two lines: One Hundred and First Ohio and Thirty-eighth Illinois in the first line, the Twenty-first Illinois and Fifteenth Wisconsin in the second. Through the cedars advanced Polk's and Wood's Confederate brigades—two thousand four hundred men. They drove in Carlin's skirmishers, but saw no line of men confronting them. They were moving joyfully forward when suddenly a staggering volley burst upon them. Some of the men started to run, but were rallied by their officers. Once more they advanced, but a second time were turned back. It was the first serious check to the Confederates, and was of vital importance to Rosecrans.

General Carlin orders his front line to advance. The men rise from their shelter and go forward with a cheer. As we look at it now, it perhaps would have been better if he had not issued the order, for the Confederates saw how few they were—only two regiments. Twice the Confederates had been hurled back by their deadly fire. Men do not like to attack an unseen foe, especially after the unseen foe has inflicted two staggering blows. The Union troops, sheltered behind rocks and trees, lying on their faces, had taken deliberate aim. They had cut down the Confederates as hailstones cut the bearded grain, and had suffered little from their volleys. But now Wood and Polk drove them through the cedar forest back to their original position.

In General Carlin's second line are the Twenty-first Illinois and Fifteenth Wisconsin. They, too, are concealed from the enemy, and deliver a destructive fire; but the Confederates under Wood are moving round upon their right flank. Colonel Alexander changes front, facing west, and makes fearful havoc in the Confederate ranks. It is a fight at close quarters. Color-bearers, one after another—four in all—are killed in the Twenty-first Illinois. More than two hundred of the regiment go down, but it holds its ground, rolling back the Confederate line. It is only for a few moments, however, for Hardee is sweeping all before him, while Polk is advancing to attack Sheridan. It is now eight o'clock. The battle has raged since daylight, resulting thus far in disaster to Rosecrans. All of his plans are upset. His right wing has crumbled; fugitives are streaming through the woods; his trains have been captured. The outlook is dark and gloomy.

Out from the cedar groves streamed soldiers, teamsters, negroes—all in confusion, moving north towards the Nashville Turnpike. It was the first information that General Rosecrans received that the right wing had been routed.

Before eight o'clock an aide from General McCook had informed him that the right wing was hard pressed and needed assistance, but McCook had not informed him that Willich's brigade had been routed, and that officer captured; that the whole of Davis's division had been driven in, and that the right wing had crumbled to pieces. It was hardly nine o'clock, and defeat stared Rosecrans in the face.

At that moment Van Cleve's division of Crittenden's command was forming in line of battle east of the river, and T. J. Wood's division was marching down to the river. On the right the whole of Davis's division had been driven, and Hardee, with his victorious divisions of McCown and Cleburne, with the cavalry, were moving on to finish the battle. In the centre Polk's cannon were opening upon Sheridan, and Cheatham was hurling his brigades upon Carlin and Woodruff.

"There is always room for a man of force, and he makes for many," said the great thinker, Ralph Waldo Emerson. The Union commander is such a man. It is genius which can change defeat to victory. These are Rosecrans's orders in quick succession:

"General Thomas will order General Rousseau to support Sheridan.

"General Crittenden will hasten Van Cleve across the river to the right of Rousseau.

"General Wood will despatch Harker's brigade down the turnpike, and form on the right of Van Cleve. The other brigades of his division will remain in reserve.

"The Pioneer brigade will stand in reserve on a knoll in rear of Palmer's brigade."

Fifteen minutes, and Rosecrans's line of battle undergoes a great change. Rousseau crosses the railroad and the turnpike upon the double-quick. "In this field the battle is to be fought," he says, as he forms his line facing west.

Van Cleve's men rush down to the river, wade the stream, gain the western bank, advance and form along the railroad and turnpike. The troops which a few moments ago formed Rosecrans's left wing now become his right wing.

The position of Cheatham's division in the Confederate line brought Vaughn's brigade upon General Sill's brigade. Up and down the line rides the fearless commander of the brigade, encouraging the men, watching every movement of the enemy; but a bullet strikes him in the face, passes into his brain, and he falls dead upon the ground. Colonel Greusel takes his place, and the battle goes on. Fearfully it rages round the Thirty-sixth Illinois; but the men from the prairies stand their ground till two hundred and thirty of their number are killed or wounded, Major Miller, commanding, among the number.

Woodruff has given way on Sill's right, and Carlin, still farther to the right, stands alone; but he can remain there no longer, for Cleburne and McCown are so far in his rear that he is in danger of being cut off.

Loomis's Confederate brigade with exultant shouts comes on, but Houghtaling's and Hescock's guns send them into the cedars.

A second Confederate brigade (Maningault's) comes to the assistance of Vaughn across a cotton-field. Men drop, but the lines close and move on with a steadiness and bravery which win the admiration of the Union men. The Eighty-eighth Illinois fired a volley that made terrible slaughter. The Confederate line came to a stand-still. The Union line with a cheer rushed forward, and the Confederates fled to the woods, leaving the cotton-field thickly strewn with killed and wounded.

Nearly all the fighting has been in the cedar woods, but the ground occupied by Roberts's brigade of Sheridan's division is along a road leading from the house of Mr. Harding to the Wilkinson Pike.

It is hard for the brave man who spiked the guns of the Confederate batteries at Island No. 10 to see the right wing crumbling piecemeal. He asks permission of Sheridan to charge bayonets. He has great faith in his men — the Twenty-second, Twenty-seventh, Forty-second, and Fifty-first Illinois.

"Yes, give them the bayonet," is the response of Sheridan.

The Eighty-eighth Illinois and Twenty-first Michigan are in his way, behind a fence.

"Throw down the fence and let me pass over you."

The fence tumbles to the ground.

"Don't fire a shot. Drive them with the bayonet."

General Roberts rides along the line swinging his cap. The air is thick with bullets aimed at him, but he heeds them not.

"Charge!" His voice rings out clear and distinct. With a hurrah the line of glittering steel sweeps on. The momentum of such a body of men is terrible. The Confederates fire, then flee across the fields to the shelter of the woods.

But Sheridan cannot hold his ground. Cleburne and McCown are so far round that he must choose a new position, and the regiments and batteries fall back into the new alignment as steadily as on parade.

General Cheatham has discovered that the Union men in front of him have the quality of staying; that to drive them he must attack with an overwhelming force. He masses his artillery, planting a battery of Napoleon guns by the brick-kiln south of Mr. Harding's house. The Union batteries reply. The artillery fire on the part of Cheatham is the prelude to a grand movement of Maningault's, Vaughn's, Maney's, and Wood's brigades, which advance through a dense cedar thicket, to be smitten with canister from double-shotted cannon and by a volley from Roberts's men. The Illinoisans hold their ground so stubbornly, and the artillery fire is so destructive, that the Confederates recoil. Cheatham called up Anderson's brigade of Mississippians, and with this reinforcement again urged on the men.

"The ground must be held!" shouted Sheridan, riding along the Union lines. The troops responded with a cheer. Sheridan rode to General Thomas and asked for help, but Thomas could not take a regiment from his own line without endangering it, as we shall see. Sheridan has fired away all his ammunition. Aides are riding over the field in the rear in search of the supply train, but cannot find it. Houghtaling and Hescock have fired nearly their last round. Since the beginning of the battle Houghtaling alone has fired nearly one thousand one hundred rounds. Most of his horses have been shot.

Sheridan knows that a critical moment is at hand, for he sees Cheatham preparing to strike another blow. Through the thicket the Confederates come once more, charging upon Houghtaling's battery, which can make no reply. The pieces which have been so powerful for the Union are dumb. Houghtaling cannot make them speak at this critical moment —cannot even take them away, for his horses are mangled and helpless.

Roberts sees that he must fall back. "Rally along the turnpike!" he shouts. "Give us ammunition!" is the cry as the troops fall back, followed by the Confederates.

Back beyond the turnpike moves the line. Conspicuous above all other men is the commander of the brigade, riding through the storm, giving his orders as upon parade. Suddenly he reels and falls from his horse. Three bullets have struck him at once.

"Boys, put me on my horse again."

The soldiers raise him in their arms, but the brave heart ceases its beating.

The Confederates are close upon them. They cannot carry the body to the rear; they lay it beneath a tree, cover it quickly with brush, and leave it on the field, trusting that it may escape the notice of the Confederates, who strip the clothes from the Union dead.

The fight is over Houghtaling's guns. Houghtaling is borne from the field wounded. Lieutenant Taliaferro is instantly killed. Nearly one-half of the Twenty-second and Forty-second and Twenty-seventh Illinois are killed and wounded. The gunners, unable to work their pieces, use their pistols and swords, until twenty-five are killed, wounded, and captured. All in vain. The advancing host outnumber them, and with exultant yells seize the cannon.

We have been seeing thus far what part the right wing took in the battle up to eleven o'clock. Johnson's and Davis's divisions have been doubled back by a superior flanking force; Sheridan's has stood immovable till, out of ammunition and nearly surrounded, it is obliged to fall back. We are not to think that there is silence everywhere else.

Let us go to another part of the field. It was past eight o'clock when the fugitives from Johnson's division, streaming across the Nashville Pike, revealed to Rosecrans the disaster that had come to McCook. We have seen Thomas sending Rousseau's division to form a line along the Nashville Pike, with Van Cleve's division forming beyond it, thus making a line of battle almost at right angles to the line as it was when the battle began. Then the troops faced mostly south-east. Negley's division still faces in that direction, while Rousseau, Van Cleve, and Wood face northwest. Towards this new line the drift of the right wing is setting.

Following, now, the wake of the advancing Confederates, we see that McCown and Cleburne have made a long march. At daylight they faced west. Their movement has been a half-wheel—facing north-east and now south. When they started, McCown was on the extreme left, but he halted to supply his men with ammunition, and Cleburne moved out upon the left, thus exchanging places.

The Confederate cavalry charged upon the wagon-trains on the Nashville Pike. Some of the teamsters fled to the woods, others stood transfixed with astonishment. The squadron of cavalry guarding the train surrendered, and the Confederates turned the train away.

Down the pike went the men of Fyffe's brigade of Van Cleve's division, the Seventh Indiana battery horses upon the gallop. Captain Swallow, commanding it, wheeled into position and sent his shells into the Confederate battalions. The Fourth United States Cavalry was General Rosecrans's escort, but General Rosecrans was everywhere over the field, and the escort, under Captain Otis, charged upon the Confederates, putting them to flight and recapturing the train.

The Confederates under Polk advanced upon Negley's division of Thomas's corps, Stewart's and Anderson's brigades falling upon Stanley's Union brigade. The shock is resolutely met, but the left wing of the Confederates is closing around Stanley, and he in turn is obliged to fall back.

It is no certain evidence of cowardice for troops to retreat, for a retreat is at times the highest possible generalship. From the first giving way of the line it was wisdom for the brigades to do what they did—fight stubbornly, and retreat when the ground was no longer tenable.

It was nine o'clock when Chalmers's division of Confederates advanced upon Cruft's brigade of Palmer's division, stationed west of the Nashville Pike and to the left of Negley's. Cruft's skirmishers fell back, contesting every inch of ground. On came the Confederates with exultant shouts, but the advancing line came to a stand-still before the volleys of the First and Second Kentucky, the Thirty-first Indiana, and Nineteenth Ohio. Every effort of the Confederates to drive them was foiled, till the troops on the right retired.

Standardt's Battery B, First Ohio, had but three rounds to each piece left when the brigade, to save itself from capture, was obliged to retire. The battery horses were nearly all disabled.

"Save the guns!" The cry came from the Second Kentucky and Nineteenth Ohio, who dragged the cannon to the rear.

It is eleven o'clock. The battle has raged since daylight. The Union line has been swung back as you would swing a door. Every division of Union troops, except Palmer's, of Thomas's corps, and Hazen's brigade, of Crittenden's corps, has been compelled to fall back. General Thomas J. Wood's division, which has held the ground between the railroad and the river, has been withdrawn and sent to the right, and Hazen holds the left of the line on the railroad. From the Confederates by Cowan's house, from the woods and fields in front, comes a terrific storm upon this one brigade, but, like a lone rock in the ocean breasting the billows, it stands there through the long struggle, never yielding an inch of ground from the beginning to the close of the battle. The position was the pivotal point of the Union line, and through the obstinacy and endurance of this brigade Rosecrans was able to reform and rearrange the other troops and continue the struggle.

In war there are narrow margins; there are only hair-breadths between victory and defeat. At eleven o'clock in the forenoon of December 31, 1862, if we could have looked down upon the battle of Stone River, we should have seen the cause of the Union trembling in the scale, with victory seemingly settling upon the banners of the Confederacy. General Bragg had driven the Union right wing, changed the front of battle, sent thousands of Union troops fleeing through the woods, captured more than twenty cannon; but there was one thing he had not accomplished—he had not conquered the indomitable wills of Generals Rosecrans, Thomas, Sheri-

28

dan, and thousands of men whose names never will be known to fame, but who were ready to lay down their lives for their country. It is the resolute determination of human wills that must be taken into account in battle—wills that know no defeat.

General Rosecrans formed his new line facing south-west. He directed General Thomas to place Rousseau's division in rear of Sheridan. He sent Loomis's and Gunther's batteries to a commanding knoll west of the railroad, and ordered Van Cleve's division to form on the right of Rousseau, to meet McCown's and Cleburne's divisions, which were coming round to seize the Nashville Turnpike.

Rousseau formed his line with the brigade of Regulars on the left, then John Beatty's brigade, with Scribner's in reserve. (We are not to confound John Beatty's brigade with that commanded by Samuel Beatty in Van Cleve's division.)

They are in an open field. In front is a cedar thicket, through which the Confederates are advancing.

"Forward and meet them!" is Rousseau's order to Colonel Shepard, commanding the Regulars. The Fifteenth, Sixteenth, Eighteenth, and Nineteenth regiments of United States troops enter the cedars and come face to face with Rains's Confederate brigade, which began the battle by routing Willich's brigade. The Confederates are flushed with success. They greet the Regulars with a yell, and the battle of the new line begins. The Regulars make a brave fight, but are forced to fall back, and the Confederates follow.

Their line of advance brings them in the rear of Grose's brigade of Palmer's division of the left wing, supporting Hazen's brigade. Palmer sees the cloud of Confederates coming down on his flank and rear.

"Change front!" he shouts, and the brigade wheels upon the double-quick.

The whole of McCown's line is advancing. Eighteen cannon on the knoll open with canister, and the Confederates are hurled back into the woods. A bullet has pierced the heart of General Rains. It is the first check which the hitherto victorious Confederate left wing has experienced.

The Confederates, commanded by McNair, with a yell advance upon Van Cleve. Rosecrans has ridden along the line and selected a place for Stokes's battery, placing it on a knoll a few rods west of the railroad, with the Pioneer Corps, composed of companies selected from several regiments—men who can build bridges, and who use axes and spades. Near the cannon is Samuel Beatty's brigade, and beyond are Fyffe's and Harker's brigades.

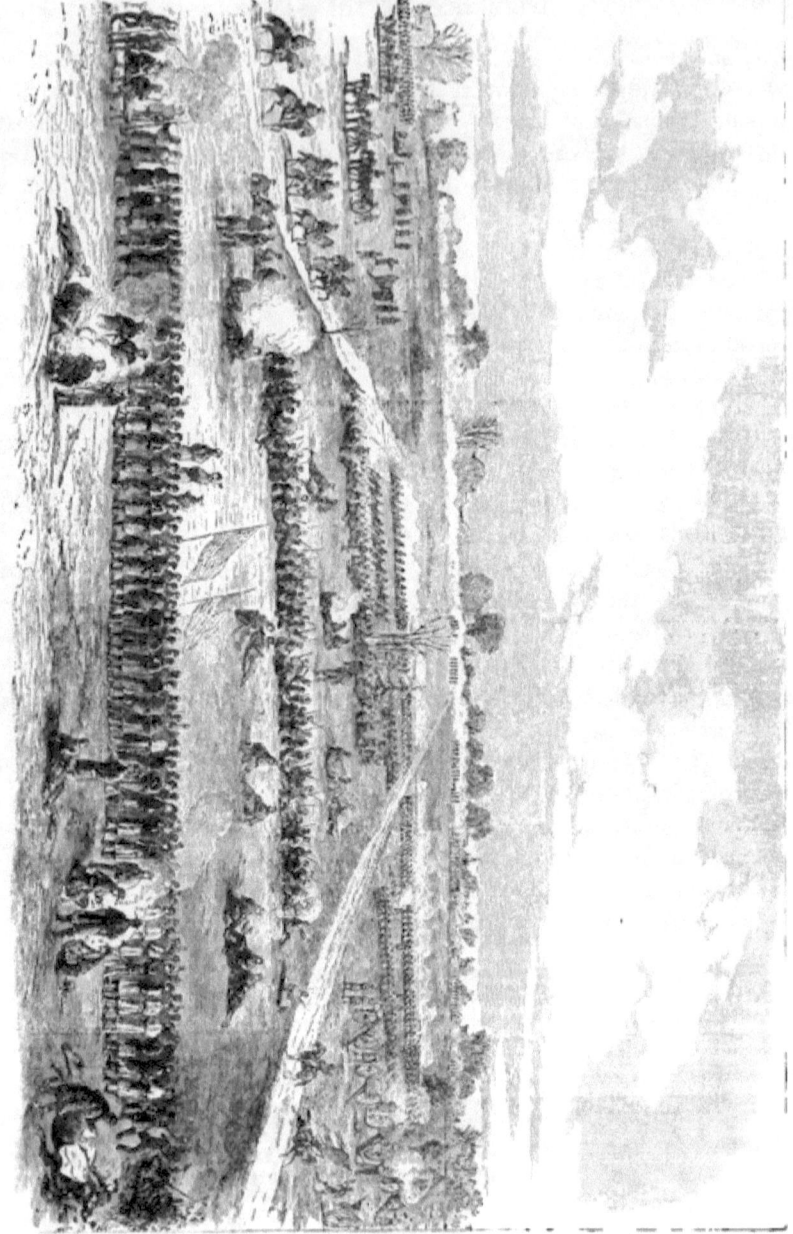

SCENE IN THE AFTERNOON AT STONE RIVER.

The Confederates come into the open field and rush upon the batteries, but are instantly overwhelmed. The Thirteenth Arkansas is all but annihilated. Ector's brigade of Texas troops is cut to pieces by the fire of Stokes's and Stevens's cannon.

Cleburne brings up all of his brigades, together with Vaughan's brigade of Cheatham's division. Bragg is still adhering to his plan of the morning, to make his left wing the sledge-hammer.

General Rosecrans is cheering the men by his presence. He understands Bragg's tactics. Samuel Beatty has formed his line, with the Ninth Kentucky and Nineteenth Ohio in front, and the Eleventh Kentucky and Seventy-ninth Indiana in rear. The front line holds its ground, delivering a destructive fire. The second line bides its time. It comes. With a hurrah the troops spring to their feet, rush upon the enemy, and drive them in confusion. The remainder of Cleburne's division fall with tremendous force upon Fyffe and Harker, who are outflanked and driven. In the retreat two guns of Bradley's battery are lost. It is a critical moment. Van Cleve is wounded; the line is broken. In a few moments the Confederates will be in possession of the turnpike. All of Rosecrans's trains will be exposed to capture. McCook and Rosecrans are riding up and down the lines endeavoring to rally the men.

You have already read of the stubborn fight made by Roberts's brigade—how their brave commander fell. His body is under the brush-heap out yonder, in possession of the Confederates. Two of the regiments—the Twenty-seventh and Fifty-first Illinois—are on their way to the rear to obtain ammunition. General Rosecrans sees them.

"Who commands these troops?" he asks.

"I do," said Colonel Bradley.

"Go into that thicket and stop the enemy. Quick—don't lose a moment!"

"I have not much ammunition, but we will drive them with the bayonet," is the reply.

The men load their guns.

"Left face; forward!"

The two regiments move on and meet the advancing foe.

"Halt! Aim! Fire!" A sheet of flame bursts from the line. "Charge bayonets!" A glittering line of steel, of men in blue, comes out from the murky cloud upon the Confederates, who flee in consternation before the impetuous attack.

The consternation runs along the whole Confederate line.

"Our flank is turned!" is the cry of the panic-stricken troops. Polk's,

Johnson's, and Liddell's brigades crumble in an instant, the men breaking ranks. The officers try to rally them, but all in vain. They flee through the woods, so demoralized and scattered that they cannot be rallied. It is a harvest-time for the men from Illinois. They gather up more than two hundred prisoners, and recapture the two cannon left behind by Harker in his retreat.

With that impetuous charge the tide of battle has turned. Bragg will not gain the turnpike or capture the ammunition of the Union army, nor its beef and bread. Not now will he see the Union troops fleeing towards Nashville or wandering like sheep along the country roads to be picked up by his cavalry; nor will he move northward once more to re-fit his army in Kentucky or redeem that State from the rule of Abraham Lincoln.

That panic in his lines, so unaccountable to the Confederate officers, is like a cold wintry blast, chilling the ardor of the troops.

General Thomas has consolidated his brigades. They are as orderly and well arranged as a class under the eye of a school-master. Rose-crans rides along the line. "You must hold the position at all hazards," he says.

"We will," is the response.

You have seen a pier in a stream with the water swirling around it. Such a breakwater is General Thomas's corps, and against which a raft of Confederate brigades is hurled by Bragg.

Rosecrans at last had his army concentrated; the front line was strengthened by the troops which had fought till their ammunition was gone, and now, with a new supply, stoody ready to respond to any call.

Hazen occupied a copse which has received the name of the Round Forest, behind which stood Sheridan's division.

General Rosecrans saw a body of Confederate troops moving west. It was General Adams's brigade of Breckinridge's division, ordered across the river by Bragg, who was vexed to find that his onward movement had been checked.

"Where shall I go in?" was Adams's question to Major-general Polk.

"Attack them and take that battery," was the reply of Polk, who pointed towards Hazen's line.

All day long Adams's troops had heard the uproar of battle, and now, as the sun was descending, they were to break the Union centre, double it back, and reap the honors of victory. It is a magnificent advance, but the lines are cut through by shot and shell—by a deadly fire of musketry.

The Fifteenth and Fifty-seventh Indiana rush forward, gather up two hundred prisoners and bring them in, with a hurrah going up from the Union line.

"Come over with Preston's and Palmer's brigades," was Bragg's order to Breckinridge.

Again Rosecrans saw the Confederates filing westward.

Bragg brought up his batteries and placed them in position. He sent word to Breckinridge's batteries across the river to open fire at long range, and solid shot and shell were poured upon the Union line.

Rosecrans was riding through the storm, paying no heed to the entreaty of his officers to take a less exposed position. His faithful chief of staff, Garesche, was instantly killed—his head severed from his body by a cannon-ball.

Under cover of the artillery fire the Confederates once more advanced, but it was a feeble attack, and the unwelcome truth came to Bragg that his troops had lost their aggressive force, while officers and men alike along the Union lines felt that the tide had turned; that no matter what Bragg might attempt, he could not move them from their chosen position. The sun goes down, the cannons' lips grow cold, the uproar dies away. In the closing hours of the year the hospital corps gather up the wounded.

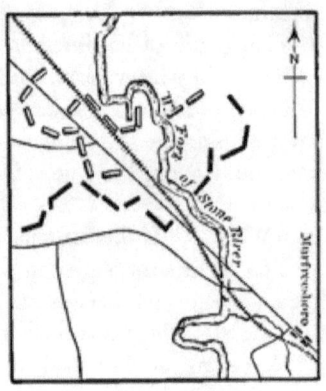

CLOSE OF THE BATTLE.

"Renew the ammunition," was the first order of Rosecrans. His officers came to his headquarters—in a little log-cabin.

"What shall we do?" he asked.

The officers were divided in opinion, but all said, "We will stand by you, whatever you desire to do."

"I will examine the ground. General Stanley, you will accompany me."

General Rosecrans looked over the ground.

"We will fight it out where we are," he said.

"Send what you can of the wounded to Nashville," was the order to the surgeon-general, and a long train of ambulances filled with wounded moved down the pike. The Confederates could hear the rumbling of the wheels, and thought that Rosecrans was retreating. Great was their surprise in the morning to see the Union lines firm and compact, with breastworks thrown up. Rosecrans supposed that Bragg would renew the attack with great vigor, while Bragg could not understand why Rosecrans, who had been whipped, did not retreat.

During the day there was cannonading, but not much fighting.

"Find the best position on the east side of the river from which you can enfilade the Union lines west of it," was Bragg's order to Captain Robertson, his chief of artillery, who reported that it was the ground held by the Union soldiers of Van Cleve's division.

"It is a very important point, for it commands General Polk's line. If you can take it you can mass your artillery there and compel Rosecrans to retreat," said Robertson.

Bragg resolved to drive out Van Cleve. He sent Robertson's own battery of six twelve-pounder Napoleon guns, Temple's battery, and two thousand cavalry to reinforce Breckinridge. As soon as the hill was taken, Robertson was to rain his shells upon the Union lines west of the river.

The afternoon of January 2d is wearing away. Breckinridge is trying to persuade Bragg not to attack.

"The Union artillery will sweep the field, and my troops will be cut to pieces," he said.

Bragg will not abandon his plan; the attack must be made. Breckinridge rides across the river to order the advance. He meets General Preston, and says, "This attack is against my judgment. I shall do my duty in obeying the order. If it ends in disaster, and if I am slain, I want you to tell the people that the attack was unwise and that I tried to prevent it."

The Union troops nearest the river on the east side were those of Price's brigade, with Livingston's Third Wisconsin battery. Next in line was Grider's, Fyffe's, and Grose's brigades.

We are to remember that the river is a small stream with a rocky bed, and easily forded. On the west bank is Hascall's division. The stream is so narrow that the right of Breckinridge's line will be within musket-range of Hascall as it advances. Between the railroad and the river, along the line occupied by Hascall's troops, is a ridge as high as that on the east side, from which Van Cleve is to be driven.

The Confederate brigade nearest the river is Hanson's; then Palmer's, forming the front line. Five hundred feet in rear are Adams's and Preston's brigades; in the third line are Wright's and Vaughan's. Out on the right is the cavalry, which will dash upon the Union troops as soon as they are put to rout.

Four o'clock. The sun is near its setting, and whatever is done must be done quickly. Suddenly the Confederate cannon, massed on the west side of the river, begin to flash. General Rosecrans believes that the movement on the east side is to be a feint, while Bragg intends to move once more against the centre. Five minutes later he sees that the massed columns of Breckinridge are advancing in earnest. They move with loaded muskets and fixed bayonets.

GENERAL BRECKINRIDGE.

Livingston's guns open upon them, but the Confederates move on, heedless of shell and canister. The Fifty-first Ohio and Eighth Kentucky open fire upon them.

The onset is so vigorous that Price's brigade is driven. The Nineteenth Ohio rushes to their relief, also the Ninth and Eleventh Kentucky, holding the Confederates in check a short time.

Let us stand for a moment on the ridge west of the river. Captain Mendenhall, Crittenden's chief of artillery, is there when Breckinridge's line begins its advance.

"This is the place for the artillery. Send all the batteries here," is the order.

Aides ride in haste. The drivers lash their horses to a run, and the cannon go rumbling up the hill. In a few minutes fifty-eight pieces are in position.

The artillerymen look down upon the scene. They see Price's and Grider's men falling back, and the Confederates rushing on with exultant yells. Suddenly the hill bursts into flame; the shells go tearing through the Confederate ranks. Negley's men rise from behind the hill where they have been biding their time, Miller's, Grose's, and Fyffe's brigades delivering their volleys. No body of men, however brave, can advance through such a storm. Cut through and through by the terrible artillery fire, the Confederates break and flee, hastening to get beyond the reach of the cannon. The Union troops follow and capture three guns.

The sun has set, and with its going down there is a great sinking of heart in the Confederate army. The troops are demoralized. In this attack nearly one thousand four hundred have been killed or wounded. Bragg has struck his last blow and been defeated. What Breckinridge feared has come to pass.

The night is dark, the clouds lowering. A cold rain sets in, the river begins to rise, and Rosecrans withdraws his troops from the east side, concentrating his army.

The Confederate generals are disheartened. At midnight they hold a consultation. Cheatham and Withers send a note to Bragg informing him that their troops are in a deplorable condition, and advise him to retreat.

"We shall maintain our position at every hazard," said Bragg, who was very angry and vexed over the failure of all his plans. Though he was so resolute, his army had lost heart. The troops expected victory. At eleven o'clock in the morning of the last day of the year they thought they had won it; but the Union troops, instead of fleeing back to Nashville, were more defiant than ever.

At eleven o'clock on the night of January 3d the Confederate army began its retreat. Long before daybreak it was miles away on the road to Tullahoma. When the sun rose not a Confederate was to be seen. With hurrahs the troops received the news. The killed and wounded in each army numbered between ten and eleven thousand men. Rosecrans had lost between twenty and thirty cannon, but he had won a victory which was of incalculable value to the country.

CHAPTER XVIII.

ON THE MISSISSIPPI.

THERE are so many turnings and windings of the Mississippi that the distance from New Orleans by river to Memphis is eight hundred miles, while in a direct line it is only four hundred. The bottom-lands below the last-named city are very wide, but two miles above Vicksburg the bluffs form the eastern bank of the river, and are two hundred and sixty feet high — not perpendicular, but very steep. Below Vicksburg they are not so high. From Cairo to New Orleans there is no other place so strong by nature.

The Confederates erected batteries there soon after the war began. In June, 1862, they had twenty-six cannon in position — some on the top of the bluffs to pour a fire down upon the Union gunboats, others but a few feet above the water, to send rifled shot into the sides of the vessels.

The river makes a very sharp bend just above Vicksburg, running north-east five miles, then turning suddenly south and south-west. The tongue of land is six miles long, but hardly a mile wide. The cannon on the bluffs could sweep it with their fire.

In April, 1862, Admiral Farragut ran past the forts below New Orleans with the war-ships and captured that city. In June he steamed up the river to bombard Vicksburg. The people living along the river were greatly astonished when they saw the great sea-going vessels, with masts and spars and rigging, moving up stream.

It was two o'clock in the morning, June 28th, when the vessels steamed towards the batteries. The vessels advanced in two columns. The Confederate cannon opened fire, and the ships replied. Slowly steamed the fleet, the sides of the vessels all aflame, pouring shot and shell upon the batteries at the foot of the bluffs. At six o'clock in the evening they dropped anchor in the bend above the city.

"The batteries have been passed, and they can be passed again as often as necessary," said the admiral.

Fifteen sailors had been killed and thirty wounded, most of them being on the gunboat *Clifton*. A shot passed through the boiler, and the men were scalded by the steam.

On July 1st the fleet of Commodore Davis—the gunboats which had destroyed the Confederate fleet at Memphis—joined Admiral Farragut just below the mouth of the Yazoo River.

For many months such mechanics as the Confederates could find had been at work up the Yazoo building an iron-clad vessel—the *Arkansas*, which was one hundred and eighty feet long, thirty wide, with a long iron beak under water, designed for running into the hulls of the Union gunboats. Its sides were stout oaken timber. Outside the timber was a plating of railroad iron. Inside were compressed bales of cotton, with a sheathing of wood to prevent the latter from taking fire. The iron, oak, and cotton made the sides so strong that cannon-balls had little effect upon it. You might as well throw peas at an iron pot. There were ten cannon—two at the bow, two at the stern, the others on the sides.

We are to remember that the war was between two systems of labor; that it was a revolt of the slave-holders against free labor; that in the North there were many mills, factories, and machine-shops; that the South had few mills or machine-shops, and very little skilled labor. Men who invented machinery, and who knew how to run engines or file iron, were not found in the slave-holding States. It did not require much skill to hew a stick of timber or to bolt the railroad iron upon the oaken sides of the *Arkansas*, but it was not so easy to build the engines. The men who undertook it had few tools; they did not know how to do it. Thus it was the engines of the steamboats were poor and constantly breaking down.

The *Arkansas* was commanded by Isaac N. Brown, who was educated by the United States Government, was an officer in the Navy when the war began, but who joined the Confederates.

The Union commanders knew that the *Arkansas* was getting ready to attack the Union fleet. Commodore Davis directed Commander Walke to go up the Yazoo in the iron-plated *Carondelet*, with the wooden gunboat *Tyler* and the *Queen of the West* (the ram) to reconnoitre. The *Arkansas* was moving down stream. Captain Walke thought it best to turn the head of the gunboat in the same direction. He made a mistake, for the stern of the *Carondelet* was not protected with iron; besides, his stern-guns were only thirty-two-pounders, while one of the bow-guns was a seventy-pounder and the other a fifty-pounder.

The *Arkansas* came alongside, and the fight began. The vessels were very near to each other, and the broadside-guns flashed muzzle to muzzle. A shot crashes into the *Carondelet*, killing and wounding ten of the crew. In turn, a shot goes into the pilot-house of the *Arkansas*, killing one of her pilots, wounding another, also Captain Brown. The broadsides of the *Carondelet* were so tremendous that when the shot struck the iron plating of the *Arkansas* they opened the seams between the timbers, letting in the water. They riddled the smoke-stack so that there was little draft in the furnaces.

All the time the *Tyler* was raining its solid shot upon the *Arkansas*, receiving shot in return, which made great rents in her sides, killing and wounding the men.

Down the river steamed the vessels into the Mississippi, the *Arkansas* running through Commodore Davis's fleet. The cannon opened fire, but the balls rolled from her iron sides as hailstones from a building.

Before the gunboats could get up steam and raise their anchors to grapple with the *Arkansas*, she was out of range and under the protection of the guns on the bluffs.

Admiral Farragut and Commodore Davis were greatly chagrined. They determined that when night came they would destroy her. The fleet advances — the ships, gunboats, and batteries flash and flame. The *Arkansas* shifts her position, and in the darkness and haze and smoke the Union vessels, one by one, pass by and thus miss her.

On the night of July 22d we see the *Essex*, under Captain Porter, with the *Queen of the West*, gliding down towards Vicksburg. The *Benton*, *Cincinnati*, and *Louisville* accompany them far enough to send their shells into the Confederate works. The *Essex*, paying no attention to the batteries, steers for the *Arkansas*, running by so close that you might leap from one vessel to the other. The gunners of the *Essex* send three shot, nine inches in diameter, into the *Arkansas*, killing or wounding thirteen of her crew. The *Queen of the West* came at full speed and rammed her prow against the *Arkansas*, giving her a great blow. All the while the batteries were raining solid shot upon the two Union vessels; but the *Queen of the West* made her way unharmed back to Commodore Davis's fleet, while the *Essex* joined Admiral Farragut.

The water was rapidly falling, and Admiral Farragut was obliged to go down to New Orleans with his fleet. The troops under General Williams landed at Baton Rouge, and Captain Porter, with the *Essex*, dropped anchor above the town, keeping a sharp lookout for the *Arkansas*.

Baton Rouge was the capital of Louisiana. The troops which had taken possession of the town were the Fourteenth Maine, Sixth Michigan, Seventh Vermont, Twenty-first Indiana, Thirtieth Massachusetts, Fourth Wisconsin, the Second, Fourth, and Sixth Massachusetts batteries—about two thousand men.

General Breckinridge, commanding the Confederate troops in Mississippi, planned an attack. The *Arkansas*, which had made so brave a fight at Vicksburg, was to descend the river and sink the *Essex* and other gunboats—the *Sumter, Cayuga, Kineo, Katahdin*—all of them small vessels, while he, with a force much larger than that of General Williams, would sweep the Union troops into the river.

"The Confederates are coming!" was the word brought to General Williams by the negroes, who placed his troops in line of battle.

The Twenty-first Indiana was on picket duty outside the town. A dense fog settled down upon the Mississippi and all the surrounding country, but through the night the soldiers stood with ears open to catch the faintest sound from the expected enemy. If General Breckinridge thought to catch General Williams asleep and unprepared, he was mistaken. At half-past three the Union troops were under arms. Many of the soldiers are on the sick-list. The malaria is in their blood; they are burning up with fever. Day by day the hospitals are filling. The regiments have been sadly thinned since they left the North.

General Breckinridge had six thousand men and thirteen cannon. The days are hot, and a number of his soldiers have dropped by the roadside, reducing his army to about four thousand. He has an understanding with Captain Brown, commanding the *Arkansas*, that the attack is to be made at daylight. If the *Arkansas* can destroy the gunboats—if the force under Williams can be swept away—the Confederates will have control of the river from New Orleans to Vicksburg, which will enable them to obtain supplies from the Arkansas River and open communication with Texas.

On through the darkness and fog move the Confederates in three brigades, commanded by Ruggles, Allen, and Clarke. The Union pickets hear the tramping of advancing feet. Day is dawning when the Confederate skirmishers come upon the Twenty-first Indiana. The Union troops, who are eating breakfast, are ready in a moment, the firing bringing the soldiers everywhere to their feet.

Very soon after the battle began, General Williams, who was riding along the line, fell mortally wounded, and Colonel Cahill took command.

The Confederates began the attack with great vigor. On the right of the Union line were the Sixth Michigan and Nims's Massachusetts battery; on the left, the Fourteenth Maine and Everett's battery. The attack was north and east of the town. The Union soldiers on the left were in an open field; the Confederates were partially sheltered by woods.

From daylight till ten o'clock the contest went on. There was first a scattering fire, then quick, heavy volleys, the artillery firing canister and making havoc in the lines; then there comes a lull for a few moments, and then the volleys begin again. Gradually the Union troops fall back, disputing every inch of ground. The Confederates get possession of a portion of the Union camp. They leave the ranks to secure the plunder, and then set the tents on fire.

BATTLE OF BATON ROUGE.

They rush upon Nims's battery and capture two of the cannon, wheel them round, load them, and open fire upon the Sixth Michigan. A Confederate officer waves a flag in triumph, and the Confederate battle-cry rings out amid the uproar; but Captain Nims's other guns are sweeping them down, and the Sixth Michigan charge and recapture the cannon, handing them over to Captain Nims, who has his own once more.

The Twenty-first Indiana holds its ground stubbornly, refusing to yield. The gunboats send their shells along the flanks of the Confederate troops. The *Arkansas* has not made her appearance. The Confederate troops lose heart. A great many of their officers have fallen, and nearly five hundred men have been killed or wounded. At ten o'clock the

GUNBOATS AT THE BATTLE OF BATON ROUGE.

battle is over, the Confederates retreating, leaving the ground strewn with
dead.

As the *Arkansas* had not come down, Captain Porter, in the *Essex*,
with the gunboats, the next morning went up the river in search of her.
One of her engines had broken down the day before, and the engineers
had been hammering all night to make it work.

"We cannot fight," said the Confederate commander; "set the vessel
on fire."

Solid shot and shell crashed against her sides. The men leaped ashore.
Up from the vessel rolled a great column of smoke from the burning cotton. Down the Mississippi floated the *Arkansas*, in flames, till the fire
reached the magazine; then came an explosion, a raining down of burning
timbers, pieces of railroad iron, cannon, solid shot, and shells.

Thus the vessel which the Confederates fondly hoped would drive
the Union fleet from the Mississippi disappeared. It had failed because
the Confederacy had no men who could file and hammer and make engines. Slavery kept men in ignorance; freedom educated them. That
was the difference.

The order issued by the War Department October 24, 1862, appointed General Grant commander of the Department of the Mississippi. He
had forty-eight thousand men in his department. Several thousand were

needed to protect the railroad over which he received his supplies. There was so much going on in Virginia and Kentucky that the War Department had not time to give much attention to affairs in the West, and Grant was therefore left to do his own planning.

The next work to be done was the taking of Vicksburg. The great question was how to accomplish it. The Confederates were making it stronger every day—planting more cannon, building intrenchments, and resolving to hold it at all hazards. Were the Union troops to capture that stronghold, the States of Arkansas, Texas, and Louisiana would be severed from the remainder of the Confederacy. It would be a crushing blow.

You remember the battle of Pea Ridge, in north-western Arkansas—the defeat of the Confederates under Van Dorn. After that battle there was no Confederate force to oppose General Curtis.

We have seen how the troops under Van Dorn were hastened to Corinth, where they were defeated by Rosecrans. General Curtis, therefore, marched east to capture Little Rock, but his provisions failed. He had to put the troops on half-rations and hasten towards the Mississippi.

DESTRUCTION OF THE "ARKANSAS."

He reached it at Helena, below Memphis, where the steamboats supplied him with food. The Union troops were widely scattered. Four thousand were at Columbus in Kentucky, whence Grant received his supplies. He was obliged to station bodies of soldiers at every bridge.

29

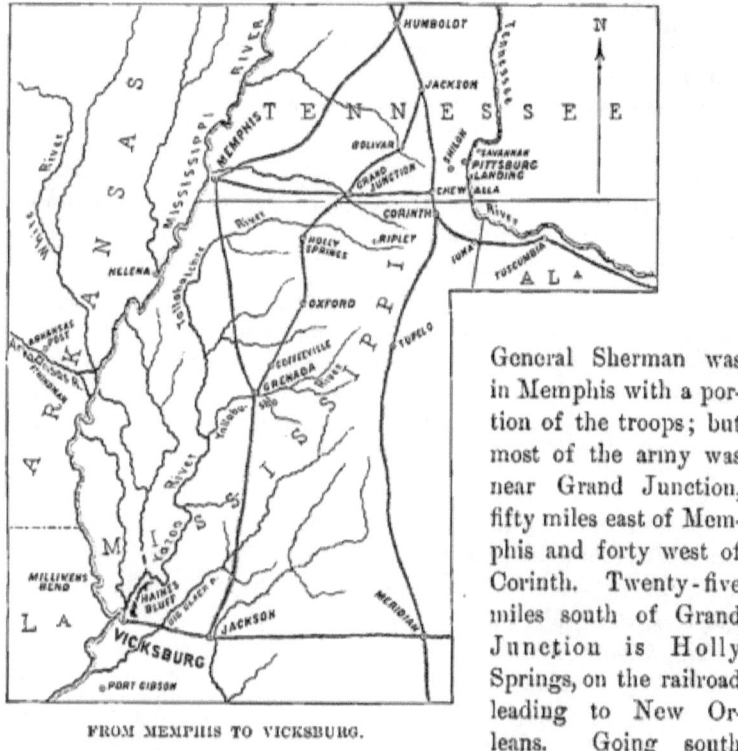

FROM MEMPHIS TO VICKSBURG.

General Sherman was in Memphis with a portion of the troops; but most of the army was near Grand Junction, fifty miles east of Memphis and forty west of Corinth. Twenty-five miles south of Grand Junction is Holly Springs, on the railroad leading to New Orleans. Going south from Holly Springs we come to the Tallabatchie River, which runs south-east to the Yazoo, which empties into the Mississippi twelve miles above Memphis. It winds through the broad bottom-lands east of the Mississippi. The bluffs are fifty miles east of the river opposite Helena. The railroad is on the table-land still farther east. There are no towns in the bottom-lands— only plantations—but along the railroad are Abbeville, Grenada, and other places.

After the defeat of Van Dorn at Corinth, Jefferson Davis appointed General Pemberton to command the Confederate army. He was at Jackson, the capital of Mississippi. Van Dorn was in command of the troops along the Tallahatchie. He had twenty-four thousand men; there were six thousand at Vicksburg, nearly six thousand more at Port Hudson, with other troops, giving Pemberton in all forty thousand.

General Grant saw that a movement from Grand Junction along the railroad would bring the army in rear of Vicksburg, which would compel the Confederates to evacuate that place. He moved south along the railroad. General Sherman advanced from Memphis November 24, 1862. General Hovey, with a portion of the troops at Helena, crossed the Mississippi and marched east, all three detachments moving towards Van Dorn, who retreated from the Tallahatchie southward, and took up a new position behind the Yallabusha River, another branch of the Yazoo.

General Grant reached Oxford, sixty miles south of Grand Junction. General Sherman was near him, at College Hill. They were one hundred and eighty miles from their base of supplies. All their flour and beef must be brought from Columbus over a single track. There were so few locomotives on the railroad that they could not do the required work. General Grant asked for more engines, but the War Department for some reason did not supply them. Foraging parties visited the plantations and brought in cows, calves, and sheep. Grant saw that if he went much farther he would not be able to feed the army, and decided to change his plan—to send General Sherman back to Memphis, put his troops on steamboats, hasten down the river, ascend the Yazoo a short distance, and attack Vicksburg in the rear, while he with the rest of the army would march from Oxford and join him. When united it would be a powerful army, which would receive its supplies by the river.

The Confederate Government in Richmond saw the great danger which threatened the Confederacy, and President Davis hastened west, taking General Joseph E. Johnston with him, and appointing him commander of all the troops between the Mississippi and the Alleghanies. He visited Jackson and Vicksburg, and was cheered by the Confederate troops. Conscripts were coming by thousands, gathered in by the conscript officers.

We come to December 11. General Bragg is at Murfreesboro'; Rosecrans at Nashville, laying his plans. Bragg has nearly ten thousand cavalry. He sees a grand opportunity to cripple General Grant by destroying the railroad over which he receives his supplies, and sends General Forrest to do the work. On the morning of the 11th Forrest leaves Columbia, Tennessee, south of Nashville, moving west.

The Union scouts bring word to Rosecrans, who before night sends this despatch to General Grant: "Tell the commanders along the road to look out for Forrest."

General Forrest crossed the Tennessee at Clifton on an old flat-boat, swimming his horses. He had two thousand five hundred men. Twenty miles west of the river he came upon Colonel R. G. Ingersoll, commanding seven hundred Union cavalry. Ingersoll and more than two hundred

FORAGING PARTIES.

of his men were captured, the rest put to flight.   Forrest had a skirmish
with two regiments near Jackson.   But he had not come to fight.   He
turns north, reaches the railroad, burns bridges, tears up the track, moving north to the Kentucky line, then turning south once more towards
Lexington.

At Parker's Cross-roads, not far from Lexington, Tennessee, he is confronted by General Sullivan, sent by General Grant with two brigades
to cut off his retreat.   Forrest begins a battle, but is put to rout with a
loss of six guns, three hundred men, and several wagons.   He had done
great damage—destroyed sixty miles of the railroad and killed, wounded,
and captured nearly two thousand Union troops.

Grant was to receive a more disastrous blow.   Van Dorn had three
thousand five hundred cavalry.   He knew that Grant's supplies were
at Holly Springs, where there was a brigade under General Murphy.
The Union cavalry was forty miles away, destroying the Mobile and Ohio
Railroad.   Now was his opportunity.   Putting himself at the head of his
cavalry he started from Grenada, and made a rapid march.

"Be prepared for Confederate cavalry, and hold your position at all
hazards," is the despatch sent by Grant to Murphy at Holly Springs, and
to the commander at Grand Junction.

Murphy has one thousand five hundred men guarding the supplies
piled up in the depot and surrounding buildings.   At daylight the next

morning Van Dorn is upon him; and the cowardly Murphy, almost without firing a shot, surrenders his whole command. A few minutes later a cloud of black smoke darkens the sky. In an hour property worth one million five hundred thousand dollars is destroyed.

Murphy was court-martialled, disgraced, and dismissed from the service as a coward.

Van Dorn attacked a small body of Union troops at Davis's Mills and was repulsed. He advanced to Bolivar and was driven off by the brave men there. He was repulsed at Middleburg. All of which shows that Murphy might have defeated him, and saved the country from the disaster which upset Grant's plan and brought defeat to Sherman at Vicksburg, as we shall see.

A great fleet of steamboats, with the divisions of Generals A. J. Smith, Morgan L. Smith, and George W. Morgan cast loose from Memphis and descended the Mississippi, to be joined at Helena by General Steele's division, making an army of thirty-two thousand with sixty cannon. It was a magnificent sight. There were sixty-seven steamboats crowded with men, who clustered on the decks like bees upon a hive.

Twenty miles above Vicksburg A. J. Smith's division landed on the west side of the river, marched south-west and reached the railroad over which the cars were bringing provisions to Vicksburg. The bridges were burned and the track destroyed. The steamboats went on to the mouth of the Yazoo, and sailed up that stream thirteen miles. The troops landed beneath the great cottonwood-trees on the bottom-lands. A. J. Smith, having destroyed the railroad, hastened on, and on December 27th the whole army was on shore.

General Sherman knew very little about the ground before him, or the Confederate forts and rifle-pits. He only knew that the Walnut Hills, as the bluffs above Vicksburg are called, were lined with forts and rifle-pits and breastworks; that thousands of slaves had been employed upon the intrenchments; that there were bayous, swamps, lakes, miry places, deep ravines, high hills, tangled thickets, and a Confederate army before him. He must feel his way.

He hoped to descend the river so rapidly that the Confederates would be taken by surprise; but before a soldier embarked at Memphis they knew all about the plan. Although Memphis had been captured, the people in that city were as much devoted to the Confederacy as ever. Along the river were detachments of cavalry, and as soon as the fleet started couriers rode with the news, so that the Confederates had full information of the movement. The troops which had been confronting

Grant along the line of the railroad were hurried west, and placed behind the intrenchments. Instead of six thousand, the Confederates numbered twelve thousand.

The bluffs were fully two hundred feet high, and the Union artillery might just as well have been left at Memphis.

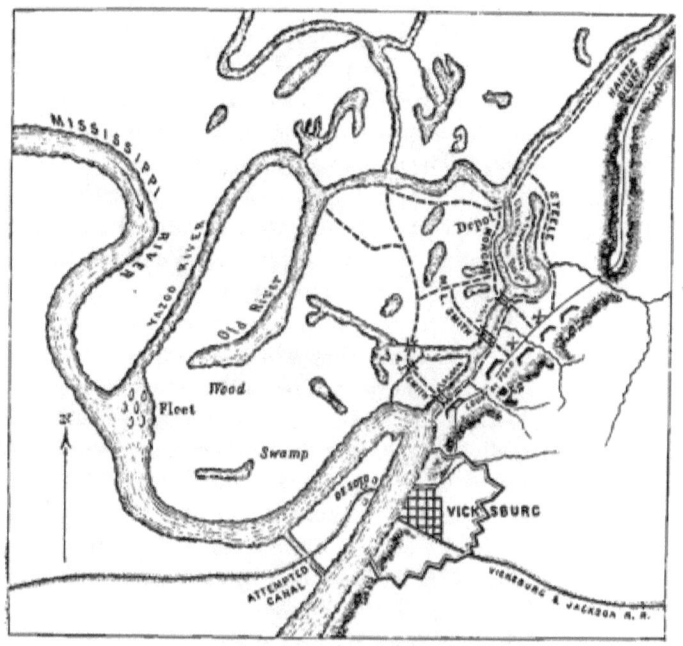

THE CHICKASAW BAYOU.

General Sherman knew nothing of what had happened at Holly Springs. He expected to hear the thunder of Grant's guns in the rear of Vicksburg; he did not know that Grant, instead of advancing to join him, was falling back to Grand Junction because of the pusillanimous surrender of Murphy.

General A. J. Smith's division was on the right, then Morgan L. Smith's, then G. W. Morgan's, and lastly General Steele's on the left. Morgan was to make the attack, supported by Steele, while the other two divisions were to make a demonstration only.

The engineers reconnoitred the ground. They found the bayou, which was from fifty to one hundred feet wide, passable only at two points—one a sand-bar, the other an old and narrow levee.

At daylight December 28th the troops advanced. They soon came upon the Confederate pickets in the edge of the woods. The morning was hazy, and they could see only a dense forest thick with tangled vines. The Confederates opened fire. The Sixteenth Ohio, Twenty-second Kentucky, Fifty-fourth Indiana, and Lamphere's battery replied. For more than an hour the soldiers fired into the dense thicket, but saw very few of the Confederates.

General De Courcey deploys his brigade, and the troops drive the Confederates, who fled across the bayou. The brigade halted, and the engineers once more reconnoitred the ground. They saw that the trees on the other side of the stream had been slashed, and that every approach was enfiladed by cannon. The soldiers bivouacked where they were, waiting till night, that the engineers might build a pontoon-bridge. The road along which they were to advance was an old path blocked with fallen trees. When morning came the engineers discovered that beyond the fallen trees was a second bayou, crossed by a log bridge. It was a half mile from the place where the troops passed the night to the foot of the bluff. Every step of the way they would be exposed to the fire of the Confederates. Down on the right, Morgan L. Smith, very early in the morning, was wounded, and the command devolved upon General Stuart. The troops of the two divisions made a show of advancing, while De Courcey's and Blair's brigades were to make the real attack. The regiments of these brigades were formed in columns to cross the log bridge, the Sixteenth Ohio leading. Blair's brigade was on the left, ready to cross the first bayou. The signal is given, and the two columns emerge from the shelter of the woods. In an instant a tempest bursts upon them. Men fall by the score. Canister from the batteries sweeps them down. Six regiments of Confederates, resting their muskets on the breastworks and taking deliberate aim, cut them in pieces. On, almost up to the trenches, rushes the Sixteenth Ohio, till half the men are disabled. It can go no farther. The men see how hopeless the task before them, and turn back. The other regiments are in confusion, and the order to retire is given. In the few moments more than one thousand men have been killed, wounded, or are captured by the Confederates, who leap over their intrenchments and gather in those who cannot get away.

Going down to the right, we see the Sixth Missouri leading the advance along a levee so narrow that only two soldiers can stand abreast. The bluff rises high and steep above them. They throw themselves under the shelter of the bank, and wait for reinforcements; but no other troops follow. They dig holes, scraping out the dirt with their hands, lying there till night, and then retreat.

General Sherman, seeing how useless it would be to make a second attack, decided to send ten thousand men up the Yazoo to Haines's Bluff. The gunboats were to take part. Morning came, but the fog was thick, and the gunboats could not move. Rain was falling in torrents. It was seen that the river might suddenly rise, flood the lowlands, and drown the army. . General Sherman consulted with his officers, who advised the abandonment of the undertaking.

A flag of truce went out, and the ambulances came back filled with the wounded. It was a sad, disheartening spectacle. The expedition was a failure, and nearly two thousand brave soldiers had been sacrificed.

Up the Mississippi steamed the fleet to Milliken's Bend, where the soldiers disembarked on the Arkansas shore, landing there January 2d, at the same hour that Breckinridge was being repulsed and the Union troops winning the victory at Stone River.

CHAPTER XIX.

THE CLOSE OF 1862.

THIS the way the people responded to the drum-beat. When Fort Sumter was fired upon, President Lincoln called for seventy-five thousand militia, and ninety-one thousand volunteered for three months. In May and July, 1861, he called for half a million, and seven hundred thousand enlisted for three years. In July, 1862, when McClellan was pleading for more troops, President Lincoln called for three hundred thousand, and four hundred and twenty-one thousand left their farms and shops to become soldiers for three years; and in August eighty-seven thousand enlisted for three months—more than thirteen hundred thousand in all. They had been armed, equipped, uniformed, and were in the field. Free labor and an unquenchable patriotism had created an army which astonished the nations beyond the Atlantic.

In the Confederate States at the outbreak of the war the drum-beat was also heard in every village. Volunteers enlisted for a year. The conspirators who had brought about the war believed it would not last longer than a twelvemonth. The first Congress which met at Richmond was called a Provisional Congress. Jefferson Davis was inaugurated President February 22, 1862—Washington's birthday. An army of four hundred thousand was authorized. It was believed that if the soldiers were allowed to go home and rest a few days that they would gladly re-enlist for the war, no matter how long it might last, and they were granted a furlough of sixty days. It was soon discovered, however, that many of the soldiers, when the sixty days had expired, did not return, and had no intention of doing so. They had no desire to endure the hardships and privations, the weary marches, to be killed or wounded in battle. The Confederate armies were rapidly diminishing. The enthusiasm which flamed throughout the seceded States at the beginning of the war had died out. The States had left the Union to protect their "rights," but the people now saw their rights and their freedom disappear as quickly as a straw in a furnace-fire, when, on April 16, 1862, the Congress at Richmond passed a law which withdrew every man between the ages of eighteen and thirty-five from State control, and placed him under the power of Jefferson Davis so long as the war should last. It set aside all agreements made by the several States with the soldiers. Those who had enlisted for twelve months were not to have the privilege of going home at the end of the year, but, just as fish are drawn into a net, they were all swept permanently into the Confederate army, to serve till the end of the war, unless relieved by death or disability. By this act all rights of States or individuals were annihilated, and the Confederate Government became a military despotism. Conscription officers issued their requisitions, and there was no escape except by flight into the mountains or to the swamps of the lowlands. It was this act that filled up the ranks of General Lee, and enabled him to drive McClellan from Richmond, defeat Pope at Manassas, invade Maryland, and confront Burnside at Fredericksburg, and which enabled Bragg to force Buell back to the Ohio River.

When the war began there were three million nine hundred and fifty thousand slaves in the United States. The soldiers of the Northern States had not enlisted to liberate them, but to avenge the insult to the flag and maintain the Union. We have already seen how the corner-stone began to crumble (page 77); how the soldiers began to see that slavery was the cause of all the trouble; how President Lincoln, after the battle of Antietam, notified the Confederates that if they did not lay down their arms he should issue his proclamation on the 1st of January, 1863, giving the slaves their freedom. Through the closing months of 1862 slaves in great numbers were making their way into the Union lines, and were no longer turned back, but were cordially welcomed.

On the last night of the year a great crowd of colored people gathered in the "Contraband Camp" at Washington. With the last stroke of the midnight bell the Year of Jubilee, the great year of the Lord which they had looked for, prayed for, waited for, was to begin. They had been slaves; henceforth they were to be free. They knelt and gave thanks to God; they clapped their hands, shouted, and sang:

> "Oh, go down, Moses,
>   'Way down into Egypt's land;
> Tell King Pharaoh
>   To let my people go.
> Oh, Pharaoh said he would not cross—
>   Let my people go;
> But Pharaoh and his host were lost—
>   Let my people go."

"Once I cried all night," said a negro, "for the next morning my child was to be sold. She was sold. I never expect to see her again. Now, no more of dat. We's free. Dey can't sell wife and child no more. No more of dat; President Lincum has done shot de gate. Dat's what's de matter."

The great multitude shouted "Amen! Glory hallelujah!"

This the song they sung:

> "John Brown, the dauntless hero, with joy is looking on,
> From his home among the angels he sees the coming dawn;
> Then up with Freedom's banner and hail the glorious morn
> When the slaves shall all go free."

The hands of the clock moved on to midnight. The great multitude knelt. There was a stillness like the silence of the grave, broken only by the bell tolling the hour. The last peal died away along the peaceful waters of the Potomac, and they were free. This the prayer of an old negro: "Almighty God, bless President Lincoln and all the soldiers." All night long they danced and sung.

From that hour, wherever the Union soldiers marched, the Stars and Stripes was not only the emblem of the Union, but of freedom and human rights. Only through disaster, defeat, disappointment, through hardship, trial, suffering, through the outpouring of the richest wine of life, had the people of the North come to a comprehension that the drum-beat of the nation, in its final outcome, was to be not only the restoration of the Union, but a wiping out of the institution which had brought about the war.

The last week of 1862 beholds the Army of the Cumberland marching through a wintry storm to fight a desperate battle and win a victory in Tennessee. The Army of the Potomac, disheartened by its many defeats and the incompetency of its commanders, is resting upon the Falmouth Hills, confronted by the Confederate army, which has hurled them back from Fredericksburg heights. This the Christmas scene as pictured by Private John R. Paxton, out on picket:

"It was Christmas-day, 1862. 'And so this is war. And I am out here to shoot that lean, lank, coughing, cadaverous-looking butternut fellow over the river. So this *is war;* this is being a soldier. Hello, Johnny, what are you up to?' The river was narrow, but deep and swift. It was a wet cold, not a freezing cold. There was no ice—too swift for that.

"'Hello, Johnny, what you coughing so for?'

"'Yank, with no overcoat, shoes full of holes, nothing to eat but parched corn and tobacco, and with this derned Yankee snow a foot deep, there is nothin' left, *nothin'* but to get up a cough by way of protestin' against this infernal ill-treatment of the body. We-uns, Yank, all have a cough over here, and there's no sayin' which will run us to hole first, the cough or your bullets.'

"The snow still fell; the keen wind, raw and fierce, cut to the bone. It was God's worst weather, in God's forlornest, bleakest spot of ground, that Christmas-day of '62 on the Rappahannock, a half-mile below the town of Fredericksburg. But come, pick up your prostrate pluck, you shivering private. Surely there is enough dampness around without adding to it your tears.

"'Let's laugh, boys.'

"'Hello, Johnny.'

"'Hello yourself, Yank.'

"'Merry Christmas, Johnny.'

"'Same to you, Yank.'

"'Say, Johnny, got anything to trade?'

"'Parched corn and tobacco—the size of our Christmas, Yank.'

"'All right; you shall have some of our coffee and sugar and pork. Boys, find the boats.'

"Such boats! Some Yankee, desperately hungry for tobacco, invented them for trading with the Johnnies. They were hid away under the banks of the river for successive relays of pickets.

"We got out the boats. An old handkerchief answered for a sail. We loaded them with coffee, sugar, pork, and set the sail, and watched them slowly creep to the other shore. And the Johnnies? To see them crowd the bank, and push and scramble to be first to seize the boats, going into the water and stretching out their long arms! Then when they pulled the boats ashore, and stood in a group over the cargo, and to hear their exclamations: 'Hurrah for hog!' 'Say, that's not roasted rye, but genuine coffee. Smell it, you-uns.' 'And sugar too.' Then they divided the consignment. They laughed and shouted, 'Reckon you-uns been good to we-uns this Christmas-day, Yanks.' Then they put parched corn, tobacco, ripe persimmons into the boats, and sent them back to us. And we chewed the parched corn, smoked real Virginia leaf, ate persimmons, which, if they weren't very filling, at least contracted our stomachs to the size of our Christmas dinner. And so the day passed. We shouted, 'Merry Christmas, Johnny.' They shouted, 'Same to you, Yank.' And we

CHRISTMAS ON THE RAPPAHANNOCK.

forgot the biting wind, the chilling cold; we forgot those men over there were our enemies, whom it might be our duty to shoot before evening.

"We had bridged the river—spanned the bloody chasm. We were brothers, not foes, waving salutations of good-will in the name of the Babe of Bethlehem, on Christmas-day, in '62. At the very front of the opposing armies the Christ Child struck a truce for us—broke down the wall of partition, became our peace. We exchanged gifts. We shouted greetings back and forth. We kept Christmas, and our hearts were lighter for it, and our shivering bodies were not quite so cold."

The soldiers of the Union army usually called the Confederates "Johnny Rebs." When and where the term was first used, and why, is not known. The Confederates called the Union soldiers "Yanks"—the abbreviation of Yankee. When the war began the newspapers of the South boastingly set forth the superior qualities and bravery of the Confederate soldiers, and had much to say about their chivalry, and indulged in many expressions of contempt for the soldiers of the Union, and employed insulting epithets. That period had passed. The men marching beneath the Stars and Stripes had exhibited bravery in battle, constancy and steadfastness under defeat, and manly qualities which ever win admiration.

The Union soldiers, when the war begun, had little doubt of their ability to brush the Confederates aside, make their way to Richmond, reopen the Mississippi, and re-establish the authority of the United States throughout the South. They did not believe that men who were not accustomed to labor would be able to endure the hardship and fatigue of military campaigns. With the progress of the war egotism, expectation, and all illusions passed away. Soldiers from the North and soldiers from the South alike had proved their manhood. Respect had taken the place of disdain and contempt. There was no personal hatred. The men in blue and the men in gray alike were fighting for ideas and principles which to them were dearer than life.

So closes the first period of the war; to the Confederacy it was victory in the East, defeat in the West, military despotism, conscription, wasting of material resources, hopes deferred, fading of expectations, future foreboding. To the people of the North, notwithstanding the victories west of the Alleghanies and on the Mississippi, it was the period of defeat, disaster, disappointment, discipline; for by these a Divine Providence was leading the nation to comprehend that Justice, Liberty, Righteousness are eternal principles which may not be violated with impunity, and which are of more value than human life. At Manassas, Fair Oaks,

Malvern, Antietam, Shiloh, Fredericksburg, Stone River, thousands of brave hearts were at rest forever, not only that the Nation might live, the Government of the people be preserved, but that Justice, Liberty, and Righteousness might be established in this Western world, and the whole human race be lifted to a larger, nobler life.

The second and third periods will be presented in subsequent volumes.

INDEX.

30

THE END.

INTERESTING BOOKS FOR BOYS.

BOUND VOLUMES OF HARPER'S YOUNG PEOPLE for 1883, 1884, and 1885. Handsomely Bound in Illuminated Cloth, $3 00 per vol. *Bound Volumes for* 1880, 1881, 1882, *and* 1886, *are out of stock.*

THE BOY TRAVELLERS ON THE CONGO. Adventures of Two Youths in a Journey with Henry M. Stanley "Through the Dark Continent." By Thomas W. Knox. Copiously Illustrated. 8vo, Cloth, $3 00.

THE BOY TRAVELLERS IN THE RUSSIAN EMPIRE. Adventures of Two Youths in a Journey in European and Asiatic Russia. With Accounts of a Tour across Siberia, Voyages on the Amoor, Volga, and other Rivers, a Visit to Central Asia, Travels among the Exiles, and a Historical Sketch of the Empire from its Foundation to the Present Time. By Thomas W. Knox. Copiously Illustrated. 8vo, Cloth, $3 00.

THE BOY TRAVELLERS IN SOUTH AMERICA. Adventures of Two Youths in a Journey through Ecuador, Peru, Bolivia, Brazil, Paraguay, Argentine Republic, and Chili. With Descriptions of Patagonia and Tierra del Fuego, and Voyages upon the Amazon and La Plata Rivers. By Thomas W. Knox. Copiously Illustrated. 8vo, Cloth, $3 00.

THE BOY TRAVELLERS IN THE FAR EAST. By Thomas W. Knox. Five Parts. Copiously Illustrated. 8vo, Cloth, $3 00 each.

PART I. ADVENTURES OF TWO YOUTHS IN A JOURNEY TO JAPAN AND CHINA.—PART II. ADVENTURES OF TWO YOUTHS IN A JOURNEY TO SIAM AND JAVA. With Descriptions of Cochin-China, Cambodia, Sumatra, and the Malay Archipelago.—PART III. ADVENTURES OF TWO YOUTHS IN A JOURNEY TO CEYLON AND INDIA. With Descriptions of Borneo, the Philippine Islands, and Burmah.—PART IV. ADVENTURES OF TWO YOUTHS IN A JOURNEY TO EGYPT AND PALESTINE.—PART V. ADVENTURES OF TWO YOUTHS IN A JOURNEY THROUGH AFRICA.

THE VOYAGE OF THE "VIVIAN" to the North Pole and Beyond. Adventures of Two Youths in the Open Polar Sea. By Thomas W. Knox. Profusely Illustrated. 8vo, Cloth, $2 50.

HUNTING ADVENTURES ON LAND AND SEA. By Thomas W. Knox. Two Parts. Copiously Illustrated. 8vo, Cloth, $2 50 each.

PART I. THE YOUNG NIMRODS IN NORTH AMERICA.
PART II. THE YOUNG NIMRODS AROUND THE WORLD.

WHAT MR. DARWIN SAW IN HIS VOYAGE ROUND THE WORLD IN THE SHIP "BEAGLE." Illustrated. 8vo, Cloth, $3 00.

FRIENDS WORTH KNOWING. Glimpses of American Natural History. By Ernest Ingersoll. Illustrated. 16mo, Cloth, $1 00.

BY CHARLES CARLETON COFFIN. Five Volumes. Illustrated. 8vo, Cloth, $3 00 each.

THE STORY OF LIBERTY.—OLD TIMES IN THE COLONIES.—THE BOYS OF '76 (A History of the Battles of the Revolution).—BUILDING THE NATION.—DRUM-BEAT OF THE NATION.

CAMP LIFE IN THE WOODS; AND THE TRICKS OF TRAPPING AND TRAP MAKING. By W. HAMILTON GIBSON, Author of "Pastoral Days." Illustrated by the Author. 16mo, Cloth, $1 00.

HOW TO GET STRONG, AND HOW TO STAY SO. By WILLIAM BLAIKIE. With Illustrations. 16mo, Cloth, $1 00.

"HARPER'S YOUNG PEOPLE" SERIES. Illustrated. 16mo, Cloth, $1 00 per vol.

THE ADVENTURES OF JIMMY BROWN. Written by Himself, and Edited by W. L. ALDEN. —THE CRUISE OF THE CANOE CLUB. THE CRUISE OF THE "GHOST." THE MORAL PIRATES. By W. L. ALDEN.—TOBY TYLER; OR, TEN WEEKS WITH A CIRCUS. MR. STUBBS'S BROTHER: A Sequel to "Toby Tyler." TIM AND TIP; OR, THE ADVENTURES OF A BOY AND A DOG. LEFT BEHIND; OR, TEN DAYS A NEWSBOY. RAISING THE "PEARL." SILENT PETE. By JAMES OTIS.—THE STORY OF MUSIC AND MUSICIANS. JO'S OPPORTUNITY. ROLF HOUSE. MILDRED'S BARGAIN, AND OTHER STORIES. NAN. By LUCY C. LILLIE.—THE FOUR MAC-NICOLS. By WILLIAM BLACK.—THE LOST CITY; OR, THE BOY EXPLORERS IN CENTRAL ASIA. INTO UNKNOWN SEAS. By DAVID KER.—THE TALKING LEAVES. An Indian Story. TWO ARROWS: A Story of Red and White. By W. O. STODDARD.—WHO WAS PAUL GRAYSON? By JOHN HABBERTON, Author of "Helen's Babies."—PRINCE LAZYBONES, AND OTHER STORIES. By Mrs. W. J. HAYS.—THE ICE QUEEN. By ERNEST INGERSOLL.—WAKULLA: A STORY OF ADVENTURE IN FLORIDA. THE FLAMINGO FEATHER. By C. K. MUNROE.—STRANGE STORIES FROM HISTORY. By GEORGE CARY EGGLESTON.

THE STARTLING EXPLOITS OF DR. J. B. QUIÈS. From the French of PAUL CÉLIÈRE. By Mrs. CASHEL HOEY and Mr. JOHN LILLIE. Profusely Illustrated. Crown 8vo, Extra Cloth, $1 75.

FROM THE FORECASTLE TO THE CABIN. By Captain S. SAMUELS. Illustrated. 12mo, Extra Cloth, $1 50.

MICROSCOPY FOR BEGINNERS; OR, COMMON OBJECTS FROM THE PONDS AND DITCHES. By ALFRED C. STOKES, M.D. Illustrated. 12mo, Cloth, $1 50.

MARY AND MARTHA. The Mother and the Wife of George Washington. By BEN-SON J. LOSSING, LL.D., Author of "Field-book of the Revolution," "Field-book of the War of 1812," "Cyclopædia of United States History," &c. Illustrated by Fac-similes of Pen-and-ink Drawings by H. Rosa. 8vo, Ornamental Cloth, $2 50.

THE HISTORY OF THE UNITED STATES NAVY, FOR BOYS. By BENSON J. LOSSING, LL.D. Illustrated. 12mo, Half Leather, $1 75.

THE ADVENTURES OF A YOUNG NATURALIST. By LUCIEN BIART. With 117 Illustrations. 12mo, Cloth, $1 75.

AN INVOLUNTARY VOYAGE. By LUCIEN BIART. Illustrated. 12mo, Cloth, $1 25.

ROUND THE WORLD; including a Residence in Victoria, and a Journey by Rail across North America. By a Boy. Edited by SAMUEL SMILES. Illustrated. 12mo, Cloth, $1 50.

THE SELF-HELP SERIES. By SAMUEL SMILES. 12mo, Cloth, $1 00 per volume.

SELF-HELP.—CHARACTER.—THRIFT.—DUTY.

PUBLISHED BY HARPER & BROTHERS, NEW YORK.

☞ HARPER & BROTHERS *will send any of the above works by mail, postage prepaid, to any part of the United States or Canada, on receipt of the price.*